CRIME AND THE CRAFT

CRIME AND THE CRAFT
MASONIC INVOLVEMENT
IN MURDER, TREASON AND SCANDAL

MIKE NEVILLE

FONTHILL

Fonthill Media Language Policy

Fonthill Media publishes in the international English language market. One language edition is published worldwide. As there are minor differences in spelling and presentation, especially with regard to American English and British English, a policy is necessary to define which form of English to use. The Fonthill Policy is to use the form of English native to the author. Mike Neville was born and educated in Bolton, Lancashire and therefore British English has been adopted in this publication.

Fonthill Media Limited
Fonthill Media LLC
www.fonthillmedia.com
office@fonthillmedia.com

First published in the United Kingdom and the United States of America 2017

British Library Cataloguing in Publication Data:
A catalogue record for this book is available from the British Library

Copyright © Mike Neville 2017

ISBN 978-1-78155-621-4

Typeset in 10pt on 13pt MinionPro
Printed and bound in England

Acknowledgements

Worshipful Brother Peter Reeve.
Brother Leonard 'Nipper' Read.
Worshipful Brother George Churchill-Coleman.
Worshipful Brother Dave Claughton.
Worshipful Brother Mike Baker.
Worshipful Brother Bob Tuthill.
Worshipful Brother Norwell Roberts.
New Scotland Yard Crime Museum.
Library and Museum of Freemasonry, London.
Sutton Masonic Hall, Surrey.

CONTENTS

Glossary of Masonic Terms

For the non-Mason reading this book, several words and phrases appear that will require clarification. The glossary below is designed to aid the reader to understand Masonic references.

Brother/Brethren: member(s) of a Masonic lodge

Chapter/Council/Conclave: alternative name for a lodge in various other Masonic Orders. Chapter is also used as a name for the Holy Royal Arch degree (and the place where it meets).

(The) Charge: a formal set of rules recited to each new member of a lodge, including his duties to God, his neighbour, and himself. It also includes his responsibilities to the country in which he resides, his 'native land', and his lodge.

Companion: a member of a Holy Royal Arch chapter (senior members are styled as Excellent Companions).

Craft: the first three degrees (Entered Apprentice, Fellowcraft, and Master Mason) are known as 'Craft Masonry'.

Deacon: the lodge officer who acts as a messenger and escorts the candidates through the different degree ceremonies. There are two deacons in the lodge: junior and senior.

Degree: a step or grade in the Masonic system.

Entered Apprentice: a Mason, who has taken his First Degree (the initiation ceremony).

Erased: the official term used when a lodge ceases to function (usually due to lack of membership) and is removed from the roll of lodges held at the United Grand Lodge of England.

Fellowcraft: a Mason who has been 'passed' to the Second Degree.

Festive Board: the meal after a lodge meeting, which includes formal toasts to senior Masons, the master, and guests.

Grand Lodge: the supreme Masonic authority for a country or state in the USA. England (including Wales), Scotland and Ireland have their own Grand Lodges. There is no American Grand Lodge; each state has its own.

Grand Lodge Above: a Masonic term for heaven, the place where a dead Freemason is said to have gone.

Grand Master: the head of a Grand Lodge. In England, authority is delegated to Provincial Grand Masters.

Initiation ceremony: the ceremony of joining a lodge as a new member.

Installation ceremony: usually the appointment of Master or head of the Masonic unit.

Joining Member: when a man, who is already a Freemason, joins another lodge or chapter.

Lodge (or Temple): term for place where Masons meet.

Mark Masonry: In England, a 'side' or additional Order in Freemasonry. In Scotland, the 'Mark' can be taken in a Craft lodge. The name of the degree is derived from the mark or symbol carved into a piece of stone, by a stonemason, to identify his work. The ceremony is based on the (fictional) method of paying wages to Masons at King Solomon's Temple.

Master Mason: a Mason, who has been 'raised' to the Third Degree.

Most Worshipful Brother: a title reserved for the Grand Master in England and his 'Pro Grand Master'.

Obligation: the formal oath recited by a candidate in each degree, including a promise not to reveal the secrets entrusted to him.

Principal: one of the three senior officers who preside over a Royal Arch Chapter. There is no Master in a Chapter. There are three Principals, known by Biblical names— Zerubbabel, Haggai, and Joshua.

Province: in England and Wales, a geographical Masonic area, usually based on traditional County borders.

Right Worshipful Brother: a very senior Mason in a Grand Lodge or a Provincial Grand Master. Just below this ranks a Very Worshipful Brother.

Side Degree or Order: a degree or Order outside the basic Craft degrees. Ranks in such do not carry weight in a Craft lodge, so a Thirty-Three Degree Mason in Rose Croix does not have power in a Craft lodge.

Steward: the lowest ranked officer in a lodge who is responsible for looking after guests; in reality, the main role is to pour wine at the Festive Board.

Tracing Board: pictorial representation of symbols on wooden boards, used in various degrees.

Tyler: a Mason who guards the door to a lodge, officially 'armed with a drawn sword'.

Volume of the Sacred Law: generally, the King James Version of the Bible or other book sacred to the members (for example, if a Muslim is a member, a Koran would be the 'VSL' for him). In some lodges, several Volumes of the Sacred Law sit on the Master's pedestal to reflect the varying beliefs of the brethren.

Wardens: in various degrees, including the Craft, these are the two principal assistants to the Master. These are named Junior and Senior Wardens and sit in the west of the lodge (senior) and south (junior).

Working Tools: representations of various tools (for example: square, chisel, mallet, axe), which are used to symbolise various moral virtues. Several degrees have their own tools, which are explained to the candidate during the ceremony.

Worshipful Brother: a Mason who has 'been through the Chair' and has been, at some point, the Worshipful Master of his lodge.

Worshipful Master: the current head of a Masonic lodge. He has a large chair in the east of the lodge. The Master-ship usually changes each year (on a set date known as 'Installation') and is (generally) the conclusion of a progressive system year by year from each office—Steward, then Inner Guard, Junior Deacon, Senior Deacon, Junior Warden, and lastly Senior Warden.

Zerubbabel: the name given to the equivalent of the Master in a Holy Royal Arch Chapter. He is addressed as 'Most Excellent'; the title is often abbreviated as 'MEZ'. See also reference to Principals.

1

Crime and the Craft:
What Happens at Masonic Meetings?

In June 1995, a young policeman in Croydon was blindfolded and a dagger was placed to his chest; however, this was not a robbery or a kidnap; no crime was being committed—it was the initiation ceremony at the Frederick Lodge of Unity No. 452. The new Mason was the author; the man with the 'sharp implement' (as Masonic ritual describes it) was Brother Duncan Hanrahan, a former police officer and seemingly ideal Mason. Injured in the line of duty, he left the force and became a private detective. However, by 1999, Hanrahan had been sentenced to over eight years' imprisonment for dealing in large quantities of the illegal drug ecstasy, conspiracy to commit armed robberies, and attempting to bribe a senior police officer to drop a serious assault charge—such was the author's introduction to *Crime and the Craft*.

I suggest, however, that such an experience is very rare. To most 'brethren' (as Masons describe each other), crime and Freemasonry will seem very strange bedfellows, but for conspiracy theorists, the two are intrinsically linked. Hanrahan's crimes were never mentioned in the lodge; he simply disappeared. Likewise, the author has sat down at a Masonic lodge with Brother Leonard 'Nipper' Read, a thoroughly incorruptible and decent man, as well as the top detective who brought the Krays' reign of terror to an end.

This book will describe all manner of crimes and scandals, from murder and treason to indecent exposure and adultery. All involve Masons—some for good and some for bad—and ask whether there is a worldwide Masonic conspiracy to commit evil deeds. Some of the most wicked men in history have been Freemasons (Andres Brevik and Kenneth Noye for example), but some of the greatest men have also been members of 'the Craft' (as Freemasonry refers to itself)—several kings of England, Winston Churchill, George Washington, and Sir Alexander Fleming. Likewise, the concept of Masonic judges and Masonic police treating their brethren differently to allow them to get away with crimes, even murder, will be considered. Rumours abound that nearly every famous criminal is a member of a lodge. Fortunately for the Craft, there are no links to such high profile offenders, much to the disappointment (no doubt) of the conspiracy theorists.

Some crimes recounted in this book involve Masonry in an incidental manner; a Freemason may be the villain of the tale or the policeman who cracks a top crime ring (for example, the investigation into the Kray Twins). In other cases, the Craft is a real

influential factor—for example, at the trial of Brother Frederick Seddon, who made a secret
Masonic sign from the dock at the Old Bailey trial to the judge, a Provincial Grand Master.
Even more Masonic is the case of a poisoner, Major Armstrong, where several members
of the Craft feature. In this investigation, nearly every person involved—suspect, victim,
local doctor, pathologist, jury foreman, and even the architect of the court building—were
Freemasons, with many from just one lodge in a small town on the England–Wales border.

Perhaps most dreadful is the death of the 10th Duke of Devonshire, the Grand Master of
United Grand Lodge of England (1947–50), who may well have been murdered for being a
Freemason (Chapter 50). What of Jack the Ripper—or was it Jack the Mason? (See Chapter
35). The several links between the infamous Whitechapel Murders and Freemasonry
have been explored in many books and even a Hollywood movie. That most modern
collection of information, the internet, is awash with rumours of Masonic skulduggery
and conspiracies—Jack the Ripper is just one of the many crimes attributed to members
of the Craft.

Furthermore, the formation of the Criminal Investigation Department (or 'CID')
at Scotland Yard was as a direct result of a scandal involving corrupt detectives, with
Freemasons appearing at the trial as defendants and witnesses both for the defence and
prosecution. As will be seen, many of the incidents described contain a combination of
these factors. The author's experience of criminal matters is London-based, so the reader
will have to forgive his bias towards the Metropolitan Police and Scotland Yard. For the
purpose of this book, 'crime', will be considered in its widest sense, so not just criminal
offences, but also scandals from the eighteenth and nineteenth century. Geographically,
the focus is narrower, and the key criteria are the links to London; this could be a crime
committed in the capital, Scotland Yard detectives (from London's Metropolitan Police)
being called in to investigate a crime in another part of the country, or a Masonic link
to London.

It would also help the reader to gain an understanding of Freemasonry. The standard
definition, as supplied to members is rather archaic—'Freemasonry is a peculiar system of
morality, veiled in allegory and illustrated by symbols', whose three 'Grand Principles' are
'brotherly love, relief and truth.' Whether the reader is a Freemason who can recognise these
references to comradeship (brotherly love) and charity work (relief), a conspiracy theorist,
a fundamental Christian who believes that the Craft is an evil thing, or just a disinterested
observer, it would make sense to briefly describe the current state of Freemasonry.

There are some 7,500 lodges in England and Wales (Scotland and Ireland have their own
Grand lodges), with one-fifth, some 1,300 lodges, in London; so, while London may have
the greatest crime rate in the country, it also seems to have the most Freemasons. Masons
are, stereotypically, white men in middle or older age, but the diversity of races and creeds
is reflected in London lodges, where it is possible to meet with Christians, Jews, Muslims,
Sikhs, Hindus, and men who follow other religions, all in the same lodge. It is important to
note that it is men. There is Co-Freemasonry (mixed male and female) and solely women's
lodges, but these are very small by comparison to the membership of the United Grand
Lodge of England. Crime, particularly violent crime, is a male preserve, with very few
women involved (some 90 per cent of recorded crime is committed by male suspects).

Freemasons' Hall in London is the headquarters of the United Grand Lodge of England.

However, what do the brethren do in their Masonic temples, locked away from the outside world? Generally, lodges meet four or five times per year, but a Mason may belong to several (and pay for the privilege). Once at the lodge, the meeting follows a standard format:

Administrative matters—reading minutes of the last meeting, financial matters (lodge subscriptions and other mundane payments), and communications from Provincial Grand Lodge and the national Grand Lodge. Though this may be routine and boring, many Masons take these instructions very seriously. Indeed, to some Masons the wearing of certain ties or cufflinks contrary to the orders of Grand Lodge is very much a 'crime'.

Ritual—a short morality play (a degree ceremony), usually based on a Biblical story where Masonic 'secrets' are communicated, so that the candidate can prove his progress to other Masons. These secrets consist of hand-signs, tokens (the infamous 'Masonic handshake' in a variety of styles) and secret passwords (invariably the names of characters or places in the Bible).

Charity Matters—reports on activities to assist local community projects (lifeboats, Air Ambulance, hospices are popular) and assistance given to elder and sick Masons or widows

The Festive Board—a meal (akin to a Wedding Breakfast or Army Regimental Dinner) with much food and lots of toasts taken with wine.

It will be noted that there are no standard agenda items, such as 'Masonic takeover of the world' or 'plan to commit crimes utilising Masonic influence.' This may sound rather facetious, but many conspiracy theorists appear to believe that such matters are discussed in open lodge. Furthermore, according to the ritual, which candidates for the Second Degree have to recite, Freemasonry is not open to those involved in crime and villainy—it is only for 'just, upright and free men of mature age, sound judgement and strict morals.' There is also guidance in 'The Charge after Initiation' (a set of rules of the Order recited by an experienced Mason to the new candidate) on what to consider before proposing anyone else as a potential candidate. They must demonstrate their commitment to the Craft 'by refraining from recommending anyone to participate in our secrets unless you have strong grounds to believe that he will ultimately reflect honour of your choice.' The same Charge also calls on Masons to never do anything which would 'subvert the peace and good order of society' and to obey 'the laws of any state which may become the place of your residence.' This, of course, does not always reflect reality and some bad Masons have joined a lodge and committed the crimes noted in this book.

Furthermore, in addition to not committing crimes themselves, Masons are also expressly forbidden from keeping the secrets of brethren involved in such dirty deeds. During the obligation taken during the Third Degree, crime is specifically mentioned. The obligation is printed below with the 'Five Points of Fellowship' (numbered to aid the reader). The candidate for the degree of Master Mason kneels before the Worshipful Master's pedestal and, with both hands on the Holy Book sacred to his faith, repeats the following:

> I, … (Candidate states his full name), in the presence of The Most High, and of this worthy and worshipful Lodge of Master Masons, duly constituted, regularly assembled, and properly dedicated, of my own free will and accord, do hereby and hereon, most solemnly promise and swear, that I will always hele, conceal, and never reveal, any or either of the secrets or mysteries of, or belonging to, the Degree of a Master Masons to anyone in the world, unless it be to him or them to whom the same may justly and lawfully belong, and not even unto him or them until after due trial, strict examination, or full conviction, that he or they are worthy of that confidence, or in the body of a Master Mason's Lodge duly opened on the Centre.
>
> I likewise solemnly engage to adhere to the principles of the Square and Compasses, to answer and obey all lawful Signs, and Summonses. I may receive from a Master Masons' Lodge, if within the length of my cable tow, pleading no excuse save sickness, or the pressing emergencies of my public or private avocations.
>
> I further solemnly pledge myself to maintain and uphold the Five Points of Fellowship in act as well as in word;
>
> 1. That my hand given to a Master Mason shall be a sure pledge of brotherhood.
>
> 2. That my feet shall traverse difficulties and dangers to unite with his in forming a column for mutual defence and support.
>
> 3. That the posture of my daily supplications shall remind me of his wants, and dispose my heart to succour his weakness and relieve his necessities so far as may fairly be done without detriment to myself or connections.
>
> 4. That my breast shall be the safe repository of his secrets when entrusted to my care–murder, treason, felony, and all other offences contrary to the laws of God and the ordinances of the realm being at all times most especially excepted.
>
> 5. I will maintain a Master Mason's honour and carefully preserve it as my own; I will not injure him, or knowingly suffer it to be done by others, if in my power to prevent it, but on the contrary, will boldly repel the slander on his good name and most strictly respect the chastity of those nearest and dearest to him, in the persons of his wife, his sister, and his child.
>
> These several points I solemnly swear to observe, without evasion, equivocation, or mental reservation of any kind. So help me The Most High and keep me steadfast in this, the Solemn Obligation of a M. M.

In his book *Inside the Brotherhood* (1993), Short makes much of the corrupt detectives and villains forming a 'column for mutual defence and support' (Point of Fellowship No. 2 above) to aid each other in their nefarious activities. He appears to have missed the later section of the ritual, which clarifies this promise as meaning 'I will support you in all your laudable undertakings'. Assisting a brother Mason to commit serious (indeed any) crime could hardly be defined as 'laudable', which means 'deserving praise and commendation'.

Furthermore, in Point of Fellowship No. 4, the Mason promises that he will keep the secrets of a brother, but only if they do not involve 'murder, treason, felony and all other offences contrary to the laws of God and the established ordinances of the realm'. This is a very wide definition, it covers the most serious crimes by name (murder and treason) and the 'ordinances' or written laws of the land cover theft, fraud, sexual crimes, and assaults. However, the 'laws of God' would include adultery and other breaches of the Ten Commandments, so there is not much a member of the Craft can actually keep secrets about, if he is to comply with his obligation as a Master Mason. As we shall see, this part of the ritual may have excused one criminal Mason giving information (or 'grassing') on another.

In addition to the many rules controlling Freemasons (there are 280 in the *Book of Constitutions*, which governs English Masonry) and the content of their obligations, members of the Craft can rightly argue that their rituals are, in the main, derived from Biblical stories. This includes Noah and the flood, Moses, Joshua seizing the Promised Land, King Solomon's Temple, the Babylonian invasion of Judah, the subsequent building of the Second Temple, and other accounts from the *Volume of the Sacred Law* (as the Bible or other religious text is described in Masonic ritual). The author has demonstrated this in the book *Sacred Secrets: Freemasonry, The Bible and Christian Faith* (Neville, 2012), with 460 of the 1,189 chapters in the King James Bible]found in Masonic ritual. It seems very odd that, if lodges were set up to plot crime and wickedness, Freemasons should base their ceremonies on religious text.

It should also be noted that lodges are completely separate—father and son, two police officers or (even) two villains could be Masons in different lodges, but unless they reveal their membership to one another, they would be unaware of the other's membership. In addition, the 'secret' signs (all can be found on the internet) vary from place to place—sometimes due to different ritual, sometimes due to lodge 'tradition' (usually meaning that someone gave the sign incorrectly for many years and the error has continued); however, this also adds to the confusion and makes the idea of any conspiracy far less likely.

Tales of Crime in Masonic Ritual

What is clear, however, is the part that tales of crime play in the ceremonies, which form the basis of the different degrees through which Freemasons pass as they progress in a lodge. The most obvious ceremony involving crime is the Third Degree, where Masons are 'raised' to the rank of Master Mason. This ritual tells the tale of a conspiracy to commit murder by fifteen Masons employed at the building of King Solomon's Temple, with the actual homicide being carried out by three of their number; according to the ritual, these had a 'more determined and atrocious character than the rest'.

The victim in this case is the main character in Craft Masonry, Hiram Abif. He does exist in the Bible; his skills and his work at the temple are variously described in the First Book of Kings (Chapter 7) and the Second Book of Chronicles (Chapter 2), but there are no further references to him. Freemasonry builds on this account and Hiram Abif becomes the chief architect at the temple and is the possessor of the 'secrets of a Master Mason', which are known only to him, King Solomon and his namesake, Hiram, King of Tyre. This secret word can only be pronounced by all three acting together, further complicating matters. The attack on Hiram Abif is described in *Sacred Secrets* (Neville, 2012) in the following manner:

Freemasons will recall that fifteen Overseers employed at the temple, aggrieved that they were not in possession of the secrets of a Master Mason, conspired to attack Hiram Abif to force them from him. In the end, only three conspirators carried out the plan and waited for him at the three entrances of the Temple, where he had gone to pray, whilst the workforce were on a break. Despite being viciously assaulted by being struck about the head with workmen's tools (a level and plumb rule) and further threatened with a heavy maul (large wooden hammer), Hiram Abif steadfastly refused to disclose the secrets. It is also stated that to do so, he would require the assistance of the other two Grand Masters—Solomon, King of Israel and Hiram, King of Tyre. This is a link to Royal Arch Chapter ritual, where the sacred word can only be pronounced by three working together.

Whilst at the east entrance (main entry) to the temple Hiram was struck on the forehead with the maul and died. The story of the murder is Masonic legend; the only Biblical feature is the use of a maul as a weapon, which is derived from the Book of Proverbs.

The murder having been committed in King Solomon's Temple in Jerusalem, Hiram Abif's body was removed some distance and buried in a shallow grave. Freemasons may wish to view the Second Degree Tracing Board in a different light—it shows two of the three crime scenes—the south and east entrances to the Temple, where the assaults on Hiram Abif took place.

Panic ensued when Hiram Abif could not be found and the twelve Overseers involved in the original conspiracy informed King Solomon of the evil plan. Three teams or 'lodges' of Fellowcrafts were then despatched to find him. One group returned having found nothing, but the second found Hiram Abif's body. To mark the spot, they placed a sprig of Acacia at the head of the grave. This is now an important Masonic symbol, which does not appear to originate from the Bible.

The third group located the murderers hidden in a cave, on their way to Joppa. There is a simple reason for their decision to make for that city. As the nearest port to Jerusalem, Joppa offered the quickest escape out of the country. They were taken back to King Solomon and sentenced to death.

Hiram Abif's dead body was recovered (in Masonic terms 'raised') from the makeshift grave, and various signs and words are derived from this incident. Once back in Jerusalem, the body was re-buried 'as near to the Sanctum Sanctorum as the Israelitish law would permit' as the Traditional History of the Third Degree relates. This means that he would have been buried somewhere on Mount Moriah.

This murder is acted out in the lodge with the two Wardens and the Master playing the part of the three villains, delivering the fatal blows one after the other on the candidate—all rather bizarre in terms of characters as the three usually represent King Solomon, Hiram, King of Tyre, and the victim, Hiram Abif, in other ceremonies. Despite the character confusion for the candidate, the message of the degree is quite clear—a good Mason, like Hiram Abif, would rather 'suffer death rather than disclose the sacred trust reposed in him.' This book will describe the likes of John Coustos, who refused to give away Masonic secrets, even when tortured by agents of the Roman Catholic Church.

The Mark Degree, a Side Order that about one-tenth of Craft Mason join, adds to the story in the Second Degree, where the Masons visit the Middle Chamber of King Solomon's Temple to receive their wages. While this chamber existed (if the Biblical account is to be believed, see First Book of Kings, Chapter 8), the use of it as a form of payment department is Masonic legend. The crime allegedly committed in the Mark Degree by the unsuspecting candidate is one of fraud; the new member plays the part of a workman, who attempts to obtain the wages due to a higher class of workmen. The ancient punishment (according to the ritual) is to have 'the right hand struck off'; fortunately for the new Mark Mason, this is not done, but the degree gives a clear warning against being involved in any form of deceit. The explanation of the Tracing Board takes it further and gives an unequivocal instruction to the candidate to 'avoid the danger of indulging in deception or attempting fraud.'

So far, murder and fraud have been covered in the ritual. Another popular crime theme used in degree ceremonies is the break-in; an illegal entry, trespass, or even burglary are the storylines in the Holy Royal Arch (also known as 'Chapter') and in several Side Orders—the Select Master degree (part of the Royal and Select Masters), the Grand Tilers of Solomon (Allied Masonic Degrees), and The Holy Order of St John the Evangelist (Appendant Orders of the Red Cross of Constantine). The latter is open to Christian Masons only, but the theme is much the same—a secret vault is found and groups of workmen enter without authority, they discover important secrets or clandestine work going on. The first three ceremonies are based on the ruins of King Solomon's Temple (destroyed by the Babylonians in the sixth century BC—a clear case of brutal war crimes, criminal damage, and arson if ever there was one) and the Christian ceremony on the ruins of the Second Temple (further criminal damage and arson, this time by the Romans). In the Chapter and Red Cross ceremony, the items recovered are welcomed—but in the Select Master and Grand Tilers, the trespasser is threatened with punishments, including death for the incursion.

It will also be noted that the Bible (or Masonic ritual) has no Human Rights Act or Geneva Convention; when King Zedekiah, ruler of Judah, flees Jerusalem and is captured by the Babylonians, he faces an awful punishment. The Super Excellent Master Degree (also part of the Royal and Select Masters) relates that he had to watch his sons murdered and then the Babylonians burned out his eyes, so it was the last thing he would see. He was then taken, bound in chains, to Babylon. As we have seen, such swift justice was also meted out to the murderers of Hiram Abif—ruthless and quick continued to be the style of justice in England, even up to the beginning of the twentieth century. This book will show how a suspect could be hanged for murder within six weeks of the crime being committed.

The English Civil War: Genesis of Freemasonry and Masons in Conflict

Masonic Connection

Claims that King James I was a Freemason
First recorded initiations in England
Prisoner of war
Executions for treason
Masonic dating system
Formation of Royal Society

Dates

1641: Robert Moray initiated in Newcastle on Tyne
1646: Elias Ashmole initiated in Warrington, Lancashire
1649: Mason, 1st Duke of Hamilton executed
1651: Mason, 1st Earl Leven imprisoned in the Tower of London
1654: Archbishop James Ussher published the Biblical chronology used to set the date of the murder of Hiram Abif
1660: Formation of Royal Society

Connection to London

Great Queen Street: named after Queen Anne, wife of James I of England
Whitehall: Banqueting House site of execution of King Charles I and Mason, 1st Duke of Hamilton
Westminster Abbey: Burial place of Archbishop James Ussher and Sir Robert Moray
Masons Avenue, City of London: Location of Ashmole's lodge meeting in 1682
Cheapside, City of London: location of first recorded Festive Board
Lambeth Road: Ashmole buried in (former) St Mary's church (now the Garden Museum)

Lodges

Unknown English lodge in Warrington
Lodge of Edinburgh (Mary's Chapel) No. 1 (Scotland)
Lodge Scone and Perth No. 3 (Scotland)

The English Civil War (1642–51) was a dreadful time for the people of the nation, but it is arguably the beginning of the Parliamentary democracy that we enjoy today and oft copied around the world. As a precursor to this conflict, Scottish armies had swept into the north of England, fighting for a religious cause. Despite all the violence, this period seems have included the birth of the Craft in England, with the first documented initiations of Freemasons. These are the first known occasions when operative stonemasons accepted speculative (pretend) Masons into their lodges. It is also a time of plots, conspiracies, and intrigue, with Masons fighting against each other and, possibly, executing each other. There are also, however, times when sworn enemies would work in peace in harmony in a lodge. As today, some did not live up to the high ideals of Masonry. Indeed, the first man recorded as being made a Mason on English soil was an invader, working for a foreign power and the second, a rogue, who saw rich widows as an easy route to riches. Most tantalising, however, is the issue of regicide—the crime of killing a king. Whether a Mason ordered the death of a Masonic monarch or not, a man who had much influence on Masonic ritual witnessed the execution.

Let us now consider one of the most important historical characters in English Freemasonry—a Scotsman, Sir Robert Moray. Moray was the first man recorded to have been initiated on English soil, but critically, this was in a Scottish travelling lodge, not an English one. Born in Perthshire in central Scotland, during the first decade of the seventeenth century, Moray enlisted in the *Garde Ecossaise*—the regiment of Scots Guards in the French Army whose duty was to guard the king of France. During this role, his skills as a spy and agent were identified. His ability to swap sides at will and find influential supporters would keep him alive in dangerous times.

At this time, religion played a great part in people's lives; it was (literally) a matter of life and death. The various factions of Christianity vied for supremacy in Britain and Europe. Those wishing to try to comprehend this issue should visit Northern Ireland or Glasgow, where religious differences still play an important part in many people's lives. The kingdoms of Scotland and England had been united under King James (the VI of Scotland and I in England) in 1603. Complete union of the countries, however, would be a complex matter. While both nations were followers of the Protestant faith, their church organisation and religious practices were different. As in Freemasonry, these variations were jealously (and zealously) guarded.

It is worth questioning whether James I of England was a Freemason. On a wall of the lodge room of Scone and Perth lodge No. 3 in central Scotland is a mural depicting the king at his initiation. It is claimed that he became a member of the Craft in 1601, but the account was not written until over fifty years afterwards. If James's Masonic links cannot be ascertained, his Danish wife, Queen Anne, is certainly recalled in English Freemasonry; the site of the United Grand Lodge of England, Great Queen Street in London, is named after her. Additionally, in 1611, the King James Version of the Bible, commissioned by the king and still used in Masonic ritual today, was published.

The leadership style of the churches in James's two nations was very different. In England, the church was ruled by bishops, while north of the border, a Presbyterian system was followed, with church elders being in charge. These elders were appointed by the congregation, rather than by the king, who selected English bishops, giving the crown great control over the church. James started to impose the episcopal (bishop led) style on the 'Kirk' or Scottish Church. It was much more in the interest of the monarch to impose church leaders, rather than leave such choices to the common folk.

Into this world was born the first Englishman recorded to have been made a Freemason in an English lodge—Elias Ashmole, who was born in 1617 in Lichfield, Staffordshire. As Ashmole grew up in the Midlands, King James continued with his controversial religious reforms and these were continued by his son, who was crowned Charles I of England and Scotland in 1625. The fact that Charles, the Protestant monarch of Great Britain, had married a Spanish Roman Catholic created more tensions in the nation, with Members of Parliament openly criticising his choice of queen.

We also do not know if Charles I was a Freemason; however, it is suggested that his father, James I, had brought the Craft from Scotland to England. If this was the case, then Charles was possibly a member. We can be sure, however, that the rules of Freemasonry were different then and it was based on Christianity. Now, the only religious requirement for membership is belief in a 'Supreme Being'—all faiths are respected. King Charles would have no deviation from the church ceremonies prescribed in the Church of England's Book of Common Prayer. Those deviating from such faced all manner of brutal punishments,

Elias Ashmole, the first Englishman known to have been made a Freemason in an English lodge.

including 'cropping' (having the ears cut off). Those Masons in the Mark Degree will recognise this as one of the 'ancient punishments' of the Order.

The royal interference in religious matters continued to cause much unrest north of the border. In 1637, in addition to the issue of bishops, the king ordered the use of a new prayer book in Scotland and riots broke out in Edinburgh. As a result of the attempt to impose bishops on the Scots, the subsequent conflicts became known as the Bishops' Wars. The first such war ended in stalemate, with the king regaining his Scottish fortresses, but allowing the Scottish Parliament and General Assembly of the Church of Scotland (with church elders, not bishops) to be convened. The commander of the Royalist forces during this conflict was a Freemason—General Sir James Hamilton, 1st Duke of Hamilton, who was later to take part in a very significant initiation ceremony.

During the uneasy peace after the First Bishops' War, the Scottish Army was enhanced by veterans of the Thirty Years War, a Europe-wide conflict. These experienced soldiers, including (future Mason) Robert Moray, were tasked by a French Cardinal, to join (and spy on) the 'Covenanters' (a Scottish Presbyterian army). These Scots had signed a 'covenant' opposing interference in their church affairs and were still in open revolt against Charles (a Protestant monarch, who had married a Roman Catholic). If nothing else, this further demonstrates the importance of religion and its influence on international and British affairs in the seventeenth century.

Throughout much of this period, Charles ruled England without a parliament and antagonised the population by demanding (what many considered to be) illegal taxes, including the infamous 'Ship Money', where inland counties had to pay for the Royal Navy. Such taxes should have been agreed by Parliament, but the king pressed on, without such authority. The conflict in Scotland had depleted England's treasury; this was one of the many reasons for the king raising taxes. Charles was also determined not to rule three kingdoms, but one united kingdom of England, Scotland, and Ireland; many of his subjects feared such a union. The English believed that this would dilute hard-fought controls imposed on the king by Parliament over many centuries. The Scots despised interference in religious matters and the Irish Roman Catholics feared the imposition of Protestantism.

In 1640, in defiance of Charles, the emboldened Scots declared that they could rule without the king's consent and crossed the English border to invade the county of Northumberland. This conflict is now known as the Second Bishops' War. Moray had been appointed to a very senior position—Scottish Quartermaster-General. The army marched south and captured the city of Newcastle, under the command of a Freemason—Major General Alexander Leslie, 1st Earl Leven.

Importantly for the Craft, Leven did not just bring his army to Northumberland—he also brought a lodge. The Lodge of Edinburgh met in Newcastle and, on 20 May 1641, Moray was made a Mason. (This lodge is the oldest in the world, with lodge minutes from 1599). Moray took Masonry seriously, often drawing his Masonic mark—he had chosen a five-pointed star—on correspondence to other members of the Craft.

In each lodge, there are two deacons, who assist the Master. The deacons at Moray's initiation were two high ranking soldiers already noted in this chapter: The Duke of Hamilton (previously a Royalist commander in the First Bishops' War) and Earl Leven, who had captured the city. Here, we have a most confusing situation—both deacons, like Moray, had fought in the Thirty Years War, but unlike the new initiate (Moray), Hamilton and Leven had fought on the protestant side with the King of Sweden. However, Brothers Hamilton and Leven had fought on different sides in the First Bishops' War; this is perhaps the best illustration of why Freemasons are not allowed to discuss religion and politics in a lodge.

Importantly, this first initiation on English soil (albeit in a Scottish lodge) was conducted by members of a rebellious army, in revolt against the king. So, while these early Freemasons could have been executed for treason, we will see that many members of the British royal family were later active members of the Craft and 'promoters of the Art' (as a new initiate is informed during the Charge) in numerous chapters of this book.

In London, King Charles grudgingly recalled the House of Commons as he needed funds to crush the Scottish rebellion. Unfortunately, his relationship with the elected members continued to deteriorate and several Parliaments came and went. Around the same time, supporters of the king attempted to kidnap Brother the Duke of Hamilton and other Scottish nobles, who supported the Covenanters cause. The plot failed as Brother the Earl of Leven heard news of the plot and warned his fellow Freemason, who managed to escape from Edinburgh. The king was suspected of being behind the kidnap attempt and this incident finally forced him to accept the religious status quo in Scotland—there would be no bishops.

Returning to England, matters came to a head in early 1642, when the king attempted to arrest five Members of Parliament for treason. The country now divided—northern and western areas (especially rural sections) supported the king, whereas the remainder, including London, favoured Parliament. The first pitched battle of the English Civil War was at Edgehill, Warwickshire, in October 1642, but neither side could claim victory.

In the same year, Elias Ashmole (already a widower as his wife had died while pregnant) had thrown in his lot with the king's Royalist forces. Ashmole left London (a Parliament supporting city) and went to his deceased wife's family in Cheshire. The Mainwarings were aristocrats, but, surprisingly, favoured Parliament. Perhaps for that reason, he returned to his home town in Staffordshire and was employed as the king's tax official. The civil war rumbled on.

Britain was not the only nation suffering from conflict. By 1643, Brother Moray had returned to duties with the French armed forces and was fighting in what is now southern Germany. During this period, he was taken prisoner at the battle of Tuttlingen. Hence he is possibly the first British Freemason to be made a prisoner of war. On release, he returned to France and duly received promotion, being appointed the commanding officer of the *Garde Écossaise*.

By now, Ashmole had served as an ordnance or supply officer in Oxford—the city chosen by the king as his temporary capital as London was a Parliamentary stronghold. Ashmole was no soldier and seems to have seen little or no fighting; however, he was a skilled mathematician. He also had a great interest in astronomy and astrology (at that time, the two were seen as the same science), as well as magic (again, a legitimate area of study in the seventeenth century). In 1645, he was posted to advise on artillery positions for use in the defence of Worcester. His mathematical skills were, no doubt, of use to calculate the accuracy of cannon fire.

In England, the conflict spread across most of the country; however, by 1645, Parliamentary forces had gained the upper hand. Oliver Cromwell had shown himself to be an excellent leader and he was appointed as second in command of the New Model Army—a highly trained and well-disciplined force. There is no documentary proof that Cromwell was a Mason; however, a contemporary image of him shows him in a very Masonic pose, stood between two pillars with a dove with an olive branch in its beak, and images of Noah's Ark (the main subject of early Craft lodges) with the sun and moon prominently displayed; perhaps this was a coincidence, or demonstrates the inclusion of Masonic symbols. We may never know, but, as we will see, at least one of his senior officers, Colonel Henry Mainwaring, would be made a Mason.

The success of the Parliamentary forces was to prove a benefit for (fair-weather) Royalist Mason, the Duke of Hamilton. His plots to force the king to accept the non-bishop led Presbyterian Church in Scotland had resulted in Charles losing his patience with him and imprisoning the Duke in two Cornish strongholds—Pendennis Castle and then St Michael's Mount. Hamilton was eventually freed when Parliamentary forces under Lord Fairfax took control of the county. Fairfax was the commander of the New Model Army and, if rumours are to be believed, was a Freemason, but there is no proof of this claim.

Worcester fell to the forces of Parliament in 1646, but Ashmole seems to have been able to leave freely. Critically, he returned to the north of England and, in his diary entry for 16 October, he noted that he was admitted to the Craft in Warrington (then in Lancashire, now in Cheshire) with Colonel Mainwaring. Ashmole's initiation is the first recorded making of a Freemason in an English lodge. The colonel was a relative of his wife and a senior Parliamentary army officer—so seemingly an enemy of Ashmole, but now a Brother Mason.

The end of the first part of the English Civil War came in 1646, with victory for Parliament. The king was imprisoned, but over the next two years, he negotiated a secret deal with the Scots to invade England and return him to the throne. Charles made further (questionable) promises that he would not interfere in Scottish religious affairs. As a result of the king's actions, several Royalist uprisings broke out, but by 1648, Parliamentary forces were once again victorious. This was to have dire consequences for the Duke of Hamilton (now back supporting the king), who had been the deacon at Robert Moray's initiation. His latest role was to command the Scottish Royalist forces at the Battle of Preston, but his army was crushed by Cromwell and the Duke was taken prisoner in Uttoxeter in Staffordshire, a few days later. He was imprisoned in Windsor Castle, but was offered the opportunity to save his life by betraying Englishmen, who had aided his army. He appears to have been a man of honour, as he refused to do so. The Duke was tried for treason against Parliament and, as the king had made him Earl of Cambridge, he was technically English and therefore subject to the High Court's jurisdiction. If he had not received the English earldom, he could have claimed to have been only subject to Scottish law. As we will see, his fate was to be the same as that of the king.

The king would not be allowed to create further problems. He was tried for high treason against his people and found guilty of being a 'tyrant, traitor, murderer and public enemy'. Cromwell was one of the commissioners whose signatures appear on the death warrant of the king, who was executed on 30 January 1649 in front of the Banqueting House in

The execution of Charles I: was he sent to his death by Brother Masons?

Whitehall in central London. It is possible to speculate that a Freemason, Cromwell, had another Freemason, Charles I, executed, as there are several Masonic links.

The execution was witnessed by Archbishop James Ussher; however, it is said that he fainted before the axe severed the king's head from his body. Significantly for Masons, it was Ussher who calculated (using Biblical 'research') that the world was created in 4,004 BC. To this day, Masonic ritual states that the central character of Craft ritual, Hiram Abif, was murdered 'three thousand years after the creation of the world' (with King Solomon's Temple being built around 1000 BC).

In eighteenth-century Germany, Baron von Hund invented a Masonic Order called the 'Rite of Strict Observance', which claimed that the story of the murder of Hiram Abif was an allusion to the execution of Charles I.

Charles, like his father James, was of the Stuart Dynasty and the later removal of this family from the throne of Great Britain in 1688 would be the cause of much conflict for many years after and several senior Freemasons favoured their cause (several chapters of this book will cover the Jacobite Freemasons).

Most bizarrely, retired Admiral and (alleged) Freemason Bertram Chambers CBE claimed that Ashmole took the place of Charles I and died on the scaffold (Lomas, 2002).

Charles I then lived on, taking Ashmole's identity. Chambers claimed that the king was the Grand Master. This strange theory was published in 1929, in the *Daily Express* newspaper. Chambers' Masonic links are unknown as his lodge cannot be identified.

With the king dead and his sons exiled, Cromwell ruled as Lord Protector. Brother the Duke of Hamilton, who had been imprisoned in Windsor Castle, was executed at Whitehall six weeks after his king. A third Civil War ensued (1649–51) led by Scottish royalists, but this again resulted in victory for Parliament. Brother the Duke of Leven, the other deacon at Moray's initiation, was again fighting for the Royalist cause, but was captured by Cromwell's cavalry and locked in the Tower of London; several other Masons would later be imprisoned in the same fortress. Fortunately for Leven, the axe would not fall on his head—having paid bail money of £20,000 (a vast fortune at that time), the Queen of Sweden secured his freedom—possibly in thanks for his service in the Thirty Years War (or perhaps there was there a more personal reason). Luckily for Leven, he was to die in his own bed in Balgonie Castle in Fife.

As an officer of the Royalist army, Brother Ashmole was banned from returning to London. He was also lacking in money and decided that the quickest method to resolve this issue was to marry a rich widow. Ashmole recorded his sexual experiences with such ladies in rather vulgar detail, and he eventually married Lady Mary Mainwaring, who was twenty years his senior and possibly related to his dead wife. This was not a happy relationship, but it did provide Ashmole with sufficient funds to continue his studies into botany and

James Ussher, the Archbishop whose Biblical research is used by Masons to date the death of Hiram Abif. He is also said to have been present at the execution of Charles I.

alchemy. Given his ruthless use of widows, we can only hope that, while Ashmole was the first known man to be made an English Freemason, he was not the first lodge Almoner. As the Almoner often looks after the widows, Brother Elias may well have abused this position.

In 1655, Ussher, the Archbishop responsible for the Biblical chronology still used in Masonic ritual, died. On the orders of Cromwell, he was buried in Westminster Abbey—such was the high esteem he was held in. The Lord Protector was to live for three more years, but his death was to throw the country into even more turmoil, eventually leading to the restoration of the monarchy, with the son of the dead king returning from exile to rule as Charles II. Sir Robert Moray, by now based in Paris, had played a key role in the negotiations with the king.

The return of Charles II to England was to mark a change in Elias Ashmole's fortunes. Now he could return to London and his loyalty was rewarded with appointment to several, lucrative government offices. Ashmole was also to join with the other 'first' Freemason, Sir Robert Moray, in forming the Royal Society in 1660. Moray, once a Scottish invader (employed by a French Catholic cardinal), but ever the chameleon, was now working for the Protestant English king. The society was established by the king to draw together the best scientific minds in the country. Science had been a dangerous business as men conducting experiments could be easily accused of sorcery and witchcraft; in the same century, the Witch-Finder General had been arresting and burning witches and there was Biblical authority for such action. Chapter 18 of the Book of Deuteronomy (Moses' second book of law) states that those who practice divination, or are a 'witch' or a 'wizard' are an 'abomination unto the Lord' meaning that a horrible death could be inflicted on any such offenders by the authorities in seventeenth century England.

Likewise, Galileo had been placed under house arrest for claiming that the sun was the centre of the solar system. Now the king, short of money and threatened by the Dutch, had to use all the skills available to him and this included scientists, or as they may have been considered at the time, magicians or wizards. Moray knew that he could be denounced at any time and noted: 'I have been reported to be writing against Scripture, an Atheist, a Magician or Necromancer.' A necromancer is someone who communicates with the dead—it was just as well for Moray that he had royal protection.

Charles II was also prepared to use the brains of all his subjects—whether Royalists (such as Ashmole and Moray) or supporters of Parliament during the Civil War. The latter group included another Freemason, Sir Christopher Wren, and most interestingly, the Reverend John Wilkins as the Royal Society's first secretary. Wilkins, the vicar of St Lawrence Jewry church in the City of London was Cromwell's brother-in-law. He was also an astronomer and wrote several books supporting the heliocentric theory proposed by Galileo. Despite being a vicar, he was prepared to risk his life arguing in a book published in 1640 that the Bible should not be quoted in scientific matters:

> It were happy for us if we could exempt Scripture from philosophical controversies. If we could be content to let it be perfect for that end unto which it was intended, for a Rule of our Faith and Obedience, and not to stretch it to be a Judge of such natural truths as are to be found out by our own industry and experience.

These words do sound like Masonic ritual, particularly 'by our own industry' from the Third Degree.

With Wilkins in the Royal Society, there was a relative of Cromwell now serving the king, who very close to several members of the Craft. The differing beliefs and allegiances of the men involved in Moray's initiation have been described and, given the bitterness of the Civil War and the religious conflict at that time, it is unsurprising (and eminently sensible) that the Royal Society forbad (as Masonry does today) the discussion of religion and politics. Until the twentieth century, the Royal Society and Freemasonry appear to have been linked, and several senior Freemasons were presidents of the Society, including Sir Joseph Banks, Sir John Soane, and the Duke of Sussex.

Brother Moray was given quarters by the king in the Palace of Westminster, but became a recluse as he grew older. He died almost penniless in 1673, but was held in such respect by the king that his body was buried in Westminster Abbey. As a soldier, spy, diplomat, and scientist, Moray, the first president of the Royal Society, had certainly lived a full life. It was also a charmed life; as an invader of England, who took up arms against the king, he could have been executed for treason. As a scientist, he could have found himself burnt at the stake for being a sorcerer. He is, however, still well respected in Freemasonry and a research lodge in Scotland, No. 1641, is named after him.

Ashmole, ever the lady's man, managed to fit in a third wife, but his love of Freemasonry is not as well recorded as his sexual encounters. The only other mention of the Craft in his diary relates to over thirty years later, when on 11 March 1682, he attended a Masonic meeting at the Worshipful Company of Masons at its hall, which then stood in Masons Avenue in London. The Festive Board was held at the long demolished Half Moon Tavern at nearby Cheapside. The meals of all present were paid for by the newly made Masons; fortunately for any potential recruits, this rule is no longer enforced. Then again, if Admiral Chambers' account is correct, it was King Charles I at the meeting and not Ashmole—now, there is a conspiracy theory.

In 1685, Charles II was to die and be replaced by his brother, James II. The latter's disastrous attempt to convert the country back to the Roman Catholic faith would end in him being deposed within three years and replaced with Protestant rulers (William and Mary). James's supporters would be known as 'Jacobites' (from the Latin form of his name). Rule of Great Britain had now passed to Protestant monarchs, but, as we shall see, many Freemasons in England and Scotland continued to support the Stuart dynasty, now exiled in Saint-Germain-en-Laye to the west of Paris. The Duke of Hamilton would not be the last Freemason to lose his head.

Ashmole died in London in 1692 and was buried in St Mary's Church, Lambeth (now the Garden Museum), adjacent to Lambeth Palace, the home of the Archbishop of Canterbury. He had been an avid collector of books and scientific objects throughout his life; these can still be seen in the Ashmolean Museum in Oxford. Within twenty-five years of Ashmole's death, Freemasonry had become more organised, with an embryonic Grand Lodge formed in London in 1717. The Civil War, with the initiations of Moray and Ashmole, can rightfully be described as the genesis of the Craft in England, despite the characters themselves being lucky to avoid being prosecuted for all manner of crimes from treason to witchcraft, as well as being rogues and chancers. However, Masons have much to thank them for.

4

Rebellion 1715:
Was there a Masonic Link to the Jacobites?

Masonic Connection
Jacobite Freemasons and Knights Templar
Establishment of Ancient and Accepted Rite
Establishment of Grand Lodge of France
Grand Master of France involved in rebellion

Date
1715: Jacobite Rebellion

Connection to London
Tower of London: Site of execution of a Jacobite Mason
Old Bailey: Former site of Newgate prison

Lodges
Kilwinning Scots Arms (Scotland)

This is a fascinating time in the history of Great Britain and appears to coincide with the growth of Freemasonry across to the continent, possibly even the establishment of the Scottish Rite or Rose Croix—the Thirty-Three Degree Masonry, so loved (or loathed) by conspiracy theorists. This is an era of king against king, possibly Mason against Mason, together with executions and daring prison escapes, making for great swashbuckling tales. This is also a time when convicted Masons lost their heads and, if less fortunate, several other body parts as well (while still alive).

It should be noted that all claims of Masonic connections to prominent men and royalty in the eighteenth century and prior to this time should be treated with caution. With the formation of Grand Lodge in 1717, a variety of Masonic scholars (and detractors) endeavoured to link Masonry to all manner of royalty; Masons will recall that in the Charge to Initiate, it is said 'monarchs themselves have been promoters of the Art' and so the 'history' of the Craft became embellished with claims of King Charles II and James II being made Masons on the continent. This is also a time when references to Masonic Knights Templar and 'Higher Degrees' start to appear.

In 1688, James II of England and VII of Scotland (part of the Scottish Stuart dynasty) fled to France; his attempts to re-convert Britain to the Roman Catholic faith had failed. He was replaced by his nephew (William of Orange) and his daughter (Mary), who ruled as joint Protestant sovereigns of the country. In 1701, the Act of Settlement ruled that the line of succession for England would pass to the House of Hanover, not a Stuart monarch. Importantly, in 1707, the Act of Union ushered in a new era; England and Scotland would be united as the kingdom of Great Britain. Furthermore, the union meant that the Act of Settlement would apply to Scotland.

The Act of Union was not universally popular in Scotland. Some saw the great opportunities in trade as the English markets were opened to them. It would also create an environment where Scottish Masons could spread their ideas more easily to England (as seen in the previous chapter, the first known making of a Freemason in England was by a peripatetic Scottish lodge). Others saw a threat to Scottish traditions and a loss of self-determination. The removal of the Stuart family from the line of succession was to be a continual source of conflict for many years. As we shall see in several chapters of this book, many Freemasons would be executed for their support for the Stuart cause.

In 1714, matters were brought to a head by the death of the last reigning Stuart monarch, Queen Anne. In accordance with the Act of Settlement, the Elector of Hanover was crowned as King George I of Great Britain. The reality now struck the Stuart family's supporters; a German king sat on the English throne, while the son of James II (recognised by the French king as James III of England and VIII of Scotland) was banished from the kingdom. The exiled Stuart court was based in the chateau at Saint-Germain-en-Laye, to the west of Paris. There, King James plotted his return to the English throne and rewarded his supporters with royal honours. This would later include the Grand Master of English Freemasons, Lord Wharton.

The supporters of the Stuart family and the exiled king became known as 'Jacobites'. The term is derived from the word 'Jacob', which is the Latin form of 'James'. The term initially referred to a supporter of James II, but was later applied to those who supported his son and then his grandson, Bonnie Prince Charlie. The aim of the Jacobites was to remove the Hanoverian kings from Britain and re-establish the Stuart line.

The motives for supporting one side or the other were complex. Not all supporters of the Hanoverian dynasty or the Jacobite cause did so out of religious zeal or loyalty to a political cause. Many would act out of self-interest and would change sides in this rebellion and in later ones, particularly in 1745; neither was the affair simply Scottish Jacobites against English Hanoverian supporters—there were Jacobites throughout England, especially in the West Country and the north east.

A classic example of the shifting nature of loyalties is John Erskine, 6th Earl of Mar, who would eventually become the leader of the Jacobite rebellion. He had initially supported the Act of Union with England, but became known as 'Bobbing John', due to his tendency to change sides whether in politics (backing the Whigs or Tories) or in his support for George I or the king in exile. There is no record of him being made a Freemason, but he is said to have been the Grand Master of the (Masonic) Knights Templar in Edinburgh. It is also worth noting that his son was, no doubt, a Mason—

Thomas Erskine joined Lodge Kilwinning Scots Arms in 1736 and would later be Grand Master Mason of Scotland in 1749.

A very active English supporter of the exiled king was James Radcliffe, the 3rd Earl of Derwentwater. He was born in 1689 in Arlington Street in London and was a grandson of Charles II. While his earldom was in what is now Cumbria, he lived in Dilston Castle in Northumberland. He was also a Roman Catholic; his religion and ancestry would make him a fervent Jacobite who refused to take an oath of allegiance to William and Mary. This resulted in imprisonment, but he was soon free and became the most feared Jacobite in the North East of England. He also visited the court of the exiled king in Paris. There is no proof of the 3rd Earl being a Mason, but it is suggested that his brother, Charles (who used the title 5th Earl) was later the Grand Master of the Grand Lodge of France and founder of the Scottish Rite. In England, this is called (dropping the reference to Scotland) the Ancient and Accepted Rite, or Rose Croix; perhaps the 'Scottish' part of the title was dropped because of the Jacobite link. Furthermore, Lord (2004) noted that the Earls of Derwentwater were believed to have been involved in lodges in the Hexham area of Northumberland, but there is no documentary proof (much like much Masonic activity from that period).

Now to the Jacobite rising of 1715. The Earl of Mar, believed to be the leader of the Scottish Knights Templar, took the initiative; in the August, he left England and returned to Scotland, where he raised the standard of the exiled King James. Mar's forces successfully captured major towns—Aberdeen, Inverness, and Dundee, but were unable to take the castles at Edinburgh and Stirling, where forces remained loyal to King George. Despite growing support (the Jacobite army had grown from a few hundred men to over 20,000 in a matter of months), Mar now became indecisive and this was to prove his downfall; it gave his rival commander, the 2nd Duke of Argyll time to build up forces in Scotland, including heavy artillery and cavalry. There are questions regarding whether Argyll was a Mason. It is known that the 6th Duke was the Grand Master of Scotland.

It was not, however, just a Scottish revolt. A major English campaign was planned in the West Country, with a diversionary rising in Northumberland. The latter became the more prominent, as the government had managed to arrest the Jacobite leaders in the south west of England. The leader of the north-eastern army was the 3rd Earl of Derwentwater.

In early October 1715, Derwentwater, together with his younger brother, Charles (later the 5th Earl) were on the march and joined with Scottish border Jacobites. This joint force then turned south, reaching as far as Lancashire by the following month. There they were joined by the future 9th Duke of Norfolk (whose older brother was Grand Master of English Masons in 1730—see Chapter 7). At the Battle of Preston in mid-November, the Jacobites were initially successful against Hanoverian troops, but the 'Government Forces' (the name used for the army of King George) were re-enforced overnight and eventually won the day. Many of the supporters of King James surrendered. The 3rd Earl (James Radcliffe) and his brother were taken prisoner. Both were taken into custody as traitors to the crown and placed in the Tower of London.

The Earl of Mar was now officially appointed by the exiled king as the commander of the Jacobite army. At the Battle of Preston, he won a partial victory over the Government Forces at Sheriffmuir, near Dunblane, but failed to finish off Argyll's army, leaving both sides to claim victory. The Jacobite general (and Grand Master of the Scottish Knights Templar) now retreated to Perth, while Inverness changed hands again—the town surrendered to Hanoverian troops. The Jacobite fortunes were now on the wane; Preston had been lost and much of Scotland was being recovered by government troops.

Three days before Christmas 1715, the Jacobite king (still styling himself James III of England and VIII of Scotland) finally arrived, landing at Peterhead on the east coast. He was too late—the Earl of Mar's army had shrunk back to a few thousand men. In contrast, the Duke of Argyll's government force was growing by day in men and materials. 'King' James was to remain in Scotland for less than six weeks, before fleeing back to France. Mar would also leave for the continent, the government stripping him of his titles and property.

In the meantime, James and Charles Radcliffe were being held in the Tower of London and escorted by armed guard each day to their trial at Westminster. In true gentlemanly style, the Lieutenant of the Tower (a senior officer) permitted them to stop and dine at the Fountain Tavern, a venue used for Masonic meetings, in the Strand. He was roundly criticised for allowing Jacobite or 'rebel lords' to do so.

James Radcliffe, or Lord Derwentwater to give him his official title, pleaded guilty to treason. He was sentenced to death with his brother, who was only twenty-two years old. They awaited their punishment in the infamous Newgate Prison, where the Old Bailey now stands. Despite appeals for clemency, there was no reprieve and on 24 February 1716, the 3rd Earl of Derwentwater was beheaded on Tower Hill. To his last breath, he continued to voice his support for the Jacobite cause and the Roman Catholic religion. Freemasons will recall that in the Third Degree prayer that the chaplain beseeches the Almighty that the candidate 'may finally rise from the tomb of transgression, to shine as the stars for ever and ever.' This seems to be case with Lord Derwentwater; when his body arrived in the north east, there was a magnificent display of Northern Lights. As with the Earl of Mar, the Derwentwater title and lands were forfeited, albeit his relatives in exile would continue to use the name.

Charles Radcliffe faced an even worse fate—being hanged, drawn, and quartered. Fortunately for Rose Croix Masons, he escaped from Newgate and the manner of his break out is worthy of note. Security at the gaol had been tightened due to several previous prison breaks. Charles, however, had the support of his fellow inmates. On the chosen night, they caused a distraction by holding a noisy party on the top floor, allowing Radcliffe to slip into the less secure debtors' part of the prison. There, he stole a brown 'tie-wig' (similar to that worn by barristers today) and convinced the turn-key (warder) that he was (in the words of the Monopoly game) 'just visiting'. He was soon back on the streets of London and managed to board a ship bound for Boulogne.

The son of James Radcliffe took the title 4th Earl of Derwentwater, despite the family being stripped of the right to do so. James had no sons, so on his death in 1731, the title was taken by his uncle, prison escapee, Charles. He now became known in the Jacobite court in exile as the 5th Earl. Some five or six years earlier, James had been assisted to form what may have been the first Masonic lodge in Paris, and this fell under the jurisdiction of the English Grand Master, Lord Wharton. As described above, Wharton was a notorious Jacobite, who had visited the exiled king. He would go on to be the only Grand Master ever wanted on warrant for treason (see Chapter 5). There is documentary proof that Derwentwater was Past Master of the Lodge that met in Rue de Bussy in Paris. The Parisian lodges had originally applied to form a Provincial Grand Lodge. In 1736, Derwentwater was appointed Grand Master of France and held this position for two years. It may have been around this time that he designed the Scottish Rite.

Charles Derwentwater, the 5th Earl, would return to England in 1745 in the last Jacobite up-rising. He was gambling on a successful restoration of the Stuart Dynasty and the grandson of James II, Bonnie Prince Charlie, taking the throne as Charles III of England. Derwentwater was, after all, still subject to a warrant of execution, having been sentenced to death in 1715. His return and subsequent fate are described in Chapter 8.

Despite these several links to the Craft, we are unlikely ever to know the extent of the influence that Freemasonry had on Jacobites, namely whether it was an important factor in the plots to return the Stuart dynasty to the throne of Great Britain or an interesting hobby that exiles practiced to remind them of home. As the respected Masonic researcher, Worshipful Brother John Hamill, noted in a paper on Jacobites and Freemasonry: 'What conclusions can we draw? That there were Jacobites who were also Freemasons is beyond doubt. That those Jacobites had influence on Freemasonry or used Freemasonry for political ends has not been proven.' For all this, subsequent chapters will describe many more Jacobite Freemasons who would fight for their cause, with many facing most dreadful punishments, sentenced to death as traitors.

5

Lord Wharton:
Grand Master, Traitor, and Flasher

Masonic Connection
Grand Master wanted for treason
Grand Master's strange behaviour

Date
1722–23: Grand Master
1726: Wedding where 'indecent exposure' occurred
1727: Arrest warrant for treason issued

Connection to London
Pall Mall: Home address of Wharton
Stationers' Hall, Ave Maria Lane: Wharton appointed as Grand Master

Lodges
Grand Lodge of England

Philip Wharton (born 1698) became Duke of Wharton at the age of sixteen on his father's death in 1715. He is a very colourful character (and Grand Master), being a man of many parts—a well-educated, travelled young man, but also a 'rake' (an eighteenth century 'hell raiser'), drunk, and founder of the Hellfire Club—a bizarre gentleman's club where blasphemy (even devil worship) and heavy drinking were alleged to have taken place. Once the Hellfire Club had been closed (after the intervention of King George I), Wharton became a Freemason joining a lodge in London, which met near St Paul's Cathedral. Newspapers of the time reported that he returned to his home in Pall Mall still wearing his new white leather apron.

Despite never having been the Master of his own lodge (and being only twenty-two years old), he was able to have himself elected as the sixth Grand Master in 1722. Wharton somehow managed to oust the previous Grand Master, the Duke of Montagu, causing much disharmony in the fledgling Grand Lodge (formed for only five years). It was reported at the time:

his Grace appointed no Deputy, nor was the Lodge opened and closed in due Form. Therefore the noble Brothers and all those that would not countenance Irregularities, disown'd WHARTON'S authority, till worthy Brother MONTAGU heal'd the Breach of Harmony.

Wharton was not to last long as Grand Master. His attempt to change the rules regarding the appointment of a Deputy Grand Master failed and this seemed to have displeased him. The Grand Lodge minutes record that, 'The late Grand Master went away from the Hall without Ceremony.' In modern parlance, it would appear that he 'stormed out' and then had little to do with Freemasonry, but did not leave completely, as we will see. Wharton is then rumoured to have been involved in the 'Gormorgons'—a strange, quasi-Masonic Order that met in 'chapters'. The Gormorgons claimed to have been founded by the first emperor of China and would only admit Masons if they renounced their membership. After the Duke's death, this odd group fizzled out.

Most importantly, Wharton was a Jacobite who gave his support to the self-styled James III of England and VIII of Scotland. James would subsequently be known as the 'Old Pretender', to differentiate him from his son (Bonnie Prince Charlie), the 'Young Pretender'. Wharton visited James III at his court in exile in France. The pretender king awarded him the Order of the Garter, which the Duke wore in public, thereby proclaiming himself an active supporter of those wishing to remove George I from the throne. Robert Walpole, King George's Prime Minister, tasked his spies to report on Wharton's activities; it is by their reports that we find that the Duke's life had descended into further scandal; often fuelled by drunkenness and debt. At his wedding in 1726, he exposed his penis not only to his bride (you may argue such is acceptable) but also to the whole wedding party, to demonstrate to his new wife 'what she was to have that night in her Gutts'—not the behaviour one would expect from a Duke and a Past Grand Master.

Worse, however, was to come. Wharton, desperate for money, sold his title back to George I. He then joined the Jacobite forces as a Lieutenant Colonel and fought with the Spanish army, who were besieging Gibraltar in 1727 (only fourteen years after the 'Rock' became a British possession). While blind drunk, the Past Grand Master led a charge against the British forces and was shot in the foot, ending his involvement in the campaign. Most significantly, Wharton had taken up arms against his native land and by doing so had committed perhaps the most serious of all crimes—treason. If he had been the Master of a lodge, the 'Antient Charges and Regulations' would have been read to him at his Installation and he would have sworn to support them. These still include 'No. 3: You promise not to be concerned in plots or conspiracies against the government.' However, he had, as we have seen, never been a Master of a lodge and these regulations had possibly never been read to him. Due to his treachery, a warrant for his arrest was issued, but the former Duke remained in Spain. Lieutenant Colonel Philip Wharton, as he now was, tried to save his skin by spying for the English against his new Spanish friends. The offer was rejected, as the intelligence he was offering was of little value.

While the English warrant of arrest was never executed, Wharton was arrested and imprisoned by the authorities in Madrid for beating his servant; his life was an amazing descent from Dukedom to incarceration. Bizarrely, he still found time to constitute the first lodge under the Grand Lodge of England on foreign soil—the Madrid Lodge in 1728.

He was, by this stage, a chronic alcoholic; this, no doubt, contributed to his death in 1731 (aged just thirty-two). He was buried in northern Spain and his tomb can still be seen in the town of Poblet. Thus ends the life of the (former) Duke, who became the Grand Master at twenty-two years old, but was also a drunk, a 'hell-rake', a flasher, and a traitor to his country.

6

Sent to the Tower:
Masons and Jacobite Plots

Masonic Connection
Grand Master and treasonous plot
Masonic connections to the Tower of London

Date
1722: Arrested on suspicion of treason
1730: Grand Master of England

Connection to London
Tower of London: Mason imprisoned at this Royal Palace

Lodges
Grand Lodge of England
Royal Somerset House and Inverness Lodge No. 4

Lord Wharton was not the only senior Freemason with Jacobite sympathies. Another supporter of the Stuart dynasty was Thomas Howard, 8th Duke of Norfolk, later the thirteenth Grand Master of the Grand Lodge of England. As a follower of the Roman Catholic faith, the Duke had every reason to desire the return of a descendant of James II to the throne; laws had been enacted to bar Roman Catholics from holding government office. As a result of his actions to return a Stuart king to the throne of Great Britain, the Duke of Norfolk was, it would appear, the first senior English member of the Craft to be locked in the Tower of London.

The Tower is an iconic London landmark; the official title is 'Her Majesty's Royal Palace and Fortress'. It was built in 1078 by William the Conqueror to secure the capital of his newly acquired country, England. Over the centuries, the fortress has been used for several purposes, including a royal palace, the treasury, Royal Mint, a public records office, and most recently, the repository of the Crown Jewels. Its most infamous use is that of a prison for dangerous and important prisoners, particularly those suspected of the most heinous crime against the state, high treason. Between 1100 and 1952, the Tower was a jail for many high-profile captives, including Anne Boleyn, second wife of Henry VIII; Sir Walter Raleigh, the famous explorer; Rudolf Hess, Deputy Fuhrer of Nazi Germany; and more recently, the Kray Twins.

Prior to the twentieth century, conditions in the Tower were, however, far more comfortable than in other London prisons, where disease was rife and cell conditions were dreadful. It is fair to say that imprisonment in Newgate and other London jails was a brutal experience. In contrast, the Tower was a gilded cage for gentlemen and ladies, who had fallen foul of the law, or more dangerously, the monarch of that time. For example, rooms were converted to enable the family of Sir Walter Raleigh to live with him and, as we will see in Chapter 10, another Grand Master, the 5th Lord Byron, was accompanied by his wife and children while awaiting his trial on a charge of murder. For all the luxuries that came with such confinement, prisoners sailing down the Thames under guard and entering via Traitors' Gate knew that they may never leave the Tower again; if they did, it would be in a coffin with their head separated from their body. The severed heads of recently executed prisoners, displayed on pikes above the infamous gate, would have further emphasised their potential fate.

In the early 1720s, the Duke of Norfolk became involved in a Jacobite conspiracy, led by the bishop of the Kent town of Rochester, the Right Reverend Francis Atterbury. The plotters included several other peers of the realm, including the exiled Earl of Mar and several government officials. Their plan was to arrest King George and, using an army of retired soldiers, seize key government buildings, including the Royal Mint, the Bank of England, and the Tower.

In the summer of 1722, the conspirators were exposed. Attempts had been made to recruit troops for the Jacobite cause from France and this information came into the hands of government officials loyal to the king. Many of the key members of the plot, including Bishop Atterbury were arrested on suspicion of treason and placed in the Tower. The government was so determined to ensure that the Jacobite threat was crushed, that the ancient law of *habeas corpus* (which prevented detention without trial) was suspended.

The Duke of Norfolk, however, was not detained in the first wave of arrests. He was taken into custody on 27 October and placed in the Tower with his co-conspirators. There was little chance that he would enjoy the presence of his family as others did. The Duke had an unhappy marriage and his wife refused to even visit him. Not all was lost; he still had two servants to ease the inconvenience of imprisonment. It was also rather fortunate that his cousin, the 3rd Earl of Carlisle, was the constable of the Tower, the senior officer in charge of the building. It should be noted that Lord Wharton, the Jacobite, was Grand Master of England at the time of Norfolk's detention.

The key allegation, which had resulted in the Duke of Norfolk's arrest, related to coded cross Channel communications with a Jacobite agent, who was based in Flanders in modern day Belgium. It was claimed that this agent then passed the messages to the Pretender King in France or James III of England. The Duke's codename was said to be 'Mrs Jones'.

In the end, the case against the Duke and many of the other suspected plotters collapsed. The allegations were vague and even if the letters had involved treachery, the Duke had worded them cleverly enough to ensure that charges against him would be very difficult to prove. After several months in custody, he was released in May 1723, initially on bail (the Earl of Carlisle stood surety), but later, he was completely exonerated.

While the Duke could not take government office due to his religious beliefs, he was appointed Grand Master of English Freemasons in 1730, fewer than eight years after he had been locked in the Tower, facing possible execution. This does demonstrate the enlightened views of Masonry and shows that the principle of accepting men of all religious creeds was active in the early years of Grand Lodge.

It is unclear where or when the Duke of Norfolk joined the Craft, but he does appear to have been an active member. It is recorded that on 12th May 1730 he paid a visit to the influential Horn Lodge No. 3 (now Royal Somerset House and Inverness Lodge No.4), which met at the tavern of the same name near the Palace of Westminster. It is recorded that 'several… persons of distinction were present' and these included a Past Grand Master, the 2nd Duke of Richmond.

As was the custom at that time, the Duke only remained in office as Grand Master for one year. He lived until he was only forty-nine years old, dying in 1732. His brother, who became the 9th Duke, was also a Jacobite. There is a Masonic footnote to this story. In 1813, when the United Grand Lodge was formed and the two rival Grand Lodges were fused, the Grand Master, the Duke of Sussex, wished to appoint a Deputy. His first choice was the 11th Duke of Norfolk, who, despite having been the Provincial Grand Master for Herefordshire, does not seem to have wanted the position. The Duke of Sussex made clear that Roman Catholic faith was no bar to the role and added that the 8th Duke had, as we have seen, been Grand Master. No reply was ever received, and the Duke of Sussex had to make do with another Deputy Grand Master.

7

Artistic Masons,
a Broken Oath, and a Runaway Bride

Masonic Connection
Artists: Hogarth and Thornhill
Third Degree obligation
Freemasonry depicted in art

Date
1728: Hogarth initiated into Masonry
1729: Eloped with Grand Warden's daughter

Connection to London
Tate Gallery, Millbank: Hogarth's engraving *Night* features a London Masonic scene
National Portrait Gallery, Trafalgar Square: Bust of Hogarth on Leicester Square side of building
Leicester Square: Hogarth's central London residence
Chiswick: Hogarth's home, off the Great West Rd (A4) is open to the public
St Paul's Cathedral: Dome interior painted by Sir James Thornhill (Hogarth's father-in-law)

Lodges
Grand Stewards'
St George and Corner Stone No. 5
Jerusalem No. 197

Now to a case of Masonic scandal and oath breaking, but not criminal acts. We will see how popular art work of the day was used to attack others, with brother Masons also falling into the firing line. It is also an interesting case as it involves two artists, whose work is still respected and can be enjoyed today in London, in the Tate Gallery and St Paul's Cathedral respectively. If nothing else, it shows the levels of influence once enjoyed by Freemasonry over many areas of life in times past, not just in the Armed Forces and politics, but also in the arts.

The 'villain' of this tale is William Hogarth, the famous artist and engraver, who created such works as *A Rake's Progress*. His work tended to be moralistic and put forward the idea that those who live by the law will be rewarded; for example, in *Industry and Idleness* (a series of engravings showing the progress through life of one hardworking and one idle young men), the conscientious man eventually attains the office of Lord Mayor of London. The indolent apprentice drifts into a life of crime and is eventually hanged (on the orders of his hard-working opposite). He received £200—at the time, the highest fee ever paid—for a portrait to paint David Garrick, the famous actor and (possible) Mason.

In Freemasonry, Hogarth joined an (unnamed) lodge No. 41, which met at the Hand and Apple Tree tavern in 1728 (the lodge was to be 'erased' just nine years later). He then joined the Corner Stone lodge (now St George and Corner Stone Lodge No. 5) and in 1735, the prestigious Grand Stewards' Lodge. Indeed, he presented the latter lodge with a hand-painted jewel for the Master to wear.

Freemasonry featured in Hogarth's art, especially in his series entitled *Four Times of the Day*. This set of four engravings is now displayed in the Tate Gallery in London and comprises *Morning* (in Covent Garden), *Noon* (in Soho), and *Evening* (in Islington), but it is the final piece, *Night*, which is of Masonic interest. The engraving is set near Charing Cross and shows a drunken Worshipful Master (his collar with square can be seen) staggering up a road with the Tyler (the lodge door guard has a sword and his keys). A lady can be seen tipping the contents of a chamber pot on their heads from an upper window.

It has been suggested that the street depicted is the original Channel Row (now Cannon Row) near the House of Parliament in Westminster, where the Rummer and Grapes Lodge met—one of the original four lodges which formed the Grand Lodge of London and Westminster in 1717. It may also be nearer Trafalgar Square, as the other tavern depicted is the Cardigan's Head, which was in Spring Gardens, just off The Mall. Given that the statue of King Charles I on horseback can be seen in the background of the engraving, this location may be correct—the statue is still at the junction of Whitehall and Trafalgar Square (the king is looking at the place where his head was chopped off). It should be noted that the Cardigan's Head was used by (the unnamed) lodge No. 80 for meetings around this time. The lodge was disbanded in 1743.

The Worshipful Master and the Tyler in this scene may well have been real men and victims of Hogarth's vicious sense of humour. While Hogarth endeavoured to send moral messages in his work, he certainly did not 'maintain a Master Mason's honour and carefully preserve it as my own' as the Third Degree requires. He used his artistic talents to attack those he was in dispute with, Mason or not. As the great Masonic researcher, Worshipful Brother Yasha Beresiner, has observed, 'Hogarth was to continue to depict Freemasons on several occasions. In doing so, as was the case with many of his other portrayals, he often antagonised his contemporaries and is seen as a controversial painter at best and cantankerous and spiteful at worst'. His vicious caricature of politician and fellow Mason, John Wilkes, was taken as a great insult and almost cost Wilkes his life. Wilkes had been initiated into the Jerusalem Lodge No. 197 in very odd circumstances (see Chapter 12).

Despite this flaw in his character, Hogarth is celebrated throughout London. He initially worked as an apprentice near Leicester Square and his statue can be found there. A bust of Hogarth also forms part of the outside decoration of the National Portrait Gallery. His home in Chiswick is now owned by the London Borough of Hounslow and is open to the public. A more unfortunate memorial is the nearby road system, which is named after him; the Hogarth Roundabout is probably best known to most west Londoners as being a cause of traffic jams.

The Masonic case of the runaway bride was in direct contravention of the Third Degree obligation. The wronged party is an older Mason, Sir James Thornhill, who was born around 1675 and, after being the Master of a lodge in Greenwich (unnamed), he achieved very high rank in the Craft—Senior Grand Warden. He was also a Member of Parliament for the area around Weymouth in Dorset. Thornhill painted the eight sections of the interior of the magnificent dome at St Paul's Cathedral in London, depicting the life of the Apostle after whom the building is dedicated. Thornhill was a director at an art academy in Great Queen Street, now the location of Grand Lodge. Thornhill later established his own academy in nearby Covent Garden and it would appear that Hogarth was a student there. This may have been how Hogarth met Thornhill's daughter. Whatever the case, Hogarth and Jane Thornhill started a relationship, which led to them eloping in 1729 and marrying in secret in a Paddington church. This is clearly in breach of the Third Degree obligation, where a Mason promises to 'strictly respect the chastity of those nearest and dearest to him in the persons of his wife, his sister, and his child'.

Sir James Thornhill.
Brother William Hogarth
eloped with the daughter
of this senior Mason.

Hogarth may have had an excuse as to the several breaches of the Obligation of a Master Mason; the Third Degree was still being developed at this point in Masonic history (his wedding was just twelve years after formation of the Premier Grand Lodge in 1717—so he may never have entered into this solemn promise). Additionally, Thornhill seems to have forgiven Hogarth, his now son-in-law and the two men remained friends. Given Thornhill's senior rank in the Craft, he could have made life in Masonry very difficult for Hogarth, if he had chosen to do so. The Senior Grand Warden died in 1734, with his son-in-law outliving him by thirty years, passing away in 1764. Hogarth is buried in St Nicholas's churchyard near his home in Chiswick and David Garrick, composed this epitaph for his tomb:

> *Farewell great Painter of Mankind*
> *Who reach'd the noblest point of Art*
> *Whose pictur'd Morals charm the Mind*
> *And through the Eye correct the Heart.*
> *If Genius fire thee, Reader, stay,*
> *If Nature touch thee, drop a Tear:*
> *If neither move thee, turn away,*
> *For Hogarth's honour'd dust lies here.*

Hogarth was loved by some Masons and hated by others. In the Ancient Charge, Masons are told to use 'the talents wherewith God has blessed you to His glory and the welfare of your fellow creatures'. Unfortunately, he sometimes used his artistic talent in a very negative manner against his brother Masons.

8

Tortured and sent to the Galleys for being a Mason

Masonic Connection
Refusal to betray Masonic secrets
Mason sentenced by Portuguese Inquisition
Vatican views on the Craft

Date
1743: Established secret lodge in Portugal

Connection to London
16 Fleet Street: Coffee house, where lodge met

Lodges
Britannic No. 33
Unnamed Portuguese lodge (erased)

This is a shocking, but inspirational story, involving a British citizen suffering dreadful torture at the hands of the Portuguese Inquisition, who demanded that he renounce his Protestant faith and reveal the secrets of Freemasonry. As punishment for his failure to comply, Brother John Coustos was then condemned by the Roman Catholic authorities in Lisbon to be a galley slave in the Portuguese navy. This case is arguably the finest example of a member of the Craft obeying his obligations and not revealing the secrets entrusted to him. As we saw in Chapter 2, the Third Degree ceremony relates how Hiram Abif, the chief architect at the building of King Solomon's Temple, was brutally beaten in a vain attempt to force him to disclose Masonic secrets. The brother, who is the subject of this chapter, found himself in a very similar situation.

Coustos was born in Bern, Switzerland in 1703, but his parents moved to England during his childhood and he became a British citizen. As an adult, he trained as a jeweller, specialising in cutting precious stones, which resulted in him travelling across Europe. He was initiated into Freemasonry in London during 1730, when he joined a lodge, then No. 75, which met at the Rainbow Coffee House in Fleet Street. Coustos's initiation is of

John Coustos was tortured and sent
to the galleys for being a Mason.

note for Masonic historians; it is the first recorded time that a new Mason was presented
with a pair of white gloves in an English lodge. His lodge would subsequently become
known as Britannic No. 33, later the Metropolitan Grand Master's personal lodge.

Coffee houses in eighteenth century London were much suited to the enlightened and
influential men attracted to Freemasonry at that time. They were a place to debate the
issues of the day and were, sometimes, a hotbed of political discussion and even, sedition.
They were perceived to be so dangerous that King Charles II had attempted to ban them.
For all the monarch's efforts, the coffee craze took off, despite the English at first not taking
to the drink—it had been described in one journal as 'bitter Mohammedan gruel'. Not only
did the caffeine fuel discussion, the coffee also helped drunks to sober up. In addition to
learned men and drunks, prostitutes often loitered in such premises, adding an element of
sexual scandal to the coffee house culture. Freemason William Hogarth depicted such in
his engraving *Morning*, as part of the *Four Times of the Day* series.

The Rainbow Coffee House was notable in the development of the culture. It was the
second such house to open in London, and was frequented by some of the most influential
men in the capital. This included Dr Desaguliers, a member of the Royal Society and the
third Grand Master of England in 1719. The Rainbow was also a meeting place for the

Huguenots, the French Protestants who had fled their homeland to escape persecution by the Roman Catholic Church. One cannot underestimate the influence of religion on the lives of men of that time. Coustos would have felt at home with the Huguenots, as he was also an ardent follower of the Protestant faith. The building, where the Rainbow was located at 16 Fleet Street, still exists, but the premises has been a legal bookshop for many years.

The Swiss born, naturalised Englishman, Coustos, further demonstrates the international nature of the Craft (even in the eighteenth century); he joined a lodge in Paris not long after his initiation. He was also a member of the London-based Union French lodge (No. 98), which met in taverns and coffee houses around the Strand. This lodge no longer exists, as it became defunct in 1753.

In early 1743, Coustos moved to Lisbon and quickly established a Masonic lodge. This was not a particularly wise decision as Freemasonry had been declared a sin by the Pope and prohibited. This was taken most seriously by the authorities in Portugal, a fervently Roman Catholic country. Furthermore, when Coustos was establishing his lodge in Lisbon, the ban was just six years old and so still fresh in the minds of the religious zealots tasked to enforce such matters.

The origin of the ban was a Vatican enquiry into Italian Freemasonry, which had been established in Florence. The Roman Inquisition investigated a lodge meeting in the city and membership was denounced as being contrary to the Roman Catholic faith by the Pope, Clement XII. In 1737, the Pope issued a Papal Bull (these orders have a lead seal or *bulla*, hence the name) banning Freemasonry and declaring members of the Craft 'depraved and perverted'. This stance has altered little and as late as 1983, at the time of Pope John Paul II, the Vatican's position was as follows: 'The faithful who enrol in Masonic associations are in a state of grave sin and may not receive Holy Communion.' It further reminded Roman Catholics, 'membership … remains forbidden.' It should be noted that Freemasonry is happy to welcome followers of the Roman faith.

In an attempt to keep the lodge secret, the brethren did not meet in a coffee house or tavern in the Portuguese capital, as it would have in London, but in a private residence. This still failed to conceal the Masonic activity and the lodge was denounced by a local woman, who informed the church that the Freemasons were 'monsters of nature who perpetrated the most shocking crimes.' To make matters worse, several local Roman Catholics had been initiated into the secrets and mysteries of Freemasonry. This no doubt aggravated the matter in the eyes of the Portuguese Inquisition—the branch of the Roman Catholic church responsible for investigating (and punishing) heresy and other religious crimes.

Many will have heard of the Spanish Inquisition, but the Portuguese version was equally as ruthless. In just under three hundred years (1536–1821), the inquisitors sentenced nearly 1,200 people to death, not just on the Iberian Peninsula, but also in the Portuguese colonies of Brazil and Goa. The Inquisition was particularly interested in witchcraft, Jews who had converted to Christianity (but, it was suspected, continued to follow their original faith), crimes of bigamy and, of course, Freemasonry. The Inquisition had much influence and power—it was led by a Grand Inquisitor, who was selected by the king and answered to the Pope. The inquisitors were made up of members of the Dominican Order, a section of the

Pope Clement XII issued a Papal Bull against the craft and described Masons as 'depraved and perverted'.

Roman Catholic Church established to combat heresy. Due to their dark cloaks, in England they were known as the 'Black Friars' (for a Masonic link to Blackfriars Bridge in London, see Chapter 57).

In early March 1743, Coustos and several other members of the lodge were detained by the Inquisition. Coustos and the lodge Senior Warden, who were both jewellers, were originally informed that they had been arrested on suspicion of being involved in the theft of a diamond, but these were trumped-up charges. Having been thrown into a dungeon and held in solitary confinement, Coustos was initially quizzed about his involvement in crimes in general, but after three days, the true reason for his arrest was revealed. During this interrogation, the inquisitors first mentioned Freemasonry, or, as they described it, 'a forbidden institution.' In their minds, he was also guilty of another heresy—being a Protestant.

For several weeks, Coustos was regularly removed from his dark cell and questioned about Masonic rituals and membership. He refused to reveal details of other members of his lodge in Lisbon. The Inquisition, however, had already arrested three of the brethren—Damaio de Andrade, Manoel de Revehot, and Christopher Diego. As Portuguese citizens and Roman Catholics, they were shown no mercy and for the crime of joining the Craft they were hanged on 8 March.

The inquisitors were tiring of Coustos's stubborn nature and refusal to answer questions. They therefore decided to apply their 'tender mercies', a rather euphemistic name for torture—often of the most brutal kind. This occurred in a specially designed room, lit only by two candles and with quilted material on the doors. This covering dampened the cries of the victim and prevented the noise carrying to the other cells. The inquisitors of the Dominican Order were officially authorised to use torture; a Papal Bull of 1252 permitted it to be used to extract confessions from heretics. The Bull did not, however, allow them to cause loss of life or limb, hence a surgeon was present. The attendance of a doctor also ensured that the tortured man did not escape by possibly the only means left to him—death.

In preparation for each ordeal, Coustos was stripped to his undergarments. Over a period of weeks, he was tortured nine times. These are some of the methods used by the Portuguese Inquisition:

The victim was secured to a scaffold by an iron collar, with iron rings fastened to each foot. These were then pulled with great force to painfully stretch the body, particularly the limbs.

Ropes were bound around the arms and thighs and then pulled tight by four men. The ropes were deliberately thin in width, so that they cut into the flesh. As they cut off the circulation, the tortured man was likely to faint.

The outstretched arms were pulled upwards by means of a rope, so that the backs of the hands came together, in order to dislocate the arms at the shoulder. The surgeons would then manually reset the joints, causing even more excruciating pain.

A thick iron chain was wound across the body, whilst the victim was fastened to a board. The wrists were also secured and the chain was then tightened to crush the stomach area. In Coustos's case, this torture also dislocated his wrists.

For all their efforts, the Inquisition extracted little from Coustos, who steadfastly refused to convert to Roman Catholicism. In relation to Freemasonry, he gave away none of the secrets and just gave some general information on the rituals. He informed his torturers that the Third Degree mentioned that three Fellowcrafts had murdered Hiram Abif. When further tortured, he mentioned that when King Solomon's Temple was destroyed, a bronze plate was found with the name of God, 'Jehovah', inscribed thereon. The name of God was known to the friars torturing him and the idea of such an engraved bronze plate was freely published in *Orbis Miraculum*, an English work from 1659, which described King Solomon's Temple in great detail.

Several weeks of torture had proved fruitless, so Coustos was sentenced to serve four years as a galley slave with the Portuguese navy. It is incredible that such slaves still existed in the eighteenth century. But exist they did and just like the Roman galley slaves, portrayed in the film *Ben Hur*, they were chained to their oar. There they ate, slept and conducted all other bodily functions. The only hygiene measure was to shave the heads of the slaves; this prevented the spread of lice. Food consisted of stale bread and bean stew. If their ship sank, the slaves went with it to the bottom of the Mediterranean; the only chance of freedom would come if their boat was captured by an enemy force (from their own country).

The Portuguese courts knew that their king needed men to power flat bottom boats, which were ideal for coastal skirmishes with Arab or Turkish pirates. As a result, those convicted of crimes (secular and religious) were often sent to the galleys. Some of those so condemned were, however, unfit for such arduous work. This included Coustos, who was in ill-health and weakened due to the torture inflicted on him. Lack of food and living in a dungeon for weeks had also worsened his physical state and he was given the task of carrying water to the other slaves. Others in his position were used to carry timber and other supplies onto ships.

The Inquisition had not given up on their duties to combat heresy. While Coustos could no longer attend a Masonic lodge while serving his sentence, he could still pray to God as a Protestant. In a further effort to convert him to the 'true faith', Irish members of the Dominican Order were sent to persuade him to convert. Despite freedom being the reward for turning to the Roman Catholic Church, Coustos steadfastly refused to renounce his Protestant beliefs.

His health waning, Coustos used a far more secular method of escape—bribery, or in his own words 'amply rewarding the overseers'—but he was still in Portugal and in danger of further torture and imprisonment. At the same time, the British Ambassador, on the orders of King George II, was attempting to have Coustos repatriated. This was to prove successful and after some eighteen months in custody, in October 1744, Coustos boarded a Dutch ship bound for London. He was to arrive on 15 December. It should be noted that George II is not known to have been a Freemason, but as a Hanoverian monarch he was a staunch defender of Protestantism against the ever-present Roman Catholic threat (with its links to the Jacobites). The fate of his Senior Warden, who had also been arrested, is unknown.

On Coustos's return, he wrote a book about his experiences in Portugal, entitled *The Sufferings of John Coustos for Freemasonry, and for refusing to turn Roman Catholic, in the Inquisition at Lisbon*. His bravery was also the subject of articles and songs. Indeed, as we will see in Chapter 11, a song written by him was a central part of celebrations held for the installation of the 5th Lord Byron as Grand Master in 1747. Some claimed that Coustos may have exaggerated the torture used against him, but he was already dead by the time of Byron's installation. He had passed away during the previous year; his treatment in Portugal had left him a broken and sick man.

Neither did the Roman Catholic suppression of the Craft end in Iberia. In 1815, the Bishop of Almeria, who also held the post of Spanish Inquisitor General, accused lodges as being 'societies which lead to sedition … and to all errors and crimes.' In Spain, as in Portugal, simply being suspected of being a member of the Craft was deemed an arrestable offence. In 1818, the Portuguese king decreed that anyone found guilty of this crime would suffer 'a cruel death' and have all property confiscated by the crown. Little wonder that the Duke of Wellington (himself an Entered Apprentice) had warned British troops serving in Iberia during the Peninsular War to desist from Masonic activities. He cautioned against engaging in Freemasonry in Portugal, describing the Craft as 'an amusement which, however innocent in itself and allowed by the law of Great Britain, is a violation of the law of this country, and very disagreeable to its people'.

Despite the activities of the Inquisition, until the Second World War and the imprisonment of Freemasons by Nazis, Coustos was one of the few men jailed for Masonic activity (see also Chapter 20 for Brother, the Count Cagliostro, who also fell afoul of the Roman church). The torture of Coustos is a warning of the ugly nature of religious extremism, which continues to rear its head in several forms throughout the world, even today. His story also shows that there are men of honour, who take their Masonic obligations seriously and would rather 'suffer death' (as the Third Degree ritual tells us) than improperly reveal the secrets of the Craft. For displaying such fortitude and bravery, Brother John Coustos deserves to be remembered by today's Freemasons.

9

1745 and the Uprising that led to the Execution of the Grand Master of Scotland

Masonic Connection
Masons fighting for Jacobites and King George
Magistrate, who sentenced Jacobites to death
Highest ranked British Mason ever executed

Date
1745–46: The Jacobite Rebellion

Connection to London
Cockspur Street: Grand Master of Scotland member of an English lodge at a coffee house at this location
Borough High Street, junction with Southwark Street: Venue of trial
Trinity Square, Tower Hill: Memorial to executed Grand Master
Kennington Common (St Mark's Church): Mason executed
St Giles's-in-the-Fields church, Camden: Mason buried there after execution
Soho Square: Past Grand Master of Scotland died in exile

Lodges
'French' or Un-named Lodge No. 44 (erased)
Vine Tavern No. 60 or No. 68 (erased)
Mother Kilwinning No. 0 (Scotland)
Lodge of Edinburgh Mary's Chapel No.1 (Scotland)
Lodge Canongate of Kilwinning No. 2 (Scotland)
Lodge Dalkeith Kilwinning No. 10 (Scotland)
Lodge St John No.16 (Scotland)
Lodge of Dundee No. 47 (Scotland)

The links between Jacobites and Freemasonry have been explored in several previous chapters. This section will cover the Jacobite rebellion of 1745, which ended in failure for the Stuart dynasty and led to the execution of several Masons who had backed that cause.

It would also pitch neighbour against neighbour and, in the style of Cain and Abel, brother against brother. The uprising saw Mason fighting Mason, even Grand Masters of England in battle against Grand Masters of Scotland.

In 1745, the leader of the Stuart court-in-exile was Charles Edward Stuart, better known today as 'Bonnie Prince Charlie', who had been born in Italy. His father, the self-styled James III, was still alive, but had named Charles as his Prince Regent. James had obtained the support of the French government for his cause and this rekindled the hope of Jacobite success.

At the time, much of the British Army was deployed on mainland Europe, fighting in the War of Austrian Succession (France being one of the main countries on the opposing side). This war would see the last time a British monarch would lead his troops in battle, with George II commanding his army at the Battle of Dettingen in modern day southern Germany. With the king and many of his battalions overseas, this presented an ideal opportunity for Jacobite leaders to return to Britain, depose the Hanoverian king and restore the Stuart line. Additionally, there were already Jacobite Englishmen in France, ready to fight for this cause. Masonically, possibly the most important from England was the 5th Earl of Derwentwater. As we saw in Chapter 5, he had already taken part in the failed 1715 rebellion and had been sentenced to death for treason, but escaped from Newgate prison and fled across the Channel. It is said that during his exile in Paris he was instrumental in forming Scottish Rite (or Rose Croix) and had been Grand Master of French Freemasonry.

As with the 1715 uprising, this was not a simple case of Scottish Jacobites fighting English supporters of King George II. Neither was it Roman Catholic supporters of the Stuarts pitted against Protestant Hanoverians—supporters of both denominations fought against each other. In addition to the Earl of Derwentwater, influential Freemasons from lodges in both countries found themselves on opposing sides:

William Boyd, 4th Earl of Kilmarnock and 7th Grand Master of Scotland (1742–43), had initially supported the English king, then switched his allegiance to Bonnie Prince Charlie. The reasons for his change of heart are unclear and he was a strong Protestant. Born in Scotland, he was seemingly a member of an English lodge prior to becoming a Scottish Mason. His lodge in London met at the 'British Coffee House', which then stood in Cockspur Street, just off Trafalgar Square. This coffee house was frequented by many Scots, who were residing in London. Lord Kilmarnock was very active in Freemasonry, being the Master of the oldest Scottish lodge, Mother Kilwinning No. 0 in 1742. As Grand Master of Scotland, he authorised the formation of the first military lodge, all the petitioners serving with the Colonel Lees' Regiment (despite being formed in Sterling, as the 55th Regiment of Foot, this unit would eventually become an English regiment, now being part of the Duke of Lancaster's). Tragically, Kilmarnock's sons, who were later members of his lodge in Falkirk (now Lodge St John No. 16), fought on opposing sides. His son James (later 15th Earl of Erroll) was an officer in King George's army, while Charles fought for the Jacobites.

John Byrom, a member of the 'French' lodge, which met in the Golden Lion inn in Dean Street—this pub still stands in London's Chinatown. His family had made their fortune in Lancashire as wool merchants, but he was heavily involved in London life and was a

Bonnie Prince Charlie, leader of the Jacobite cause in 1745 and possible Freemason.

Earl of Kilmarnock, the
highest ranked British
Freemason to be executed.

member of the Royal Society. He had many talents, being the inventor of an early version of shorthand, a composer of hymns and, possibly, a Jacobite spy. It is now argued that he may have been a double agent working for King George's government, who can be described as a Masonic 'man of mystery.'

General John Campbell, 4th Earl of Loudoun (which is in Ayrshire, less than ten miles from Kilmarnock) was the Grand Master of England 1736–37. He raised a regiment of Scottish infantrymen to fight for King George's 'government forces' on the opposing side from his near neighbour, Lord Kilmarnock.

Sir Robert Dickson of Carberry a member of Lodge Dalkeith Kilwinning No. 10, and was Master of that lodge and Senior Grand Warden in the Scottish Grand Lodge in 1742; he was selected by Lord Kilmarnock, the Grand Master, as one of his most senior assistants. However, they now found each other on opposing sides, as Sir Robert raised troops for the defence of Edinburgh against the 'Highland Army' or Jacobite forces.

Prince William, Duke of Cumberland, son of King George II, was the ruthless commander of the government forces and victor at Culloden. He was later known as 'Butcher Cumberland' due to his suppressing of the Highlands after the defeat of the Jacobites. According to the Library and Museum of Freemasonry in London, Cumberland may have been initiated in Germany. He should not be confused with the subsequent Duke of Cumberland, the first royal Grand Master of England—the grandson of George II.

General Campbell, the Earl of Loudoun, past Grand Master of England, but a poor military commander.

'Butcher' Cumberland, leader of the Government Forces and Prussian Mason.

James Drummond, 3rd Duke of Perth was a member of a Scottish lodge (now called the Operative Mason Lodge of Dundee No. 47). He should have been the 6th Earl of Perth, but the earldom had been taken from his father for his involvement in the Jacobite uprising in 1715. Given the family's sympathies for the Stuart cause, in July 1745 the London government thought it wise to detain the young Duke, before he followed in his father's footsteps. Sir Patrick Murray and others visited Drummond under the pretence of having dinner, but the true aim was to make an arrest. The Duke of Perth consumed his meal, but then made his escape by a back door. After hiding overnight in a ditch, he borrowed a peasant's horse and galloped (without a saddle or bridle) to Perth to join the Jacobite army. As with the Earl of Derwentwater, this Mason's exploits are worthy of their own book.

William Home, 8th Earl of Home had been the Master of the Kilwinning Scots Arms Lodge (number unknown). Despite marrying for money, he deserted his wife and took a commission in a dragoon regiment of the Government Forces. A scoundrel, but, as we shall see, a brave man.

Lieutenant General John Lindsay, 20th Earl of Crawford, was the Grand Master of England in 1734, but had been initiated into Scottish Masonry the previous year into Lodge of Edinburgh (Mary's Chapel) No.1. He was also a Fellow of the Royal Society, as were many eminent Masons of that time. He was a career soldier who had served in some of the most famous regiments of the British Army, including the Grenadier Guards and the Black

Duke of Perth, Freemason and daring Jacobite leader.

Watch; he was the first colonel of that great Scottish Regiment. He had also seen service attached to the Russian and Austrian armies and fought, under George II, at the Battle of Dettingen and continued to serve the Government Forces.

Charles Lennox, 2nd Duke of Richmond was the Grand Master of England in 1724. Given that his father was a Mason in Chichester, where Lennox was also the Member of Parliament and mayor, he may well have been initiated there. He was also involved in establishing lodges in France at Metz and Paris. During the uprising, he served as a Lieutenant General under Cumberland.

George McKenzie, 3rd Earl of Cromartie (Cromarty is in the Highlands of Scotland, north of Inverness) was the Grand Master of Scotland 1738–39. He fought for the Jacobite cause.

John Mackenzie, Lord MacLeod and son of the Earl of Cromartie, also served in the army of Bonnie Prince Charlie. He is believed to be a Mason, but this may have been later in life, as he was only eighteen years old in 1745.

Lord George Murray was a veteran of the Jacobite cause, having fought during the 1715 rebellion. He was made a Lieutenant General under Bonnie Prince Charlie in 1745. There is no documentary evidence of his being a Freemason, but a badge has been discovered with crossed quill pens (the Masonic symbol for a secretary) engraved 'Lord George Murray, scribe to the Grand Lodge, 23rd September 1745'. Murray was a capable commander, who brought discipline to an army made up of various competing clans.

Sir James Murray of Broughton was a Scottish Mason and member of Lodge Canongate of Kilwinning No. 2. He served as secretary to Bonnie Prince Charlie during the rebellion. As we shall see, his loyalty was questionable.

Sir Archibald Primrose, like Lord Kilmarnock, was a member of the lodge in Falkirk (now Lodge St John No. 16). He had joined some five years before the uprising in 1740 and supported the Jacobites.

Sir John Wedderburn, 5th Baronet of Blackness, a member of the Lodge of Dundee (as was the Duke of Perth) served as a colonel in the Highland army.

So it can be seen that the idea that Freemasonry was a uniquely Jacobite issue is clearly wrong—the majority of brethren listed above did support the Stuart cause, but some senior figures fought for the Government Forces. There is no evidence that Bonnie Prince Charlie or his rival, George II were members of the Craft.

James Cranstoun, 6th Lord Cranstoun, was the Grand Master of England in 1745, but he was Scot from Midlothian. His politics are unclear, but in 1715, his uncle had assisted in the defence of Scotland for King George I. Likewise, the involvement of James Wemyss, 5th Earl of Wemyss (in Fife), who was the Grand Master of Scotland at the time of the rebellion, is uncertain. He had married the daughter of an infamous Scottish soldier (and non-Mason), Colonel Francis Charteris, a man who had made his fortune by gambling and was nicknamed the 'Rape Master-General', following his conviction for a vicious sexual assault on a servant. He was sentenced to death and imprisoned in Newgate Prison, but released after a campaign by his son-in-law. Charteris's despicable life inspired the painting *A Rake's Progress* by Freemason William Hogarth. Wemyss, the Grand Master, does not seem to have taken an active part in the 1745 rebellion, but the same cannot be said for his son, David, Lord Elcho, who was a colonel in Jacobite cavalry.

In July 1745, Bonnie Prince Charlie took his chance and sailed from France to Scotland. This Italian-born prince convinced the leaders of the Highland clans to join his cause, and the Jacobite standard was raised. In mid-September, the ever-growing army had reached Edinburgh and on the 17th, the gates were thrown open and Bonnie Prince Charlie entered the capital of Scotland. It can only be assumed Brother Sir Robert Dickson of Carberry, who was responsible for the government troops defending the city, had fled. Bonnie Prince Charlie's father was now proclaimed as King James VIII of Scotland and the union with England was declared 'at an end'.

The Jacobite army now turned towards the coast and met the poorly equipped government regiments at Prestonpans, some fifty miles from the border town of Berwick on Tweed. Bonnie Prince Charlie's forces were further strengthened by two Masons described above—the veteran, Lord George Murray and the Duke of Perth. Assisted by a local farmer, the Highland army was able to move silently by night on 21st September through marshland, so that a surprise attack could be launched. Despite being on the losing side, Brother the Earl of Home fought well and was given command of a government unit tasked to guard Stirling. The earl was seemingly a better soldier than a husband. Not so competent was the former Grand Master of England, General Campbell, Earl of Loudoun. His regiment was tasked to guard the money, arms and ammunition belonging to the Government Forces, but over one hundred soldiers were allowed to leave their posts and told to report back in the morning.

The Jacobites were not prepared to wait for the earl's troop to return to the battlefield. At 6 a.m., the Highlanders charged into the unsuspecting Government Forces, with battle cries and bagpipes wailing. They achieved complete success, with the engagement over in ten minutes. Over 1,500 government soldiers were captured, together with £5,000 (a small fortune) and many muskets. Fortunately for Loudoun's soldiers, who had still not appeared, they had missed the battle and had not been taken prisoner. The victory at Prestonpans was a great morale boost to the Jacobite cause and resulted in more Scots joining the army to fight for the Stuart cause.

While Bonnie Prince Charlie may have publicly declared an end to the union, he seems to have been determined to seize the crowns of Scotland and England for his father. In November, the Jacobite forces crossed the border into what is now Cumbria. The city of Carlisle was quickly taken, after a short siege led by Brother, the 3rd Duke of Perth. This then led to an argument with his superior officer, Brother Lord George Murray, whereupon the Duke resigned—surely two Masons would not argue and one then submit his resignation? Many Masons will, no doubt, be familiar with such an incident. Fortunately, the dispute was resolved and the two Masonic commanders were back on good terms. Amusingly, when Carlisle fell, the Duke of Perth found Sir Patrick Murray, who had deviously tried to arrest him at his home. The Duke was obviously forgiving type, as he did nothing to his former friend, except sarcastically to inform him, 'Sir Patie, I am to dine with you to-day.' It is unknown if the dinner took place.

One Mason determined to assist the Jacobite cause was the 5th Earl of Derwentwater. He had set sail to join the Jacobite forces (as he had in 1715), but was captured at sea in November 1745. Charles Radcliffe was never to join his beloved Bonnie Prince Charlie, but he would later pay the price for this loyalty. The authorities well knew that he was still under death sentence from his involvement in the 1715 uprising. The Grand Master of France would never see Paris again.

Following on from securing the border at Carlisle, the Jacobites took Preston in Lancashire and, after advancing into the east Midlands (the army had marched along roads, which are now the A6), on 4 December, Derby fell. This was to be the high point for the Highland army. Fortune now turned against Bonnie Prince Charlie on several fronts. The expected support of English Jacobites failed to materialise and neither did the promised French invasion ever come. Additionally, the government in London had recalled a large number of battle hardened troops from the continent and was preparing to repel the invading force. Perhaps most effectively, King George's commanders had planted a double agent in the Jacobite camp, who convinced the leaders that there were three (in reality there were two) armies ready to advance on the Highlanders.

Bonnie Prince Charlie was determined to march on London, but his support was frittering away. The main opponent to any further advance into southern England was a Jacobite Mason—Lord George Murray. His stance was supported by Lord Elcho, the son of the Grand Master of Scotland at that time. Reluctantly, the Young Pretender had to give the order to return north. It must be said, however, that the retreat was disciplined and well organised.

In London, the threat of a Jacobite attack resulted in harsh treatment of Roman Catholics. Priests were hunted down and diplomatic immunity did not appear to exist—a chaplain from the Portuguese embassy was thrown into Newgate Prison. It should be noted that this was only two years after British Protestant John Coustos had been tortured by the Portuguese Inquisition in Lisbon for being a Freemason, so there was no love lost between the two nations.

The Highland Army fell back, following a similar route to its advance and pursued by the Duke of Cumberland. The two sides would fight at Clifton, a small village near Penrith in Cumbria, six days before Christmas 1745. Brother Lord George Murray commanded the Jacobites, with orders to conduct a rear-guard to allow the main part of the army to retreat to Carlisle. In, arguably, the last battle on English soil, (it could be more realistically described as a 'skirmish') fewer than thirty soldiers (in total, from both sides) were killed.

Over the Christmas period Carlisle, taken by the Jacobites just a few weeks before, was now under siege by Government Forces commanded by Cumberland. On 30th December, the city fell and the last Jacobite stronghold in England was gone. A whole regiment of Jacobites, who had been recruited in Manchester, were taken prisoner. These were cruelty treated and later the many rebels would be tried in the city. The fighting now returns to Scotland, whence it began, with the Highland Army being pushed further and further back towards their homeland. The last major Jacobite success was at the Battle of Falkirk. Mason Lord George Murray was present as a Jacobite commander and his opposite number was the inept, but brutal General Henry Hawley. Despite this victory, the retreat northward continued. The former Grand Master of Scotland, the Earl of Kilmarnock, also fought for the Jacobites at this battle, as did Lord MacLeod, son of the Earl of Cromartie (also a Past Grand Master of Scotland).

The Past Grand Master of England, General Campbell (the Earl of Loudoun) pursued Bonnie Prince Charlie north, with the intention of capturing the Young Pretender and putting an end to the rebellion. This operation was to end in embarrassing failure.

The Jacobite leader stayed in the village of Moy on 16 February. Well knowing that the Hanoverian troops were advancing up the road from Inverness, the lady of the manor sent her son and a blacksmith with two other servants to create a diversion. During the twilight, they ran around shouting war cries and banging swords on rocks; Loudoun's force of several hundred soldiers believed that they had fallen into an ambush and beat a hasty retreat, which became known as the 'Rout of Moy'.

Further military calamity was to befall the Earl of Loudoun. In March 1746, there was a clear Mason versus Mason skirmish. The ever-adventurous Brother, the Duke of Perth, led a commando style raid on the Government Forces commanded by the hapless Past Grand Master of England. Using over thirty commandeered fishing boats, the Duke crossed Dornoch Firth in the Highlands and led a surprise attack on the camp of the opposing army. Loudoun's army was scattered and a large quantity of arms, food and other supplies fell into Jacobite hands. Once again, the former Grand Master had allowed valuable resources to fall into enemy hands.

These small victories were not enough to turn the tide. By April, the Jacobite army had been pushed into the northern tip of Scotland. The Government Forces were not the only ones being raided; the forces of King George had also captured supplies belonging to the Highlanders. On the 15th of that month, the former Grand Master of Scotland, the Earl of Cromartie, a Jacobite commander, led an attempt to take back vital food and arms. This attack, known as the Battle of Littleferry, was to end in failure, despite Cromartie commanding some of the best Jacobite forces. The earl and his son, Lord MacLeod, fled the battlefield, but were captured later the same evening in nearby Dunrobin Castle. Both men were taken to London, as prisoners, on board a Royal Navy vessel.

The following day, 16 April 1746, was the date of the fateful Battle of Culloden. This was to mark the end of the Jacobite up-rising. Brother Lord George Murray had attempted to repeat the night raid tactic, so successful at the Battle of Prestonpans, but confusion and disorder caused by the darkness and lack of tracks resulted in failure. This was a pity as every regiment in the Duke of Cumberland's government army had been issued with two gallons of brandy to celebrate their commander's birthday.

The battle on Culloden Moor commenced early in the morning. On the Jacobite side, senior Masons commanded the right wing (Lord George Murray) and the left (the Duke of Perth). The Earl of Kilmarnock was present with his infantry regiment as was Sir Archibald Primrose. It was to be a brutal affair; the Highlanders had (allegedly) issued an order that prisoners were to be killed. This would later be used in evidence in the trials against the Jacobites, including the former Grand Masters of Scotland. Although Cumberland may have been a member of the Craft, there do not seem to have been any Masons as commanders in his army, albeit a company of soldiers from the Earl of Crawford's regiment was present. As we have seen, the earl was the former Grand Master of England. In the end, the Government Forces routed the forces of Bonnie Prince Charlie, who fled the battlefield and eventually sailed to France. He was never to return to Scotland again.

Significantly for members of the Craft, the Earl of Kilmarnock, the former Grand Master of Scotland, was captured by the Government Forces at Culloden. In the heat of battle, he had mistaken a cavalry regiment as being part of the Jacobite forces and had ridden into captivity. His foolish mistake was witnessed by his son, who was serving with the opposing army. Brother Primrose managed to escape, but was arrested in Aberdeenshire and taken to Carlisle. Sir John Wedderburn, 5th Baronet of Blackness was also taken prisoner on the battlefield, but his fellow lodge member, the Duke of Perth was (initially) more fortunate. Once again, the Duke was able to escape and having evaded Cumberland's army, board a French warship. A bold and brave Mason, he was to die, exhausted, on the ship before it ever reached the continent. Others were able to evade being arrested as traitors. Lord George Murray retreated, in good order, with some of the remaining Jacobite forces to Ruthven Barracks. He was, however, rather ungraciously dismissed by Bonnie Prince Charlie, but escaped to mainland Europe and eventually died in Holland.

Now followed a brutal suppression of the Highlands and the Jacobite cause, so much so, that the Duke of Cumberland, will forever be remembered as 'Butcher Cumberland'. Now that the government in London was certain that victory was theirs, action could be taken against the Jacobites. The evidence against the Jacobites was bolstered by the capture of Mason, Sir James Murray of Broughton. He was found in his sister's home and, despite being the secretary to Bonnie Prince Charlie, he soon gave evidence against his former comrades. It did save his own neck, but it resulted in him being dismissed from his Scottish lodge. Sir James died a natural death in Cheshunt, Hertfordshire over thirty years later.

In August, the trial was held of the Jacobites, who had been detained in London. This included two former Grand Masters of Scotland, the Earl of Kilmarnock and the Earl of Cromartie. The hearing was held at what was then called 'St Margaret's Hill' in Southwark (this is now the site of Town Hall Chambers on Borough High Street) on the first floor above a tavern (which it is now). At least one of the judiciary present was a Mason—Sir Thomas de Veil, a member of a lodge that met in the Vine Tavern in London. He was later the founder of the famous Bow Street Magistrates' Court. The charge of treason laid against the Jacobites was as follows:

Not having the fear of God in their hearts, for having any regard for the duty of their allegiance, but being moved and seduced by the instigation of the devil, as false traitors and rebels against our said present sovereign lord the king, their supreme, true, natural, lawful, and undoubted sovereign lord, entirely withdrawing that cordial love, true and due obedience, fidelity, and allegiance which every subject of right ought to bear towards our said present sovereign lord the king; also devising (and as much as in them lay) most wickedly and traitorously intending to change and subvert the rule and government of this kingdom... and also to put and bring our said present sovereign lord the king to death and destruction, and to raise and exalt the person pretended to be Prince of Wales—during the life of the late king James the second of England—to the crown and royal state and dignity of king, and to the imperial rule and government of this kingdom.

Kilmarnock and Cromartie pleaded guilty and threw themselves on the mercy of the court. The fate of the two Grand Masters of Scotland was to be very different. Both were sentenced to that most dreadful of executions—to be hanged, drawn, and quartered. Both made pleas for clemency, but only Cromartie's were heard. Stripped of his rank, he was pardoned, but forbidden from travelling north of the River Trent—in effect, unable to travel to northern England or Scotland again. The fact that he had a heavily pregnant wife may also have assisted his cause. He was to die, a broken man, in Soho Square London in 1766. His son, Lord MacLeod, as we shall see, was to reintegrate himself into British society.

On 18 August 1746, Brother Kilmarnock was to face execution, but (fortunately), he was only to be beheaded. This may sound dreadful, but it was far better than being slowly strangled to death and then having his bowels cut out, while still alive, as was the original sentence. Rank has its privileges, and he was the first to face death; as an earl, he held the highest title. Surrounded by troops, the former Grand Master of Scotland was taken to the place of execution on Tower Hill (the spot, now on Trinity Square, is marked by a plaque). He continued to be contrite and publicly confessed his guilt. With one blow of the axe, his head was severed from his body. Next on the scaffold was non-Mason, Lord Balmerino. He showed no guilt at all, laughing as he 'inspected' his coffin and professing his continued support for the Stuart cause. Perhaps to teach this unrepentant Jacobite a lesson, the executioner took three blows to remove his head.

Less than a month later, on 9 September, a special commission in Carlisle dealt with the prisoners detained in the city castle and sentenced thirty-three to death, including Brother Sir Archibald Primrose. He was part on the last group to be executed. On 15 November, at the aptly named Gallows Hill, he was hanged with ten others. Brother Primrose also acknowledged his guilt. Prior to his execution, he had written to his sister, stating 'I repent most heartily for what I did and I merit this death as punishment.'

The trials also continued in London. In November, Brother Colonel Sir John Wedderburn, 5th Baronet of Blackness, also appeared before the court in Borough High Street. He attempted to claim that he had not taken up arms against King George II, but he was found guilty of treason. On 28 November, he was taken to Kennington Common and, unlike others, actually suffered the awful death of being hanged, drawn, and quartered. The location of the gruesome penalty is now the site of St Mark's church opposite Oval tube station.

Less than two weeks later, on 8 December 1746, justice would eventually catch up with the Earl of Derwentwater. On Tower Hill, some thirty years after his original death sentence, the execution was finally carried out and Charles Radcliffe lost his head. As he had been captured at sea, *en route* to England, he had taken no active part in the 1745 uprising. The earl had faced death bravely and paid his executioner ten guineas. The body of the man, who had managed to escape from Newgate Prison some thirty years previously and (apparently) established the Scottish Rite, was buried in St Giles's-in-the-Fields church in Camden.

Back in France, Bonnie Prince Charlie allegedly became involved in further developing the Masonic Scottish Rite. There is, however, no proof that he did so. We can be sure that he turned to drink and womanising. He also sneaked back to London and converted to the Protestant faith, which he saw as a necessary step to be accepted as a British king. In 1759, he had a further chance; the French were planning another invasion of England, but it fell apart due to two factors—firstly, the Royal Navy scored a series of victories, making a sea crossing a very risky scheme; secondly, Bonnie Prince Charlie simply failed to impress the French authorities. He would later return to Rome, the place of his birth, where he died in 1788, at the age of sixty-seven. His conversion to Protestantism was forgotten and he was buried in the Vatican.

Of all the Jacobites, Lord MacLeod seems to have fared best. He had pleaded guilty to treason, but was pardoned, as was his father, Past Grand Master of Scotland, the Earl of

Cromartie. MacLeod's youth was very much on his side, but he had to forfeit his titles. He sailed to mainland Europe and served in the Swedish and Prussian armies, but returned to Britain in 1771 to become a colonel in two Scottish regiments. He eventually became a Major-General in the British Army, as well as a serving Member of Parliament. Unlike his father, his later life was a success. MacLeod's grave can still be seen in Canongate Kirkyard in Edinburgh.

The Masons in the Government Forces were not guaranteed long and happy lives, simply for being on the winning side. Their lives, however, tended to end in a better manner than the Jacobite brethren.

The Duke of Cumberland continued in military service, but in 1757 he agreed a peace with the French, allowing them to occupy Hanover. His father, George II, never forgave him and the Duke resigned all military offices. Once his nephew, George III, took the throne, he became an influential advisor and died in his bed in London in 1765. There is no mention of any further Masonic activity by him.

John Byrom, the spy (or double agent), continued to move in mystical circles and was buried in Manchester in 1763. His lodge seems to have been No. 44 in 1725 and met in Dean Street, Soho in London. It has long been erased.

We can only hope that the Grand Mastership of England General Campbell, the Earl of Loudoun, in the 1730s was more successful than the military skills, which he displayed in the Jacobite campaign. As has been noted, he lost his supplies twice and was tricked into thinking his regiment was being ambushed, by four men shouting and banging swords. Despite these apparent failings, he was to achieve high office, being the Governor of Virginia (several towns and counties in the USA are named for him), but was soon removed due to incompetence and failures against French forces in North America. The residents of the colony observed that he was like 'Saint George on the tavern sign—always on horseback, but never advancing.' In 1763, he returned to Scotland as the Governor of Edinburgh Castle, an office he held until his death nearly twenty years later.

Sir Robert Dickson returned to his duty as 'Chief Bailie' or magistrate of Musselburgh on the south-east coast of Scotland, where he died in 1760. General Lindsey, the Earl of Crawford, the Past Grand Master of England, was dead within three years of the executed peers. He died on Christmas Day 1749 in Upper Brook Street, Mayfair (this street would later be the headquarters of the Grand Lodge of Mark Master Masons for many years). The earl had been badly wounded during the Austrian War of Succession, fighting near Belgrade and this injury finally proved fatal. Charles Lennox, Duke of Richmond, died at the age of just forty-nine years old in 1750. He is now remembered as a driving force in the development of the game of cricket. William Home, Earl of Home, rose to the rank of lieutenant-general and became the Governor of Gibraltar, where he died in 1761.

The Jacobite Rebellion had ended and the Earl of Kilmarnock, Past Grand Master of Scotland, had paid the ultimate price (becoming the most senior British Mason to be executed). The Earl of Derwentwater, Grand Master of France, and apparent founder of the Scottish Rite, had also faced the executioner's axe. Furthermore, the Jacobite rebellion had given the Masonic authorities in England good reason to play down any Scottish influence in the origins of the Craft. The name 'Scottish Rite' is still used in the USA and many parts of the world, but, in England, it is the 'Ancient and Accepted Rite'.

10

The 'Wicked Lord':
Grand Master, Killer, and Vandal

Masonic Connection
Grand Master of England
Highest ranked English Mason ever tried for murder

Date
1747–52: Grand Master
1765: Charged with murder

Connection to London
Mortimer Street, near Cavendish Square: London home of 5th Lord Byron
Drapers' Hall, Throgmorton Street, London: Installed as Grand Master at this venue
Devil's Tavern, Temple Bar, the Strand (site now marked by a plaque): Used for Grand Lodge meetings when Byron was Grand Master
Star and Garter Tavern, 44 Pall Mall (current site of the Institute of Directors): Location of murder
Tower of London: Bryon held in Tower prior to trial
Westminster Hall (House of Lords): Location of trial

Lodges
Grand Lodge of England
University No. 74 (erased)

William Byron, 5th Lord Byron of Rochdale in Lancashire (1722–98) was the great uncle of the famous Lord Byron, the poet and hero of the Greek independence movement. The 5th Lord was also the Grand Master of England for five years from 1747 to 1752. He was, however, to become known as the 'Wicked Lord' or 'Devil Byron' and was to be the only Grand Master ever charged with murder, being tried by his peers in the House of Lords. He also presided over one of the most troublesome periods of English Freemasonry, when a rival Grand Lodge was formed.

Byron was only fourteen years old when he inherited his title on the death of his father. In 1736 he left the family home at Newstead Abbey in Nottingham and was commissioned in the Royal Navy. As a naval officer, he was trained in the art of fencing and taught to use a sword to quickly kill an enemy. This skill was to haunt Lord Byron in years to come. During his naval career, he served on HMS Falkland as a lieutenant and was then transferred to HMS *Victory* (this ship predates the famous flagship of Nelson). In 1744, the Victory was lost with all hands in a violent storm off the Channel Islands. Fortunately for Byron, but possibly not for Freemasonry, he was safely on land at that time.

Byron became a Mason at the age of twenty-one, but the details of his initiation have been lost—no record is held at Grand Lodge. He may have joined in London, Lancashire (due to Rochdale connection) or Nottinghamshire (the family seat). He did appear to have the right qualities for the Craft and in the true sense of Masonic charity, he acted as a governor for a Foundling Hospital, a London based charity that cared for abandoned babies.

Despite owning the magnificent Newstead Abbey and coalmines in Lancashire, Byron was not a rich man. His estate had still not recovered from the Civil War, some one hundred years earlier. Bryon did, however, find a solution to his cash-flow problems. He married a young girl, Elizabeth Shaw, who was nine years his junior. She was the only daughter of a rich Norfolk landowner, who also owned estates in Cambridgeshire and Nottinghamshire. Most importantly, Elizabeth arrived with a dowry of £70,000, a vast fortune at that time, which was spent on travel, luxury items and the high life.

At only twenty-five years old, in April 1747, Byron was elected as Grand Master and was later installed at Drapers' Hall. A concert at the theatre (now Theatre Royal) Drury Lane was held in his honour, where the first three rows were reserved for members of the Craft. This included a song selected by the new Grand Master written by Brother John Coustos, who had been imprisoned in Portugal by the Roman Catholic inquisition for forming a

Newstead Abbey, home of the fifth Lord Byron—the 'Wicked Lord'—and Grand Master of England.

lodge in Lisbon. He had been tortured, but refused to renounce his Protestant Faith or disclose the secrets of Freemasonry (see Chapter 9).

Byron was Grand Master for five years. He also was held in high regard at the court of George III, as he was appointed 'Master of the Staghounds' (in charge of the king's hunting dogs) for two years. There is no record of his achievements in the world of canine care, but he does not appear to have been a committed ruler of the Craft. He was often absent from Grand Lodge meetings, despite many of the meetings being held at the (aptly named) 'Devil's Tavern' at Temple Bar on the Strand (a plaque now records the location of this inn). Byron seemed to be more focused on gambling on horse races, even riding his own horse to victory at Northampton.

During Byron's tenure as Grand Master, a prominent brother, Horace Walpole MP, 4th Earl of Orford (the son of the first Prime Minister, Sir Robert Walpole) was scathing about the public perception of the Craft. In 1743, Walpole observed, 'The Freemasons are in … low repute now in England … I believe nothing but a persecution could bring them into vogue again.' Most importantly, it was during Byron's watch that the rival Antients Grand Lodge was formed in London (in 1751). While this schism appears to have been many years in the making, Byron's neglect of his duties no doubt exacerbated the issues. In the end, he was forced out of office and replaced by a Member of Parliament as Grand Master—John Proby, 1st Baron Carysfort.

Following his removal from Grand Lodge, his life descended into madness and scandal. Byron was already a womaniser; he had fathered nine children. He also became violent when drunk and this was nearly his un-doing. On 26 January 1765, he killed a distant relative, William Chaworth, who also had inherited estates in Nottinghamshire. The two men were part of a group, including members of both Houses of Parliament, who met as part of a Nottinghamshire County Club in London. The meeting took place at the Star and Garter Tavern, then located at 44 Pall Mall. During the course of the evening, an argument ensued over a trivial matter—how to preserve the level of a game on an estate and how poachers should be treated. A witness to the drunken row described it as a 'silly business' in his evidence at the later trial.

To settle their differences, the two drunk men agreed to fight a duel in a small room lit by only one candle. The score was settled very quickly; as they entered, Byron thrust his blade straight through Chaworth's body. It was said that Byron stabbed his rival in the back before the duel could be properly fought. Two doctors were called, but nothing could be done; Chaworth was mortally wounded and died the next day. It is to be remembered that Byron was no amateur swordsman; the Royal Navy training had been very effective. Tragically, Chaworth's wife was to give birth to a daughter a few days later.

Due to the allegation that the duel had not been fairly fought, Byron was charged with murder and held in the Tower of London, although not under close arrest—he was allowed to wander around the interior. He was even allowed to dine with Lady Elizabeth and three of their children. After several weeks in captivity (of sorts) on 16 April, he was brought, under guard, to Westminster Hall for his trial. As a member of the House of Lords, he was entitled to be tried by his peers. These included the Dukes of York and Gloucester; the latter was later made a Past Grand Master in 1767. Such was the interest in this scandalous case, that tickets for the event were advertised in the press. These could be obtained (for free) from the Lord Chamberlain, but a Mr Robson, a bookseller from New Bond Street, advertised that he was willing to pay five guineas to 'any person having one to dispose of.' Ticket touts have long existed.

The court was presided over by the Lord Chancellor, who was not a Mason, but during the hearing, Byron was questioned by the 14th Earl of Morton, a fellow Past Grand Master of England (1741). Morton was an eminent man, who had also been Grand Master of Scotland (1739–40) and President of the Royal Society. In 1730, he had been initiated into the (lodge defunct) University Lodge (then No. 74), which met in a tavern at Temple Bar.

The official House of Lords records note that Lord Bryon, the former Grand Master, was accused in the following terms, that 'being moved and seduced by the instigation of the devil… feloniously, wilfully, of his malice aforethought … did kill and murder.' Byron pleaded 'not guilty'. Was the wording of the indictment the origin of his nickname 'Devil Byron'?

The case revolved around whether Byron had unfairly drawn his sword before Chaworth had a chance to do. Some witnesses suggested that Chaworth had drawn quickly himself, but as he attempted to strike his rival in the dimly lit room, the sword had become entangled in Byron's waistcoat. It was at this point that the former Grand Master ran him through. Byron did not give evidence to the court, but his solicitor read out a statement, giving his version of events. The statement also expressed his 'deep and unfeigned sorrow' about the death and 'reposed himself, with utmost confidence on their Lordship's justice and humanity.' The members of the House of Lords then retired to consider the verdict and subsequently acquitted him of murder, but found him guilty of manslaughter. At this point, Byron knew that he could receive a long prison sentence or even the death penalty.

To save his neck (literally), he threw himself on the mercy of the court and claimed the 'Benefit of Clergy'. Given Byron's devil-like qualities and the fact that he had never been a vicar, claiming such a right to reduce his sentence may, at first sight, appear odd. The original concept of the 'benefit' was introduced after the murder of Thomas a Becket, the Archbishop of Canterbury. Henry II, the king, who had ordered the killing, was forced to concede that any crime (with the exception of treason) committed by a clergyman would not be tried in a secular court, known as the Assizes. Rather, it would be heard by a bishop, who would (invariably) hand out a far lesser punishment.

When initially introduced, any person claiming it had to appear dressed in ecclesiastical dress, with the top of the head shaved, in the style of a monk. Over time, this was replaced by a literacy test and this was formalised in law in 1351 and (importantly) extended to all who could read. As printed volumes were few in those days, it became the tradition that the person claiming the benefit had to read a section of the Bible, the most widely available book. The passage selected was, rather aptly, Psalm 51: 'O God, have mercy upon me, according to thine heartfelt mercifulness.'

This became known as the 'neck verse' as it could save a criminal from being hanged. Many an illiterate villain would learn the verse off by heart and pretend to read, just in case he faced the death penalty. If the crime was particularly heinous, then a suspicious judge would ask the defendant to read another passage, thereby exposing those who had simply recited the verse. Many Masons will know some who, in similar fashion, can regurgitate the ritual, without actually knowing the meaning. The penalties for doing so, are of course, somewhat less than that faced by a criminal in times of old.

The reading test was abolished in 1706 and by the time of the Byron trial, the 'Benefit of Clergy' had morphed into a means in which all first offenders could plead for a lesser punishment, once they had been convicted. Members of the House of Lords had even more favourable treatment. By an Act of Parliament passed in 1537, a peer could be released without any punishment at all, if the conviction was his first offence. This applied to every crime, except murder or malicious poisoning. Such was the means that the former Grand Master was able to walk free, after being found guilty of manslaughter, despite it being defined as a felony—a serious crime. It should be noted (for anyone considering using this obscure law) that the benefit was abolished in 1827.

A contemporary newspaper reported that he left the court a free man and 'took a chair' (that is a Sedan Chair, carried by two men), through St James's Park to his London residence in Mortimer Street, off Cavendish Square. Initially, Byron appeared to enjoy his new-found notoriety—he mounted the sword used to kill Chaworth in his bedroom at Newstead Abbey and he reveled in his new nickname 'the Wicked Lord'. His behaviour then turned erratic and violent. He once shot his coachman (while on a journey); his solution was to leave his wife to deal with the injured servant while he took the reins. He further alienated his wife by throwing her in the lake at Newstead Abbey, leaving a gardener to rescue her from drowning.

Byron also appears to have enjoyed reliving his military career, as he had a castle and two forts built on his estate. These were equipped with cannons, so that he could stage mock naval battles. It was also rumoured that the former Grand Master held orgies in his private fortresses. All this proved too much for Lady Elizabeth, who left the former Grand Master to his devices (and his mistress, a household servant). This lover, Elizabeth Hardstaffe, was referred to as 'Lady Betty'.

The next stage of Byron's ruin and irresponsible (if not criminal) acts related to his son, who was also named William. Lord Byron was running short of funds—Elizabeth's dowry having been spent. He perceived that if his son married into money, the family would be saved from ruin. William Junior, however, had no intention of being involved in his father's plan and duly eloped with his cousin, Juliana Byron. Lord Byron claimed that his objection to this relationship was nothing to do with money—such inter-family marriage could result in children suffering from all manner of mental illness (he was after all, an apparent expert in madness).

William Junior refused to listen to such 'reason' and his father exacted revenge— he decided that his son would inherit a worthless property. He committed wholesale vandalism—allowing Newstead Abbey to fall into rack and ruin, cutting down all timber and killing thousands of deer. Even fire places where ripped out and sold. He also sold off the family coal mines in Lancashire and spent the proceeds on drink and debauchery. Fortunately, in some ways for William Junior, his father was to out-live him, and so he never had to deal with the tragic mess created by Lord Byron.

Lord Byron, despite his violent and unhealthy lifestyle, was to live to the ripe old age of seventy-five. It is said in a local legend that towards the end of his life, he would feed the hundreds of crickets that infested Newstead Abbey and that when he passed to the 'Grand Lodge Above' (or is it Grand Lodge Below in his case?) the insects marched out and disappeared.

The 5th Lord Byron, Past Grand Master, is buried in the family vault under the floor of the church of St Mary Magdalen in Hucknall near Nottingham. He remains the only Grand Master to have been charged with murder. Given his early military career and charitable work, it is a shame that he brought such disgrace to Freemasonry. Perhaps it is due to his conduct that no file exists on him in the archives of the United Grand Lodge of England.

11

Bow Street Court, a Masonic Magistrate, and Reading the Riot Act

Masonic Connection
Famous court opened by a Mason
Masonry depicted in art

Date
1740: Bow Street court opened
2006: Bow Street Magistrates' Court closed

Connection to London
Bow Street Magistrates Court (now closed): Established by De Veil
Canon Row (formerly Channel Row): De Veil depicted in Hogarth's engraving *Night*

Lodges
Vine Tavern No. 60 or No. 68 (erased)

Bow Street Magistrates Court is possibly one of the most famous courts in the world—the home of the Bow Street Runners, said to be the first professional police in London. From 1740 until its closure in 2006, Bow Street would deal with all manner of petty crimes, but would also hold the pre-trial hearings for many of the most infamous trials in England, including numerous cases featured in this book—Crippen, the Kray Twins and other murderers appeared there before being sent to the Old Bailey for trial. But how many are aware that it was a Freemason who set up this court? The Mason concerned was Brother Sir Thomas De Veil.

De Veil was the son of a French clergyman, who had immigrated to England and settled in London. Sir Thomas was born in a house in St Paul's Churchyard in 1684, the same location of the Goose and Gridiron inn, the tavern where the Grand Lodge was established in 1717. Details of his military service are unclear, but he served in Portugal (most likely during the War of Spanish Succession) and Ireland, leaving the British Army with the rank of colonel. His Masonic career is equally shrouded in mystery, but he appears to have been a member of a lodge, which met at the Vine Tavern in Long Acre, Covent Garden. This is possibly an unnamed lodge (No. 68, then No. 60—but 'erased' in 1740).

Bow Street Magistrates' Court was opened by Freemason Colonel Thomas de Veil.

In 1729, he was appointed a Justice of the Peace, a Magistrate, for the County of Middlesex and the 'Liberty of Westminster' (the southern part of what is now the City of Westminster). At this time the population of London was expanding—between 1715 and 1760, the number of people in the capital increased by over 100,000 to reach a total of 740,000. There was much poverty and destitution, particularly during long periods of bad weather and economic depression. In such circumstances, a rise in crime was inevitable. While attacks on the rich invariably received more publicity, the poor were also victims of violence and petty crime.

One way that the poor could escape their awful existence was drunkenness; and the cheapest way to achieve such a state was to drink gin and lots of it. This alcoholic drink had originally been created in the Netherlands, but with William of Orange becoming King of England is 1688, its popularity spread to the British Isles. Two other major factors resulted in British produced gin being very cheap and therefore the choice of the poor—firstly, grain unfit for use in brewing beer could be used to make it and secondly, the government placed heavy duties on other imported spirits, making them expensive.

Some thousands of gin-shops sprung up in London during what was known as the 'Gin Craze'. Like illegal drugs of today, gin was blamed for a variety of social problems and early rates of death. Even today it is still referred to as 'mother's ruin'. Freemason William Hogarth immortalised the problem in his engravings *Beer Street* and *Gin Lane*. While *Beer Street* was depicted as a scene of happy and industrious London (beer being shown as the decent, English drink), *Gin Lane* is set in the St Giles' area (a notorious slum of that period) and features madness, infanticide, prostitution, and greed. Gin is therefore depicted as a wicked, foreign influence on the masses.

The government attempted to legislate against the problem and placed taxes on gin. Sir Thomas De Veil was one of the most active magistrates in implementing the Gin Act of 1736. The rise in cost of the once cheap drink led to disorder on the streets, which were further suffering from gangs of robbers. While accused of being a 'Trading Justice' (the name given to a magistrate willing to take bribes) and also of accepting sexual favours from prostitutes (it was said that he had a small room off the court to receive such sexual 'payments'), no evidence has been produced to prove such corrupt conduct. On the contrary, he seems to have enforced the law with common sense, realising that harsh enforcement would have lost him the support of the public. This did not always have the desired affect and violent gatherings continued to occur. Once, a mob tried to storm his house; he dispersed them by reading the Riot Act:

> Our Sovereign Lord the King chargeth and commandeth all persons, being assembled, immediately to disperse themselves, and peaceably to depart to their habitations, or to their lawful business, upon the pains contained in the act made in the first year of King George, for preventing tumults and riotous assemblies. God save the King!

One man was arrested, but the rest of the mob dispersed. They knew that failure to disperse within one hour was a serious offence, punishable by death. Luckily for the arrested man, he was later found not guilty.

Night, an engraving by Mason William Hogarth. The man is the foreground with the Master's collar (and square) is said to be Colonel de Veil.

It must be recalled that, at that time, there was no professional police force in London (the Metropolitan Police were not formed until 1829) and the organisation of the justice system was equally chaotic. To provide a better service for victims of crime, magistrates established 'rotation offices' where Londoners could find a Justice of the Peace at certain times of the day. Herein lies the origin of Bow Street Magistrates Court. In 1739, Sir Thomas De Veil was living at 4 Bow Street, just off Covent Garden; he set up such a 'rotation office', and later, a court. Under De Veil's successor, Henry Fielding, this would become the headquarters of the 'Bow Street Runners'.

Around the same time, Hogarth and De Veil appear to have fallen out; both were Masons and it would seem met in a lodge at the Vine Tavern, a short walk from Bow Street in Long Acre. It will be recalled that Hogarth had studied in Covent Garden, also a stone's throw from the inn. Whatever the reason for the disagreement, Hogarth used his artistic talents and cutting humour to ridicule his fellow Mason. Hogarth used his engraving entitled *Night* to ridicule the efforts of Sir Thomas to deal with the Gin Craze. The drunken Worshipful Master depicted in *Night* has been identified as De Veil by Worshipful Brother George Speth of the respected Quatuor Coronati Masonic research lodge. The Tyler is said to be the Grand Tyler, Brother Montgomerie. By showing De Veil as a staggering drunk, unable to see the chaos around him (such as a coach on fire), and being outside two inns used for Masonic meetings, he is being depicted as a hypocrite. Furthermore, the chamber pot being tipped over De Veil's head may be poking fun at the unfortunate occasion when the magistrate mistakenly drank a bottle of urine, which he mistook for illicit gin on an inspection of a tavern.

If nothing else, Hogarth's efforts have ensured that Sir Thomas and early London Freemasonry have been depicted for all to see today; the engraving can be seen in the Tate Gallery. De Veil died in 1746 and his efforts to stamp out the undesirable impact of gin on society appear to have been a success; the 'Craze' was petering out just a few years after his death. Additionally, there can be few occasions when a Freemason has literally read the Riot Act. More importantly for London, the court at Bow Street, which Brother Colonel De Veil established, was to dispense justice for over two hundred and sixty years.

12

'Mr John Wilkes, are you Free and of Good Report?' … 'No!'

Masonic Connection
Unusual initiation ceremony

Date
1769: Initiation took place
1774: Lord Mayor of London

Connection to London
Houses of Parliament: Wilkes served as an MP
Britton Street, Clerkenwell: Jerusalem Tavern (where Wilkes' lodge met) still stands there
Borough High Street and Harper Street (site of Inner London Crown Court): Former location of King's Bench Prison
Drury Lane: Scene of riot, following Wilkes' imprisonment
Mansion House, City of London: Residence of Wilkes during his year as Lord Mayor
Fetter Lane: Cross-eyed statue of Wilkes
Carlton House Terrace: Current location of the Royal Society

Lodges
Grand Stewards'
Royal Somerset and Inverness No. 4
Lodge of Friendship No. 6
Lodge of Emulation No. 21
Jerusalem No. 197

John Wilkes was born in Clerkenwell, London in 1725 and was an English journalist, politician, and campaigner for liberty and the rights of voters. He was made a Fellow of the Royal Society when just twenty-four years old, and this may have influenced the decision to allow him to become a Mason in very unusual circumstances many years later. Wilkes was elected to the House of Commons in 1757 and was the Member of Parliament for constituencies in Buckinghamshire and Middlesex over a long political career. He was instantly recognisable, being the only cross-eyed (and possibly the ugliest, by his own admission) MP in the country. Indeed, he is celebrated in the form of the only cross-eyed statue in London; wander up Fetter Lane to see him. Another Freemason, the famous artist William Hogarth, created a satirical engraving of Wilkes, adding a devil-like wig to the crossed-eyes. Hogarth may have been responding to Wilkes' attacks on him in his newspaper, *The North Briton*. Hogarth's portrait of Wilkes may have been unkind, but it was very accurate—so much so that, while in Paris, Wilkes was challenged to a duel by a Jacobite supporter who had identified him from it.

Wilkes was an early campaigner for what would now be called 'freedom of information'; in 1771, he forced the government to produce verbatim records of parliamentary debates (Lodge secretaries please note). He also secured freedoms for the press. As we shall see, this was a dangerous time to attack the 'Establishment'.

Prior to joining Freemasonry, Wilkes (like Lord Wharton) was a member of the infamous Hellfire Club, with several other prominent members of society. Wilkes is said to have worn a baboon costume, complete with horns, when bizarre rituals were performed among the drunken members. Anyone thinking that Masons perform odd rituals should consider the activities of the Hellfire Club.

His journey from Parliament to prison cell (and Freemasonry) began with him using his newspaper to criticise the monarch, George III, regarding the peace terms agreed with France following the successful campaign in Canada. Wilkes considered that the agreement was over-generous to the defeated French. The king, stung by the criticism, issued a warrant for the arrest of Wilkes for the offence of seditious libel. Wilkes, as a Member of Parliament, was able to claim that parliamentary privilege protected him from such charges. Thus, he avoided being convicted at this stage. Emboldened by this success, he continued his attacks on the king and, as a consequence, was challenged to a duel by Samuel Martin MP, a supporter of the monarch. During the duel in Hyde Park, Wilkes was shot in the stomach; more dangerously for him, his fellow MPs passed a law removing parliamentary protection for anyone publishing seditious libel.

Wilkes then enraged a fellow Hellfire Club member, the 4th Earl of Sandwich, by writing a pornographic (by eighteenth-century standards) poem about the latter's mistress. The earl read out the poem in the House of Lords, and Wilkes was further charged with obscene libel in addition to his earlier charge. Realising his number was up, Wilkes fled to France. Back in England, he was tried in his absence and found guilty of both forms of libel. He was also declared an outlaw.

Wilkes remained in France until his funds ran out. He returned to England after four years, intending to stand as an MP. The government were loath to arrest him, as he still commanded popular support as a campaigner for liberty. Wilkes was quick to win back his seat in Parliament, being elected to a seat in Middlesex. Having made his point, he then surrendered to the authorities. He was then sentenced to two years in prison and a fine of £1,000 (around £150,000 today). He was, however, no longer declared an outlaw (so at least he had some rights under the law of England). Wilkes was committed to the King's Bench Prison in Southwark, just south of London Bridge.

The sentence of imprisonment caused outrage, and a crowd gathered outside the prison on the night he arrived, 10 May 1768. Wilkes's supporters chanted slogans against the king, resulting in troops firing on the unarmed protesters, killing seven. A riot also broke out at the theatre on Drury Lane as the playwright had supported the army's tactics. It should be noted that the Theatre Royal on Drury Lane has one of the most Masonic statues in London; outside the entrance is a bust of Sir Augustus Harris, flanked by two square and compasses. This is unrelated to Wilkes, but is worth visiting.

While still serving his sentence, on 3 March 1769, members of the lodge held at Jerusalem Tavern (now Jerusalem Lodge No. 197) visited him and 'made Mr Wilkes a Mason', hence the title of this chapter. Masons will recall that when they enter the lodge room blind-folded, the first question the Worshipful Master asks is 'Are you free and of good report?' The answer is invariably 'Yes', but Wilkes was not 'free'—he was in a prison cell. It should be noted that one of the Masons involved in the initiation of Wilkes was Brother Edmund Burke, another libertarian, who is believed to be the author of the oft used saying, 'The only thing necessary for evil to triumph is for good men to do nothing'.

Wilkes was not the only man admitted to the Craft that evening; the Lodge of Jerusalem also admitted four more 'Gentlemen' (as they are described by the secretary in the minutes of the meeting) named as George Bellas, Lewis Francis Bourgeois, Captain Read, and John Churchill. The lodge had high level support to conduct this very odd initiation. The Master, Worshipful Brother Thomas Dobson, acted with the written authority of the Premier Grand Lodge; the Deputy Grand Master, Charles Dillon, 12th Viscount Dillon had signed a dispensation (a Masonic document allowing changes to be made to agreed meeting venues and dates), permitting the initiations to take place in the jail and not at the Jerusalem Tavern in Britton Street, Clerkenwell, where the lodge was registered to meet. Dillon was an active Freemason, being a member of several lodges including Old Horn No. 2 (now Royal Somerset and Inverness No. 4), Lodge of Friendship (now No.6), Lodge of Emulation (now No. 21), and the Grand Stewards' Lodge. The Viscount was also the First Grand Principal in the Holy Royal Arch 1770–71. Critically, Dillon had been made a Fellow of the Royal Society in 1767; this was possibly his link to Wilkes.

Given the number of visitors to the jail to conduct the ceremony, the staff must have suspected something unusual was afoot. The 'Turnkey' (prison warder) was given twenty guineas for the 'poor prisoners' to turn a blind eye to the Masonic business taking place in the jail. It is unclear if the money ever reached its intended recipients or if it stayed in the guard's pocket; the latter is most likely.

The term of imprisonment does not seem to have damaged John Wilkes; in 1774, he became Lord Mayor of London; the vast majority of those holding this influential office, even to the present day, have been Freemasons. Wilkes was also a Fellow of the Royal Society, which has had a major influence on Freemasonry, particularly when the Craft evolved into its current form in the eighteenth century. Later in life, he was a magistrate, despite his conviction and imprisonment. He did, however, lose some of his popularity when he was involved in cracking down on those involved in the Gordon Riots in 1780.

That said, Wilkes gained further prominence during the American War of Independence (1775–83). Wilkes became popular in the American colonies, where his views on liberty struck a particular chord. Despite being born in England, he supported the rebels, as they had not been allowed representation in the British Parliament. He was particularly critical

John Wilkes, the man made a Mason in prison.

King's Bench Prison, where Wilkes was initiated by the Lodge of Jerusalem.

of King George III and railed against him for sending 'German troops to suppress the American-English'. It will be recalled that George III was of the House of Hanover and was concurrently the King of England and ruler of part of modern north Germany.

If Masons have ever admired an amusing speaker at the Festive Board, they would enjoy the quick-fire wit of John Wilkes. When Wilkes was campaigning for re-election, a constituent declared that he would rather vote for the devil, to which Wilkes responded, 'And if your friend decides against standing, can I count on your vote?'

The Earl of Sandwich told Wilkes, 'Sir, I do not know whether you will die on the gallows or of the pox', to which Wilkes retorted: 'That depends, my lord, on whether I embrace your lordship's principles or your mistress'.

His last years were spent on the Isle of Wight; he died in 1797. The tragedy of this great man is that he is immortalised for all the wrong reasons. We have seen that he was revered in America for his support for their cause. As a result, a distant descendant was named after him—John Wilkes Booth, the man who assassinated President Lincoln in 1865. However, perhaps, Freemasons will now remember him as one of the only men known to have been initiated in prison by other Masons who were also supporters of liberty and freedom.

13

Grand Chaplain, Grand Swindle

Masonic Connection

Swindler was first Grand Chaplain

Victim of fraud

Date

1775: Made Grand Chaplain

1777: Convicted of forgery

Connection to London

West Ham: Dodd was a curate at a church in this district

Hanover Square, Mayfair: Attempted to become priest of church in this affluent area

St James's Street: Meeting venue of lodges

Wood Street, City of London: Imprisoned in jail, which stood in this street

Old Bailey: Court where tried and convicted

Marble Arch: Hanged at Tyburn (original name of location)

Lodges

St Albans No. 29

Lodge of the Nine Muses No. 235

Minerva of the Three Palm Trees (Germany)

The office of Grand Chaplain is one of the most senior in the United Grand Lodge. It is held by a man in holy orders; this has included Christian clergymen and Jewish rabbis, a great advertisement for the inclusiveness of Freemasonry and its ability to bring men of all faiths together. Perhaps the most notable Grand Chaplain was the Most Reverend Geoffrey Fisher, the Archbishop of Canterbury (1945–61) and when he held this post, was also the most senior clergyman in the worldwide Anglican Church. Indeed, it was this Freemason who placed the crown on Queen Elizabeth II's head at her coronation in 1953.

Regrettably, the first officially appointed Grand Chaplain, the Reverend Doctor William Dodd, is remembered for all the wrong reasons; he is possibly the most senior English

William Dodd, the highest ranked English Freemason to be executed.

member of the Craft to be hanged. As will be seen, this Mason is also the origin of a famous phrase, composed by that great wordsmith, Samuel Johnson. Johnson was a friend of Dodd, as was John Wilkes MP. In the previous chapter, it was shown that Wilkes, like Dodd, spent time in prison. The ultimate outcomes of their periods of incarceration could not have been more different.

The Reverend Dodd, born in 1729, originated from the village of Bourne in south Lincolnshire. He was a clever man, achieving much academic success at Cambridge University and was ordained as a deacon in the Church of England in 1751. He was to serve as a curate in West Ham (in East London) and then as a priest in various places across the country, including the City of London, Bedfordshire, and Oxfordshire.

Unfortunately, Reverend Dodd also liked to live life 'on the edge', riding his luck. On the upside, he won £1,000 on a lottery, worth nearly one hundred times that amount in 2014. However, on the downside, his extravagant spending often exceeded his income. Due to his taste for the 'good life' and un-vicar like lifestyle, he was known as a 'Macaroni Parson' (a 'macaroni' was a dandy, a fancy dresser, who wore the latest fashions). The reader will recall the American song 'Yankee Doodle', who 'placed a feather in his cap and called it macaroni'.

The lottery winnings had been spent by 1774 and in need of more cash, Dodd attempted to bribe his way into a very lucrative priestly position—vicar of St George's in Hanover Square. This church sat in the fashionable district of Mayfair and was frequented by the great and the good, and, most importantly for Reverend Dodd, the very rich. His attempt to become the vicar by dishonest means was found out and he was dismissed from his existing church posts. He was also subject to much ridicule and, in consequence, he fled to Switzerland, then France, remaining out of the country for much of the next two years, while the scandal subsided. He did, however, find time to become the Grand Chaplain of the Grand Lodge of England in 1775.

Dodd had been initiated into St Albans Lodge No. 29, a London lodge. He also became a joining member of the Lodge of the Nine Muses No. 235—a lodge not formed until 1777, the year of his death. Both met in the Thatched House Tavern in St James's Street, the current location of Mark Masons' Hall.

Despite the high ideals of Masonry, the Reverend Dodd had to turn to crime to fund his ever more expensive life style. At least one of his former pupils was very rich—the 5th Earl of Chesterfield. The earl was also a member of the Craft. In 1773, he had joined a lodge named *Minerva zu den drei Palmen* (or in English 'Minerva of the Three Palm Trees') in Leipzig in modern day Germany. It must be recalled that King George III of England (father of the Duke of Sussex, the first Grand Master of the United Grand Lodge of England) was also Prince-Elector of the Holy Roman Empire, of which Leipzig was part.

In February 1777, Dodd forged a bond in the Earl's name, to the value of £4,200; this was a substantial amount of money and worth in the region of £500,000 today. Henry Fletcher, a banker, accepted the document as legitimate and the dishonest vicar received the funds. Unfortunately for Dodd, the banker noticed a small error on the bond and had a copy produced for the Earl to re-sign. When it was presented for signature, the forgery was discovered; the Earl must have been rather rich, as the missing cash had not been noticed until this point. The eighteenth century was a dangerous time to commit criminal acts; over two hundred offences carried the death penalty, including forgery and counterfeiting.

Earl of Chesterfield, Freemason and victim of Dodd's fraud.

Dodd was apprehended and confessed, but pleaded to be given time to pay back the stolen money. This was refused and he was placed in the Wood Street Compter, a small jail in the City of London, where debtors were imprisoned. He was tried at the Old Bailey; the indictment is in the same style of language as a Masonic oath. It was alleged:

[Dodd] feloniously did falsely make, forge, and counterfeit, and cause and procure to be falsely made, forged, and counterfeited, and willingly act and assist in the false making, forging, and counterfeiting a certain paper writing, partly printed and partly written, purporting to be a bond, and to be signed by the Right Honourable the Earl of Chesterfield, with the name of Chesterfield, and to be sealed and delivered by the said-Earl; the tenor of which said false, forged, and counterfeit paper writing, partly printed and partly written, purporting to be a bond.

In both the law and Masonic oaths, the rule appears to be 'why use one word, when you can use twenty?'

Dodd was found guilty and sentenced to death by hanging. Samuel Johnson wrote articles supporting him, including helping to compose the errant Mason's sermon 'The Convict's Address to his unhappy Brethren'. It would seem Johnson endeavoured to give Dodd full credit for writing this piece, but was challenged by a friend. Johnson's support for the vicar's authorship of the sermon has become famous: 'Depend upon it Sir, when a man knows he is to be hanged in a fortnight, it concentrates his mind wonderfully'.

Despite his dishonesty, Dodd remained popular with over twenty thousand people signing a petition pleading for a king's pardon. It was all to no avail. On 27 June 1777, the Grand Chaplain climbed the scaffold at Tyburn, the infamous scene of public executions. This place is now marked by a plaque at the site of Marble Arch and there, Dodd met his maker.

However, rumour persisted that his unconscious body had been taken down from the scaffold and he had been revived, fleeing to France. The rich could pay for such an escape, whereas the relatives of a poor criminal could hand a few pennies to the hangman, so that they were permitted to hasten the death of their loved one. Terribly, they were allowed to pull on the feet of the condemned prisoner to quickly bring on death, rather than watch him slowly being strangled to death, as the noose was not designed to break the neck at that time.

Whether Dodd died or not, the brutality of the age can clearly be seen; the other criminal hanged on that day was a twelve-year-old boy. If the errant vicar did die on the gallows, his body was buried in Cowley in Middlesex. Dodd was the first Grand Chaplain and the last man to be hanged for forgery at Tyburn. For all his flaws, he paid a heavy price for his attempt to swindle a brother Mason, the Earl of Chesterfield, out of a large sum of money.

14

Benjamin Franklin:
Science, Revolution, Sexual Desires, and the Mystery of a Mass Grave

Masonic Connection
American War of Independence
First Masonic book printed in North America
Provincial Grand Master of Pennsylvania

Date
1730–31: Franklin initiated in Philadelphia
1734: Provincial Grand Master
1757: Arrived in England as representative of his colony
1775: Returned to America

Connection to London
36 Craven Street: Franklin lived at this house (now a museum in his honour)
St Bartholomew the Great, Smithfields: Franklin worked in a printing shop in the Lady Chapel
John Adam Street: Royal Society of Arts
Carlton House Terrace: Current location of the Royal Society
The Strand: Franklin attended the Grand Lodge of England in a tavern

Lodges
St John's (Philadelphia)
Loge Les Neuf Soeurs (Paris)
Loge de Bon Amis (Rouen)
Loge de St Jean de Jerusalem (Nancy)

Benjamin Franklin was a great man—a scientist, a writer, a founding father of the United States of America, an inventor, and a Freemason. An innovator who did nothing by halves, he was not just one of the founding fathers, he is described as the 'First American'; he was also not just any Freemason, he was the Grand Master of Pennsylvania. His discoveries regarding electricity and lightning are well documented, but it was another discovery made in his London home, many years after his death that, perhaps, is the strangest.

The fact that Freemasons were involved in the American Revolution is in no doubt. Together with George Washington, nearly half of the commanders of the United States Continental Army, which fought the British forces, were Masons. Furthermore, Franklin and seven other Masonic brethren were signatories on the Declaration of Independence. Ironically, it was the idea of a Mason, linked to Franklin, who suggested a revenue raising law, which would spark the split between Great Britain and the North American colonies. Grievances relating to this Stamp Tax would result in the rallying cry of the Americans: 'no taxation without representation.'

The Stamp Tax, as we shall see, was the brain-child of Sir William Keith, 4th Baronet, later a member of the Grand Lodge of England, who was born in Peterhead, Scotland in 1669. His family were loyal to the Jacobite cause and, in 1703, Sir William was arrested on suspicion of plotting treason against Queen Anne, but was released without charge. The intrigue and plots continued and in 1715, with the first Jacobite Rebellion, Keith's father fled to the court in exile in Paris. This does not seem to have affected his son's career with the government in London, as Keith was appointed as Lieutenant Governor of the colony of Pennsylvania.

On that side of the Atlantic, Benjamin Franklin had been born in Boston, Massachusetts in 1706. Despite his formal schooling ending at ten years old, Franklin educated himself by reading vast amounts of books. As a teenager, his life-long religious views were formulated from writings criticising Deism—the belief that God is found by logic and reason and not, as in Christianity, by revelation. The books had the opposite effect on Franklin; he became a convert to Deism and saw the world around him as part of a 'clockwork universe', which, although created by God, operates without His intervention.

By the age of twelve, Franklin was working in the printing trade for his older brother, who had founded a newspaper. Dissatisfied at being a bound apprentice, he fled from his brother's employment and made his way to Pennsylvania, where he again found work as a printer. It was in this state, in 1723, that the young Franklin was to meet the Lieutenant Governor, Sir William Keith. The Scotsman convinced Franklin to go to London to purchase the printing equipment for a new American newspaper. The Lieutenant Governor promised the adventurous young man that he had several backers for his new paper in Great Britain and his mission would result in financial rewards for both of them. Unfortunately, on arrival in London, Franklin found no such support for the venture and had to find work in a printer's shop. This was situated in the Lady Chapel of St Bartholomew he Great in Smithfields, which the church hired out to raise funds.

In 1726, Keith and Franklin both sailed across the Atlantic to return to their native lands: Franklin journeying to Philadelphia and Keith to London. Sir William's return was not by choice; he had fled the colony, owing much money. It was during the voyage that he was to write *A Short Discourse on the Present State of the Colonies in America with respect to the Interest of Great Britain,* which included the Stamp Tax, to fund the stationing of British Army regiments in North America. The 'stamp' in question was not a postage stamp; it was an embossed mark on all paper, thus legal documents, newspapers, and possibly even the Book of Constitutions printed by Franklin in 1734 (the first Masonic book produced in the New World) would all fall into the scope of the tax.

Benjamin Franklin,
Provincial
Grand Master of
Pennsylvania.

It is unclear when or where Sir William Keith became a Freemason (he may have joined in Scotland), but by 1733, he is recorded as being in the Grand Lodge in England. He had sufficient influence to second a vote, proposed by the Deputy Grand Master, to send aid to the colony of Georgia. Unsurprisingly, the Grand Master at the time, James Lyon, 7th Earl of Strathmore, was, like many members of the Keith family, a Scottish Jacobite sympathiser. The date when Franklin joined the Craft is also unclear. It occurred some five years after arriving back in America, in 1730 or 1731. The place, however, is of no doubt—Franklin was made a Freemason in St John's lodge in Philadelphia. His growing influence in the colony is demonstrated by the fact that, within three years, he had been appointed the Provincial Grand Master of Pennsylvania. Today, each state has a Grand Master (there is no overall control of Masons in the USA), but in Franklin's time, the colony was a Province of the Grand Lodge of England.

Returning to his non-Masonic roles, Franklin established newspapers in several colonies and made further money by printing magazines and a popular Almanac. At the same time, he conducted many of his famous scientific works, such as using a kite to demonstrate that lightning was composed of electricity and charting (and naming) the Gulf Stream.

The latter changed the route used by ships to cross the Atlantic. Franklin's scientific work resulted in him being made a Fellow of the Royal Society and later, of the Royal Society of Arts. While Brother Franklin's fame and influence was increasing, Brother Keith's life was, however, on the decline. The Scotsman ended his days in ignominy—financially ruined and in 1749, he died in the debtor's prison at the Old Bailey.

In 1757, Franklin was sent to England to represent the affairs of the colony of Pennsylvania and he was to spend the next eighteen years in Europe, travelling across Britain and Ireland and later to Germany. While in England, he would spend much of his time in rented rooms at 36 Craven Street, near Charing Cross in London. He remained at an active Mason attending the Grand Lodge of England meeting in 1760, which was held in the Crown and Anchor tavern, which then stood on the Strand.

While in London, Franklin's influence continued to increase and he was called to give evidence at the House of Commons, regarding the hated Stamp Act. His efforts resulted in the repeal of the law and Franklin became the leading spokesman in England for the North American colonists, hence his title, 'the First American'. However, despite the repeal of the Act, the damage had been done to the relationship between the Americans and their British masters. The revolutionary spark would soon be ignited.

Initially, Franklin took a consolatory position and supported the idea of the colonies remaining part of the British Empire. This view gradually changed with Parliament continuing to demand that the colonists should pay for the cost of troops fighting the French in the New World, as well as protecting settlements from attacks by Native Americans. A visit to Ireland further convinced Franklin that British taxes could unfairly control and stifle parts of the empire, but the final turning point for Franklin was the 'Hutchinson Affair'. This related to letters written by Governor Hutchinson of Massachusetts to Parliamentary officials in London. These were very inflammatory, as they suggested methods of enforcing the unpopular British laws in his colony and cracking down on those who protested against them. Franklin came into possession of the letters and forwarded them, secretly and in confidence, to America. Franklin had intended that only a select number of influential Americans would see the correspondence, but the letters were published in a Boston newspaper and later throughout the thirteen colonies.

In England, the source of the leak was a matter of great debate. With accusations flying, Franklin came forward and admitted his actions. He was hauled before Parliament and lambasted by the Solicitor-General (who does not appear to have been a Mason, despite being the 1st Earl of Rosslyn, where the chapel of Masonic folklore stands). After this treatment by a British official, he was committed to independence. Franklin would return to America in 1775 and, with the Revolutionary War won, he would help to draft the Declaration of Independence. Thirteen of the fifty-six signatories are claimed to be Masons: with some, there is little proof as to their membership of the Craft; with Franklin, the most famous of names on the document, there is no doubt.

Franklin would become the USA's ambassador to France and, while in Paris, he found time to become the Master of the *Les Neuf Soeurs* from 1779 to 1781. During his membership, he persuaded the French philosopher, Voltaire to become a Freemason; it should be noted that Voltaire also lived in the Covent Garden area of London, albeit many

Franklin's home in Craven Street, London; fifteen dead bodies were found buried in the garden when it was renovated.

years earlier than Franklin. A plaque in Maiden Lane commemorates the writer's London residence. Voltaire died a few months after joining the lodge in Paris and Franklin presided over the 'Lodge of Sorrow' to mark his passing. He would also join lodges in Nancy and Rouen during his time in France.

Franklin died in Philadelphia in 1790 at the age of eighty-four. During his life, he had served his country, Freemasonry, and science well. There is some irony in the fact that the Mason who sent him to England, Sir William Keith, may well have caused the War of Independence with his Stamp Tax, a law which Franklin played an enormous part in bringing to an end. He was not, as the Earl of Rosslyn described him during the 'Hutchinson Affair', a thief or dishonest, but he could be a rogue, with a weakness for women. He had been brought up by Puritan parents, but freely admitted using prostitutes in London and one of his letters ('Advice to a Friend on Choosing a Mistress') was deemed so scandalous that is was not published for many years. Indeed, this letter was used in arguments to overturn obscenity laws in twentieth century America. For those interested, Franklin advises taking an older woman as a mistress, as such a lady is more likely to be discreet, unlikely to get pregnant and has more experience in pleasing a man.

But what of the mystery of a mass grave? Over two hundred years after Franklin's death, his London home in Craven Street was converted to a museum in his honour. During this work, some ten dead bodies—of men, women and children—were found buried in what had been the garden of the house. The bones, including many sawn through limbs and a skull with holes drilled into it, were dated to the time of Franklin's residence. It would appear, however, that the 'villain' was another man, who shared the premises, Dr William Hewson. Hewson was not a Mason, but neither was he a mass murderer. It would appear that he was using dead bodies robbed from graves in order to conduct medical experiments. Such work, while producing vital scientific knowledge, was frowned upon at that time. Given Franklin's interest in science, there is little doubt that he would have known of this work and assisted with the *post-mortem* examinations.

The Strange Case of the Cross-Dressing Mason, Soldier, and Spy

Masonic Connection
Transvestite Mason
Membership of women
Assisted by former Grand Master of England

Date
1766: D'Éon joined London lodge
1770: Went into hiding fearing kidnap
1810: Died in London

Connection to London
Arundel Street/the Strand: Lodge met at now demolished tavern
Brewer Street, Soho: Resided at this venue
Carlton House Terrace: D'Éon fought a duel at the now demolished Carlton House, the
    home of Freemason the Prince of Wales (later George IV)
Milman Street, Holborn: Resided at this venue later in life
Trafalgar Square: Portrait in National Gallery (Room 12)

Lodges
Grand Stewards'
Royal Somerset and Inverness No.4
L'Immortalité de L'Ordre No. 303 (erased)
Les Amis Réunis (Tonnerre, France)
Loge Les Neuf Soeurs (Paris)

Many Freemasons will have heard of the case of Elizabeth St Leger, who was made a Mason in Ireland sometime around 1710, after accidentally (or deliberately) seeing part of a Masonic ceremony through a crack in the wall in a house in Cork. At least the brethren concerned knew that Miss St Leger was a woman. This chapter will describe an even more unusual Mason, who until death, no one was ever sure if the person was male or female.

Legally, he was a woman, as a court had declared him to be such. Once d'Éon had passed to the Grand Lodge Above, the body was examined by a panel of experts, who finally confirmed the gender of the deceased. It is also a fascinating tale of a swashbuckling spy and diplomat, who was an expert with a sword, even while wearing the restrictive and flamboyant dress style of an eighteenth-century lady. The revelation of this Mason's true sex is said to have sent King George III mad. It also involves a Grand Master of England offering shelter to this rather unusual brother.

The Mason involved in this bizarre tale is Charles d'Éon, or to give him his full (and rather exotic) identity: Charles-Genevieve Louise-Auguste-Andre-Timothee d'Éon de Beaumont, who was born in 1728 in the French town of Tonnerre in the Burgundy district, some 125 miles south west of Paris. His mundane childhood revealed nothing of the exciting life he was to lead, but he progressed through university, earning a law degree. He also enjoyed learning other languages and was very good at memorising text (no bad thing for a future Freemason). D'Éon worked in several roles for the government, working in a finance office and later censoring books.

In 1745, the king of France, Louis XV, formed an intelligence gathering unit named the *Secret du Roi* (in English, the 'Secret of the King' or 'King's Secret'). D'Éon joined this undercover organisation and was posted to the east, to find opportunities to spy on the Russian court. Here are the origins of d'Éon's bizarre double-life. The Empress of Russia wanted to recruit a secretary, but, unfortunately for the French spy, she would only employ a woman. As a result, a rumour was created that d'Éon had been born a woman, but chose to live as a man. This rather incredible story was believed and so his alter ego, 'Madame d'Éon' was born and the French government had a spy in the Empress's court in St Petersburg.

Between 1756 and 1763, Europe was at war in what has become known as the Seven Years' War. Britain, Prussia, and Portugal fought against France, Russia, Austria, and Spain, with the conflict spreading to the New World, with fighting in North and South America. Returning to France, d'Éon switched back to his male identity and took a commission, serving as a captain in a cavalry regiment. He fought with some distinction during the war and was rewarded for his service with a medal for bravery and the title '*Chevalier*' (or in English, a knight). Once the war was over, and given his spying and diplomatic skills, he was sent to London. Overtly, he served as part of the team tasked to negotiate a peaceful conclusion to the war. Covertly, as a member of *Secret du Roi*, he was establishing intelligence to aid a potential French invasion of England. Such action was required to restore Gallic pride, which had been badly dented as all New France (a vast part of North American stretching from Louisiana to Canada) had been lost.

D'Éon, however, had a problem—he was short of money. He had hoped to become the French ambassador to England, but that appointment was not forthcoming. He would have to be innovative. Given that the district of his birth was Burgundy, it can come as no surprise that he saw wine as a potential solution. He used government funds to purchase and import thousands of bottles of expensive French wine, which were much sought in England. His French masters were outraged by his abuse of government money and, possibly more important, that his conduct would draw attention to himself. A spy should operate in the shadows; d'Éon was far too visible.

MADEMOISELLE de BEAUMONT, or the
CHEVALIER D'EON.
Female Minister Plenipo. Capt. of Dragoons &c. &c.

Charles d'Éon, the cross-dressing Freemason.

The French Ambassador tried to deal with d'Éon and ordered him to return to Paris, to 'face the music' for his actions. D'Éon refused to obey such orders twice. He was determined to remain in England and it was at this time, in 1766, that he joined a London-based French speaking lodge that met at the Crown and Anchor Tavern (long since demolished), which stood in Arundel Street near the Strand. Within a couple of years, he was the Junior Warden of *L'Immortalité de L'Ordre* (Lodge of Immortality), by this time numbered No. 303 on the roll of the Modern's Grand Lodge.

As well as Freemasonry, d'Éon indulged in another hobby—dressing as a woman. His effeminate looks added to the realism. By the time he was serving as the Junior Warden in 1770, rumours (and a newspaper report) started to spread around London that d'Éon was, in fact, a woman. Bets were even taken as to his true sex and Masons wondered if they had allowed a lady to join their lodge.

The betting became so intense that d'Éon feared being kidnapped by gamblers determined to prove his gender, and, of course, claim the winnings. As a result, he decided to go into hiding and get out of London. The membership of the lodge in the Strand had produced a useful and, given the circumstances, an unusual, ally—the 5th Earl Ferrers, Grand Master of England (1762–64). The earl was a committed Freemason, being a member of Horn Lodge No.2 (now Royal Somerset and Inverness lodge No.4) and was instrumental in forming the Grand Stewards' Lodge. The former Grand Master had obtained his title in very unfortunate circumstances: his brother, the 4th Earl, had been convicted of murder after shooting his servant in a drunken rage. In true English style, as a peer of the realm, he was hanged with a silk rope. D'Éon was to hide away in the earl's country home in Staunton Harold, north Leicestershire. Unpleasantly, this was the site of the murder committed by the previous earl, but at least it was well away from London gamblers, who were intent on a forceful and intimate examination of d'Éon.

As a result of the failure to find the cross-dressing Mason, an insurance company asked a court to adjudicate on d'Éon's sex. Following evidence from witnesses, the magistrate declared the French spy to be a woman. Perhaps sick and tired of the speculation, d'Éon now decided to return to his native land. His transvestite behaviour had to be explained to the French authorities and he fell back on the story used to gain his roll with the Russian empress—he had been born female. He further embellished the tale, adding that he had been brought up as a boy as his family stood to inherit a fortune, but only if they had a son.

The French king was, by now, Louis XVI, who was later executed after the French Revolution. He permitted the cross-dressing Mason to return in 1779. Oddly, the king insisted that d'Éon continued to act as a woman and as such he would be known as Lady (in French, *Chevalière*) d'Éon. This was agreed, and d'Éon returned to his mother's home in Tonnerre. He even found time to join the lodge in his home town, *Les Amis Réunis*, or Lodge of Reunited Friends. D'Éon also found time to study Jansenism, a Roman Catholic theological study movement at that time. Many in French society were convinced that d'Éon was, indeed, a woman. His fellow Freemason, Voltaire, the great philosopher was not so easily duped. He called d'Éon an 'amphibian'; he even ridiculed his facial hair. Voltaire had joined the Lodge of Nine Sisters or *Loge Les Neuf Soeurs* in Paris the year before d'Éon's return to France.

Never one to let the grass grow under his feet, d'Éon was back across the Channel in 1785 and was never to return to his native land. He moved back to 38 Brewer Street in Soho. The French Revolution began in 1789 and the king, Louis XVI, was executed in 1793, freeing d'Éon from his obligation to live as a woman. Unfortunately, the removal of the French monarchy resulted in d'Éon's pension being stopped. As a result, he was, as ever, short of money and had to tour England showing off his duelling skills, with spectators paying five shillings a head to watch. His victories were reported in the press at that time. During the contests, he sometimes dressed in the uniform of a dragoon, on other occasions in the voluminous skirts of a lady (but wearing his military decorations). Fellow Freemason, the Prince of Wales (later George IV) was to witness the female alter ego giving a great display of fencing ability at Carlton House. This royal residence has since been demolished and replaced with Carlton House Terrace. As evidence of d'Éon's cross-dressing at this time, a portrait of him in female garb was painted in 1792 and still can be seen in the National Gallery.

He was, however, getting rather old for a contact sport. In 1796, when in his late sixties, his luck ran out. He was badly injured when an opponent's sword entered his armpit. He was bed-ridden for months and his duelling career was at an end. D'Éon moved in with Madame Marie Cole at 26 Milman Street in Holborn. Madame Cole was French, but had been married to an English engineer. The elderly widow seemed to have been convinced that she was living with a distinguished French lady. They survived on gifts from friends, including a £50 annual allowance from Queen Charlotte, the wife of George III. D'Éon still, however, kept spending and had to spend a short spell in a debtors' prison.

His health having been in decline for some years, d'Éon died in 1810 in England, at the age of eighty-one. Madame Cole and even the queen tried to prevent examination of the body, but to no avail as there was too much interest. A French professor of anatomy, two surgeons, a lawyer, and a journalist were called to examine the body. The panel announced that he was man. The result was said to have caused a bout of madness in George III; the king suffered much from mental illness.

So passed the life of a Mason described in 'The Gentleman's Magazine' as 'he/she' and who spent much of his life dressed as a woman, convincing most that he was a lady. The fascinating life of Brother Charles d'Éon involved being wounded in battle, working as a spy, negotiating peace between the great powers of Europe, fighting duels, and sending the king of England mad. He was, no doubt, a rogue, who could always spend more money than he could earn and would abuse any authority he was given. As a Freemason, he could count some of the most influential members of the Craft amongst his friends—the Prince of Wales and the Past Grand Master, the 5th Earl Ferrers. Finally, he was, possibly, the earliest accepted transvestite in London society.

16

The First Royal Grand Master and his 'Criminal Conversation'

Masonic Connection
Grand Master
Royal Family and Holy Royal Arch

Date
1767: Initiated into Freemasonry
1769: Sex scandal involving Lady Grosvenor
1771: Breached Royal Marriage Act
1782–90: Grand Master

Connection to London
Leicester Square: Place of birth
Cavendish Square: Location of 'criminal conversation'

Lodges
Royal Alpha No. 16
Thatched House Tavern (erased)

Prince Henry, Duke of Cumberland and Strathearn was born in 1745 in Leicester House (which was located near the present-day Leicester Square). He was a younger brother of George III and uncle to the Duke of Sussex (the first Grand Master of the United Grand Lodge of England). The Duke of Cumberland served as Grand Master of the Moderns Grand Lodge 1782–90 and was the first Royal Grand Master, perhaps the opportunity to have a Royal Grand Master resulted in those who selected him being rather forgiving in relation to the several sexual scandals he had been embroiled in—one of which ended in court and another which resulted in an Act of Parliament.

Women appear to have been the Duke's continual downfall. He enraged his brother, the king, by marrying a commoner (Olive Wilmot) in a secret ceremony in 1767. At least as a Freemason, he was not concerned with 'rank and fortune'; Masons, according to the initiation ceremony, should focus on 'honour and virtue' in a person. Indeed, 1767

Prince Henry, Duke of Cumberland, the first Royal Grand Master.

appears to have been the year of secret ceremonies as the Duke was initiated into a lodge at the Thatched House Tavern in St James's in that year. Two months after his initiation and passing (on the same day), he was installed as Master of the New Horn Lodge (a very apt name, given his sexual prowess). He was also the first member of the Royal Family, who is recorded as being exalted into the Holy Royal Arch. New Horn (later known as the Royal Lodge) was amalgamated with the Alpha Lodge in 1824 to form the Royal Alpha Lodge No. 16.

The Duke then entered the Royal Navy, at the fairly late age of twenty-two; possibly, he was sent to sea to keep him out of trouble, but it did not work. His ship was recalled to England due to the threat of a French invasion. This gave him the opportunity start an affair with Lady Henrietta Grosvenor, the attractive wife of Lord Grosvenor, a politician and racehorse owner. Lord Grosvenor seems to have neglected his young wife and spent much of his time gambling or frequenting brothels.

Henrietta and the Duke met in private, under the pretext of her seeking his aid for her relative, who was in the Royal Navy; however, it was to end in discovery in 1769. While pursuing their affair at a friend's house in Cavendish Square (some accounts give the location as an inn in St Alban's), they were found *in flagrante delicto*; Lady Grosvenor with her 'petticoats up' on the couch with the Duke's 'breeches unbuttoned' according to evidence given by witnesses. Lord Grosvenor sued the Duke for 'criminal conversation' or adultery. In what must be possibly the most expensive sexual encounter in Masonic history, the future Grand Master had to pay damages and costs to the tune of £13,000 (some £1.5 million today).

Once this scandal had passed, Prince Henry found himself embroiled in another one; in 1771, he married another commoner, a widow named Anne Horton. She was, at least, the daughter of an earl, but she was seemingly happy to please many men of a certain rank. Such was her beauty that Gainsborough painted her several times. The king, however, was not impressed and responded by forbidding any of his relatives to marry in future without his express permission; this was enshrined in law as The Royal Marriages Act 1772. Despite all these misdemeanours, the Duke of Cumberland was to become an admiral and hold the office of Grand Master from 1782 until his death in 1790 (at only forty-five years old). He was also the Grand Patron of the Royal Arch from 1774. The first Royal Grand Master had lived a short, but eventful life.

17

Mutiny on the Bounty: the Masonic Links

Masonic Connection
Proposer of mission
Evidence that captain of HMS Bounty was a Mason

Date
1789: Mutiny occurred

Connection to London
Crane Court, Fetter Lane: Headquarters of Royal Society (1710–80)
100 Lambeth Road, Kennington: Bligh's London home
St Mary's, Lambeth (now the Garden Museum): Bligh's tomb

Lodges
Royal Somerset House and Inverness No. 4

There can be few more serious crimes than mutiny in the Armed Forces. Until 1998, overthrowing or resisting the lawful authority of senior officers was punishable by death. Neither is there a more famous (or infamous) mutiny than that which occurred on HMS *Bounty* in 1789. Who involved was a Mason, and did Masonry play a part in the selection of the captain of the ship?

It must be said that Masonic records, particularly of Naval lodges in the formative years of English Masonry, are incomplete. For example, it took many years of research to finally show that Admiral the Lord Nelson was a member of the Craft. Likewise, at this time there were two (if not more) Grand Lodges, further confusing matters. The Royal Navy helped to take Freemasonry across the globe and some of the most influential men in the Craft at that time were sailors, including Thomas Dunckerley, a Chief Gunnery Instructor, who must take much credit for promoting the Royal Arch. Importantly, he introduced (or perhaps, re-introduced) Mark Masonry to England at Portsmouth, one of the Royal Navy's principle ports.

There is no doubt, however, that the proposer of the breadfruit expedition, which later involved HMS *Bounty*, was a Freemason. Sir Joseph Banks (1743–1820) was a member of the Old Horn Lodge No. 2 (now Royal Somerset House and Inverness Lodge No. 4), which, in 1767, met at the Fleece Tavern in Tothill Street, London. He was a renowned botanist and the year after his initiation, he took part in Captain Cook's epic voyage of discovery. This took him across the southern Pacific and to the South Sea Islands. Banks, it would seem, was the first Freemason to set foot in Australia and New Zealand. He was later the President of the Royal Society for over forty years and made Kew Gardens the world's leading botanical gardens. For his services to science, he was made a baronet by George III.

At this time, slavery was permitted in the British Empire and plantation owners in the West Indies required a cheap and high-energy food to feed their workforce. During his travels across the Pacific, Banks had noted that the local Polynesian people ate what was later called 'breadfruit'. This versatile fruit could be boiled, roasted, or fried, and tasted like potatoes or (unsurprisingly) a freshly made loaf. Banks offered a cash reward and gold medal for the leader of an expedition to take samples from the island of Tahiti to the Caribbean.

Sir Joseph Banks, the Freemason who arranged the Bounty's expedition and appointed (Brother) Bligh as captain.

Furthermore, as President of the Royal Society, Brother Banks was able to lobby the Admiralty to send an official Royal Navy expedition to undertake this task. A merchant ship, which was suitable for carrying the delicate botanical cargo, was purchased by the government and renamed HMS *Bounty*. In 1787, Lieutenant William Bligh (1754–1817) was appointed to lead this mission. Bligh was a highly experienced sailor—he had been enlisted into the Royal Navy at the age of seven as a 'young gentlemen'. He had also sailed the South Seas with Captain Cook in his later voyages. He was certainly a Fellow of the Royal Society, but there are no official records of his membership of the Craft; however, as we will see, there are two pieces of evidence that suggest that he had joined a lodge at some point in his naval career.

On 23 December 1787, the *Bounty* departed Portsmouth with Bligh as captain of the ship. After a difficult voyage of over ten months, the ship reached Tahiti on 26 October 1788. The crew were supposed to complete their work on the island within six weeks, but the beauty of the island (and female inhabitants) appears to have created delays. While over one thousand breadfruit plants were eventually collected, it took over five months to do so. The sailors, no doubt, enjoyed their extended stay in paradise and were probably loathe to return to the disciplined life on-board a ship. In addition to the return to a life of strict routine, the living conditions were even worse than the outward voyage. Vast numbers of plant pots now took up much room, giving the men little space. HMS *Bounty* set sail for the Caribbean on 5 April 1789; it was never to arrive.

Less than four weeks into the voyage, on 28 April, eighteen members of the crew mutinied, led by Fletcher Christian. Christian has been Bligh's second-in-command, but despite being long-standing friends, animosity had grown between them. It will never be clear if Bligh's leadership style caused the men to seize his ship. Films portray him as a tyrant, but the evidence of the punishments awarded by him, recorded in the ship's log, tend to suggest that he was not as cruel as Hollywood would have us believe. This would not be the last time men under his command would turn on him.

Whatever the case, Bligh was cast adrift with loyal members of his crew. By fantastic seamanship, he was able to navigate the open boat over four thousand miles to the island of Timor. By March 1790, he was back in Portsmouth and exonerated for the loss of HMS *Bounty*. The mutineers made for Tahiti, where some remained, while others sailed to Pitcairn Island—an excellent hiding place as it was incorrectly charted on British maps. Fletcher Christian's fate is unknown, but the mutineers on Tahiti were found by the Royal Navy; four drowned when the ship collided with rocks and three were eventually hanged.

Bligh's leadership style let him down on several more occasions. Crews under his command were to mutiny at Nore (on the Thames) and later at Spithead, near Portsmouth. These were wider disputes, with sailors angry at the poor conditions on board Royal Navy ships, but Bligh's reputation followed him. The seamen often referred to him as the 'Bounty Bastard'.

A further blight on the Bligh career was to occur in Australia. He was appointed as the Governor of New South Wales in 1806 on the direct recommendation of Sir Joseph Banks. Bligh's authoritarian style resulted in a dispute with the colonists and the Army officer in charge of the New South Wales Corps. By early 1808, the Australians placed Bligh under house arrest. Order was eventually restored and Bligh sailed to England in 1810, where Major George Johnson was court martialled for seizing power. While found guilty, the court appears to have had some sympathy with his actions. His only punishment was to be cashiered—thrown out of the Armed Forces in disgrace.

Bligh's navel career continued and he achieved the rank of Rear Admiral in 1814. He was to die three years later. His tomb in Lambeth is topped with a stone carving of a breadfruit. His great supporter, Sir Joseph Banks, was to outlive him and died in 1820.

It is unlikely that we will ever know if Bligh was a Mason, but there is evidence that he may well have been 'on the square'. Displayed at the Australian National Portrait Gallery in Canberra is a painting entitled 'Midshipman Bligh', which shows him wearing the square and compasses on a chain around his neck. The symbol can be seen poking out of his waistcoat. Bligh held the rank of midshipman between 1771 and 1774, while serving on two ships—HMS *Hunter* and HMS *Crescent*. He had joined the Royal Navy as a boy and would not have been eligible to join the Craft until his eighteenth birthday. He had left the *Hunter* before that time and so if Bligh did join a lodge, he did so during his service on HMS *Crescent*. So was a Masonic ceremony held on a thirty-two-gun ship, a renamed captured French vessel, to initiate a young William Bligh?

Perhaps this explains the great support that Bligh received from Sir Joseph Banks. There may be another piece of evidence to support Bligh's membership, which seems to have continued throughout his life. In letters to Banks, sent during his time in New South Wales, Bligh refers to God as the 'Great Architect'—a very Masonic term and used by him over thirty years after the painting showed him wearing square and compasses.

18

Yorkshire Mason Hanged in London: the Bizarre Inventor turned Counterfeiter

Masonic Connection
Bizarre inventor
Counterfeiter

Date
1774: Initiated into Freemasonry
1789: Executed for offence of 'coining'

Connection to London
Haymarket: Denton resided in Coventry Court
Schomberg House, Pall Mall: Assisted to build a sex-aid bed located in the 'Temple of Hymen'
Gray's Inn Road: Counterfeiting implements found at (now demolished) Bell Court, Holborn
Old Bailey: Court where tried, convicted and executed

Lodges
Moriah No. 176 (erased)
York No. 236

This is the tale of a clever man and Freemason who was seemingly determined to make his fortune (by hook or by crook), but who ultimately ended up on the gallows—having been convicted of counterfeiting coins, which sadly for him was a treasonous act.

Thomas Denton was born in North Yorkshire around 1746 and was an apprentice tinsmith. He quickly became bored of making pots and kettles and, being an entrepreneur, with a taste for literature, opened a book shop in York. There he found the Craft and in 1774, was initiated into Moriah Lodge No. 176, which met in the Star and Garter Tavern in Nessgate. His Mother Lodge closed in 1777 and so he became a founder member of Union Lodge No. 507 (known as York No. 236 since 1870) and the following year, he was installed as its second Master. Denton soon gave up the life of a bookseller and headed to the bright lights of London.

On arrival in London, by chance, he visited an exhibition of an automaton in Westminster. This bizarre device, designed in Austria, was (supposedly) a man-like robot chess player, dressed, rather exotically, in Turkish garb and a turban. It was, of course, a trick. A human chess master was inside the device, controlling the metal arms, which moved the pieces around the board (beating many eminent men along the way). Those defeated by the automaton included Mason Benjamin Franklin, various Dukes, and even Napoleon Bonaparte.

Denton, using his metal work skills, is said to have designed a similar device, which was superior to the original as it was also a 'speaking machine'. It is unclear quite how this worked, but it may have been another scam designed to trick an unsuspecting public. It could, however, have been an intricate clockwork device; a 'writing boy' still exists in a Swiss museum—this writes text and even moves its eyes, following the text. Whatever the case, Denton then toured the country exhibiting the robot, making a substantial sum. Returning to London, he continued to invent devices and turned his hand to chemistry, even translating a book on the subject from Italian into English. There is little doubt that this selfmade Yorkshireman was very clever and resourceful.

Possibly the most bizarre aspect of Denton's inventing career was his work with (self-styled) 'Doctor' James Graham, a Scottish proponent of all manner of odd cures for sexual problems, including magnetism and electricity. Denton constructed parts for Graham's 'Grand State Celestial Bed'—a giant leap forward in the field of sexual pleasure. The enormous bed included flashing lights, music, erotic images, and mirrors. It also sprayed perfume and pleasant-smelling aromas and tilted to achieve the best position for the couple to conceive. Above the bed was a dome with fresh flowers and even live turtle doves. There was also an electric sign flashing God's words to Noah as recorded in the Book of Genesis—'Be fruitful, multiply and replenish the earth' (Never has Royal Ark Mariner Masonry been so much fun). Well-to-do London couples, with sexual problems, could hire the bed for £50 per night (over £5,000 at today's value).

The magnificent bed was located in Graham's 'Temple of Hymen' (named after the Roman God of Marriage) at Schomberg House on Pall Mall, which opened in 1781. Although the interior has been rebuilt, the façade of the building is the original. Graham gave the aim of his institution:

Preventing barrenness, and propagating a much more strong, beautiful, active, healthy, wise, and virtuous race of human beings, than the present puny, insignificant, foolish, peevish, vicious, and nonsensical race of Christians, who quarrel, fight, bite, devour, and cut one another's throats about they know not what.

The Temple of Hymen was frequented by Lady Emma Hamilton, the lover of Mason, Lord Nelson. Dr Graham employed her as a 'model and a dancer' and taught her to pose ('gracefully') as the Goddess of Health.

In 1785, Denton was living not too far from Schomberg House at Coventry Court in Haymarket (where there is still a Coventry House). While there, he produced a book entitled *The Conjurer Unmasked*. Showing his language skills, this was a translation from the French original, *La Magie Blanche Dévoilée*. The book was subtitled, 'A clear and full explanation … of all the surprising performances … of Professors of Slight [sic.] of Hand.' This gave detailed disclosures of how the automaton was actually operated and the methods used by conjurers, including card tricks and how to make doves 'magically' appear—a standard illusion, even today. It was lucky for him that the 'Magic Circle' was not formed until 1905, for they would have been mightily displeased.

Around this time, Denton moved to Holborn and resided in Bell Court, which has long been demolished. It appears to have stood at the Holborn end of Gray's Inn Road near Chancery Lane underground station. By this time, he was married, with a child. In Holborn, Denton ran another successful business—adding metal plates to coach harnesses. The plates seem to have been nothing more than an accessory, with little practical purpose, but they were in fashion and the rich were willing to pay. Most importantly, Denton's metal work skills were back to the fore. At some point, he began to produce counterfeit silver coins. This remains a serious crime, but even more so in the eighteenth century as it was considered a form of treason as counterfeiting coins involved reproducing images of the king's head.

The illegal activities of Denton and his men came to the attention of the police force of the day, the Bow Street Runners. Unfortunately for Brother Denton, two of the Runners on his case, Charles Jealous and John Clarke, were two of the most prolific officers. These officers were responsible for a large proportion of the convictions of London's villains.

On 25 March 1789, Jealous and Clark raided Bell Court and found Denton and two men, William and John Jones, potentially the same 'John Jones' who was the first master of York Lodge No. 236. In Denton's pocket was a key for a bureau—an office desk. John Jones had the key for the cellar. When these were searched, implements for making false coins, including shillings and half-crowns, were discovered. No actual counterfeit coins were found, but the three men were arrested and kept in custody. On 3 June, they appeared at the Old Bailey, charged with several offences of 'coining'. The most serious accusations related to actually making coins, but they also faced lesser charges concerned with possessing implements to do so. A guilty verdict for any would be fatal as all the offences carried the death sentence.

Luckily for William Jones, the judge soon declared that there was no evidence against him and he was free. The other two accused were not so fortunate. Denton tried to use a scientific defence—the dyes were not made of steel and were too soft to make an impression on the metal. Neither the judge nor the jury were impressed; both he and John Jones were found guilty and sentenced to death by hanging. It could have been worse; most offences relating to treason carried the awful death of being hanged, drawn, and quartered.

Just six days after the sentence had been delivered, Denton and Jones, together with other criminals—a gang of burglars and a highwayman—were brought out of Newgate Prison to face the noose in front of the Old Bailey. Their execution was reported across the country. For example, the Hereford Journal reported that Denton behaved with the 'greatest levity' prior to his execution. It further noted that 'If he had gone to a wedding he could not be merrier', telling its readers that Denton even threw a bunch of sweet smelling flowers into the crowd. The *London Chronicle* recorded that Denton used 'abominable and blasphemous expressions' and continued to laugh with the crowd, even when the black cap was put over his head. It was unusual that such a criminal would have had public support; coiners and counterfeiters were hated, especially by the poor. The shilling was the highest denomination coin a labourer would receive for many hours of hard work. To receive a counterfeit coin in payment for such would mean a family would go hungry.

Denton had written a letter to his parents in Yorkshire ('Dick' was his son, Richard):

> When you receive this I shall be gone to that country from whence no traveller returns. Don't cast any reflections on my wife, the best of mothers, and the best of women; and if ever woman went to heaven, she will. If I had taken her advice I should not have been in this situation. God bless my poor Dick. The bell is tolling. Adieu!

While his parents in the north were aware of Denton's execution, his brother Masons in York were seemingly not, although the *Leeds Mercury* newspaper carried a report of his hanging. It took twenty-two years for the Provincial Grand Secretary to record the incident in the Yorkshire Masonic records. That said, his name lived on; as late as 1795, a Richard Denton (possibly the son) was advertising the services of Thomas Denton printer, engraver and translator of magic books. This was in Mead Row, next to the current Kennington Police Station. A man called Richard Denton was sentenced to prison for forging notes in 1811—like father, like son? Denton junior would have met one Mason—the prison chaplain at Newgate was a Freemason, Worshipful Brother the Reverend Doctor Brownlow Forde.

It is a pity that such an ingenious man and Mason as Thomas Denton should use his talents for crime rather than the good of society. The Yorkshireman was blessed with inventive genius, business acumen, and the ability to speak several languages, but this was all wasted and his life ended, swearing at the crowd, before dangling on the gallows.

19

A Masonic Swindler and
the Downfall of the French Monarchy

Masonic Connection
Fraudster involved in swindling French royal family
Device used to execute French king and queen
Vatican stance on membership

Date
1776: Initiated into Freemasonry
1786: Tried for involvement in 'Diamond Necklace Affair'
1789: Imprisoned for being a Mason

Connection to London
Gerrard Street, Soho: Cagliostro's lodge met in King's Head Tavern
Sloane Square: Residence of Cagliostro
Warwick Court, Gray's Inn: Residence
Whitcomb Street: Residence
Stationers' Hall, Ave Maria Lane: Cagliostro gave lectures at this venue

Lodges
Lodge of Antiquity No. 2
L'Esperance No. 369 (erased)
La Parfaite Union (France)

This chapter involves a European count (or perhaps a commoner), an elaborate swindle, alchemy, and mystical beliefs, ending in an arrest for simply being a Freemason. The main Mason in this strange affair is Brother Count Alessendro di Cagliostro, who appears to have been born in Sicily in the mid-1740s. His identity is shrouded in mystery, as he may have been born simply Joseph Balsamo. Whether a real count or not, he studied medicine, magic, and alchemy; to enhance his mystical persona, he visited Arabian holy sites in Mecca and Medina, as well as travelling to the pyramids in Cairo. Importantly, one of his (alleged) criminal activities was to play a part in the downfall of the French monarchy. The king and his family were then executed using a device invented by another member of the Craft.

Count Alessendro di Cagliostro, a Mason who helped to bring down the French monarchy.

Despite the mysteries surrounding Cagliostro (or Balsamo), it is certain that in 1768, he married a young woman; she was fourteen years old at the time. The couple then travelled throughout Europe, where Cagliostro met a forger, who taught him his trade. Now a mystic and a fraudster, Cagliostro paid his teacher in a most unusual manner; he was allowed sex with his teenage wife, who was now styled as Lady Cagliostro.

For their first dishonest scheme, the count and his accomplice opened a casino in Naples, where rich foreigners were cheated out of money. The swindle was uncovered and Cagliostro was forced to leave the city. Moving to Rome, his strange mysticism resulted in the attention of the Papal authorities and he was accused of heresy. Well aware of the power of the Roman Catholic Church, Cagliostro and his wife quickly returned to his home town of Palermo in Sicily. This would not be the last time that the count would fall foul of the Pope. While the Roman Catholic Church did not approve of his odd religious beliefs, and others may have questioned his dishonest conduct and use of his wife's sexual favours to pay for services rendered, none of this seems to have damaged Cagliostro's reputation. In Paris, he was even recommended to be a physician to Freemason Benjamin Franklin.

Around the same time, a sexual scandal was encompassing the French king, Louis XV, who had become infatuated with Madame du Barry—a beautiful woman, who was, unfortunately, of common birth and, therefore, deemed not suitable to associate with royalty. Unperturbed and determined to impress the lady of his desires, the king decided to present her with the most impressive diamond necklace ever made. Jewellers across the nation searched for the best stones to complete the piece, but by the time they had done so (over ten years later), the king was dead and his grandson (crowned Louis XVI) had assumed the throne. He offered the necklace to his wife—the infamous Marie Antoinette— but she refused it. It is said that she thought the money could have been better spent on the nation's armed forces, but it is suspected that she hated Madame Du Barry, who had held great sway in the French court, and did not want to wear jewellery designed for her.

During the period of these changes in the French royal court, Count Cagliostro had not remained in Paris. Continuing his travels, he had found time to become a Freemason in London. In April 1776, he had joined the (long disbanded) French-speaking L'Esperance lodge, No. 369, which met in the King's Head Tavern in Gerrard Street in London's Soho. Cagliostro would have felt at home; as well as French brethren, many of the members were Italian. He seems to have enjoyed Masonry, as it fitted in with his mystical beliefs, so much so that he invented new ceremonies, seemingly based on the beliefs of ancient Egypt. In 1784, he was to form such an 'Egyptian' lodge in Lyon. He was, however, soon to return north to Paris. In the capital, he continued to practice his own form of medicine, sell potions and organise séances.

Never one to let the grass grow under his feet, Cagliostro was back across the Channel the following year and living in Sloane Square, London. Here, he made a living selling 'Egyptian Pills'—a rather dubious treatment, but at 36 shillings a box, they are perhaps proof that a 'fool and his money are easily parted'. He was still active in the Craft, visiting the Lodge of Antiquity No. 1 (now No. 2), to try and promote his supposedly Egyptian Masonic ceremonies. His attempts to convert the brethren to his new degrees failed and he was ridiculed for dressing like a 'drum major'. He was not, however, without influence, and had met the Prince of Wales, a fellow Freemason and the future King George IV.

While making a decent living from quack medicine and mystical nonsense, an opportunity to obtain a large sum of money in France was soon to materialise. This conspiracy would also play a significant role in the downfall of Marie Antoinette and the French monarchy. The Parisian jeweller, who now owned the extremely valuable, but unwanted, diamond necklace was faced with bankruptcy and was desperate to sell the piece. This situation presented unscrupulous criminals with the chance to make money. A French female swindler, the self-styled Comtesse de la Motte, was able to use her sexual charms on Louis de Rohan, a cardinal and bishop of the Roman Catholic Church, who was eager to ingratiate himself with Queen Marie Antoinette. By use of forged documents and dishonest advice proffered by Brother the Count Cagliostro, the cardinal came to believe that the queen wished to buy the necklace. He was further convinced when he had a secret, night time, meeting with her royal majesty. He had been tricked; the 'queen' was, in fact, a prostitute, in disguise, but the deception had worked. The cardinal obtained the necklace and passed it to Comtesse de la Motte. Unsurprisingly, the jewellery never reached the queen. Within days, the Comtesse's husband had broken down the necklace and was busy selling the diamonds in London and Paris.

Outraged by the swindle, the king ordered the arrest of Cardinal de Rohan, together with Count Cagliostro, for their involvement in the fraud. As a result, Cagliostro was imprisoned in the Bastille Prison for several months. The king and queen were keen to distance themselves from the affair and show that they had played no part in trying to

This piece of jewellery played a major part in the downfall of the French royal family during the Diamond Necklace Affair.

obtain the valuable necklace, but their public relations scheme backfired, with the French populace convinced that their greedy queen had some involvement. The cardinal and Cagliostro were found not guilty in 1786, but, angry with the 'wrong' verdict, the king had them exiled. One party was found guilty—the Comtesse—and she was sentenced to be whipped. The punishment was never to be given, as the (ever resourceful) lady escaped from prison disguised as a boy and fled to London. Public opinion continued to see the queen as the villain of the affair. She would never be forgiven and so began the long road to the guillotine.

Exiled from France, Cagliostro returned to London, claiming that the governor of the Bastille prison had stolen his fortune. It was in England that Charles de Morande, a French spy (and journalist), denounced Cagliostro as a commoner named 'Joseph Balsamo'. He vehemently denied this accusation and the two men began a very public disagreement, having letters published in various London newspapers. This affair may have been an attempt to extort blackmail money from Cagliostro or the work of the French king to discredit the count in revenge for the diamond necklace affair. Short of cash (again), Cagliostro made money by giving talks on his imprisonment in France, speaking at Stationers' Hall in London.

Cagliostro was also using his skills as an alchemist to (apparently) turn base metal into gold. He also claimed that he possessed an ancient Egyptian manuscript that enabled him to predict the results of games of chance. Thus, he was able to extract large sums of money from London's greedy and gullible. Such deeds did, however, draw him to the attention of the authorities, as several of his victims informed the local magistrates about his activities. For a time, Cagliostro was imprisoned in the King's Bench jail in Southwark where some twenty years before, Brother John Wilkes had been made a Mason in his cell. By now, the count had moved to Whitcomb Street, not far from Leicester Square, but such were the frequency of his arrests, that he transferred his residence to Warwick Court in Gray's Inn, so that he could be nearer to the Court of Justice and its officers (and, perhaps, bribe them); the house he lived in belonged to a court official.

Cagliostro's mystical life story now became even more bizarre. He claimed that he had been born before the Flood and had assisted at the wedding in Cana (where Jesus turned water into wine). For all his strange tales, he did have his loyal supporters. Volunteers still joined his Egyptian Masonic lodge, but he left for the Netherlands and travelled across Europe. In late 1788, the press in England reported that Cagliostro had been expelled from Vienna and forbidden from practising his style of medicine. Now, the Count was on his final journey—to Rome. In the Eternal City, for all his fraudulent exploits, bizarre medical practices, and dishonest alchemy, Cagliostro was arrested by the Papal Inquisition for the heretical offence being a Freemason and trying to set up a Masonic lodge. If convicted, he would face torture or worse.

Brother Cagliostro was not the only person facing trial and dreadful consequences. Events in France were now reaching a climax and the population were in revolt against King Louis XVI and his Austrian wife, Marie Antoinette. On 14 July 1789, the Bastille Prison, where the Count had once been imprisoned, was stormed; this signalled the beginning of the end of the French monarchy.

The Bastille—the dreadful Paris prison where Brother Cagliostro was held after being arrested for his part in the Diamond Necklace Affair.

While the French royal family was being held captive, Cagliostro also found himself in prison. He had been detained just after Christmas 1789 and kept in custody at the Castel Sant'Angelo in Rome. He had possibly been denounced by his wife, who was possibly exacting revenge for her husband's use of her as a payment device so many years before. Pope Pius VI would not permit Freemasonry to flourish in a Catholic country and the count was sentenced to death.

Fortunately for Cagliostro, this was commutated to life imprisonment and he was moved to the Fortress of San Leo in the north of Italy. He did attempt to escape, but he was never to taste freedom again. He died in the castle in 1795, aged fifty-two. The strange nature (and unfairness) of his sentence is summed up in an English translation of the *Life of Joseph Balsamo, commonly called Count Cagliostro*, originally published in 1791, before his death:

> Cagliostro, after committing a multitude of rogueries in various kingdoms, and escaping from the hand of justice in almost every capital in Europe, has at length, by an uncommon fatality, been arrested in his career, and condemned to death in the only metropolis, perhaps, in which he could not have been convicted of a breach of the moral obligations that connect man with society. Whatever motive may have influenced the court of Rome, it will be a lasting reproach on the reign of Pius VI to have detained, tried, and inflicted the punishment of perpetual imprisonment on a man, against whom he could only prove the crime—of being a free Mason!

So ends the life of a Masonic rogue. Pope Pius VI was not to have a happy end either. The French Revolution resulted in the rise of Napoleon, who attacked the Papal States (the Pope ruled a considerable part of Italy at that time) and took him prisoner in 1799. The pope was to die a short time later, having been forcibly moved around Italy by his French captors.

Pius VI, the pope when Cagliostro was sentenced to death for being a Mason.

Louis XVI and Marie Antoinette, as well as Madame du Barry, were to face a more violent death, at the hands of the executioners of revolutionary France. In the name of equality, the new French Republic decided that all condemned citizens, whatever their status in life, should face the same form of death. In the past, the rich had been beheaded with swords or axes, while the poor had been hanged—or rather slowly strangled to death, dangling from a rope. The new form of egalitarian punishment was proposed by Brother Joseph Guillotine, who had been initiated into the La Parfaite Union lodge in Angouleme, in south west France, some fourteen years before the revolution. By 1772, he was Deputy Grand Master of the French *Grand Loge* and attended lodges in Paris. The mechanical beheading machine adopted by France was to bear his name. While his suggested device may have brought untimely deaths to many of his countrymen (and women), Brother Guillotine was to die, peacefully, in his own bed, in 1814.

Thus, it can be seen that a Mason and swindler, Count Cagliostro played a part in the Diamond Necklace Affair, which was to damage the already unpopular French monarchy and another Mason, Joseph Guillotine, would provide the means whereby the king and queen would lose their heads. Along with Brother Coustos, the count would be one of the few members of the Craft to be imprisoned simply for being a Mason until the rise of Nazi Germany.

20

Unlawful Societies, Unlawful Masons?

Masonic Connection
Attempt to make membership illegal
Legislation requiring list of lodge members
Negotiations with British government

Date
1799–1967: Period law in force

Connection to London
Downing Street: Location where Grand Masters met with the Prime Minister
Houses of Parliament: Legislation debated on making secret societies, including Freemasonry, illegal

Lodges
Grand Lodge of England (Moderns)
Grand Lodge of England (Antients)
Grand Lodge of Scotland

In early 1799, a Member of Parliament in London, Henry Thornton, wrote to the Home Office with concerns about the threat of revolutionary groups. He had been informed by the owner of a distillery in Battersea that one of his workers had been asked to join a radical group (believed to be a republican society called the United Englishmen). One of the criteria for membership was like that of a Masonic lodge—he would be required to swear a secret oath.

The 'Establishment' (as it would now be called) saw threats all around. The American War of Independence and the French Revolution, which had begun only ten years before in 1789, were still major influences on radical minds, who wished to be rid of the king and establish new forms of government. By 1799, General Napoleon Bonaparte had seized power in Paris and had already fought against the British forces in Egypt. A French invasion of England was a continual threat.

Likewise, memories of Jacobite plots (as shown in this book) created an atmosphere of suspicion in the court of King George III. The Prime Minister, William Pitt the Younger, observed that Jacobinism was a 'restless and fatal spirit' capable of 'assuming new shapes, and concealing its malignant and destructive designs under new forms and new practices'.

Another factor was republicanism in Ireland. The Society of United Irishmen sought Catholic emancipation and radical reform. They also made efforts to gain French support for an uprising and a united Ireland, free of British rule. The United Englishmen and United Scotsmen were formed to in the footsteps of the Irish group, no doubt influenced by the ever-increasing flow of immigrants from Ireland to London and the new industrial cities of the north of England. These threats were not all in the minds of politicians—the Despard Plot, which included Freemasons, was a real conspiracy, which aimed to start a British Revolution.

The government moved fast, but quick legislation often results in bad law. Within weeks of Thornton's letter, the Prime Minister had made clear which type of groups he was determined to stamp out:

> [those with] mutual fidelity and secrecy by which the members are bound; the secrecy of electing the members … secret appointments unknown to the bulk of the members; presidents and committees, which, veiling themselves from the general mass and knowledge of the members, plot and conduct the treason—I propose that all societies which administer such oaths shall be declared unlawful confederacies.

Unfortunately, these criteria could be applied to Masonic lodges. Even one hundred years before, a Presbyterian minister in London had printed the first known anti-Masonic leaflet. This accused Masons of 'secret swearings' and being a 'devilish sect'. Religious belief had far more influence in the eighteenth century than now. If the proposed legislation went through unchanged it would mean that the taking of a Masonic oath could be a crime.

The two Grand Lodges of England—nicknamed the 'Moderns' (formed in 1717) and the 'Antients' (formed in 1751)—were quick to act. On the last day of April, a delegation was sent to meet the Prime Minister in Downing Street. They proposed a system of self-regulation by the Grand Lodges to ensure that no radical elements could infiltrate the Craft. The two representatives had considerable influence:

Moderns Grand Lodge—Representing the Grand Master (the Prince of Wales, later George IV), was the Acting Grand Master, the Earl of Moira (later known as the Marquess of Hastings), a retired general, who had served with the 'Grand Old Duke of York'—the second son of the king and a Mason with the rank of Past Grand Master. The earl had been a member of the government and some had supported him as a future Prime Minister.

Antients Grand Lodge—Grand Master was the 4th Duke of Atoll, a Scottish peer and therefore a member of the House of Lords. He had vast Masonic experience, being Grand Master of England and Scotland 1778-1780. He served as Grand Master of the Antients 1775–1781 and 1791–1812.

The Earl of Moira, the Acting Grand Master of the Moderns' Grand Lodge who convinced the government to exempt Freemasonry from the Unlawful Societies Act.

Unfortunately, Pitt had received information from Ireland from a Roman Catholic priest that he was aware of at least one Mason, who had also claimed to be a Knight Templar and member of the United Englishmen. These societies also appeared to copy the style of Masonic oaths and signs. Furthermore, a Mason visiting a lodge in the rapidly growing city of Leeds in Yorkshire, reported that the brethren from the 'lower class' obeyed the rules of Masonry by not discussing politics within the lodge, but once at the Festive Board, they expressed support for the radical French government.

When the matter was debated in the House of Lords, it seemed that the legislation would be passed and that there would be no exemption for Freemasons. The day was saved by Lord Grenville, Leader of the House of Lords and Foreign Secretary (but not a Freemason). He suggested, rather than self-regulation by Grand Lodges, each lodge would have to submit an annual return to the local Clerk of the Justices of the Peace. This document would list the names of the members and the detail of meeting dates and locations. This law was not repealed until 1967. If nothing else, it has proved a valuable source of information for Masonic historians, albeit by 1920, half the lodges did not bother to submit the return and no one was ever prosecuted for failing to do so.

The Act still, however, has an impact on lodges, despite being repealed nearly fifty years ago. When it was introduced in 1799, the Grand Secretary at Freemasons' Hall misinterpreted it. It was believed that, while existing lodges were allowed to continue, no new ones could be formed. To get around this problem, new lodges were given the numbers of defunct ones, and even given the warrant and minutes books of such lodges. As a result, lodges applying to the United Grand Lodge of England for recognition of being in existence for 250 years have to be told, 'I am afraid you are not as old as you think you are.'

21

Newgate Prison and the Mason who Ministered to the Condemned

Masonic Connection
Architect and designer of the building
Prison chaplain

Date
1798–1814: Mason held the post of Prison Chaplain
1856: Old Bailey designated the 'Central Criminal Court'
1907: Current court building opened

Connection to London
Haymarket: where chaplain was previously an actor
Old Bailey: former location of Newgate Prison

Lodges
Robert Burns No. 25
United Industrious No. 31
Constitutional No. 55
Merchants' No. 241
Lurgan (Ireland)
Carlow (Ireland)

'As black as Newgate's knocker' is a saying still used in London, which emphasises that this dreadful prison lives on in the minds of Londoners despite it being demolished over one hundred years ago in 1902. The site is now occupied by the Central Criminal Court, or as it is better known, 'The Old Bailey'. The famous Victorian writer and social commentator, Charles Dickens described the jail as a 'gloomy depository of the guilt and misery'.

The name of the prison comes from one of the gates in the Roman wall of London. The gatehouse (which was also used as a prison) was rebuilt in the twelfth century and remained in use for over seven hundred years, during which time more than one thousand people were executed at the site. Over the long period of its existence, it was extended and

Newgate Prison, where Brother Brownlow Forde ministered to the condemned.

renovated on several occasions. When the famous Lord Mayor, Dick Whittington, died in 1423, his will allocated funds to conduct works on Newgate. Along with many buildings in the City, the prison was destroyed in the Great Fire of London in 1666.

The prison was redesigned in the mid-eighteenth century by George Dance the Younger, who may have been a member of the Craft; his father (George Dance the Older) certainly was. In 1767 (the year could relate to father or son), a George Dance, whose employment is described as a surveyor, joined lodge No. 84 (now Constitutional Lodge No. 55), which met at the Half Moon Tavern in Cheapside, in the City of London. The Younger Dance also trained Freemason Sir John Soane, the designer of the Bank of England and the second Freemasons' Hall, which has been replaced by the current building.

In 1780, Dance's rebuilt Newgate was ready for use, when it was stormed by the mob. In June of that year, the 'Gordon Riots' broke out; initially Anti-Catholic protests, they soon turned into a riot, with looting all over the City of London. As an aside, this was a turning point for the popularity of Brother John Wilkes, the man made a Mason in prison. Now, the voice of the people was leading government troops against them. Newgate further cemented its frightful image in 1783, when public executions were moved to the site from Tyburn and these drew huge crowds. With these connections to famous people and events, it is little wonder that Newgate Prison is burnt into the collective conscience of London.

Ministering to the condemned in the jail was the role of the chaplain or, to give him his correct title, the 'Ordinary of Newgate'. Despite being an unpleasant role for a clergyman, it was not without its benefits. The Ordinary was entitled to publish accounts of the prisoners' speeches on the scaffold and their behaviour. This was done (it was said) to deter others from offending, but it was also quite lucrative, earning the chaplain over £200 per year—a small fortune at that time. The prison had its own chapel and, when the condemned attended their special service, a coffin was placed on the table, to remind them of their fate (a dreadful variation on the Third Degree ceremony, it would seem).

Towards the end of the eighteenth century, the man to hold the position of Ordinary of Newgate was a Freemason—Worshipful Brother the Reverend Doctor Brownlow Forde. He was present when several famous prisoners, as we will see, met their end, but his own journey to prison chaplain is also noteworthy. The acting profession and the clergy have little in common, but these are just two of the career paths pursued by this Mason.

Forde was a native of Ireland and was born in Dublin. Despite obtaining a doctorate in medicine, he began an acting career in his home town. By 1769, he was in London, taking the leading role in a play entitled *The Minor* in the Haymarket. In the same year, he had been initiated into a lodge in Lurgan, County Armagh (then No. 394 in the Grand Lodge of Ireland). Leaving London, he moved back across the Irish Sea and in 1774, joined a lodge in Carlow in the south of Ireland (then No. 493, Irish Constitution).

Haymarket Theatre. From actor to vicar: Brother Forde performed here as an actor, before becoming a 'man of the cloth'.

He returned again to London in 1782, where he seemingly held a theatre management role, as the Lord Chamberlain (the government censor) granted him a licence to put on plays. By 1784, he had swapped the stage for the pulpit and took Holy Orders with the Church of England, initially preaching in London. He subsequently found a position at St Catherine's (also known as the Octagon Chapel) in Liverpool. Reverend Forde appears to have been committed to helping the poor. He founded several Sunday Schools, where children were taught to read and write. It is while he was in the North West of England that he joined the Merchants' Lodge No. 522 (now No. 241) in Liverpool in 1786 and was the Master within three years. The lodge then met in the Shakespeare Tavern in Sir Thomas's Buildings, a street that still exists in Liverpool city centre.

Forde returned to London in 1798 to take up the post of Ordinary at Newgate. It would appear that he continued with his Masonic activities, but did not join a London lodge. In *Book for a Rainy Day,* John Thomas Smith notes meeting Forde in a London inn as follows 'upon entering … a public house, we found the said doctor most pompously seated in a superb Masonic chair'. During his time as the prison chaplain, the doctor ministered to many prisoners, who had been condemned to death. Of note are the following, who were executed in the years shown:

Joseph Wall (1802) was an Army officer and former Lieutenant Governor of the island of Goree, a British possession off the West African coast. Wall was convicted of murder as he had had three soldiers flogged to death. The actual crime occurred twenty years before on Goree, when a drunken Wall had (without holding a court-martial) ordered the three men to be given nearly two thousand lashes between them on spurious charges of mutiny. He evaded justice for many years, but was finally arrested in London.

Colonel Edward Despard (1803) plotted with several men, including two Freemasons to kill King George III and start a revolution. When convicted of treason, they were the last men to England to be sentenced to be hanged, drawn, and quartered.

Women such as Elizabeth Godfrey (1807) were also held in a separate area of Newgate, sometimes with their children, sleeping on straw. Godfrey had rented rooms in a house 'of ill repute' in the Marylebone area of London. She soon became involved in a dispute with the man who lived in an adjacent room. Matters came to a head on Christmas Day 1806, when Godfrey stabbed her neighbour in the eye when he opened his door to her. The wounded man knew he was done for, but he took over three weeks to die; Godfrey was convicted of murder. When Brownlow Forde led her and two condemned men out of the prison at 8 a.m., there was an enormous crowd; this was not unusual. Tragically, however, the three murderers were not the only ones to die that day. A massive crush ensued and twenty-seven people, including children, were crushed to death. Brother Forde truly witnessed a disaster on that day.

John Bellingham (1812) had murdered the Prime Minister, Spencer Perceval in the House of Commons. This is the only ever assassination of a British Premier. Bellingham was detained at the scene and identified by the Member of Parliament he had been in correspondence with regarding a grievance with the government. That MP, General Isaac Gascoyne, was a Liverpool Freemason like Forde.

Forde's enthusiasm for his spiritual work appears to have waned over time. At a committee meeting in 1814 (the year he left), he admitted to not visiting sick prisoners. It was noted that his sole activity appeared to be visiting the condemned inmates twice per week. Gone were the days of setting up Sunday Schools and the zeal of helping the young; the committee observed that Forde had failed to hold any classes or instruction for young prisoners who had been incarcerated at Newgate. The committee also noted that services in the prison chapel were ill-disciplined affairs with shouting, talking, and even yawning.

Not everyone was dissatisfied with his efforts. Forde gained great support from Basil Montagu, a barrister and later founder member of the RSPCA. In 1815, he vigorously defended the doctor in a publication entitled, *An Inquiry into the Aspersions upon the Late Ordinary of Newgate, With Some Observations upon Newgate and upon the Punishment of Death*. In this, Montagu praised Forde's 'commendable … efforts in the prison's deplorable conditions.'

Once Brother Forde had left, a school was established for juvenile prisoners by his successor. He was paid a pension and lived for ten more years, dying in 1824 at eighty years old. His path certainly was a strange one—from medicine to acting to the church, thence to one of the most notorious prisons in England. He is probably the Mason who ministered to more condemned men (and women) than any other.

Around the time of Forde, Newgate was the first jail visited by the great prison reformer, Elizabeth Fry. A statue of this great woman now stands in the Old Bailey, which as stated, occupies the site of the prison. Newgate was closed in 1902 and demolished two years later. A court house also known as the Old Bailey had been adjacent to the jail for many years, but it is because of a Mason that it is officially known as the 'Central Criminal Court'.

When it was first established, the court's purpose was to hear cases relating to crimes committed in London and Middlesex. This changed due to a notorious Staffordshire murder, where it was felt that the accused could not have a fair trial at a local court, as feelings were running high in the area. Hence, in 1856, a law was passed to allow any case, wherever the location, to be heard at the Old Bailey. (For similar reasons, the Yorkshire Ripper case was tried at the court, despite all the murders being committed hundreds of miles from London). The original case concerned Dr William Palmer, who was known as the 'Rugeley Poisoner'. He was convicted at the Old Bailey of murdering his friend, John Cook, with strychnine. He was, however, suspected of killing several relatives in Staffordshire by poisoning; this included his brother, mother-in-law, and four infant children. Palmer was motivated by greed and obtained vast sums of money from life insurance payments, but he seems to have gambled away his ill-gotten gains. Palmer had been initiated into Robert Burns Lodge No. 25 in London, shortly after he qualified as a surgeon in 1847. He did not progress any further in the Craft on his return to his native county.

On a positive side, it was a Mason who helped to send him to the gallows; the prosecution barrister at his trial was John Huddleston, a member of a Canterbury lodge, United Industrious No. 31. The current court building was officially opened in 1907. As we will see, it has hosted trials involving more Masons good and bad.

22

The Despard Plot:
Masons Sentenced to be Hanged, Drawn, and Quartered

Masonic Connection
Masons executed for treason
Masonic-style oath
Masons gave character evidence at trial

Date
1803: Plot discovered

Connection to London
Mount Pleasant Mail Centre, Clerkenwell: Former location of Cold Bath Fields Prison
Tower of London: Plot involving seizing the Tower
Bank of England: to be seized to control finance for the revolution
Pratt Walk (then Pratt St), Lambeth: the two executed Masons were initiated in the (demolished) Spread Eagle Public House
Spring Gardens, just off Trafalgar Square: Army Agent had offices at this location
Borough High St (formerly Blackman St): location of meeting between Despard and the informer
St James's Park: Intended location of the murder of King George III
Baylis Road (formerly Oakley St), Lambeth: Location of arrest of the plotters
Union St, Southwark: Location of Magistrates' Court, where plotters were originally held in custody
Old Bailey, City of London: Site of the former Newgate Prison, where Despard met the (Masonic) chaplain
Harper St (formerly Horsemonger Lane), Southwark: Location of execution
St Paul's Cathedral, City of London: Burial place of Colonel Despard, leader of the conspiracy
St George's Cathedral, Southwark: Burial place of the Masons and other men executed

Lodges
Merchants' Lodge No. 241
Lodge of Unions No. 256
Amphibious Lodge No. 407 (erased)

The last time Englishmen were sentenced to the dreadful punishment of being hanged, drawn, and quartered was in 1803. A senior Army officer and six other men, including two Freemasons, were condemned to that awful method of execution for their treasonous conspiracy, known as the 'Despard Plot'. Once again, nineteenth century justice is shown to be brutal and very swift. The ruling classes were determined to deal with the many revolutionary groups that threatened to bring down the established order.

The leader of the conspiracy was Colonel Edward Marcus Despard, a British Army officer of Anglo-French stock. Despard was born in to a distinguished military family in 1751 in Queen's County, Ireland (now County Laois), which was then ruled by Great Britain. His brother, John, was to achieve the rank of general. There is no evidence that the Despards were Freemasons in England or Ireland. However, several of his associates certainly were Freemasons—some of the highest men in the country and some of the lowest. This sorry tale is about as close as one can get to a 'Masonic conspiracy to take over the country.'

Edward Despard was commissioned into the 50th Regiment of Foot (now the Princess of Wales's Royal Regiment) and saw service in the American War of Independence. During this time, now a captain, Despard was to form a close bond with a naval officer who was later to achieve great fame—Horatio Nelson. As we will see, Nelson would later defend Despard's character.

A question that has been asked many times is whether Nelson was a Freemason. As early as 1839, claims were made that the hero of Trafalgar was a member of the Craft, but no evidence could be produced. Now, it would seem that proof has finally been uncovered by the expert Masonic researcher, John Hamill of the United Lodge of England. It would

Colonel Edward Despard, leader of a plot involving Masons to kill the king and seize the country.

appear that Brother Nelson visited a lodge for Royal Navy officers (the long disbanded Amphibious Lodge No. 407) in Plymouth in August 1787. In the same year, Nelson attended a Masonic stone laying ceremony with the lodge with the future King William IV, who was also 'on the square'.

During the American War of Independence, the Spanish Empire took advantage of the situation, by attempting to seize British possessions in the Caribbean, while the Royal Navy and British Army were distracted elsewhere. They had little success in their campaign. During 1782, at the Battle of Black River (in modern day Honduras), Colonel Despard proved his soldiering ability by fighting a successful action against a Spanish force. As a result, he captured nearly eight-hundred prisoners, together with a significant prize—three Regimental standards. The victory was so significant that these standards were despatched to England and paraded before King George III, whom Despard would come to despise.

The colonel had served his country well and was to be rewarded. His military engineering skills were also worthy of note and were praised by Nelson. Despard was appointed the superintendent of the Bay of Honduras colony (now Belize) in central America. There, he married a local woman—a freed black slave—and made it his aim to give former slaves the same rights as white settlers. Such progressive views were not, however, welcomed by many of the newcomers from England. Complaints were forwarded to London as to his conduct and he was suspended by the Home Secretary, Lord Grenville (not a Mason). As a result of the allegations, Despard was returned to England, where he demanded that a full investigation be conducted to clear his name. In the meantime, he was suspended on half pay. The enquiry was to last for two years and following further charges of misconduct, he was arrested and placed in the King's Bench Prison for two years (1792–1794). It was here that nearly thirty years earlier, John Wilkes had been made a Mason while in a cell. The time in this dismal jail, no doubt, caused Despard (once a loyal and brave soldier) to feel anger and bitterness towards the king and his government.

Once released, Despard joined the London Corresponding Society, a political group mainly composed of the working class, with an aim of extending the right to vote. It also included a freed black slave among its members. Despard seemed to have an affinity with those who would have been considered the 'lower orders' by many of his peers; perhaps, his army service had brought him closer to such men. Additionally, being born in Queen's County, the authorities had reason to suspect him of being a member of the United Irishmen, who had organised a rebellion against British rule in 1798. These were worrying times for the Establishment, as Ireland was not the only source of potential unrest; the French Revolution, American War of Independence, and Jacobite rebellions were all fresh in the mind. Napoleon was sweeping across Europe and an invasion of Britain was a real threat. As a result, in 1794, the government had suspended the law of *Habeas Corpus*, as it had done before; this meant that the government could arrest any suspected traitors and intern them indefinitely.

Despard was to fall foul of this latest purge and found himself incarcerated in several jails, including Coldbath Fields Prison in Clerkenwell, now the site of the central London Post Office sorting office. One can only imagine the bitterness felt by Despard as he was released in 1801. He had fallen from a being a respected officer who had bravely served his country to being a suspected revolutionary, imprisoned without charge for three long years. As he walked out of the prison gate, he would have observed that London's population was swelling and living conditions for the working classes were appalling. Disease and death were rife. At this point, it would seem, Despard decided that revolution was the solution to the country's ills.

Around the same time, two men who would share his awful fate were joining Freemasonry. On 29 January 1801 and 17 January 1802 respectively, Arthur Graham and Thomas Broughton joined the Lodge of Unions (then No. 390, now No. 256), which met at the Spread Eagle Public House in Pratt Street, Lambeth, on the south bank of the River Thames, near the Archbishop of Canterbury's Lambeth Palace. Given that crimes were about to be committed by them, it is ironic that this site is now occupied by the Metropolitan Police Forensic Science Laboratory. Graham and Broughton were tradesmen (a slater and a carpenter) with little in common with a senior army officer.

Despard, however, was now frequenting taverns in the nearby (and equally poor) area of Southwark. He had now decided what action was required to change British society. His plan involved the most serious of crimes—high treason and murder. Most importantly, he had decided that the king must die—the same monarch, who, two decades before, had reviewed the Regimental standards captured by this very colonel. Despard also planned to take the Tower of London, to take control of the vast quantity of arms and ammunition held there. In his mind, this would be the spark that started an English Revolution. Finance would be provided by taking control of the Bank of England. Despard believed that there would be countrywide support for his actions and he particularly saw the new industrial towns—he named Leeds, Sheffield, Manchester, and Birmingham—as being ripe for rebellion.

At some point during his visits to the inns of south London, he recruited Brothers Graham and Broughton into his plot. Several other men also joined the conspiracy: another carpenter, John Macnamara; a shoemaker, James Sedgwick Wratton; and two low ranking soldiers, John Francis and John Wood. These men were privates in the 1st Regiment of Foot Guards (now the Grenadier Guards) serving at Windsor Castle. Private Wood appears to have been very active in attempting to entice more servicemen to join the plot. Each member of the conspiracy had to swear an oath to bind them into the conspiracy. Copies of the oath were then supplied to each new member so that they in turn could recruit more like-minded men. The aims of the conspiracy were also shared. These were not unreasonable; the means to obtain them—murder and revolution—were. The objectives of the Despard Plot were as follows:

> Constitution and Independence of Great Britain and Ireland; an equalization of civil, political, and religious rights; an ample provision for the families of the heroes who fall in the contest; a liberal reward for distinguished merit; these are the objects for which we contend, and to obtain these objects we swear to be united.

The oath was in the same legalistic and archaic language as Masonic obligations. It is also fascinating to note that the oath refers to a 'Supreme Being', a term often used in the Craft.

Evidence at the later trial noted that having recited the words, the new member had to kiss the card on which the oath was printed. This was the version produced at the court:

In the awful presence of Almighty God, I, A. B. do voluntarily declare, that I will endeavour, to the utmost of my power, to obtain the objects of this union, namely, to recover those rights which the Supreme Being has given to all men, that neither hopes, fears, rewards, nor punishment, shall ever induce me to give any information, directly or indirectly, concerning the business, or of any member of this Society, or of any similar society, so help me God.

The brazen and open recruitment was foolish and would lead to the exposure of the enterprise. As shown in 'The Charge after Initiation', Masons are taught not to expose their lodge to danger 'by refraining from recommending anyone to a participation in our secrets unless you have strong grounds to believe that he will ultimately reflect honour of your choice.' A soldier named Thomas Windsor was encouraged to join the plot. He was from a different unit from Francis and Wood, serving in the 3rd Foot Guards (now the Scots Guards). Windsor did not comply with his oath and soon began to give information to an Army agent named Thomas Bownas. Windsor was told to remain in the gang, gather further information, and identify those involved. In this plot, there was more than honour at stake; by introducing an infiltrator, the gang were now in danger of facing the full wrath of the law.

The reader should be aware that an 'Army agent' was not an undercover spy in the mode of James Bond. Bownas was an agent who arranged the buying and selling of Army commissions, as was the custom at this time. Neither was his profession secret; his offices were listed as being in Spring Gardens, just off Trafalgar Square. It is likely that Bownas was a retired Army officer who had the confidence of Guardsman Windsor.

It was Brother Broughton who was to seal Despard's fate, by introducing him to Windsor. Broughton had arranged the meeting in the Flying Horse public house on Blackman Street, Southwark (now Borough High Street in the area of the police station). This inn also hosted a Masonic lodge, long defunct, named the Lodge of Constitutional Attachment (then numbered 178). Records at the United Grand Lodge of England show that no (known) members of the conspiracy were members; however, Broughton might have known this location as a result of visiting this lodge.

The make-up of the membership of the lodge clearly demonstrates that it was vastly different from many in the more affluent areas of London. While there were some middle-class professionals in the lodge—for example, a school master, a clerk, and a doctor—the majority are from the working classes and include ironmongers, a coal merchant, a bricklayer, at least two coopers (barrel makers), sailors (unsurprising given that ships from across the world sailed up the Thames), and several victuallers (pub landlords). The age profile of the lodge is also of note—there were sixty members on the register of the United Grand Lodge of England at this time; the majority of these were in their twenties or thirties.

Broughton had told Windsor, who was still passing information to Mr Bownas, that they would meet a 'nice man' at the Flying Horse; this was the codename adopted by Despard.

At this meeting, the necessity to kill the king was emphasised by the disgraced colonel. The informer further established that the mail coaches were to be stopped as a signal to the populace that the revolution had begun. He was then invited to a second meeting on the following day to plan the taking of the Tower of London. This took place at the Tiger Tavern on Tower Hill (only demolished in 2002). The plotters, especially those in the Guards, knew the 'Ceremony of the Keys', where the Tower is formally locked at night. This appeared to be an ideal time to storm the building.

While at the tavern, Windsor learnt that the attack on George III would occur two days later, as the king travelled to the Houses of Parliament. The location of the attack was described at the time as 'the Park'—this would seem to be St James's Park (George III had purchased Buckingham Palace and also used St James's Palace as an official residence—both would require crossing St James's Park to reach Parliament). Windsor was not the only one leaking information about the plot. Numerous other members, including several soldiers, were readily passing information to the authorities and would later give evidence on behalf of the Crown.

Windsor informed Bownas of the identity of the leader of the plot and Despard's plans to start a revolution. The Army agent quickly passed this information to the authorities, who acted decisively. It was known that on 16 November 1802, Despard and a large group of working men, many of them Irish immigrants, would be meeting in the Oakley Arms, Lambeth. This inn was located on Oakley Street (now Baylis Road, between Lambeth North and Waterloo). A squad of police officers descended on the Oakley Arms and all present were arrested. They were held in custody overnight and appeared before the magistrates in Union Hall, Union Street; the façade of this building still exists.

It is interesting to note that the contemporary account of the trial refers to the arrests by 'police officers'. These events in 1802 were, of course, prior to the formation of the Metropolitan Police in 1829. The government had, however, created seven police offices throughout London in 1792. Encouraged by the success of Bow Magistrates Court (which had been established by a Mason), these police offices consisted of three paid magistrates and up to six constables. The major difference of these offices with the Metropolitan Police was that they were localised and lacked any form of centralisation or control from the Home Office.

As a result of the magistrates' hearing, the main offenders were identified and the remainder released without charge; ten men had been in an entirely different room in the inn, but had also spent the night in the cells. Despard was committed into custody and was held in Newgate prison, where he would have met Brother Reverend Brownlow Forde of Merchants' Lodge No. 241, the chaplain. Twelve other plotters, six soldiers among them, were placed in Clerkenwell jail.

A Special Commission was established by the Privy Council, the 'privy' (private) advisors to the king. Despard was interviewed several times, but simply refused to answer any questions. As now happens in the American system, a Grand Jury was formulated to decide whether sufficient evidence existed to charge the arrested men. Treason required more than actual words; overt acts were required. Such acts were deemed to have occurred—the Crown were in possession of printed copies of the aims of the plot and the oath sworn by those involved.

The trial of Despard, who was arraigned alone, began on 7 February 1803, at Sessions House in Newington, Southwark (now Inner London Crown Court), a short walk from the Flying Horse public house. He was charged with the most serious of crimes—high treason. The indictment alleged that they had committed several treasonous acts, including plotting to kill the king, encouraging soldiers of the Crown to join the conspiracy and administering unlawful oaths. The presiding judge was Baron Ellenborough, the Lord Chief Justice, who was not a mason.

It took some time to form the jury. The Crown challenged ten potential jurors and the defence twice as many more; in those times, no reason had to be given (defence counsel could have challenged up to twenty-five). Several men (as only men were allowed to be jurors) were excused jury service for a variety of reasons—two were deaf and one was a male midwife (an unusual occupation then, as now). In the end, the twelve men selected did represent the working-class nature of the area. They included a lighter-man (a man who operated a light, flat bottomed boat), a candle-maker, a hat manufacturer, a hops trader, and at least two merchants. That said, all jurors at that time had to fulfil the 'property qualification' and either be a freeholder or a least own £50 worth of personal property (around £4,000 today). This qualification applied until 1974.

Many witnesses gave evidence for the prosecution, outlining that Colonel Despard had been the leader of the conspiracy and had encouraged them to join the plot. These witnesses were also able to recall Despard's oath. Several soldiers, mainly serving with 1st Foot Guards, gave evidence that attempts had been made to recruit them; Thomas Windsor was the key witness in this respect. The evidence was damning, but Despard chose not to give evidence in his own defence; instead, he called on three influential men to support his character. Lord Nelson (a Freemason, as we have seen) and General Alured Clarke, who had served in the same regiment as Despard, both described the colonel as a loyal and brave officer. The Crown were able to counter this evidence by showing that Nelson and Clarke had not seen Despard for over twenty years. More recent character testimony was given by Sir Evan Nepean (also believed to a Mason, but the records of the Grand Lodge in London appear to refer to his son), a colonial administrator and Secretary to the Admiralty. Unfortunately, Nepean's reference was only up to 1798 and Despard's prison terms had been after that date. The colonel's chances of freedom were slipping away.

After just three days, the jury were sent out to consider their verdict. It took them little more than twenty-five minutes to find Colonel Despard guilty. Brothers Broughton and Graham, together with ten other plotters, were tried immediately afterwards, with the same witnesses called; the trial of the working-class prisoners lasted just one day. The two Masons and seven others were also found guilty of high treason. Three lucky men were acquitted.

Despard and the other convicted plotters then faced the wrath of the judge. Lord Ellenborough informed them that they had endeavoured to bring about a 'wild system of anarchy and bloodshed', with 'the annihilation of all legitimate authority and established order'. He further observed that 'their atrocious conspiracy' had a 'wicked and abominable purpose'. The jury had recommended mercy for some of the men, including Despard, due to their Army service, but the tone of the judge showed that he was not prepared to show any such thing.

His Lordship then pronounced the sentence, named each defendant, and informed them thusly:

> [They would be] taken from the place from whence you came, and from thence you are to be drawn on hurdles to the place of execution, where you are to be hanged by the neck, but not until you are dead; for while you are still living your bodies are to be taken down, your bowels torn out and burned before your faces, your heads then cut off, and your bodies divided each into four quarters, and your heads and quarters to be then at the King's disposal; and may the Almighty God have mercy on your souls!

At this, Despard and the Irishman, Macnamara, attempted to profess their innocence, but it was far too late. The condemned men were placed in the cells at Horsemonger Lane by the court in Southwark. The following day, 10 February 1803, the Lodge of Unions met. It was noted in the minutes of the meeting that Brothers Graham and Broughton were 'now under sentence of death for being found guilty of the most wicked and diabolical design of contriving, encompassing and imagining the death of our dearly beloved and Most Gracious Sovereign Lord the King...'. Therefore, the lodge was informed:

> In consequence of their guilt [the men] had forfeited the countenance of the… Society of Freemasons, whose known attachment to their Sovereign and Constitution, together with the principles of the Order, renders it impossible for them to continue their fraternal attachment to any brother who acts repugnant to those excellent rules and orders to which they are subject.

> At that meeting, Brother Jones proposed and a senior member, Right Worshipful Brother Archer seconded the motion that Graham and Broughton be 'expelled from Masonry on this night, on account of their guilt.' This was unanimously agreed by the brethren of the lodge (Davis, 1885). The Freemasons' Charge demands that members of the Craft must show the 'allegiance due to the sovereign or ruler of your native land'. Graham and Broughton had clearly breached this Masonic law by plotting to kill their king.

Three non-Masons in the gang, who had been sentenced to death, were pardoned. The others were not so fortunate. On Saturday, 19 February, the remaining convicted plotters were informed that the warrant of execution had been confirmed and that it would be carried out two days later. There was a chink of good news, if it could be described as such—the king had remitted part of their sentence. No longer would their bowels be taken out and burnt before their face, nor would their bodies be quartered; at least this way, their deaths would be swifter. Last minute attempts to save Despard were made by Nelson, who appealed to George III, but with no success.

On the Sunday, the men would have heard the gallows being built on the flat roof of the prison. These were not the only preparations made by the authorities who feared that revolutionary associates of the gang could stir up the vast crowd which was expected. As a result, constables and military units were drafted south of the River Thames to patrol the area throughout the night and following day. Detachments of the king's Life Guards also patrolled the streets of Southwark on horseback.

As the sun rose on 21 February, the men were released from their iron shackles and bound with ropes. Together with the colonel, Graham, and Broughton, four other men were to be executed—Macnamara, Wratton, and the two soldiers, Francis and Wood. Soon, an enormous crowd had gathered to witness the public execution—some 20,000 people. Rumours had been rife that the prisoners had been cruelly chained together and tortured to obtain confessions. Little wonder the authorities were concerned about a potential riot. This, it is believed, is the reason the king rescinded the worse aspects of the sentence; such butchery and brutality may have inflamed the masses. Hanging and beheading were one thing—cutting bowels out and chopping people up were another.

The prison governor was keen to see the remaining aspects of the traditional punishment carried out. A horse drawn sledge (or 'hurdle') was ready in the yard, which would ensure that the condemned men were 'drawn' to the gallows. Unfortunately, the packed streets made it impossible to carry out this part of the execution process. To satisfy this aspect of the sentence, each prisoner had to sit, facing backwards, in the hurdle and be hauled across the enclosed, cobbled yard. Despard seems to have been in good spirits, denouncing the pointless symbolical 'drawing' of himself and the others around the prison as 'nonsensical mummery'. No one else laughed, but the colonel's fortitude in the circumstances has to be admired.

With the initial section of the punishment having been completed (in a fashion), the men were taken to the scaffold on the roof by foot, where the Sheriff of Surrey and clergymen were gathered. The roof had been designed to facilitate public executions. Looking rather like a Masonic possession, the governor led the way with a white wand (as does a Director of Ceremonies), while the executioner was at the rear, 'armed with a drawn sword' (like the lodge Tyler).

On the scaffold, the head of each condemned plotter was placed in a noose and just before 9 o'clock, the trap doors fell open, sending the two Masons (possibly) to the 'Grand Lodge Above' and the non-Masons to a similar place of the dead. The bodies were left hanging for half an hour and then cut down. The dead men had their heads placed on a block, on an area covered with sawdust, where they were beheaded one at a time, with Despard first. To complete the brutal ritual, the masked executioner held up his severed head by the hair and announced to the crowd, 'This is the head of a traitor, Edward Marcus Despard.' This was witnessed by the now widowed Mrs Despard. The same act was carried out six further times.

The bodies and heads were then placed in the pre-prepared coffins. The disgraced colonel was interred in the graveyard of St Paul's Cathedral. The others were buried in one grave in the chapel in London Road, where St George's Cathedral now stands. The reaction of the crowd was closely watched by the City Marshal, a uniformed official, employed by the Lord Mayor of London to enforce the law with a team of ten officers. While Southwark was on the south side of the river, it was only walking distance for any riotous mob to cross London Bridge and cause mayhem in the city. Additionally, inside the jail, the head warden was issued with six rockets, which would be fired as a signal to the Army and police units that a disturbance had broken out. There was, however, no riot or revolution.

Thus the sad tale of Colonel Despard and of two Masons, Arthur Graham and Thomas Broughton ends—the last men in England sentenced to be hanged, drawn, and quartered. The swift and brutal justice in early 19th century England is clearly shown. There were only three months between arrest and two trials, which took up all of three days. The jury convicted Despard in twenty-five minutes, and there was only a fortnight between conviction and execution. The involvement of Lord Nelson as a character witness, at long last proved to be a Freemason, also adds an interesting Masonic aside, as does the presence of another member of the Craft, who was the chaplain at Newgate Prison.

The lower social status of the lodge members and those executed contrasts with the general view of the Craft, at that time, as being the preserve of the upper classes. That said, snobbery has always existed. In 1778, Laurence Dermott, the Grand Secretary of the Antients Grand Lodge, criticised the rival Moderns Grand lodge for allowing servants to be initiated (in Southwark, of all places). He observed:

> This may seem a very ludicrous description of making Freemasons. But (the) master of the lodge No. 11, London, declared that he was present in a modern Lodge not one mile from the Borough of Southwark, when two or three persons dress'd in liveries with shoulder tags, booted and spurr'd, andc., andc., were initiated into modern Masonry; and upon enquiring who they were, he was told they were servants to Lord Carysfoot, then Grand Master of modern Masons.

Masons should also note the Biblical justification for the awful punishment of being hanged, drawn, and quartered. All members of the Craft are exhorted to a 'serious contemplation of the Volume of the Sacred Law'—for Christians, the King James Bible. Sir Edward Coke (pronounced 'Cook'), the sixteenth and seventeenth century judge and legal scholar, who presided over such cases as the Gunpowder Plot and wrote on such matters as the 'right to silence', offered these Biblical examples to justify the brutal punishment:

> Drawn—Joab was dragged out of the Tabernacle and killed on the orders of King David (1 Kings 2). As with Despard, Joab was a disgraced senior Army officer.
>
> Hanged—Baanah was hanged and had his feet and hands chopped off, again on the orders of David (2 Samuel 4). Baanah was a captain in the Army of the rival to, the ever ruthless, King David. He slew his leader and expected a reward. Instead, David had him executed for High Treason and murder.
>
> Quartered and Embowelled—Judas Iscariot, betrayer of Jesus, is said to have hanged himself (Matthew 27), but he is also said to have died after his bowels burst out (Acts 1).

23

The Grand Old Duke of York, He had Ten Thousand Men … and a Military Scandal

Masonic Connection
Past Grand Master
Mason allegedly involved in corruption

Date
1787: Duke of York initiated into Freemasonry
1809: Scandal occurred

Connection to London
Horse Guards: Office of Commander-in-Chief of the Army
Pall Mall: Location of now demolished Star and Garter Tavern, where his lodge met
Wimbledon Common: Location of duel with Colonel Lennox
Waterloo Place: Statue atop a large pillar

Lodges
Britannic No. 33
Prince of Wales's No. 259

'The Grand Old Duke of York'—or more properly in Masonic terms, Most Worshipful Brother, His Royal Highness, Prince Frederick Augustus—was born in 1763. He was the second son of George III (and hence the older brother of the Duke of Kent, Grand Master of the Antients Grand Lodge, and the Duke of Sussex, Grand Master of the Moderns and then United Grand Lodge of England). He also possibly holds the record for the fastest Masonic promotions—initiated in 1787 into the Britannic Lodge (now number 33) and within one week was promoted to Past Grand Master. His lodge met at the Star and Garter, a seemingly popular venue with gentlemen. The Duke of York is also one of the most visible Freemasons in London, as his statue is on top of a very high pillar just off Pall Mall. According to wits of the day, there are good reasons for him being placed so high up in the sky, as will be revealed.

The Duke had a long military career, but it was blighted by a scandal. Anyone visiting his statue may wonder why he is shown as Commander-in-Chief of the British Army from

1795–1809 and then 1811–1827, and what happened to the missing two years. His career began well enough (as with Masonry) with a very high rank. At just seventeen years old, his father appointed him a colonel.

By 1789, he was a Lieutenant-General and was involved in a duel with another officer, Colonel Charles Lennox (later 4th Duke of Richmond). The colonel felt insulted as the Duke had made disparaging comments about him in a gaming club. The origin of the dispute appears to be that Lennox had been promoted in the Coldstream Guards (the Duke of York was the Honorary Colonel of this regiment) without the Duke being consulted. The duel was arranged to be fought with pistols on Wimbledon Common. Such a contest was contrary to military regulations; the last thing the Army needed was an officer with good shooting skills 'calling out' more senior officers and killing them to clear the way for further promotion.

In the end, the duel was a rather Masonic affair. The Duke's 'second' was the Earl of Moira (later Marquess of Hastings), who went on to be Acting Grand Master of the Moderns Grand Lodge just prior to the Union of the Grand Lodges in 1813. He was later the Acting Grand Master of Scotland. Lennox, who also went on to be a Right Worshipful Brother as Provincial Grand Master of Sussex, actually fired at the Duke of York, but deliberately only 'grazed his Royal Highness's curl'. Uninjured, the Duke refused to continue the duel stating that he held 'no animosity' towards Colonel Lennox. With their honour settled, the matter was at an end.

By 1793 (aged just thirty), the Duke had been made a full general and was given his first field command in Flanders. Here he commanded the British Army's contribution to a force made up of several European allies fighting against revolutionary France. Throughout two years of fighting, the army had mixed success and the Duke returned to England. He was promoted to Field Marshal and, in 1795, made Commander-in-Chief of the British Army.

His next campaign was to result in him being immortalised in a children's song. He commanded a joint British and Russian force in a campaign against the Dutch. The campaign went well at the beginning, but soon ground to a halt. The Duke's tactics of constantly re-positioning his forces gave rise to a satirical song, which became the nursery rhyme, 'The Grand Old Duke of York', who 'marched his troops to the top of the hill and he marched them down again'.

For the early part of the nineteenth century, the Duke remained in England as Commander in Chief, enabling him to commence a lengthy affair with a beautiful, but vengeful lady called Mary Anne Clarke. This is start of the scandal, which was to remove the Duke from office. Clarke's lavish lifestyle was funded, in secret, by the Duke's civil list payment from the government. When the relationship ended in 1805, Clarke's silence was bought with an annual pension. In 1809, the Duke (foolishly it would seem) ended this payment without notice and Clarke exacted her revenge.

As noted in the previous chapter, commissions for officer ranks in the British Army were purchased via Army Agents; this provided a ready supply of money for the government and ensured that only the ruling classes could command regiments as they were less likely to use the army to start a revolution. The Duke is said to have been in favour of merit-based promotion in the army; however, encouraged by a radical MP, Gwyllym Williams, Miss

Mary Anne Clarke, the lover of the Duke of York, who accused him of being involved in a financial scandal.

Clarke alleged that she had been selling commissions for her former lover. The Duke would be guilty of taking bribes if it could be proved that it was done with his knowledge.

This, then, is the scandal. In 1809, a cartoon was published showing the Duke fawning over Clarke, who was wearing his cloak, under which were exposed her under-garments and a note stating 'Who'll buy promotion tickets?' The Duke resigned as commander-in-chief (hence the dates on his statue in London). Parliament held an enquiry and the star witness was the attractive Mary Clarke. The Duke, however, was acquitted of any wrong-doing by the House of Commons, but only by a rather unconvincing 278 votes to 196. In 1811, it was alleged that the accusing MP, Williams, had bought Clarke's testimony and as a result, the Duke of York was re-instated as commander-in-chief that year.

The Duke spent much of his time working at Horse Guards, then the headquarters of the British Army. While this demonstrated his commitment to the troops, it also enabled him to live the 'high life' in London. He indulged in excessive gambling on cards and gaming, leaving him continually in debt until he died of natural causes in 1827. He remained a Freemason throughout his life, being the permanent Master of the Prince of Wales's Lodge (now No. 259) from 1823 until his death. His funeral also killed off another Mason, Prime Minister George Canning. The chapel in Windsor, where the funeral of the Duke was held, was so cold that it was the final blow to the already ill Canning.

It is said that every soldier in the British Army voted to give up one day's pay to build a monument in his memory (any former soldiers will rightfully be suspicious of such a 'vote'). The monument paid for by the soldiers is the Duke of York's column in Waterloo Place. It is quite a magnificent column, in the Tuscan style (as mentioned on the Second Degree Tracing Board) and over 137 feet (nearly 42 m) high. The height of the monument caused commentators to jest that the Duke was trying to escape his creditors, as he died owing vast sums of money in gambling debts. The column is now closed to the public as it had been used too often by those committing suicide.

The Grand Old Duke of York. This statue is on top of a pillar in Pall Mall.

24

Prime Minister's Assassin:
Identified by a Mason

Masonic Connection
Killer identified by a Mason
Prison chaplain

Date
1812: Assassination occurred

Connection to London
Audley Square, London: Victim born in this location
Palace of Westminster: Location of murder
Old Bailey: Executed at Newgate

Lodges
Ancient Union and Princes No. 203
Merchants' No. 241
Prince of Wales No. 259

The United States of America have had four presidents assassinated, but in the United Kingdom, only one Prime Minister has suffered such a fate—Spencer Perceval in 1812. The killer was Henry Bellingham; unfortunately for conspiracy theorists, he was not a Mason, but the man who identified him certainly was a member of the Craft. Let us deal with each of the characters involved in this crime in turn.

The victim, Spencer Perceval, was born in 1762 in Mayfair, London. He was from the aristocracy; his father was an earl and his mother the grand-daughter of another. He was educated at Harrow and Cambridge, but as the second son of a second marriage, he was likely to inherit very little. He had to make his own way in life and chose the law as his career. In 1796, he was elected as the Member of Parliament for Northampton. His work as a barrister had honed his debating skills and he was soon identified as a future minister. He went on to hold senior government roles, including solicitor and attorney general from 1801–06. As such, he was involved in the prosecution of Colonel Despard for his plot to kill the king and set off a British Revolution. His next post was as Chancellor of the Exchequer, during which time he defended the Duke of York; Right Worshipful Brother, Prince Frederick Augustus, second son of King George III, was the Commander-in-Chief of the British Army, but was alleged to have been involved in the corrupt sale of Army commissions by a former lover. At this time, George Canning, a Freemason and another future Prime Minister, served in the cabinet as Foreign Secretary. His statue can be seen in Parliament Square. Canning was a member of the Prince of Wales's own lodge, No. 259.

Higher office was to follow and, in 1809, Perceval was appointed Prime Minister. This was a difficult time for the nation: the king was mad; Napoleon was rampaging across Europe; and the social changes brought about by the Industrial Revolution were exacerbating the division between rich and poor. Perceval appears to have been a decent and honourable man, a devout Christian who opposed slavery and supported charity, and a committed father to his twelve children.

John Bellingham was born around seven years after his victim in Huntingdonshire. His family then moved to London and he became involved in international trade, travelling across the world, including to China and Russia. For a merchant, a seaport was the obvious place to live and Bellingham settled in Liverpool, marrying Mary Neville (perhaps a distant relative of the author). In 1803, he was in Russia, where he became embroiled in an investigation into a shipwreck. The merchant vessel had been lost in the White Sea off the north coast of Finland and Russia, but the insurers had refused to pay the owners the value of the ship. An anonymous letter had been sent to Lloyds of London, which alleged that the shipwreck had been caused by sabotage and was part of an insurance fraud. The owner of the ship suspected Bellingham of being the author of this information. To exact revenge, he accused Bellingham of failing to pay a debt. The owner then 'persuaded' (most likely by handing over roubles) the Russian authorities to imprison Bellingham in Archangel. He would later tell the Old Bailey that he was locked in a dungeon and fed on bread and water while in Russian prisons. Legal wrangles continued and despite being released from custody, Bellingham was further imprisoned in St Petersburg; he was not to return to England until 1809. Financially ruined and riddled with grievance, he bombarded the government with petitions for compensation.

The MP for Liverpool—Bellingham's adopted home town—was a Freemason, retired Lieutenant General Isaac Gascoyne. He was a distinguished British Army officer, having served in several infantry regiments, which are now the Coldstream Guards, Royal Regiment of Fusiliers, Royal Anglians, and The Rifles. In 1796, he was elected to Parliament as a member of the Tory Party. Gascoyne was an ardent supporter of the slave trade, which made money for merchants in his constituency. In the same year, he joined the Ancient Union Lodge No. 276 (now known as the Ancient Union and Princes Lodge No. 203), which then met in the centre of Liverpool in various taverns. From 1811, Gascoyne began to receive letters from his constituent, Bellingham, demanding compensation for his treatment at the hands of the Russians. General Gascoyne also met his aggrieved constituent and knew him well enough to later identify him. Bellingham had also been to the MP's home. Attempts to resolve the issue were further aggravated by Britain breaking off diplomatic relations with Russia. For a while, Bellingham's wife was able to persuade her husband to drop the matter.

Unfortunately, the matter festered in Bellingham's mind and, in April 1812, he visited the Foreign Office but was fobbed off. He now decided to take direct action. On 20 April, he bought two pistols and, as evidence of his intent, he had an inside pocket sewn into his coat so that the weapons could be concealed. He also began to frequent the lobby of the House of Commons. It was there, on 11 May, that he was to murder the Prime Minister. At 5 p.m., when Spencer Perceval entered the lobby, Bellingham produced a pistol and fatally shot him in the heart. According to William Smith MP, the Prime Minister staggered forward and collapsed face down, muttering 'murder'. He was carried to the office of the Speaker's secretary and laid on a table, but was dead within minutes.

The lobby was crowded with around twenty people and the assassin had little opportunity to escape. He was quickly detained and General Gascoyne was able to identify Bellingham as the gunman, who still presented grave danger to all present as he still had one loaded pistol in his possession. According to Gascoyne, Bellingham appeared to be about to shoot himself, raising the pistol to do so. Brother Gascoyne, who we should recall was a retired soldier, acted with great bravery, pulling Bellingham's arm down with all his strength (as later he told the Old Bailey jury) and allowing Henry Burgess, a solicitor, to take the weapon. Burgess then sat with the killer and asked about his motives. Burgess was later to recall that Bellingham had said words to the effect of, 'want of redress of grievance, and refusal by government'. Once Bellingham was in custody, a Bow Street Runner, John Vickery, searched his home at 9 New Millman Street, near Grays Inn Road. Vickery found a pistol key that fitted the seized weapons and a mould for making the lead balls, the ammunition for such handguns.

The trial opened at the Old Bailey on 15 May, just four days after the murder. Bellingham could have pleaded insanity, but he insisted on not doing so, despite both him and his father having suffered from mental illness. Witnesses testified that he was mad, but the judge, Sir James Mansfield, discounted the evidence. The case against Bellingham was overwhelming; General Gascoyne was a key witness to the murder and identification. Additionally, Vickery, the Bow Street Runner, gave what must be some of the earliest ballistics evidence ever. He compared the mould found in New Millman Street to the ammunition made by Bellingham and stated that there was a match. The accused had little tangible to offer in his defence. In the court, he made a long rambling statement, quoting all manner of letters sent to him by officials (who had done nothing to help him with his grievance). He stated that he had no malice against the dead Prime Minister and that the attack on him was, simply, an attack on the government. Once the judge had summed up the evidence, it took the jury all of fourteen minutes to convict him.

The sentence was inevitable—death by hanging. This swift justice was carried out on 18 May. Worshipful Brother the Reverend Brownlow Forde, the Newgate Prison chaplain was present. He was also a member of a Liverpool lodge, Merchants' No. 241. It is interesting to note the latter part of the judgement: 'you shall be hanged by the neck until you be dead; your body to be dissected and anatomized.' Condemned prisoners were useful to the ever-progressing field of medical science.

This marks the end of the life of the only man to have assassinated a British Prime Minister. A Freemason's evidence and identification ensured he was brought to justice and the chaplain, who was with him at his execution, was also a member of the Craft.

25

Sir John Soane:
Iconic Architecture, Great Mason,
Dreadful Son

Masonic Connection

Famous architect

Designer of Freemasons' Hall

Date

1813: Initiated into Freemasonry

1828: Commissioned to build the second Freemasons' Hall in London

Connection to London

Design of red phone boxes

Banqueting House, Whitehall: Prize awarded to Soane for drawing of building early in his career

Christ Church, Blackfriars Rd, Southwark: Soane married Eliza in this church

10 Downing Street, London: Dining room in Prime Minister's official residence designed by Soane

Lincoln's Inn Fields: Former home and now museum relating to Soane

Threadneedle Street: Location of Soane's Bank of England (now demolished)

St James's Palace, Westminster: Soane appointed Clerk of Works

Houses of Parliament: Soane appointed Clerk of Works

Royal Hospital, Chelsea: Sections rebuilt by Soane

Dulwich Picture Gallery, Gallery Road, SE21: Designed by Soane

Great Queen Street: Location of Soane's Freemasons' Hall (part of which remains)

St Pancras Old Church, Camden: Location of Tomb

Lodges

Grand Master's No.1

Royal York Lodge of Perseverance No.7

Constitutional No. 55

Throughout history and in the Bible, there is clear evidence that great men do not necessarily produce great sons. Oliver Cromwell rose from country gentleman to Lord

Protector of England, but his son, Richard, was a miserable failure as a leader. The prophet Samuel was chosen by God and, as the last Biblical judge, led Israel, but his sons were thieves and rogues. It was the same with Freemason Sir John Soane, whose life was blighted by his wayward offspring. For all of his problems in life, Soane's legacy can still be seen all over London. As we will see, a copy of his self-designed tomb is an iconic image of London. He also designed the Bank of England and the second Freemasons' Hall, part of which can be seen today and a museum in his honour stands at his former home in Lincoln's Inn Fields, a short walk from Freemasons' Hall in Great Queen Street. This self-made man and wonderful architect was, however, the victim of blackmail at the hands of his own son.

Soane was born in Oxfordshire in 1753, the son of a bricklayer. After the death of his father, when only fourteen years old, his mother moved the family to Chertsey in Surrey, the home of his elder brother. There, young Soane was introduced to colleagues of George Dance (the Younger), an established architect, who was responsible for redesigning the Newgate jail in London. Either Dance or his father, who shared the same name, was a member of Lodge No. 84 (now Constitutional Lodge No. 55), which met in the City of London.

By the age of fifteen, Soane was working for Dance at his offices in the City of London and before he had attained the age of twenty years, he had moved to be an understudy

Sir John Soane, the Mason who designed several iconic buildings, including the Bank of England.

of another established architect, Henry Holland. Among other buildings, Holland had redesigned the Theatre Royal, Drury Lane. Soane's skill began to be noted at this time and he was awarded prizes for his drawings, including one of the Banqueting House in Whitehall, where Charles I had been beheaded two hundred years earlier.

In 1778, and by now a published author on architecture, Soane set off on his Grand Tour, travelling via Paris to Rome. In the Eternal City, he paid particular interest in the Coliseum; here lies another tale of crime. This was built using funds from the treasures of the temple at Jerusalem, looted in AD 70 by Titus. Soane then travelled throughout Italy, making observations and drawings of the classical buildings. Tragically, many of these were lost on the return journey to England. When passing through Switzerland, his trunk broke open while on a coach and many of his books were lost.

Soane was back in England by the summer of 1780, his mind full of ideas, but his bank account drained of funds. He travelled all over the kingdom looking for employment, even as far as Londonderry in Ulster. Various associates gave him work, including Dance Junior, who required further work conducted on Newgate Prison. His financial situation had become so desperate that Soane even entered a competition to design a new prison. Unfortunately, his was not the winning design.

Despite the slow start, Soane's career did, eventually, take off. In 1783, he was commissioned by several landowners in East Anglia to plan and build homes in Norfolk and Suffolk. As his fame spread, he was offered work closer to London, in Harrow and Keston, Kent, where he redesigned Holwood House, which was owned by William Pitt the Younger, twice Prime Minister of Great Britain (this has now been converted into private flats). Soane was then commissioned to draw the plans for the first public picture gallery in England and (no doubt through the Pitt connection) remodel the dining room at number 10 Downing Street. This new-found stability allowed him to take a wife and in 1784, he married Eliza in Southwark. Within six years, they were to have four sons, but only two survived infancy—the first child, John and the third, George. Following the death of Soane's father-in-law, the family were left an inheritance, which enabled him to buy properties in Lincoln's Inn Field and eventually build the home, which is now the museum in his honour.

Thanks to the influence of Pitt, Soane was appointed to a most prestigious role in 1788—architect and surveyor of the Bank of England. He would almost rebuild the entire establishment during the forty-five years that he would spend in the role. This appointment was the making of Soane and significantly increased his influence (and bank balance). Further opportunities followed: in 1791, he was appointed the Clerk of Works for St James's Palace and the Palace of Westminster; in 1807 came another important surveyor post, this time at the Royal Hospital.

In late 1813, Soane became a Freemason. He was proposed into the Grand Master's Lodge No. 1 by James Perry, who had been the Deputy Grand Master of Antients Grand Lodge from 1787 to 1790. Perry was a most interesting character. A radical journalist, he had been charged with seditious libel on several occasions, usually being acquitted. While serving as Deputy Grand Master, his luck ran out and in 1798, he was found guilty of libelling the House of Lords and was sentenced to three months' imprisonment in Newgate. Quite what the Grand Master at the time, his Royal Highness the Prince of Wales (later King George IV), made of the affair is unclear.

Despite the anti-establishment conduct of his proposer, Soane achieved rapid Masonic promotion and was quickly appointed to the rank of Grand Superintendent of Works. Furthermore, he was employed by Grand Lodge some eight years later to extend Freemasons' Hall and in 1828, to completely rebuild it. Soane's Grand Lodge was later demolished to make way for the current structure.

Soane had hoped that his two sons would follow in his footsteps, but neither John, who was frequently ill and of an idle disposition, nor George, with his violent temper, made any effort to study architecture. Likewise, both seemed to have made a poor choice of bride. While taking the sea air in Kent, John married Maria Preston with the promise of a £2,000 dowry. Unfortunately, this never materialised. His brother then married a woman named Agnes Boaden, while at university and freely admitted doing so to spite his parents. George, like his older brother, failed to achieve a degree despite trying medicine and law. He was also rejected by the Royal Navy, the army, and the church.

George's conduct was to worsen. In 1814, he demanded that his father pay him £350 (over £20,000 in 2016) or he would be forced to become an actor; this shows the view held of those on the stage at this time. Soane senior refused to pay and his son turned to crime. His criminal career was short lived; within months, George was in prison for fraud and being in debt. His mother came to the rescue and paid his accuser, thus securing her son's release from incarceration.

Despite their help in releasing him from prison, George Soane remained embittered and angry with his parents. To exact revenge, he then published anonymous articles in 'The Champion' newspaper, criticising the standards of the arts and architecture in England, and particularly the work of his father. The identity of the author was soon exposed and the affair may have contributed to his mother's death; she had been ill for some time, but this would have been a bitter psychological blow.

Eliza was buried in the grounds of St Pancras Old Church in London. Soane was devastated by his wife's death in 1815 and designed a magnificent tomb. Interestingly, the memorial is devoid of Christian symbols; it should be noted that at the same time, the Duke of Sussex, the first Grand Master of the United Grand Lodge of England (just two years prior to Eliza's death) was busily de-Christianising Masonic ritual to ensure Jews and men of other faiths could join. Soane himself was a Deist; he rejected organised religion, but believed in a supreme being. The ritual relating to the First Degree Tracing Board states that 'the usages and customs of Freemasons have ever corresponded to those of the ancient Egyptians...' and the roof of the tomb is topped with a pinecone, as was the staff of Osiris, the Egyptian god of the afterlife. There is also a carving of a serpent swallowing its own tail; this is a symbol of eternity and features on the collar of a Rose Croix Freemason. It is the roof of the tomb that has, however, gained most fame; its design was copied for the red telephone boxes that adorn many streets throughout Britain.

It is worthy of note that in 1821, Soane became a Fellow of the Royal Society, an organisation that has links to Freemasonry from its foundation after the English Civil War. His membership of this organisation demonstrates the influence he was gaining in society.

Sir John Soane's tomb. The roof of the famous London phone box is based on this design.

While his career and professional standing was flourishing, Soane's private life was a source of unhappiness. Within two years of him being admitted to the Royal Society, his eldest son, John, had joined his mother in the tomb and his last remaining son was to be the cause of further misery. George Soane was now living in a bizarre *ménage à trois* with his wife and her sister. He had even managed to have a further son by the latter. George's temper continued to be a blight on his family's life and he was violent towards his wife and first child (Frederick had been born in 1815 by his wife). Soane senior intervened and while trying to persuade Agnes to leave his son, he paid for his grandson's education. Once again, Soane was hoping that architecture would be continued in the family.

Once Frederick Soane had left school, his grandfather secured him a place with John Tarring, an architect (but not a Freemason) responsible for several churches still standing in London today. The opportunity was to pass Fred by; like his father, he was not going to be an architect. Tarring soon dismissed the young Soane, who was staying out late and spending time with a homosexual Army officer—a grave matter (and possibly criminal) at that time. Soane's grand-daughter caused him further grief, by eloping to Gretna Green and marrying a navy officer.

Soane determined to cut his last surviving son, George, out of his will. The house in Lincoln's Inn Fields was filled with all manner of valuable items—antiquities from Rome and Greece, all manner of books, drawings of Sir Christopher Wren and other famous architects and paintings by contemporary artists, including fellow Freemason, William Hogarth. Soane, now knighted by William IV, reasoned that his son would sell anything of value and waste it on a decadent life. He was determined to stop this and by an Act of Parliament, Sir John Soane left his home and its contents to the nation.

Sir John died in 1837 and, true to form, his greedy son challenged his last will and testament. George Soane's efforts failed and the home became the museum we see today. In the Picture Room in the house, Soane can be seen in a portrait wearing his Masonic regalia. The wayward son was to die himself in 1860, but his role in Masonry is debatable. In 1830, a man named 'George Soane' was initiated into a London lodge, Royal York Lodge of Perseverance No. 409 (now No.7). At that time in England, there only appears to be two men of that name - Sir John Soane's son and a man born in Sussex in the same year. If it was the greedy George Soane, his initiation into Masonry would have been another blow to his father.

In addition to blackmail by his son, Sir John was also the victim of another type of 'crime', which can either be described as 'progress' (by those who commit it) or 'cultural vandalism' (by those who disagree with it). The demolition of the Bank of England to make way for the current building was described by architectural historian, Sir Nikolaus Pevsner as 'the greatest architectural crime, in the City of London, of the twentieth century.' Prior to the destruction of the bank, his Freemasons' Hall was demolished and the rebuilt between 1927 and 1933. Another of his works, an extension to the Royal Hospital (the home of the Chelsea Pensioners), was destroyed by the Luftwaffe in 1941 during the Second World War (this is now the site of the National Army Museum). For those wishing to enjoy his architecture, the Royal Hospital guardhouse and other buildings still stand today.

It is a great shame that a self-made man, a wonderful architect and Freemason should have such dreadful off-spring. Unlike his selfish sons and grandson, many of Soane's contributions to London are still standing. While the main part of his Grand Lodge was demolished, a small section remains. If the reader stands outside Central Regalia, the Masonic shop in Great Queen Street and looks across the road, part of the Soane building can be seen between the current Grand Lodge and the Grand Connaught Rooms.

The First King and the Craft: The Scandalous Life of George IV

Masonic Connection
First English king acknowledged as a Mason
Prime Minister
First Mark Mason in England

Date
1787: George IV (as Prince of Wales) initiated
1790: Appointed as Grand Master of England
1795: Start of disastrous marriage to Caroline of Brunswick
1805: Appointed as Grand Master of Scotland
1821: Coronation and death of Caroline

Connection to London
St James's Palace: King born and married in the palace
Pall Mall: Joined Freemasonry in a tavern, now demolished
Westminster Abbey: Coronation
Trafalgar Square: Statue of George IV

Lodges
Royal Somerset House and Inverness No.4
Prince of Wales's No. 259

'The King and the Craft' is a Masonic toast that has been used over the centuries, but some debate remains over who the first monarch to be honoured in lodges in this manner was. While some Masonic historians have attempted to claim monarchs of old—such as Solomon and Athelstan—for the Craft, the first king of England recognised as a Freemason by the United Grand Lodge of England is George IV. When Prince of Wales, he was to hold the two most senior positions in the Craft, Grand Master of England and Grand Master of Scotland. Unfortunately, his life was one tarnished with scandal—a wild lifestyle, an illegal marriage, outrageous treatment of his wife (or is it wives?), and a possible drug addiction.

George IV, the first English king recognised by Grand Lodge as a Freemason.

For all this, his lifetime saw great events in Masonry—the making of the first Mark Mason and the Union of the two Grand Lodges in England. His patronage would also encourage many of the Establishment to join the Craft, increasing the influence of the Craft.

George IV was born in 1762 at St James's Palace, the first child of George III. Prior to ascending to the throne, he was styled Prince George Augustus Frederick. As the eldest son of the king, he was given the title Prince of Wales. He appears to have been a clever child, quickly learning several European languages. However, once given the free run of his own affairs at the age of eighteen, he threw himself into a life of extravagance and scandal, drinking heavily and taking several mistresses. At the age of twenty-one, he received an annual allowance of £60,000 (over £6 million today) and nearly as much again from his father, the king. Unbelievably, this was still insufficient to pay for this royal wild-child.

An important aspect of the prince's Bohemian and debaucherous lifestyle was the theatre. The young prince, loaded with too much money for his own good, fell for a twice-widowed actress, Maria Fitzherbert. Like his younger brother, the Duke of Sussex (the first Grand Master of the United Grand Lodge of England), the Prince of Wales seemed to have enjoyed the talents and pleasures of an older woman. Mrs Fitzherbert was six years his senior, but more importantly in the religious conscience society of that time, she was a Roman Catholic. The Royal Marriage Act 1772 forbad marriages between the Protestant royal family and followers of the Church of Rome. Additionally, the consent of the king was required for a prince to marry anyone. Throwing convention (and the law) aside, the prince married the actress in 1785. The ceremony was secretively conducted in her home in Park Street, London and performed by a vicar in need of cash. Despite being a royal chaplain, the Reverend Robert Burt had been placed in Fleet Prison as he owed some £500; the prince paid off this debt as reward for his services. There was every reason to hide this wedding—to marry a Catholic would mean forfeiting the prince's right to the throne.

Possibly seeking some security and an escape from all his troubles, while in his mid-twenties, Prince George became a Freemason at a special meeting held at the Star and Garter Tavern in Pall Mall (where his younger brother, the Grand Old Duke of York had also joined the Craft; see Chapter 24). Fittingly, in 1787 he was initiated into the Horn Lodge No. 3 (now Royal Somerset House and Inverness Lodge No.4), by another relative, his uncle, Prince Henry, Duke of Cumberland and Strathearn. As we have seen in chapter 17, the Duke was also involved in a variety of scandals with ladies. Indeed, as a result of his actions, the Royal Marriage Act had been created.

The Prince of Wales, for all the other distractions, appears to have taken to the Craft. Within a year of his initiation, he had formed his own lodge,using his title to name it and this is now lodge No. 259. Initially, the membership had consisted of staff in the Royal Household, but then other influential men and Masons joined, such as Royal Navy officer Thomas Dunckerley and politician (and later Prime Minister) George Canning. In relation to Dunckerley, the first evidence of Mark Masonry in England is in 1769 in Portsmouth, when he made a Chapter member a Mark Man. Dunckerley was the Provincial Grand Master and Grand Superintendent for the Royal Arch in several parts of England. Indeed, he appears to have amended the ritual so that the Third Degree story of a lost secret flows into the Royal Arch ceremony (where a Mason finds it). He was also influential in several other Masonic Orders, including Royal Ark Mariners and Knights Templar. Most importantly, on her death bed, his mother had identified his father as the Prince of Wales (later George II)—yet more royal scandal. To his credit, George III accepted the retired naval officer as a half-brother, so this man of great influence was another Masonic uncle to Prince George Augustus Frederick, the Duke of Sussex and first Grand Master of the United Grand Lodge of England.

In 1788, the year after Prince George became a Freemason, the mental illness of his father was to start to impact on the young prince's life. The 'Madness of George III' has been the subject of studies and even films, but the cause is unclear (most bizarrely, finding out the true gender of a transvestite Mason may have pushed him over the edge on one occasion). Whatever disease (or circumstances) were the origin of these issues, the government were aware that they could not carry on with a constitutional monarchy, where the head of state was deranged. On this occasion, the king was to recover his sanity and by February of the following year, George III was fit enough to carry on as the ruling monarch.

In 1790, high honour was bestowed on the Prince of Wales, Grand Master of England, but he seems to have enjoyed the social side of Masonry, rather than any administrative duties or leadership roles. Fortunately for him, the Acting (or what would now be called the Pro-Grand Master) was the Earl of Moira. As a retired Army general, he had the qualities required to lead the Craft. Indeed, in 1799, he possibly saved it from extinction when the government attempted to have all 'unlawful' or secret societies banned.

Returning to the Prince of Wales's private life, the hidden marriage to Mrs Fitzherbert was to continue for over nine years, until 1794. In a rather cool manner, he ended the marriage by letter. The prince's reason for dumping the love of his life was simple—money. He was terribly in debt and his father, the king, had promised that if he did the 'right thing', his debts (by now £600,000, more than ten times his annual allowance) would be paid off in full. Accordingly, he was betrothed to his German first cousin, Duchess Caroline of Brunswick of the Kingdom of Hanover. This was no strange place to the English kings at that time, as they also ruled that part of Europe.

George married Caroline in 1795 in the Royal Chapel in the palace of his birth; they had poor opinions of each other, even on their wedding night—he thought she was unhygienic, unattractive, and not a virgin; Caroline claimed the Prince was a drunk. Indeed, the Prince was so disappointed on first meeting Caroline that he had to ask for a glass of brandy. To further aggravate the situation, the Prince had a new lover, Frances Villiers, the Countess of Jersey and she was installed as 'Lady of the Bedchamber', Caroline's personal assistant. Having a lover and wife so closely linked was never the recipe for a happy marriage. Lady Jersey was a determined social climber, who came from an unusual background. Her father, an Irish bishop (another clergyman in debt) had been shot, while robbing a stagecoach. Despite being (officially) married, the prince continued to be a young man with too much money and too much time on his hands.

Additionally, the Prince of Wales, notwithstanding the charms of Lady Jersey, could not forget his actress 'wife'. Despite Caroline giving birth to a daughter, Princess Charlotte in 1796, the prince continued to fixate on the woman whom he described as 'my wife, the wife

Queen Caroline died of 'natural causes' just three weeks after being refused admission to the coronation service of her husband, George IV.

of my heart and soul.' Indeed, just three days after the birth, he wrote a secret will leaving everything to Mrs Fitzherbert. In the document, the prince bequeathed his legitimate wife, Caroline, just one shilling—five pence in today's currency.

Given all these factors, it is unsurprising that the relationship between the Prince and Princess of Wales deteriorated. In a parallel to recent events in the modern world, the general populace sided with the princess, as Caroline had become, seeing her as a victim and wronged wife. As a result, she became popular, which was aided by her easy-going nature. Princess Caroline was often cheered in public, while the Prince of Wales was widely regarded as an adulterer. His extravagant and wasteful lifestyle also did nothing to endear him to the masses.

While his Masonic career was at its height as Grand Master of England, his marriage was in a state of collapse. By 1797, Caroline had moved into her own residence in Charlton, south London, then later Blackheath. There she is rumoured to have had affairs with several men, including George Canning, the Prime Minister. If he did, Brother Canning was in breach of the Third Degree obligation, which notes that a Master Mason should 'most strictly respect the chastity of those nearest and dearest' to a brother Mason, 'in the persons of his wife, his sister and his child.'

Attempts were made to find an amicable solution, all to no avail. The government also conducted what was known as the 'Delicate Investigation'—a secret enquiry into Caroline's alleged adultery—but no evidence was found. In another similarity to modern events, Caroline was offered the title of Duchess of Cornwall, rather than Princess of Wales. Additionally, the Prince was being drawn again to Mrs Fitzherbert. He was bored of Lady Jersey and was seeking reconciliation with his first 'bride'; even the Pope deemed the marriage to Mrs Fitzherbert as legitimate. Being head of the Roman Catholic Church, the Pope, no doubt, was keen to cause mischief for a Protestant monarchy.

In 1805, the Prince of Wales was also appointed Grand Master of Scotland, but there is no evidence that he ever travelled north of the border to receive this title. His interest in Masonry started to wane. His carefree lifestyle as eldest son of the monarch was to end, as in 1811, George III was deemed to be permanently insane. Consequently, Prince George was appointed as Regent. This scenario was to continue for nearly ten years until the king died. This was an unsettled time—the following year, the Prime Minister was assassinated. George's appointment as Regent appears to have been the final nail in the coffin regarding his active involvement in Freemasonry. After 1813, the prince would attend no further meetings, but he did accept the title of Grand Patron of the Order.

During the Regency, as the period became known, the ill-feeling between the Prince of Wales and Caroline fared no better. George made every effort to get rid of his German wife with little success. Caroline could not return home to Brunswick, even if she had wanted to, as much of the continent had been overrun by the French army. All this was to change and after the defeat of Napoleon, Caroline could return to the continent. First visiting her homeland, she then made for Switzerland and Italy, where she hired an Italian man servant. Rumours soon spread that they were, in fact, lovers. This was not helped by the future queen creating the 'Order of St Caroline' and making her servant the Grand Master.

Caroline's position was further weakened in 1817 by the death of her only daughter in child-birth (Charlotte was only twenty-one years old); Caroline was no longer the mother of the heir to the throne. Around the same time, lurid tales of her affairs in Italy were to reach London. In January 1820, George III died and the Prince of Wales succeeded him as George IV. Much to the latter's disgust, Caroline was now Queen Consort. The new king therefore decided to use legal means, including a trial, to obtain a divorce. In consequence, he introduced the Pains and Penalties Bill into Parliament in an attempt to 'to deprive Her Majesty Queen Caroline…of the Title… of Queen Consort of this Realm; and to dissolve the Marriage between His Majesty and the said Caroline'. Specifically, the allegations relating to her conduct with her Italian servant resulted in the charge that Caroline had had sexual liaisons with a 'foreigner of low station'—scandalous conduct, indeed.

In August 1820, the Queen Consort appeared at the House of Lords, where the Pains and Penalties Bill was to be debated. This was effectively a trial of her conduct. Various prosecution witnesses thrilled the gallery with sordid tales, giving accounts of Caroline and her 'lover' bathing together or being in each other's presence in various states of undress. Another servant even admitted spying through the keyhole—was there ever a truer case of 'what the butler saw'? The defence team only hinted at the hypocrisy of the Prince of Wales, who had engaged in several affairs. The lawyers well knew that if the truth about his marriage to Mrs Fitzherbert, a Roman Catholic, was revealed, it could spell the end of the monarchy. In private, Caroline was to jest that she had committed adultery once, and that was with the husband of Mrs Fitzherbert. After several days, the Lords voted, narrowly, in favour of George. The votes for him included one from his older brother, the Grand Old Duke of York, but not his younger one, the Duke of Sussex. The recently made Grand Master of the United Grand Lodge of England (the Modern and Antient Grand Lodges having joined) asked to withdraw from the debate due to the family connection. Despite winning the vote, the government feared a revolution and so withdrew the Bill, meaning that it could not become law. Caroline was still on track to be Queen of England.

No doubt angry at his plan being foiled, the new king threw his energy into a new project. Despite all the troubles in the country and in Europe, George IV spent nearly eighteen months planning his coronation. He was determined that it should be finer than Napoleon's coronation as Emperor of France. A small fortune was spent on the ceremony, using money, of course, that the king did not have. He was even forced to wear hired jewels. Despite all the planning and finery, there was still one person who could ruin the day—Caroline.

On 19 July 1821, London was ready for the coronation service, which was to take place in Westminster Abbey. George IV had added to the security arrangements by insisting that armed guards be posted at all entrances to the cathedral to prevent Caroline from claiming her own crown. Prize fighters were also hired and dressed as servants, in case of crowd trouble. Caroline entered London, but the sentries did their duty and she was forced away from the Abbey at the point of a bayonet. She tried to enter three times, but was stopped at the east and west entrances and also after trying to sneak in via Westminster Hall. The failure appears to have broken her spirit, and lost her public support. Perhaps she misunderstood the English people, who have a love for all things ceremonial. By attempting to wreck the coronation, she seemingly insulted them.

Tragically, Caroline died less than three weeks later. Her death occurred in a riverside mansion house in Fulham, but her body was transported back to Brunswick and buried there. The cause of her death is unclear. It may have been cancer or it may have been more suspicious. At the time, there were rumours that she had been poisoned.

George IV was to outlive Caroline by nearly nine years. During the first few years of his reign, he also turned against Mrs Fitzherbert, but her veiled threats to 'go public' ensured that she continued to receive an annual payment from the king. In 1827, he appointed Canning as the Prime Minister. If the king was aware of the politician's affair with Caroline, he did not hold it against him. Brother Canning was to die in office and still holds the record of being the Prime Minister for the shortest period (119 days).

As his reign progressed, the king grew more obese and disliked by the public. On his death in 1830, *The Times* newspaper was scathing, noting, 'There never was an individual less regretted by his fellow-creatures than this deceased king. What eye has wept for him? What heart has heaved one throb of unmercenary sorrow?' Perhaps, however, Mrs Fitzherbert was the one person that wept for him. For all his anger and foul moods, the king never seems to have forgotten his first 'wife', nor did she forget him. At his request, the king was buried with a tiny painting of her eyes about his neck.

Thus the first King of England in the Craft was dead. He was to be succeeded by another Mason, his brother, the Duke of Clarence (who managed to have ten illegitimate children by another actress—a common thread, it would seem). The Duke would rule as William IV. George appears to have been a dreadful individual—wasteful with money, irresponsible, and selfish. A fellow Freemason, the Duke of Wellington, even described him as 'without one redeeming quality'. For all this, his patronage of Freemasonry allowed the Craft to flourish. George IV is also remembered as the 'First Gentleman of England', so he must have had some redeeming qualities and his support of the arts and science can be seen today; he commissioned the building of Brighton Pavilion, founded King's College London, and supported the establishment of the National Gallery. A statue of George IV can be seen in Trafalgar Square, near another Freemason (the nemesis of his father), Brother George Washington.

27

The Duke of Sussex: Breaker of the Royal Marriage Act Three Times

Masonic Connection
First Grand Master, United Grand Lodge of England
Masonic statues

Date
1798: Initiated into Freemasonry
1813: United Grand Lodge of England formed

Connection to London
Great Queen Street: Statue in Grand Lodge
John Adam Street: President of Royal Society of Arts

Lodges
Grand Stewards'
Lodge of Antiquity No. 2
Lodge of Friendship No. 6
Royal Alpha No. 16
Lodge of Jerusalem No. 197
Prince of Wales's No. 259
Lodge of Victorious Truth (Berlin)

Prince Augustus Frederick, the Duke of Sussex, will be known to many Freemasons, especially in England, as he was the first Grand Master of the United Grand Lodge. He was born in 1773, the sixth son of George III. He was well suited to his Masonic appointment, as he was a Biblical scholar with a great knowledge of the Hebrew language.

Like his uncle, the Duke of Cumberland, and his brother, the Duke of York, he was to achieve much in Freemasonry, but also like them, he was involved in various scandals involving women. As has been related, due to the unsuitable choice (in the view of George III) of wives by the Duke of Cumberland, the Royal Marriages Act 1772 had been enacted. This forbade marriages of senior royals without the king's permission. Indeed, as late as 1967, it was a criminal offence to officiate at a wedding in contravention of the Act.

Duke of Sussex, First Grand Master of the United Grand Lodge of England and offender against the Royal Marriage Act.

The Duke of Sussex fell afoul of the Act three times. At twenty years old, when travelling in Italy, the Duke fell for the charms of Lady Augusta Murray (described as 'rather bossy'), who was five years his senior. It was an unlikely match as her grandfather, the 3rd Earl of Dunmore, had been a Jacobite who had been convicted of high treason against the Duke's grandfather (George II). However, previous family conflicts forgotten, they married in a secret ceremony in Rome, where few Protestant clergy were to be found. Their happiness was not to last long; the king sent a minister to escort young Prince Augustus Frederick home. Not to be thwarted, the couple married again just six months later in London, failing to disclose their identities. Both these marriages were annulled under the Act.

In 1798, the Duke was initiated into Freemasonry while in Prussia, modern day Germany. He joined the Lodge of Victorious Truth in Berlin. He would also join several English lodges—Prince of Wales No. 324 (now No. 259), Lodge of Friendship No. 6, and Lodge of Antiquity No. 2. He also played a key role in the formation of Royal Alpha No. 16, which is still the Grand Master's personal lodge.

It will be recalled that at this time, there were two Grand Lodges in England—the Moderns (the Premier Grand Lodge formed in 1717) and the Antients (which broke away in 1751). By 1811, both had appointed Commissioners to negotiate an amalgamation and within two years, an Article of Union had been agreed. In 1813, the Duke of Sussex succeeded his brother, the Prince Regent (later George IV), as Grand Master of the Moderns. Likewise, his other brother, the Duke of Kent, became the Grand Master of the Antients for a matter of days before resigning, so that on 27 December of that year, the United Grand Lodge of England was constituted, with the Duke of Sussex as its head. Outside of the Craft, he was also President of the Royal Society and the Royal Society of Arts.

Returning to his less successful personal life, Lady Murray was kept well by the Duke, but she died in 1830. The following year, again without obtaining his father's permission, the Duke married Lady Cecilia Letitia Gore, a widow who was twelve years his junior. This irregular marriage was also declared null and void. It is unclear if any of the clergymen involved in these unlawful ceremonies were ever prosecuted.

Prince Augustus Frederick died in 1843. It is an odd coincidence that Anthony Sayer and the Duke, as the first Grand Masters of the Premier Grand Lodge in 1717 and United Lodge of England in 1813 respectively, should both be involved in what were classified as 'clandestine marriages'. These were weddings that took place without any banns being read out in a church. They were often officiated over by disgraced priests, who had been sentenced to prison, but bribed the prison warders to allow them to live outside the walls of the jail.

For all this scandalous conduct, the Duke did much for Freemasonry. To show his importance to the Craft, his statue used to stand behind the Grand Master's throne in Grand Lodge. The statue was moved in 1933, when Freemason's Hall in London was demolished and rebuilt; it now stands in a ground floor corridor. The statue was created by E. H. Baily, another Mason and a member of Lodge of Jerusalem (then No. 233), now No. 197, Prince of Wales's No. 259 (the same lodge as the Duke of Sussex), and the Grand Stewards' Lodge. Baily also produced the statue of Nelson that stands on top of the famous column in Trafalgar Square. The sculptor was often in financial difficulties, once caused by Buckingham Palace not paying its bills.

28

General Napier: Military Mason and Crime Prevention Officer

Masonic Connection
Famous general
Lodges in India and Pakistan

Date
1807: Napier initiated into Freemasonry
1850s: Stopped deadly Indian tradition

Connection to London
Trafalgar Square: Statue of Napier on south west plinth

Lodges
Doyle's Lodge of Fellowship No. 84
Ancient Union No. 13 (Ireland)

General Sir Charles Napier was born in 1782 in Whitehall Palace, London; he had royal blood—his mother was a direct descendent of Charles II. His statue now stands in Trafalgar Square, looking down towards the place of his birth. He was a career soldier, first joining the 33rd Regiment of Foot (later known as the Duke of Wellington's Regiment). By the time of the Peninsula War, where coincidentally, the future Duke of Wellington was in command of the British Army, Napier was the colonel of the 50th Regiment. For military buffs, these were to become the Royal West Kents; their cap badge was worn by other Freemasons, Arnold Ridley and Ian Lavender, when they played Mr Godfrey and Private Pike in *Dad's Army*.

During the conflict in Spain, Napier was badly wounded and taken prisoner by the French, but he managed to return to British lines. After his wounds had recovered, he quickly returned to active service. He proved a gallant officer, being decorated for bravery under fire in several battles, including the siege at Badajoz. By now, he was the colonel in charge of the 102nd Regiment; this ultimately became the Royal Dublin Fusiliers. The wounds suffered during this conflict would trouble him for the rest of his life.

General Sir Charles Napier. This statue stands in Trafalgar Square.

It was around this time that he became a Mason—in 1807, he joined Doyle's Lodge of Fellowship on Guernsey, then No. 99 (now 84). As he was due to sail from the Channel Islands imminently for further active military duties, he was initiated, passed, and raised in all three degrees on one day.

He remained in the army and more promotions followed. In 1838, he returned to Britain and was based at Chester as the general commanding all troops in the north of England; at that time, there was much unrest in the new industrial cities and the army was used as a form of police force. He was active in Freemasonry and required details of his initiation— he had to write to his Mother Lodge as all his Masonic paperwork had been lost in a shipwreck.

Four years later (and now sixty years old) he was posted to the east, to command the Indian Army. At that time, a number of Muslim chieftains in the Sindh Province (part of modern Pakistan) had refused to accept British rule. Napier dealt boldly with this threat, defeating the tribes in two decisive battles. His original orders were simply to deal with the threat of rebellion, but now he had conquered the whole of Sindh, together with surrounding provinces. It is said that he sent the one-word message '*Peccavi*' (Latin for 'I have sinned', a play on words) to London. This is a great story, but not entirely true, as it was invented by a schoolgirl. His Masonic career continued; his conquest of the area enabled him to lay the foundation stone of the Masonic Hall in Karachi (then in British India) in 1845. Freemasonry would be banned in Pakistan in 1972.

Despite his successes in India, he fell out with the British East India Company, which controlled trade and had its own private army out of British government control. He returned to Ireland (where he had attended school) to great acclaim. In 1848, the brethren of the Ancient Union Lodge No. 13 (Irish Constitution) in Limerick invited him to be an Honorary Member. His reply sums his view of Freemasonry and its benefits to mankind:

> The honour, which you have bestowed upon me, is most flattering to me both as a soldier and a Mason. The troops which served under my orders (among whom were many Masons) won a country by their courage, and held it by their good conduct. To them I owe the honour, which you have raised today. It will I hope gratify the Worshipful Master, Officers and Brethren to know that we built and established a Masonic Lodge in Scinde and thereby found many natives who were, I believe, initiated into the mysteries of the Craft previous to the arrival of our Countrymen among them, and thus was an additional bond of union established here. I have great pleasure in accepting the offer of Honorary Member of the Masonic Lodge No 13.

The penultimate sentence (referring to ancient Masonry in India) has a similar feel to Rudyard Kipling's Masonic story *The Man Who Would Be King*. He continued to promote the Craft on the sub-continent and, in 1849, attended a Masonic dinner in full uniform of the Commander-in-Chief of India, with the addition of Royal Arch regalia. During the after dinner speech, he acknowledged the debt he owed to Masonry.

It could be argued that Napier was instrumental in stopping many murders in India. At that time, the Hindu population practiced *Sati* or *Suttee*; when a man died, his wife was thrown alive onto the funeral pyre. Napier intervened and the local priests objected, saying that he was interfering with local customs, something that the British had promised not to do. The general told them that they could, of course, continue with their tradition in the following manner:

> Be it so. This burning of widows is your custom; prepare the funeral pile. But my nation has also a custom. When men burn women alive we hang them, and confiscate all their property. My carpenters shall therefore erect gibbets on which to hang all concerned when the widow is consumed. Let us all act according to national customs.

As a result, this wicked practice was brought to an end. Napier again argued with the authorities in India and returned to England. He was still suffering from the many wounds he had sustained as a young officer in Spain and Portugal. He died in 1853 in Portsmouth and was buried in the Royal Garrison Church in Southsea; his tomb can be seen outside the building to this day. In addition to his statue in Trafalgar Square, many other places were named after him, including a city in New Zealand and several barracks. He was a Mason, a brave soldier, and a man who prevented the deaths of many unfortunate women, whose husband had died before them. Perhaps, as a Mason, he remembered that Hiram Abif was a widow's son.

29

As Drunk as a Lord!
(and a Lodge named after a Magistrate)

Masonic Connection
Police officer
Magistrate

Date
1861: Arrest occurred

Connection to London
Coventry Street, Westminster: Scene of the crime
Marlborough Street: Case heard at Magistrates Court

Lodges
Royal Alpha No. 16
Scientific No. 88
Bedford No. 157
Domatic No. 177
Prince of Wales's No. 259
Apollo University No. 357
Beadon No. 619
Staffordshire Knot No. 626 (erased)

In the middle of the nineteenth century, one of the several police officers in the Domatic Lodge No. 177 was George Silverton. In 1861, Silverton was an acting inspector in central London; on 6 March of that year, one of his constables had little option but to make an arrest in Coventry Street, just off Leicester Square, where a drunken man was throwing his money and cigars at a large crowd of some five hundred people. He was arrested for disorderly conduct and after a violent struggle with the constable, was taken to Marlborough Street Magistrates Court (or Police Court as it was known at that time). This was, however, no ordinary drunk; the arrested man was a Member of Parliament and the son of a peer of the realm.

Lord Adolphus Vane-Tempest (not a Mason) was the son of the Marquis of Londonderry and represented Durham in the House of Commons. This troubled man seemed to be suffering from what would now be called post-traumatic stress disorder after serving as a British Army officer at the brutal siege of Sevastopol, during in the Crimean War. On his return to civilian life, he began drinking to excess and behaving in a bizarre manner; even Queen Victoria was aware of his crazed behaviour.

The arrest had proved difficult; the (not-so-honourable) Member of Parliament was extremely aggressive and spat in the police officer's face. Having been taken in a cab to Marlborough Street Magistrates Court, Vane-Tempest had to be carried up the stairs to the court room by six officers and placed in the dock while still heavily under the influence of alcohol. The Justice of the Peace presiding is the second Mason in this case, and a very senior one—Right Worshipful Brother William Frederick Beadon. Beadon was a qualified barrister and experienced magistrate, having worked for many years at courts in Hammersmith, Wandsworth, and central London. He also held two of the most highly ranked Masonic positions in England: Junior Grand Warden of the United Grand Lodge and Grand Scribe Nehemiah in Supreme Grand Chapter.

It is unclear when Beadon joined Masonry, but he may have been initiated into the Scientific Lodge, Cambridge (then No. 131, now No. 88) in May 1828, when he was aged twenty-one and studying at St John's College, or his first lodge may have been Bedford No. 183 (now No. 157) in London. There is confusion as he is shown as a rejoining member of the latter in 1833, but it is unclear when he actually became a member of Bedford Lodge. He was a very active Mason and joined several lodges across the country, including Staffordshire Knot Lodge No. 626 in Stafford in 1836 (this lodge closed three years later), Prince of Wales Lodge in London (then No. 324, now No. 259) in 1845, and Polish National Lodge (then No. 778, now No. 534) in 1848. The records also show one William F. Beadon in Royal Alpha No. 16, the Grand Master's personal lodge and Apollo University No. 460, but it is unclear whether it is the same man. Perhaps most importantly, he was a member of Beadon lodge (then No. 902, now No. 619), a lodge named in his honour. The Lodge was consecrated at the Star and Garter Tavern, in Kew, west London in 1862 when he was fifty-four years old, with Beadon performing the Consecration Ceremony. To hold such senior rank in the Holy Royal Arch implies that he was also a member of several chapters.

Despite Beadon's high professional and Masonic standing, Lord Vane-Tempest was in no mood to be respectful to the 'Beak' (as magistrates are called in London), pompously shouting 'I suppose you know I am a Member of Parliament'. When Beadon replied in the negative, the lord called him a liar. Vane-Tempest continued to shout, swear, sing opera songs, whistle, and bang tunes on the witness box, which did little to aid his case. Beadon had little sympathy and held him in custody, unless bail of £1,000 (a small fortune at that time) was paid. The magistrate's patience was, no doubt, further tested as he was in constant pain, but continued with his duties. The Member of Parliament for Durham was then taken off to the 'house of correction' and locked in a padded cell. His family later paid for him to he placed in a private lunatic asylum. The press had a field day reporting the incident, with the *Western Daily Press* describing it as a 'scene seldom seen in a court of justice'.

None of the participants in this tale of the drunken lord fared well. Beadon died just over one year after the case and would never become the master of the lodge that still bears his name. Vane-Tempest's stay in the 'private lunatic asylum' achieved little and he continued to drink to excess, even when in Parliament. During a debate on the American Civil War in the House of Commons, he made a fine speech (while drunk), but then fell over backwards into the row of seats behind him. He died while fighting with attendants in another asylum just three years after the arrest in Coventry Street. Lastly, in 1871, Inspector Silverton's thirty-year police career ended when he was accused of attempting to pervert the course of justice by planting evidence on a man accused of robbery. This case even prompted questions in Parliament. He was never convicted, but left the Metropolitan Police under a cloud, albeit with his pension of 50 shillings per annum intact.

Unlike Vane-Tempest, Beadon went to his grave a respected man. When he was buried in Taunton, Devon, at the age of just fifty-four, hundreds of mourners lined the streets. The local paper, *The Western Times* reported that the crowd was present to pay a 'last tribute of respect' to the deceased magistrate and local land owner. This could have been a simple Victorian phrase, or the reporter could have been making a cryptic reference to the Third Degree ritual. The dead man was, after all, a very committed Mason who had served the people of England for many years, despite often being in great pain. The Beadon lodge still meets and continues as a memorial to this senior Mason.

30

Scotland Yard's First Top Detective: a Mason

Masonic Connection
Senior police officers
Detectives
Judge
Symbol on gravestone

Date
1829: Metropolitan Police formed, with at least one superintendent being a Mason
1842: Detective Department established
1864: Inspector Tanner initiated into Freemasonry and murder by Franz Müller

Connection to London
Great Scotland Yard: Location of Detective Department
Hackney, East London: Murder occurred on a train
Cadogan Terrace, E9: Victim died in public house
Cheapside: Stolen property identified in a jeweller's shop
Old Bailey: Trial and execution of murderer

Lodges
Union Waterloo No. 13
Lodge of Fortitude and Old Cumberland No. 12
Domatic No. 177
Socrates No. 373
Star No. 1275 (erased)
Abbey No. 2030
Domatic Chapter No. 177 (Royal Arch)
Rose of Denmark Chapter No. 975 (Royal Arch)

With the Industrial Revolution, London expanded rapidly in the nineteenth century; between 1801 and 1851, the population doubled to two million people, making it the world's biggest city. While this presented many with opportunities to make money, it also resulted in a massive increase in crime and disease. Rich and poor were thrust together in a way that would not have happened in the countryside.

The centuries-old system of local watchmen supplemented by the Bow Street Runners was exposed as insufficient to maintain law and order. Sir Robert Peel, the Home Secretary, successfully appealed to Parliament to form a police force for London; thus, the Metropolitan Police was established in 1829, with its headquarters at 4 Whitehall.

The new force was led by two commissioners, assisted by eight superintendents. At least one of the eight was a Mason—Brother David Williamson, a Scot, who had served at the Battle of Waterloo in 1815 as a Sergeant-Major in the Royal Artillery. Williamson had been initiated (unsurprisingly) into the Union Waterloo Lodge No. 13, which then met in Woolwich (a large artillery garrison). Williamson's son, who would also join the Craft, would achieve even higher rank at Scotland Yard and features later in this section.

The Metropolitan Police covered all of London, except for the 'Square Mile' or City, which ultimately would have its own force. Significantly, the rear entrance opened onto Great Scotland Yard, historically an area used by the kings of Scotland during visits to London. The Scotland Yard name was born and the officers were known as 'Bobbies' or 'Peelers', as Robert Peel had created the new force.

The force was initially made up of uniformed officers, who wore blue civilian style uniforms, armed with wooden truncheons so that the government could not be accused of using para-military troops to control the population, as happened on continental Europe.

Scotland Yard. This plaque, just off Whitehall, marks the location of the original 'Yard'.

Importantly, there were no plain clothes officers who might be seen as spies, persecuting anyone who was seen as a political undesirable. Gradually, however, a detective capability was built up and the attempted assassination of Queen Victoria in 1840 showed the need for an investigative branch in the 'New Police'. As a result, the Scotland Yard Detective Department was formerly opened in 1842. Initially, this was just a small unit with only two inspectors running the teams.

These officers soon caught the imagination of the public and the press. Perhaps the greatest accolade any detective can receive is to have the title 'of the Yard' after his name. The first officer to have this honour was Inspector Richard 'Dick' Tanner. Tanner of the Yard was also a Mason; he joined the Domatic Lodge No. 177 in January 1864, the same year as his most famous case. This involved the first murder on a British railway and a transatlantic pursuit—albeit possibly the slowest ever police chase. The crime occurred on 9 July, some six months after Tanner's initiation into Masonry.

After dining with friends near the Old Kent Road on a Saturday evening, Thomas Briggs, a chief bank clerk, was murdered on the 9.50 p.m. train travelling from Fenchurch Church towards Chalk Farm on the now defunct North London Railway. Briggs, a Lancastrian by birth, was an easy target—he was nearly seventy years old. At that time, carriages were divided into small, separate compartments with no corridor—ideal for privacy, but also for the commission of crime. For anyone being attacked, there was no escape and, with the noise of the steam engine, little hope of anyone hearing a cry for help.

The attack on Briggs occurred very soon into the journey, as within ten minutes of the train departing, his unconscious body was spotted by a train driver travelling in the opposite direction, on the tracks between Bow and Victoria Park and Hackney Wick stations (this is now part of the route of the A12 road). The murder scene is just near where the A12 crosses the River Lee Navigation on a canal bridge, originally built for the railway. The elderly man had been badly beaten about the head seemingly by a blunt instrument, with his left ear almost severed. The latter injury was probably caused by being thrown onto the track, rather than during the attack. The victim had also been robbed of a pocket watch and gold spectacles. Importantly, as we shall see, his hat was missing, but the robber had failed to take four sovereigns from his pocket, a diamond ring, and a silver snuff box.

The badly injured Briggs was carried to a nearby public house, the Mitford Castle in Cadogan Terrace, Hackney (this is now called the Top o' the Morning), but he died of his injuries. Several doctors and surgeons would later give evidence of his wounds and their efforts to save him. The newspapers made much of the case and the fear of crime gripped London. The middle classes were afraid of further attacks, as trains provided the perfect venue for robbers to attack with little chance of being captured.

As a murder had been committed, Scotland Yard took over the case from the local police and Dick Tanner inspected the railway carriage where the robbery had taken place. There were blooded handprints on the walls, but it would be nearly fifty years until the Fingerprint Department opened. A black beaver skin hat was also found, but the Briggs family were adamant that it was not headdress worn by the victim. It appeared to have belonged to the killer, so one hat had been stolen and another left at the scene of the murder. This would prove critical as the case progressed.

The first clue to the identity of the killer came from a jeweller, with the unfortunate name of Death. John Death ran a shop in Cheapside; he told the police that, on 11 July, two days after the crime, a German man had entered his premises and exchanged one gold chain for another. The chain exchanged by Müller was later identified as the one stolen from the victim. Death added that the foreigner had acted suspiciously, standing in such a way as to not to fully expose his face.

To encourage the public to give further information, a reward of £300 was offered, made up of £100 each from Mr Briggs's bank, the railway company, and the government. This was a vast sum (worth up to one thousand times this amount today) and this, together with newspaper coverage, soon produced valuable information. Nine days after the robbery, a cab driver, Jonathan Matthews, came forward with the name of a possible suspect.

While on a cab rank, the driver had heard the story of the chain from the murdered man possibly being found at the jewellers with the rather gruesome name. Matthews then realised that his daughter's former boyfriend, Franz Müller, could be the suspect. The ex-boyfriend had given the cab driver a gold chain, in a box marked 'John Death, jeweller'. He informed the police of his suspicions and a photograph of Müller was taken to the shop in Cheapside, where Mr Death identified Müller as the suspicious looking German. Furthermore, Matthews was able to identify the hat found in the railway carriage as belonging to Müller.

Enquiries by Inspector Tanner's team revealed that Müller was a tailor, in his early twenties (his age on official reports varies from twenty-three to twenty-five years old) and born in Saxe-Weimar, then Prussia, in what is now central Germany. While in England, he had been living, as a lodger at 16 Park Terrace, Bow, and so had reason to travel on the train from Fenchurch Street station. As a result of all this evidence, much of it circumstantial, a warrant was issued for the arrest of the suspect by Bow Street Magistrates Court on 19 July.

The bird, however, had flown, albeit at slow pace. Some four days prior to the warrant being granted, Müller had boarded the *Victoria* in London, a ship bound for New York. While he would escape Britain, he would do so on an old-fashioned boat that only used sail power. Tanner realised that he could still catch the suspect if he used a faster ship to arrive in the United States before Müller disappeared into the ever-growing metropolis on Manhattan Island. Hence, on 20 July, Tanner departed Liverpool on the steam-powered *City of Manchester*, with his assistant, Sergeant George Clarke. Clarke would be initiated into the Domatic Lodge in 1869 and it is likely that he would have been proposed by Tanner, the only police officer who was a member at that time. Clarke would later join Abbey Lodge No. 2030, but most importantly, he would feature in the Trial of the Detectives in 1877.

Tanner was so determined to convince the US authorities of the strength of the evidence and grant the extradition of Müller that the inspector also persuaded (or told) the two key witnesses to accompany him. As well as Tanner and Clarke, the jeweller, Death, and the cab driver, Matthews, also boarded the steamer for the ocean voyage. This was not an unusual police tactic—officers took a witness to Spain to identify Freemason Kenneth Noye as a murderer some 140 years later. Tanner and his party arrived in America in early August 1864. Unlike the Crippen case, there was no method of communicating with a ship in the middle of the Atlantic at this time; they would simply have to wait for the 'Victoria' to arrive.

Franz Müller was the first man to commit murder on a train; he was captured by a Freemason.

Unfortunately, this was not the best time to be an Englishman in New York. The American Civil War was at its height and many in the USA suspected the British of supporting the Confederate States.

On 25 August, Müller's ship arrived in New York harbour. Inspector Tanner and Sergeant Clarke, accompanied by an officer of the New York Police Department, boarded the *Victoria* and arrested him. A search of Müller's possessions by Clarke resulted in the recovery of a hat, believed to be the one stolen from Mr Briggs. A gold watch was also found, sewn up and concealed in a piece of cloth (the watch was later identified by the victim's son as one of the stolen items). Tanner then found eight volunteers and placed Müller in an impromptu identification parade, where Death picked him out as the man who had brought the gold chain into his shop. The evidence against the German was becoming ever stronger.

Now, an extradition warrant had to be applied for. Müller was placed in front of a New York court, where his lawyer made every effort to block it, appealing to the contemporary anti-British sentiment. He argued that, as the English had supplied a warship to the Confederacy, any treaties with the USA were null and void. Therefore, the application for extradition was a 'dead letter'. Unsurprisingly, the funding for the lawyer had been arranged by German immigrants living in New York. The judge, however, found on behalf of Inspector Tanner, and Müller was placed in his custody. The actual warrant allowing Müller to be returned to England was signed by the President, Abraham Lincoln. Despite the extradition being authorised at the highest level, there was still much anti-British sentiment and Tanner kept his prisoner under close guard; he feared that a mob might attempt to free him.

Tanner did not fail in his task and, on 3 September, Müller was taken on board an England-bound ship. The party arrived back in Liverpool in just under two weeks and the suspect was taken to London, where he was remanded in custody by Bow Street Magistrates Court. The trial at the Old Bailey opened on 24 October, with the senior judge presiding also being a Mason—Sir Frederick Pollock, the Lord Chief Baron. He had joined Socrates No. 511 (now No. 373) in 1833, when the Member of Parliament for Huntingdon, where the lodge was situated.

Müller pleaded not guilty to the charge of murder and the prosecution counsel set out the case against him, speculating that the dozing victim had been attacked with his own heavy handled walking stick. Much was made of the evidential value of the two hats, one found at the scene of the crime and the other found in Müller's possession. The cab driver, Matthews, reiterated that the hat from the carriage belonged to Müller, as did the wife of a German tailor, who was an associate of the defendant. Both identified it by its unique (or as they said in Victorian times and still in Masonic ritual, 'peculiar') lining. The hat seized in New York was shown to Mr Briggs's hat maker and he verified that, while alterations had been made, it was headwear that he had made for the murdered man.

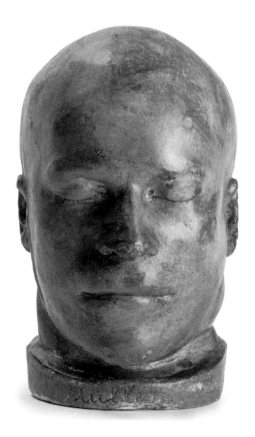

Death mask of Franz Müller, arrested by a Masonic detective and condemned to death by a Masonic judge.

The defence tried to discredit Matthews, the cab driver, suggesting that he was motivated by the reward money. Müller even called a prostitute to give evidence on his behalf, but it was all in vain. The German tailor was found guilty and sentenced to death by Worshipful Brother, His Honour, Sir Frederick Pollock. The King of Prussia pleaded for a stay of execution, but was unsuccessful, and on 14 November, Müller was taken onto the scaffold outside Newgate Prison, having (allegedly) admitted his guilt to the Lutheran pastor, who took his last confession. Watched by a vast and drunken crowd, the murderer was hanged. Once declared dead, Müller was cut down and taken back into Newgate Prison. A plaster cast was taken of his shaved head and this 'death mask' can still be seen in the Metropolitan Police crime museum. Müller was not the last public execution, but by the Capital Punishment within Prisons Act of 1868, this grisly form of mass entertainment finally came to an end.

Matthews did eventually receive the reward money of £300 offered for information leading to a conviction. The large sum would bring him little happiness, as owing much money and failing to repay it, he was detained in the debtors' prison. The vast majority of the cash went to his creditors, with Matthews later complaining that his family had been left to starve while he was incarcerated.

More positively, this crime was to have an impact on railway safety. In 1868, trains were required by law to have a communication cord, so passengers could summon help from the railway crew. Newly built carriages also had corridors, ensuring an escape route for any passenger under attack. These changes took place slowly; a further murder on a train occurred in 1881 in very similar circumstances to the murder of Thomas Briggs.

While safety would be improved, jurisdiction relating to responsibility for investigating crimes committed on trains was often unclear. As in this case, policing of railway crime at first fell to the local force, but over time, the railway companies formed their own separate police, but these officers could have other non-police duties. It was not until 1949 that this would become one national force—the British Transport Police.

Returning to the nineteenth century, this investigation by Tanner added to the growing reputation of the Scotland Yard Detective Department. Tanner also enjoyed his Masonry. Within eighteen months of being initiated, he was exalted into the Rose of Denmark Royal Arch Chapter No. 975. He was the founder member of the Star Lodge No. 1275 in 1869, which originally met in the Marquis of Granby Tavern in New Cross Road, South East London (the publican was also a founder) and later in Greenwich; while these locations may be considered now as London, historically they were in Kent and the lodge was controlled by that Masonic Province. Tanner appears to have been the only police officer in the lodge, with the membership made up of men from many professions, from a vicar to an artist. The Star folded in 2010 due to lack of members. Most importantly, Tanner was the 'Most Excellent Zerubbabel' of Rose Denmark Chapter in 1872, but beyond his installation, he never attended any further meetings as his health was failing. That said, he was able to attend the Domatic Chapter No. 177 in the November of that year as a guest.

Brother Dick Tanner died in 1873; he was only forty-one years old and his demise is shown in the Domatic Lodge records the following year—news, like sailing ships, travelled slowly at that time. He had been medically retired from the police for some three years

Sir Frederick Pollock, the judge and Mason who sentenced Müller to death.

Grave of Inspector Tanner. The Star of David is a Masonic symbol, not an indication that Tanner was Jewish.

and became the licensee of the White Swan public house in Winchester, Hampshire. The cause of his death was recorded as 'apoplexy'; in Victorian times, this meant death after suddenly falling into an unconscious state. His funeral was attended by many Scotland Yard detectives, including the head of the department, Superintendent 'Dolly' Williamson, a member of the Lodge of Fortitude and Old Cumberland No. 12 (the son of one of the first superintendents appointed in 1829).

Herein lies another mystery. Brother Tanner is buried in Winchester's Roman Catholic cemetery. Unusually, for such a place, the Star of David is displayed on his gravestone. The evidence suggests that he was not of the Jewish faith, as records show that he was baptised in 1831 at St John's in Egham, Surrey and married in 1857 at St Martin's-in-the-Field in Trafalgar Square, both Anglican churches. His wife, Emma Jane (*née* Beecher) may have been Jewish, as there appears to be no baptism record, but this may just have been lost. In any case, she died thirty years after her husband and was placed in the same grave. The Star of David, in this case, is a Masonic symbol as used on the Holy Royal Arch breast jewel. As further evidence of the use of Masonic symbolism in his cemetery, a few feet away from Tanner's burial plot is a gravestone decorated with the Square and Compasses.

Domatic No. 177 grew in popularity with police officers and several other members of the Metropolitan Police joined the lodge, including Chief Inspector William Palmer, Inspector William Turpin, and Police Constables George Silverton, Edward Hancock, and George Mumford. By the time of Tanner's death, Brother George Clarke had been promoted to Chief Inspector, but Clarke and Palmer would soon find themselves on the wrong side of the law.

31

A Right Royal Scandal and the Seeds of a Masonic Conspiracy Story

Masonic Connection
Grand Master
Several lovers at the centre of the scandal

Date
1868: Prince of Wales initiated into Swedish Masonry and scandal begun
1870: Divorce Hearing
1874: Prince of Wales installed as Grand Master
1901: Coronation as Edward VII

Connection to London
Westminster Hall: Location of divorce hearing

Lodges
Grand Masters' No.1
Royal Alpha No. 16
All Souls No. 170
Prince of Wales's No. 259
Apollo University No. 357
Navy No. 2612
Household Royal Brigade No. 2614
Sancta Maria No. 2682
Kells No. 244 (Ireland)
Enniskillen No. 891 (Ireland)

Now we turn to a scandal that erupted in 1870 involving the Prince Albert Edward, Prince of Wales, son of Queen Victoria, and later King Edward VII. He is the last Grand Master to have been called to give evidence in court, in a case that was a great Victorian scandal that shocked society. This sorry story may, as we shall see, be the origin of one of the most damaging Masonic conspiracy stories. Worst of all, it shows how the Establishment could imprison someone, without trial, for the rest of their life, to look after 'its own'.

Edward VII. As Prince of Wales, he was Grand Master of England.

The prince, like many of the royalty featured in the Bible (King David, King Solomon, and others), had a weakness for women; consequentially, he was known as 'Dirty Bertie' (to the Royal Family he was 'Albert'). Like David's outrageous treatment of his loyal general, Uriah (whom he placed in the worst part of the battle to ensure he died so that he could steal his wife, Bathsheba; see II Samuel, Chapter 11), the Prince of Wales would also take advantage of his loyal subjects and their wives.

For many at that time, divorce was unimaginable and challenging the behaviour of the Royal Family even more so. One man who did not follow this line was Sir Charles Mordaunt, a Conservative MP who lived in the magnificent Walton Hall near the village of Wellesbourne in Warwickshire; he was the MP for the south of the county. In 1866, Sir Charles married a pretty young lady, Harriet Moncreiffe, the daughter of a Scottish nobleman. Despite her beauty, Charles seems to have been more interested in hunting and fishing. Lady Harriet also seemed to have enjoyed hunting, albeit for lovers.

Perhaps it was Harriet's love of horses that drew her to Sir Frederick Johnstone, a racehorse owner and later Conservative MP. She also had secret liaisons with Viscount Lowry Cole, also a Tory MP (and later the 4th Earl of Enniskillen) and, most scandalously, the Prince of Wales. Her affairs usually took place in hotel rooms, away from prying eyes, but, as we shall see, possibly also at Walton Hall. Oddly, unlike her husband, all her lovers appear to have been Freemasons.

Viscount Cole had been initiated into an Irish lodge, Enniskillen No. 891 (unsurprising, given his later title) in 1875; he later joined another lodge, this time in the south of Ireland in County Meath, Kells No. 244.

Sir Frederick Johnstone had been initiated into an Oxford lodge in 1859, where the Prince of Wales was later a member, Apollo University No. 357. He had several connections to Dorset; he was a member of the local yeomanry regiment and joined All Souls Lodge No. 170 in Weymouth in 1871.

The Prince of Wales was initiated in Stockholm in 1868 by the Swedish king into the *Nordska Forsta* lodge, where he received all ten degrees of the Swedish Rite (Scandinavian Freemasonry follows a very different degree system from England). On return to London, he was able to prove himself a Master Mason to the then Grand Master, the Earl of Zetland. He was then given the honorary rank of Past Grand Master (within a year of being initiated). In addition to his Swedish and English Masonry, the future King Edward VII was also to become Patron of the Grand Lodges of Scotland and Ireland. The Prince seemed to thoroughly enjoy the Craft and joined several lodges within the next twelve years—Royal Alpha No. 16, Apollo University No. 357, Prince of Wales No. 295, and the Grand Masters' lodge No. 1. Additionally, he was founder and first Master of three lodges—Household Royal Brigade No. 2614, Navy No. 2612, and Sancta Maria No. 2682.

The scandal began to unfold in the summer of 1868, the same year as the Prince of Wales's initiation. Sir Charles returned home to Walton Hall to find the prince enjoying a demonstration of Lady Harriet's carriage driving skills. She was using her favourite pair of white ponies. Sir Charles was outraged; he knew the Prince's reputation and ordered him to leave. He also knew how to hurt his wife; he shot the horses in front of her. This brutal act would have done little to endear him to his young bride.

Matters came to a head in 1869 when Harriet gave birth to a daughter who was initially thought to be blind. In the mind of the new mother, this affliction was due to a sexually transmitted disease, which she must have caught from a lover and passed on to the unborn child. She was also unsure if Sir Charles was the father and riven with guilt, she confessed to her numerous affairs with Lord Cole, Sir Frederick, the Prince, and other men. It should be noted that the child actually suffered no defect at all, but guilt can play strange tricks on the mind.

Sir Charles was outraged and planned his revenge. He knew that naming the Prince in a divorce case would show him as a cuckolded fool, but it would be far more damaging to the Royal Family. Harriet received no support from her family. Her mother declared her mad. She was then removed from Walton Hall and imprisoned in various rented houses (or gilded cages) where her husband's loyal servants could spy on her behaviour. It was reported that she was indeed of disturbed mind, with reports of the (former) lady of the house smashing crockery, eating coal, and chewing the carpet, as well as binge eating or starving herself. We will never know if this was an act or real, but perhaps Harriet was aware that if declared insane, she could not be divorced by her husband.

Numerous doctors examined Harriet as to her mental state. Significantly, she was seen several times in Worthing, Sussex and Bickley, Kent by the surgeon to the Prince of Wales, Sir William Gull. This man has become a major character in Masonic conspiracies. At the later divorce hearing, Gull was to note that Lady Harriet had 'no mental comprehension' with 'a meaningless laugh'. In consequence, he concluded that she was mad, or as he explained it, 'incapable of mind.'

Sir William Gull. A long-time Jack the Ripper suspect, this doctor gave evidence to show that Harriet Mordaunt was mad.

The divorce hearing was held in Westminster Hall (part of the Houses of Parliament) in February 1870. The Prince was not named in the case (Mordaunt *v.* Mordaunt, Cole and Johnstone), but he was subpoenaed to attend. The hearing was a sell-out—but ladies were forbidden from the public gallery. The Prince eventually gave evidence on the fifth day and strongly denied any impropriety. The audience in the gallery were, however, to be disappointed, as the barrister for Sir Charles failed to ask any questions of the Prince, allowing him 'off the hook'. Furthermore, the lawyer failed to prove that Lady Harriet was guilty of adultery and therefore failed to obtain a divorce for his client. Some years later, it would seem that Brother, the Lord Cole 'fell on his sword' and accepted that he had had an affair with Harriet and the matter was at an end. It has been suggested that he was offered an inducement by the Prince of Wales to 'draw a line under the matter' (as we would say in modern speech).

It would appear that Lady Harriet was placed in various asylums including a house in Sutton, Surrey. She was to spend the remaining thirty-five years of her life in such establishments. If she was sane, this was a disgrace and an abuse of power. She died in 1906 and was buried in Brompton cemetery in west London.

Freemasonry has much reason to be grateful for the patronage of Prince Albert Edward, the Prince of Wales, who became Grand Master in 1874. In 1814, there were under seven hundred lodges, but by the end of his Grand Mastership (he resigned on his ascension to the throne as Edward VII in 1901), the number had grown to 2,850—a four-fold expansion. However, his scandalous conduct with Lady Harriet Mordaunt may have sown the seeds

Walton Hall, the Warwickshire house where a Member of Parliament believed that the Prince of Wales had seduced his wife.

for a Masonic conspiracy story that has possibly damaged the Craft more than any other—Jack the Ripper. The reader should consider the similarity between the Walter Sickert tale of alleged Masonic involvement in the Whitechapel Murders and the Mordaunt divorce scandal. Perhaps the most obvious are as follows:

Involvement of a Royal prince, who is heir to the throne
Illicit affair
Baby born
Involvement of Dr William Gull
Women involved in affair silenced

As we will see, another scandal would draw Most Worshipful Brother, his Royal Highness the Prince of Wales to court again.

32

Trial of the Detectives:
Masonic Evidence at the Old Bailey

Masonic Connection
Honest and corrupt detectives
Dishonest lawyer
Masonic influence used on a prosecution witness
Attendance at a lodge meeting used as an alibi
Prosecution and defence counsel at court

Date
1877: Corruption exposed

Connection to London
Great Scotland Yard: Headquarters of Detective Department
Northumberland Street: Criminals ran their racket from a ground floor office
Charing Cross Railway Station: Corrupt information given to criminals under the railway arches
The Silver Cross, Whitehall: Corrupt payments made to officers in this public house
Fleet Street: Location of lodge meeting used as alibi
Marlborough Street: Attempt made to persuade a 'brother' Mason to change evidence outside the magistrates' court
Old Bailey: Court where trials held

Lodges
Grand Master's No. 1
Lodge of Friendship No. 6
Lodge of Fortitude and Old Cumberland No. 12
Robert Burns No. 25
Domatic No. 177
Zetland No. 511
Royal Alfred No. 780
Dunheved No. 789
Southern Star No. 1158

St Peter and St Pauls' No. 1410
Chine No. 1884
Gallery No. 1928
Abbey No. 2030
Avondale No. 2395
Justicia No. 2563
Mendelssohn No. 2661 (erased)
Sir Edward Clarke No. 3601
Lodge of Independence with Philanthropy No. 2 (India)
East Medina Chapter No. 175 (Royal Arch)

The 1877 'Trial of the Detectives' or 'Turf Fraud Scandal' was a shock for Victorian Society as it was the first high-profile case of police corruption. It involved Freemasons as police officers (honest and corrupt), the accused and lawyers (again, good and bad), together with witnesses both for the prosecution and the defence. It has been claimed that the most corrupt detective was a Mason, but there is no evidence of his membership. There can be few cases at the Old Bailey where the secretary and several other members of a lodge have given evidence about the proceedings of a Masonic meeting and whether the Junior Warden was present. At the time, it was also the longest ever trial, lasting over two weeks.

The trial had a major impact on the organisation of the Metropolitan Police and the Detective Department at Scotland Yard. The lack of supervision highlighted by the case resulted in the creation of the Criminal Investigation Department (CID). This case also shows how criminals seize on advancements in communication to find further methods of committing crime. At this time, the railway network covered the United Kingdom and journeys that had taken days now took just a few hours. The telegraph had revolutionised international communication and sending messages to Europe and even the United States of America was commonplace. As will be explained, Paris and Rotterdam both feature in this case; crime was becoming international.

The 'Turf' in this investigation relates to a horse racing track. In the nineteenth century (and indeed until 1961), it was illegal to place bets on horse racing, except at the race course itself. This created an underground network of illegal bookmakers (who took bets), often composed of men involved in all manner of other crime. As a result, bookmakers were seen as ideal informants for the detectives at Scotland Yard. If the police officers associated with such 'scoundrels' (as one of the fraudsters was referred to during the trial), then intelligence on more serious crimes could be obtained. One of the witnesses at the trial, Detective Inspector George Greenham, observed, 'when I want to get information I often have to mix with very bad company.' This is still in the same today; the worst criminals can give the best information. Greenham would later become a Mason.

The origin of the 'Trial of the Detectives' was at a meeting in 1872 at the Angel Hotel, Islington in North London, between two Scotsmen—Sergeant John Meiklejohn (by 1876, a Chief Inspector in the Detective Department at Scotland Yard and later Superintendent of the Railway Police) and William Kurr, a bookmaker (or, as he described himself 'a racing man') who had been convicted of forgery. Kurr had originally been employed as a clerk by South Eastern Railways, but he soon found horse racing to be a far more profitable business.

It has been suggested by some, including Short (1993), that Meiklejohn and Kurr's initial encounter was at a Masonic meeting, but there is no record of any lodge ever having used the Angel Hotel. It was certainly not said to be a Masonic gathering at the subsequent trial, where other Masonic issues, including details of other meetings, were freely discussed in evidence. Neither is there any record of Meiklejohn being a member of the Craft in England or Ireland (albeit he could have joined in Scotland).

Kurr also used the name 'Gifford' and was from Dunblane, near Stirling in central Scotland. Meiklejohn originated from the same area, and this was to give the corrupt officer an advantage when receiving large amounts of cash; Scotland used different banknotes, but they had the same face value as the English currency. Moreover, the Scottish banks kept fewer records of transactions and therefore this offered an opportunity to launder English notes. As we have seen, rail travel had made the journey from London to Scotland a few hours rather than a week in a stage coach.

Taking advantage of the new means of communication, Kurr planned an audacious scheme to swindle French 'punters' out of large sums of money. The fraud was simple; an article would be written in an Edinburgh newspaper, *The Sport*, stating that bookmakers were not giving proper odds at races, but if they placed their bets through the (fictitious) Mr Montgomery, he would negotiate better odds and advise on the best horses to bet on. By bribing jockeys, the gang could also guarantee some winning advice to further convince their victims of Mr Montgomery's expertise. Additionally, the newspaper report was to be translated into French and thereby attract money from abroad. Quick and easy money has always attracted investors. The fraudsters needed, however, to ensure that the police were kept 'onside' and would not interfere in their money-making scheme.

Kurr joined forces with a convicted criminal, Harry Benson (by now calling himself George Yonge), as his main accomplice. It should be noted that there is no record of any such Benson or Yonge joining an English Masonic lodge. Kurr and Benson had originally met on the Isle of Wight. The latter had been brought up in Paris and spoke fluent French, an important skill for the fraud he was to commit with Kurr. His first attempt at making money from crime involved a swindle playing on the sympathies of Londoners for the victims of the Franco-Prussian War. Many northern French towns had suffered badly in the fighting and Benson claimed to be raising funds for them; however, he pocketed the cash. He was caught and imprisoned in 1872. In an attempt to commit suicide, he had set fire to his cell and had been badly burnt on the buttocks, leaving him crippled.

Kurr's brother Frederick and two other men (Bale and Murray) were recruited into the gang. To further ensure the success of the criminal enterprise, Kurr enlisted the aid of a corrupt solicitor, to deal with any legal problems. This man was Edward Froggatt, whose practice was based in Argyle Street in central London. Froggatt was a Mason; he had joined Robert Burns Lodge No. 25 in March 1869, which met at Freemasons' Hall in Great Queen Street. Froggatt also appears to have had a home on the Isle of Wight, as he joined a Chapter there—East Medina No. 175.

An office was required to give the appearance of a legitimate business. On behalf of Kurr and Benson, Froggatt rented 8 Northumberland Street, a short walk from Great Scotland Yard and the gang's corrupt police contacts. The office was hired in a false name, demonstrating Froggatt's criminal conduct. As proof that not all members of the Craft are of questionable character, the owner of the premises, Brother George Flintoff, would later appear as a prosecution witness against his brother Masons. Flintoff, a civil engineer, who lived on the Strand, had been initiated into Royal Alfred Lodge No. 780 in 1868. At the time, it met near Kew Bridge.

Kurr and Benson's fictitious company in Northumberland Street was styled 'Brooks and Co. of Glasgow'. At this time, such a betting agency was known as a 'sworn bookmaker's bureau'. Other premises in central London were also rented as accommodation for the gang members, all under false names. Even a bank was invented to facilitate the fraud; cheques from the 'Royal Bank of London' were printed to pay the victims of their crimes.

While the major fraud was being planned, Kurr and Benson ran other dishonest schemes to bring in cash. To guarantee police 'protection', they paid Chief Inspector Meiklejohn large sums of money and valuable jewellery. Given that the value of money has increased one hundred-fold since 1877, the dishonest detective was regularly receiving pay offs worth today up to £20,000. As a result, he was even able to buy a large house in Lambeth for cash. These payments were often made in public houses in south and central London, particularly the Silver Cross, which was walking distance from Great Scotland Yard. In return, Meiklejohn ensured that the fraudsters were warned of arrest warrants issued against them in several places, including Scotland and Ireland.

Meiklejohn was seemingly able to draw more officers into his web of corruption; this included two more Chief Inspectors in the Detective Department—Nathaniel Druscovich and William Palmer. At the trial, it would also be suggested that Chief Inspector George Clarke had also been involved in assisting the fraudsters. It is worth examining the backgrounds of the other senior officers in the Department:

Druscovich was born in the East End of London, but lived for part of his youth in what is now Romania, from whence his father originated. He joined the Metropolitan Police and was promoted to sergeant at just twenty-two years old and around his thirtieth birthday, he was appointed a Chief Inspector in the Detective Department. This surprised some of his colleagues; he was fluent in several languages, but not English. His knowledge of French and other European tongues was, however, most useful as crime spread its tentacles ever wider. For example, Irish republicans were committing acts of terrorism at that time and used Paris as a base. Despite his successful Scotland Yard career, Druscovich was in debt. Foolishly, he took Meiklejohn's advice and borrowed £60 from Kurr, a known criminal. He is likely to have associated with Meiklejohn off duty, as the two officers lived only a few hundred yards apart in south London—Druscovich at 64 South Lambeth Road and Meiklejohn at 202. As with Meiklejohn, there is no evidence that Druscovich was a member of a Masonic lodge.

Palmer was born in Carshalton, Surrey on the outskirts of London and joined the Metropolitan Police in 1861. He was another rising star, making Chief Inspector at Scotland Yard in less than ten years. He was also a Freemason in the Domatic Lodge, together with Chief Inspector Clarke (both men joined in 1869) and other members of the Detective Department. In the Craft, he was progressing towards the Worshipful Master's chair; at the time of his trial he was Junior Warden, and as the usual procedure is that promotion is granted annually, he was just two years away from being the head of the lodge.

8 Northumberland Street, the ground floor office from where Kurr and his gang ran the 'Turf Swindle'.

The main characters in the Trial of the Detectives: William Kurr in the centre, in prison uniform, with Harry Benson gave evidence against the four police officers (Meiklejohn, Druscovich, Palmer, and Clarke) and the dishonest solicitor, Froggatt.

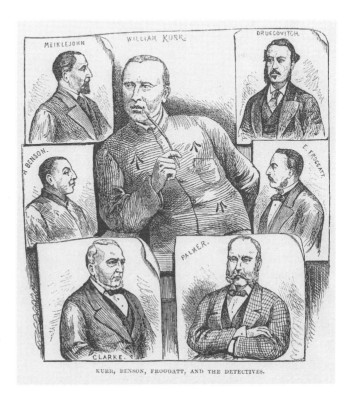

KURR, BENSON, FROGGATT, AND THE DETECTIVES.

George Clarke was the senior Chief Inspector in the Detective Department and was known as the 'Chieftain', possibly due to his age. Clarke was sixty years old, some twenty years older than his colleagues Meiklejohn, Druscovich, and Palmer. Clarke was the senior Chief Inspector and second in command to the head of the department, but while he was senior to Palmer at work, he was three ranks below him in the Craft. In 1877, Clarke was the Inner Guard; to progress to be Master, he would have to be Junior, then Senior Deacon, before being Junior Warden. As a sergeant, Clarke had travelled to the USA to arrest a murder suspect with another member of the lodge, Inspector Dick Tanner. In May 1877, Clarke became a joining member of the Abbey Lodge No. 2030, which then met in Caxton Hall (a short walk from the New Scotland Yard, which opened in 1967).

Superintendent Adolphus 'Dolly' Williamson was the head of the Detective Department. He had been a Freemason since May 1859 and was in a senior lodge—the Fortitude and Old Cumberland No. 12. He had worked at the 'Yard' for many years, and his work address is shown as such when he was initiated.

Kurr's plan was initially successful and money was paid into the fraudulent business by naïve gamblers. A French woman, Madame de Goncourt, 'invested' £10,000 (today about £1 million) in the form a cheque; this was paid into an account opened in a false name and the cash withdrawn. If they had been satisfied with this significant amount of money, they may well have escaped justice, but the gang then became greedy. They attempted to persuade the French lady to place another £30,000 into the scheme, but she was warned by her banker that she was being swindled. She therefore did not transfer the second sum to England. Madame de Goncourt then crossed the Channel and instructed a solicitor to help her recover the

Trial of the Detectives, 1877. A sketch of the Old Bailey court room, with the defendants to the left and the jury in the centre rear.

money. Her lawyer went to Scotland Yard on 25 September and reported the matter as a criminal fraud. At this point, Chief Inspector Druscovich, who was already receiving bribes from Kurr, was appointed as the investigating officer for the Turf Fraud case.

Given that the office of the gang was a stone's throw from Scotland Yard, their arrests could have made very quickly, but, rather than being apprehended, the fraudsters were tipped off by Druscovich (under the arches of Charing Cross Station). He informed Kurr that Scotland Yard was aware of the gang's activities and that warrants had been issued for their arrest. Druscovich also warned that the police knew the serial numbers of the English bank notes drawn out of the bank following Madame de Goncourt's first payment by cheque. Kurr shut the 'bureau' and made his way to Derby (in a circular route via Carlisle and Leeds) and then stayed in the Midlands town with Meiklejohn, who owned a house there. The corrupt detective promised to find out if the bank notes had been 'stopped'—i.e. deemed worthless. To prevent this happening, Kurr and Benson made their way to Scotland to change the notes into (what they believed to be) untraceable Scottish currency.

The cash was paid into a Glasgow bank and then to further dampen the trail, the money was then drawn out from the Berwick branch (on the English side of the border), but in Scottish notes. Some of these notes (not as untraceable as the gang thought, it would seem) were later found in Meiklejohn's possession and others had been used to purchase jewellery that was recovered from Druscovich.

Meiklejohn also travelled north of the border and introduced Kurr and Benson to a bank manager near his home town, the Bridge of Allan. Here is a clear demonstration of the scale of his corrupt involvement; not only was he giving them information, he was actively assisting them to evade justice and to keep their ill-gotten gains. With a Scotland Yard senior officer acting as a reference, the bank manager had no reservation in opening an account for Captain Gifford and Mr Yonge (or as we know them, Kurr and Benson).

Benson decided to return to familiar territory, the Isle of Wight, to 'keep his head down'. Perhaps, he also met Froggatt 'on the island'; as we have seen, the corrupt solicitor had Masonic business there too. Unfortunately, other (honest) Scotland Yard detectives received information about Benson's whereabouts and were planning to detain him. The date by now was 10 November 1876 (this date became significant at the later trial of the officers) and a telegram was sent to Captain Gifford (Kurr) in Scotland by 'W. Brown' from the Strand in London. This advised Kurr to warn Benson, who was laying low in Shanklin (the main town on the Isle of Wight), of the threat of arrest. At the later trial, it would be suggested that Chief Inspector Palmer was the true author of this telegram.

As a result of the message, Benson and two other gang members left England and sailed to Rotterdam in Holland. While improved international communication can provide criminals with opportunities to commit crime, it can also be used by the police. Superintendent Williamson had sent a 'wanted poster' to European police forces and Dutch officers spotted and detained Benson. Froggatt, the dishonest solicitor, made efforts to have him released, but without success. Corrupt as ever, Meiklejohn even considered sending a false message, purporting to be from Superintendent Williamson, stating that the wrong man had been arrested.

Williamson, still unaware of the involvement of Druscovich, sent the Chief Inspector to Rotterdam to collect Benson, so that the villain could face justice in England. Druscovich initially returned empty handed and went on leave—much to the annoyance of his superior officer, who ordered him back to Holland. Under such pressure, the corrupt detective had little option but to bring Benson back to London.

Druscovich knew that his poor handling of the Turf Fraud was impacting on his career. A Detective Sergeant from Scotland Yard later gave evidence that he asked the Chief Inspector how the case was progressing, to which he replied 'Damn the turf swindle! I wish I had never heard anything of it.' Druscovich also intimated that he suspected that Meiklejohn was corruptly involved, but later admitted that he had not informed Superintendent Williamson of his suspicions. Given that he was also taking bribes from the gang, this is unsurprising.

On New Year's Eve 1876, Brother Kurr was arrested after a short chase in Essex Road, Islington and taken to the local police station. His arrest had been made by a future Mason, Detective Constable John Littlechild, who would later be initiated into Zetland Lodge No. 511 in London in 1894. Once he had retired from the police, Littlechild joined Mendelssohn No. 2661 (now defunct) and Justicia No. 2563, now in Twickenham. He was involved in several famous cases as a police and private detective, even putting forward a suspect for the Jack the Ripper murders.

A search of Kurr at the police station revealed that he was in possession of a loaded revolver. Superintendent Williamson then searched his home at 29 Marquess Road, Islington and, under the mattress, discovered a wrap of tissue paper containing twenty-one diamonds and three rubies. Littlechild continued the enquiries at the police station and during the same evening, Flintoff, who had legitimately rented out 8 Northumberland Street, was taken to Islington and shown Kurr. Flintoff had no difficulty in identifying the Scot as the man who had rented his office. This placed Kurr at the heart of the criminal activity.

The following day, an initial hearing case was held at Marlborough Street Magistrates' Court. At the entrance to the building, the dishonest solicitor, Froggatt, endeavoured to pervert the course of justice by making two attempts to persuade Flintoff to change his identification evidence. The first was the cheap option; he appealed to Flintoff's sense of Masonic brotherhood. Froggatt gave a Masonic sign and told him that Kurr 'was a Freemason in distress.' During this conversation, Flintoff tried to confirm if Froggatt was, indeed, a Mason and asked 'How old is your mother?' (a Masonic method of discretely establishing the number of a brother's first or 'Mother' lodge). Evidence was given by Froggatt's clerk that his employer had said to Flintoff, 'She was once twenty-five, but now I am in the Chapter … something was then said about some number, 175.' The first reference is to the Robert Burns Lodge No. 25 in London, but the second relates to the East Medina Holy Royal Arch Chapter, which still meets on the Isle of Wight.

Despite Froggatt revealing himself as a Craft and Royal Arch Mason, Flintoff refused to budge and firmly stated that 'Freemasonry was not intended to assist persons of that description.' Having failed with the Masonic method, the next tactic was more direct—money. Froggatt offered the landlord £50 to state that Kurr was not the man who had rented his office. Again, Flintoff refused. This meeting at the court would later land Froggatt in the dock himself. With Kurr in custody, Benson and the other members of the gang were rounded up by the Metropolitan Police.

The Turf Fraud gang were tried at the Old Bailey in April 1877. Benson was defended by Horace Avory, a barrister later known as a 'Hanging Judge'. Avory had been initiated into the St Peter and St Pauls' Lodge No. 1410, which met in Newport Pagnall in Buckinghamshire. The prosecution was led by a future Mason—the Solicitor-General, Sir Hardinge Giffard QC, later 1st Earl Halsbury and not to be confused with 'Gifford' (the alias used by Kurr). Sir Hardinge would subsequently become a very senior member of the United Grand Lodge of England and hold the office of Grand Warden. Four years after this trial, he was initiated into the Lodge of Friendship No. 6 and later joined Dunheved Lodge No. 789 in Launceston, Cornwall, where he was the Member of Parliament. This eminent Mason would serve as Lord Chancellor on three occasions.

The evidence presented by Sir Hardinge was overwhelming and the whole gang was found guilty. Kurr, Benson, and the other members were given long sentences—ten years imprisonment with hard labour. The Treasury Department, who had been involved due to the currency issues raised in the case, then wrote to the Home Office, who were responsible for the Metropolitan Police. Grave concerns were raised about the conduct of Chief Inspectors Meiklejohn and Palmer, and the possibility of a corrupt relationship between officers and the fraudsters.

The authorities took their time and it was not until July of that year that arrests were made. By now, Druscovich's conduct was under suspicion and he, Meiklejohn, and Palmer were all taken into custody and refused bail. Chief Inspector Clarke was to be arrested later. Kurr and his gang were visited in prison and offered a deal; their sentences would be reduced from ten years to just two, in return for giving evidence against the corrupt officers. It was an offer they could not refuse, especially considering the harsh conditions in nineteenth century jails.

The Trial of the Detectives would now expose large-scale police corruption to a shocked Victorian public. On 22 October 1877, the four officers found themselves in the dock at the Old Bailey, together with the solicitor, Froggatt, all charged with perverting the course of justice. It was just six months since the Turf Fraud gang had appeared at the same court. By this time, Meiklejohn was a superintendent in the Railway Police at Derby. It is ironic that as this case involved allegedly 'bent' detectives, Chief Inspector Druscovich's barrister was named Mr Straight. Brother Douglas Straight QC had been initiated into the Grand Master's Lodge No. 1 in 1874 and would later continue his Masonry in British India. While serving as a judge in the city of Allahabad, he joined the Lodge of Independence with Philanthropy (then No. 391, but now Lodge No. 2 under the Grand Lodge of India). Straight was also a member of Gallery No. 1928 in London.

Chief Inspector Clarke (a Mason) was defended by his namesake and a fellow brother, Sir Edward Clarke. The latter was to gain such eminence in the Craft that a lodge (No. 3601) would be named after him. Brother Froggatt's defence counsel was also a member of the Craft—Brother Avory, who had defended Benson at the first court case.

As the trial began, Kurr accused several members of Victorian society of being involved in corruption, including a lord, an 'honourable' gentleman, an army captain, and several officers; these wild exaggerations tainted his account. The case against Meiklejohn and Druscovich, however, was strong; there was correspondence between Meiklejohn and Kurr. Likewise, money and jewellery connected to the fraudsters had been found in the possession of the officers. The enquiry had been extensive and a wine merchant from Leeds was brought to London to state that Meiklejohn had changed a £100 Scottish bank note into English notes. His sister gave evidence that he had sent £100 to their father's farm near Dunblane, but the family had refused to receive it. Even his brother, a former police sergeant in the Metropolitan Police, was called to give evidence against him.

The case against Palmer was less convincing and revolved around the telegram sent to Kurr telling him to warn Benson to leave the Isle of Wight. Frank Rayner, the postmaster in Shanklin, confirmed at the Old Bailey that this message was received and passed to 'Captain Gifford'. Rayner subsequently joined the Chine Lodge No. 1884 in 1881. While, as we have seen, the message was signed 'W. Brown', Superintendent Williamson and Henry Wilson, a clerk at Scotland Yard, gave evidence that the handwriting belonged to Palmer. Here is a Mason and a police officer (Williamson) having no qualms about giving damning evidence against another Mason and police officer (Palmer).

The message in question had been sent on the evening of 10th November 1876– at the same time as a meeting of the Domatic Lodge. The secretary, Worshipful Brother Thomas Williams, produced the attendance register, to show that both Palmer and Clarke had been present at that time and therefore could not be responsible for sending the telegram. The meeting had taken place at the (now demolished) Anderton's Hotel, 162–164 Fleet Street and the presence of the two police officers between 4.30 p.m. until nearly 11 p.m. was verified by other Domatic members—Brothers Edward White, George Everett, and William Foxcroft, together with a visiting Freemason, John Willis. Despite many members of the Metropolitan Police being in Domatic, none of these witnesses were officers and their jobs included telegraphic cabinet maker, builder, and leather seller. All four gave evidence that they had not seen Palmer (or Clarke) leave or send messages out of the room. As Junior Warden, Palmer occupied a large distinctive seat in the meeting and at the subsequent banquet (as the Festive Board was then called). If he had left his seat, Masonic tradition is such that another brother would have to occupy it. Additionally, unlike Meiklejohn and Druscovich, there was no tangible evidence of any bribes accepted by Palmer (or Clarke), simply the word of Kurr and his associates.

Superintendent Williamson freely admitted at the Old Bailey that he had given the alleged author of the telegram time off to attend such meetings. Brother 'Dolly' stated in his evidence:

> I had frequently given Palmer leave to quit the office early in the afternoon for the purpose of attending the lodge. I should think it would take about forty minutes to walk from his house to Fleet Street.

While the issue of the telegram was the only tangible allegation against Palmer, the evidence against Clarke was particularly weak and consisted of little more than vague allegations made by Kurr. Additionally, several Scotland Yard colleagues including Colonel Henderson, the Commissioner of the Police, gave strong character reference on his behalf. It is notable that such character evidence was not given for the other officers in the dock. In his defence speech for Chief Inspector Clarke, barrister Sir Edward Clarke was damning regarding Kurr and Benson, describing them as 'creatures… with smiling lips and glossy words'.

Unsurprisingly, Meiklejohn and Druscovich, together with Froggatt, were found guilty. Despite the strong evidence of his innocence provided by the brethren of his lodge, Palmer was also found guilty. Clarke was acquitted and continued to attend Domatic Lodge; he is shown at the Centenary meeting in 1886. The guilty men were all given two years in prison. This does seem unfair given the different scales of corruption. Meiklejohn is possibly the most corrupt officer to have served at Scotland Yard. He received vast amounts of money, gold, and jewellery and had actively assisted the criminals to launder their stolen loot. In a supporting role, Druscovich had also taken bribes and met the villains to give them warnings instead of arresting them. On the other hand, Palmer had sent a telegram (and this was disputed) and there was no evidence presented that he had received any money from the villains.

On various anti-Masonic internet sites, this case is used as an example of conspiracy and corruption, but when analysed, this theory simply does not add up. Firstly, there is no evidence that the most corrupt officers, Meiklejohn and Druscovich, were members of the Craft. Many of the meetings between Meiklejohn and Kurr often took place in the Silver Cross public house, not at a Masonic lodge. Likewise, if Freemasonry has such power, Palmer, the Mason, being found guilty despite several other members of the Craft giving evidence in his defence is hard to believe. Furthermore, his sentence was the same as non-Masons, Meiklejohn and Druscovich, who, as we have seen, committed far more corrupt deeds. Indeed, the jury recommended mercy for Palmer (and Druscovich) due to their long police service, but this was ignored. Kurr, the gang leader, was said to be a Mason by his corrupt solicitor, Froggatt. However, Kurr was found guilty at the original trial and Froggatt was also sentenced to two years' imprisonment with the Scotland Yard detectives. Critical to his conviction was the damning evidence of a Brother Mason, Flintoff, who gave his account of Froggatt's attempt to use Masonic influence and bribery on him. Having a Mason as his barrister does not seem to have helped Froggatt or Druscovich either. Brother 'Dolly' Williamson, the superintendent, also had no compunction in arresting his friend, Brother Clarke, or giving evidence against Brother Palmer.

In addition to the major scandal that this case caused at the time, it has had a long-term impact that lives on to this day. The Metropolitan Police Detective Department was disbanded and the Criminal Investigation Department was formed under the direct supervision of a Director, who later became an Assistant Commissioner. The CID still exists and has been copied by every police force in Britain.

In 1977, one hundred years after these events, Operation Countryman was launched to investigate corruption in the Metropolitan Police. It is possible that Meiklejohn inspired this operation name; throughout his correspondence with Kurr the fraudster, this devious officer used the nickname 'Countryman'.

Kurr and Benson took their criminal skills abroad, initially committing fraud in Europe. Benson was convicted of selling bogus shares in Belgium and was thrown out of the country. He then teamed up with Kurr and the two men swindled a retired Army doctor out of £7,000. Both then crossed the Atlantic and at this point, Kurr disappears from history. Benson, however, continued to attract the attention of the authorities and he was convicted of a $25,000 swindle in New York. Here, he was sentenced to imprisonment in the notorious Tombs Prison on Manhattan Island. This was to prove too much for Benson; he committed suicide by throwing himself over a top floor railing in May 1888. After serving their sentence, Meiklejohn and Druscovich became private investigators, but the latter died at a young age. Meiklejohn was able to supplement his income by writing in newspapers about his Scotland Yard investigations.

Palmer the Mason became the landlord of the Cock Tavern in Kennington. It was highly unusual for the local magistrates to allow a man with a conviction to run a public house, possibly indicating that they suspected he was innocent all along. The previous landlord had given evidence in Palmer's defence at the trial. He noted that a 'club' met at his pub and Palmer was the chairman, potentially a reference to a Lodge. However, there is no record of a Craft lodge meeting at these premises, but it may have been a Royal Arch Chapter or a lodge of instruction. Palmer resigned from Domatic Lodge in November 1877, shortly after being convicted. The lodge eventually moved from the hotel in Fleet Street to the Masonic Centre in Clerkenwell, where it met until 2014; it now meets at Great Queen Street.

Chief Inspector Clarke was soon to be forced to retire from Scotland Yard as his presence was an embarrassment to the Metropolitan Police.; he left in early 1891. Superintendent Williamson fared better and his career survived the scandal. Despite the level of corruption uncovered in his department, 'Dolly' was promoted to Chief Constable (in the Metropolitan Police, this rank was not the head of the force, but what is now called a commander). As such, he was Deputy Director of the newly formed CID.

Detective Inspector Greenham, who had given evidence at the trial, citing the need to deal with criminal informants, was not put off Masonry. In 1880, he was initiated into Southern Star Lodge No. 1158—but his occupation is shown as an 'engineer'; it is possible that he wanted to keep his real occupation secret. The following year, he joined another lodge that met in Brixton in South London, Avondale No. 2395. Ironically, this lodge now meets in the Civil Service Club in Great Scotland Yard, where Greenham was employed at the time of the Trial of the Detectives. The Avondale Lodge register shows him in his true role, as a Chief Inspector of the Criminal Investigation Department. Given that three of the four Chief Inspectors had been sent to prison, it is unsurprising that he had been promoted from Detective Inspector. Finally, in 1895, he joined Justicia No. 2563 (the same lodge as Littlechild, the officer who arrested Kurr).

Most interestingly, in 1888, Meiklejohn was shown to be involved in investigating the 'Whitechapel Mystery' (what we call the Jack the Ripper murders) while running his detective agency in Heaver Road, near Clapham Junction. It is unclear as to his involvement in this infamous case, which also has many Masonic connections.

It should also be noted that the ironically named barrister, Mr Straight, had also found himself on the wrong side of the law several years before the Trial of the Detectives. In 1870 (it will be recalled that he joined a lodge in 1874), as the newly elected Conservative Member of Parliament for Shrewsbury, he was accused of all manner of electoral fraud offences. The defeated Liberal candidate alleged that Brother Straight had bought votes and bribed officials. Oddly, it was even alleged that a local vicar had influenced the result by toasting the health of the Conservative candidate. Straight was represented in court by Hardinge Giffard (the future Mason and Attorney General noted in this chapter). The court found in Straight's favour, but some of the local townsfolk were angry with the decision, as a local newspaper reported that there was 'shameful rioting' in the centre of Shrewsbury. Brother Straight would, as has been described, serve as a judge in India, for which he was knighted. Sir Douglas died in 1914.

33

The First 'Photofit' image:
Masons investigate the murder of a Mason

Masonic Connection
Victim
Murderer
Doctor
Chief Constable of Brighton Police
Railway police officer
Scotland Yard detective
Police Surgeon
Lawyer
Witness at trial
Coroner

Date
1881: Murder occurred

Connection to London
Mile End Road: Victim grew his successful business in this area
London Bridge: Victim boarded at this station and crime occurred on the Brighton-bound train
Great Scotland Yard: Detectives investigated the crime
Charing Cross Police Station: At the time, Charing Cross Hospital was where the Police Surgeon was based
Bouverie Street (number 17/18): While on the run, the suspect stayed at the (now demolished) Sussex Hotel
Blackfriars Bridge: Stolen property thrown into the River Thames from this location
Smithy Street, Stepney: Criminal arrested at a house in this street

Lodges
Tuscan No. 14
Old Union No. 46
Domatic No. 177

Phoenix No. 257
Royal Clarence No. 271
South Saxon No. 311
Royal York No. 315
St Helena No. 488
Yarborough No. 554
Ockenden No. 1465
Elliot No. 1567
Welcome No. 1673
Jubilee Masters No. 2712
St Peter's No. 284 (Scotland)
Ubique No. 411 (Mark)

The use of an artist's impression or 'Photofit' of a criminal is now a familiar method of identifying suspects and solving crime. No 1970s police show is complete without the composite image of a bearded white man wanted for several murders in the north of England. Once Peter Sutcliffe was identified as the 'Yorkshire Ripper', the accuracy of the image could clearly be seen. Now such images are even more lifelike, as they are created with computer programmes by skilled police operators.

The first use of such an image in an investigation was in 1881. The crime committed was a murder and robbery of a Freemason on a train between London Bridge station and Brighton. The suspect was eventually arrested and brought to justice by another member of the Craft, Detective Inspector Donald Swanson of Scotland Yard. Swanson was originally from Thurso, in the very north of Scotland, but he had joined the Metropolitan Police in 1868. He maintained his connections with the Highlands, as he joined the St Peter's Lodge No. 284 in his home town in 1885 and was later 'Advanced' to the Mark Degree the following year. He obviously enjoyed that aspect of Freemasonry as he later joined an English Mark lodge (Ubique No. 411), which met in London.

The offence involved a vicious attack on a businessman, Frederick Isaac Gold (known by his middle name), who had originally been a baker in the East End of London, but had made his fortune as a corn dealer and owned several shops. In 1848, while living in the Mile End Road, he had been initiated into the newly formed Yarborough Lodge, then No. 812 (now No. 554). As a result of his commercial success, he had been able to move to a fashionable part of Brighton. On 27 June 1881, the sixty-four-year old businessman travelled to London to collect rents from his shops as he did every Monday morning. Returning to London Bridge station, he boarded the 2 p.m. train to return to his home on the south coast. For the initial part of the journey, Brother Gold was alone, but when the train stopped at East Croydon, another man got into the First-Class compartment. This was no ordinary passenger; Percy Lefroy Mapleton had just redeemed his pistol from a local pawnbroker and was intent on committing violent robbery.

Mapleton was over forty years younger than Gold and ironically, he was a 'Lewis', or son of a Freemason; his father, Henry Mapleton, was an officer in the Royal Navy, who had joined the St Helena Lodge No. 718 (now No. 488) on the remote South Atlantic island of the same name. As his father was at sea and his mother had died when he was just six years old, Mapleton had been brought up by an aunt. His childhood was spent in south London and Surrey, but Mapleton travelled as far as Australia, attempting to become an actor or theatrical agent. He also discovered that he was a very good liar and this had enabled him to make money by fraud, but now he was back in England and had so little cash that he had to pawn his belongings, even his clothes.

Before travelling to London Bridge, Mapleton had borrowed sufficient money to purchase the first class ticket to give him the opportunity of robbing a rich passenger. As evidence of his intention to use extreme violence to these ends, as well as the pistol, he also had a cut-throat razor in his pocket. The much older businessman, who was wearing a gold pocket watch, must have seemed to be easy prey for the desperate villain and, as we saw in the Müller murder case, the men were alone in a sealed compartment and unlikely to be disturbed. After the Müller trial, the law required safety cords to be fitted in all carriages, but these were a recent innovation and it appears that Brother Gold was unaware of the device or never thought of using it.

The train departed East Croydon, quickly building up steam as it sped towards the Surrey and Sussex countryside. Perhaps Mapleton believed that the noise of the engine in a confined space would provide ideal cover for the victim's cries and as the train entered the Merstham tunnel between Croydon and Redhill, passengers in an adjacent carriage heard a strange sound—gun shots. It does not appear, however, that Brother Gold was fatally injured at this point, as a mother and daughter were later to relate that they had seen two men engaged in a violent struggle as the engine steamed past their cottage in Horley, further down the line than Merstham. The final murderous assault appears to have taken place as the train entered the lengthy tunnel between the towns of Balcombe and Three Bridges. Gold was fighting hard for his life, despite being shot several times and slashed with the razor, but Mapleton managed to throw him from the fast-moving train into the dark tunnel, causing the final fatal injuries to the businessman. During the robbery, Mapleton had snatched Brother Gold's watch and a purse, containing just ten shillings and some distinctive (but valueless) coins; a murder had been committed for this pitiful hoard.

Mapleton quickly threw his weapons out of the window, but these were not the only evidence of a violent crime; Gold's fight for life had left the robber covered in blood and his hat, collar, and tie had been ripped off, making him very conspicuous. He would also have been hobbling around as the stolen watch was concealed in his shoe and this drew him to the attention of the ticket collector, who joined the train at Preston Park station to check fares. Mapleton attempted to cover his tracks by claiming that he was, in fact, a victim of robbery inside the Merstham tunnel. He alleged that two men had viciously attacked him and knocked him out. As a further precaution, he slightly changed his name, using 'Lefroy' as his surname. Mapleton had considered alighting the train at Preston Park—a far quieter station than busy Brighton—but the arrival of the ticket collector had scuppered his plans and proved to be the initial step in his downfall. The railwayman, not satisfied with the account related to him, insisted that Mapleton should accompany him on the train to Brighton. Once there, a report was given to the Station Master and Mapleton reiterated his story, adding that the watch had been placed in his shoe for safe keeping.

A Freemason would later be a key witness to the appearance of Mapleton on his arrival at Brighton Station. Local councillor, Oliver Weston, gave evidence at the subsequent trial that he saw blooded finger and thumb marks on Mapleton's neck, as though he had been grabbed around the throat. Weston was a member of the Royal York Lodge No. 315, which met in the Royal Pavilion in the seaside town. The councillor related at the subsequent trial that he believed that Mapleton had committed a crime, while the railwaymen simply thought him to be a 'lunatic'.

The Railway Police were called and Mapleton made a formal complaint about the fictitious robbers, whom he claimed had attacked him. The police were, however, rightfully suspicious of his story. This was exacerbated when his injuries were examined at the County Hospital, where the doctor could not understand how such superficial wounds had resulted in Mapleton being covered in blood. The injured man then announced that he had to return to London for an 'urgent' appointment. Perhaps because he knew he was an excellent liar and could exonerate himself, he returned to Brighton Police Station (wearing a new shirt and tie) to be interviewed by local detectives. He was even interviewed by Chief Constable, James Terry, who was also a Freemason (like Councillor Weston, he was a member of the Royal York Lodge). The initial conclusion of the police was that he had attempted to commit suicide and had invented the robbery to conceal the truth (attempting suicide was, at that time, a crime).

In addition to interviewing Mapleton, the police also located the carriage in which the attack had occurred. This resulted in three bullet holes being found, together with signs of a violent and bloody struggle. There was, however, nothing tangible to challenge his account, but, rightfully suspicious, the police ordered a search of the track, while Mapleton (still calling himself 'Percy Lefroy') was escorted by Detective Sergeant George Holmes to a relative's boarding house in Cathcart Road, Wallington, Surrey, on the outskirts of London. DS Holmes was a Metropolitan Police officer, but was paid for by the London, Brighton and South Coast Railway, in effect seconded to the Railway Police. There is no record of Holmes being a Mason.

At the same time as Mapleton was being accompanied to Wallington by the Detective Sergeant, Gold's body was found in the tunnel, together with a knife. The Station Master at Balcombe used the quickest method of communication at that time—a telegram—to send the following message to the police, 'Man found dead this afternoon in tunnel here. Name on papers 'I Gold'. He is now lying here. Reply quick.' The unfortunate victim's body was then removed to Balcombe and placed in a shed adjacent to the Railway Arms Hotel.

The railway workers, who had transported Gold's body to the inn, believed that he had been struck by a train and called a local surgeon, Dr Thomas Byass, to pronounce death and give his view on the cause of the many injuries suffered by the victim. Like Gold, Byass was also a member of the Craft; he had been initiated into the Royal Clarence Lodge No. 338 (now No. 271) in Brighton in 1862 and had also joined Ockenden No. 1465 in his home town of Cuckfield. The doctor quickly established that the deceased was not the victim of an accident; his injuries were consistent with a violent assault.

This damning information was related to DS Holmes at Three Bridges Station, but Mapleton was still not arrested for no clear reason. The officer was, however, told to maintain a sharp watch on 'Lefroy' and not let him out of his sight, but he failed to carry out such instructions. On arrival at Wallington, the Detective Sergeant received a telegram via Croydon Police Station, asking him to check the watch in possession of Mapleton. This, no doubt, belonged to Brother Gold, but the hapless DS simply accepted his prisoner's explanation when given an incorrect serial number for the watch. DS Holmes then allowed Mapleton to change his clothes in private and the murderer (unsurprisingly) escaped, making his way to London on foot and staying for one night in a hotel in Bouverie Street (off Fleet Street). Mapleton knew he had to get rid of incriminating evidence and the stolen watch was subsequently thrown into the Thames from Blackfriars Bridge (the later scene of a possible Masonic crime). The bungling by the police, in allowing a murderer to flee, resulted in ridicule in the press and in music halls, especially against DS Holmes and Brother Terry, the Chief of the Brighton Police.

In the meantime, 'Mr Lefroy' was identified as Percy Lefroy Mapleton and Scotland Yard now took charge of the man-hunt. As part of the investigation, the victim's body was further examined by Dr Thomas Bond, the Westminster Division Police Surgeon. The doctor had been initiated into Old Union Lodge No. 46 in 1876. He also offered expert advice during the Jack the Ripper case. Dr Bond stated that the victim had fought hard for his life, but the bullet wound in his neck would had considerably weakened his resistance. He also noted several slash wounds on the body that had been caused by a razor or a knife; these would have resulted in much blood loss.

Just two days after the murder, an inquest into the death of Isaac Gold was opened and presided over by a Freemason—London coroner, Wynne Baxter. Coincidentally, given the location of the murder, Baxter was a Sussex Mason who had trained as a lawyer. In 1886, he had been appointed coroner for the County of Middlesex (Eastern District). Baxter was a member of the South Saxon Lodge No. 311, which met in Lewes. The inquest heard that the victim had suffered horrific injuries, being stabbed in the eye and having his throat cut. His wife had been so distressed that a neighbour had to formally identify the body. The jury had little difficulty in finding that Gold had been the victim of 'wilful murder' by the man named as 'Lefroy'. DS Holmes and other officers were heavily criticised for the blunders that had allowed the suspect to flee. Scotland Yard was quick to point out that the hapless officer now worked for the railway company (the 'blame game' is not new).

To rally public assistance, a £200 reward was offered by the railway company for Mapleton's apprehension. Additionally, the head of the Metropolitan Police CID (then known as the 'Director of Criminal Investigations') commissioned an artist to draw an impression of the suspect. Colonel Howard Vincent was responsible for establishing the CID following the corruption trial in 1877 (see the previous chapter). Vincent was certainly not a Mason in England, but his full name was Charles Edward Howard Vincent and he served as a soldier in Ireland, where Grand Lodge records show several possible matches to his name.

The image created was published on 'wanted posters' and in *The Daily Telegraph* on 1 July 1881 (Colonel Vincent had worked as a correspondent for this newspaper). The article also carried a very detailed (but rather uncomplimentary) description of Mapleton:

Very thin, sickly appearance, scratches on throat, wounds on head, probably clean shaved, low felt hat, black coat, teeth much discoloured ... his thin overcoat hangs in awkward folds about his spare figure. His forehead and chin are both receding … he is inclined to slouch and when not carrying a bag, his left hand is usually in his pocket.

The publishing of such an artist's image was a first. The publicity resulted in all manner of false sightings of Mapleton; the use of Photofit images is a useful tool, but it can lead to all manner of incorrect information that diverts the investigating officers. In the end, it was not the artist's impression which located the murderer, but his desperation for cash. He fled to the East End of London and hid behind the closed blinds of a house at 32 Smith (now Smithy) Street, Stepney, calling himself 'Mr Park'. For all these efforts to conceal his identity and whereabouts, he asked his employer to send his wages to the address.

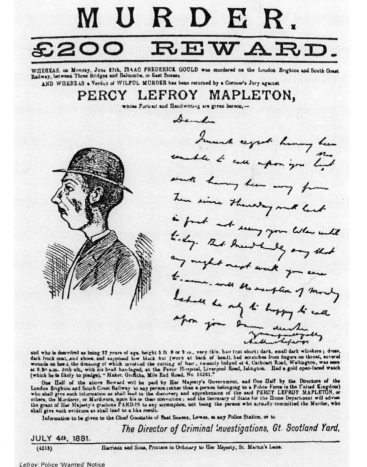

Percy Lefroy Mapleton featured on this wanted poster, with the first use of a sketch to locate an offender.

Scotland Yard was informed and, on 8 July, less than a fortnight after the murder, Mapleton was re-arrested by DI Swanson. A search of his hideout resulted in the blood-stained clothing being recovered. Further enquiries established that he owned a revolver and was in possession of coins similar to those stolen from the victim. He still, however, denied the offence. When cautioned by the Detective Inspector, Mapleton, no doubt realising the overwhelming evidence against him, replied, 'I think it better not to make any answer.' He then added, 'I will qualify that by saying I am not guilty.'

The suspected murderer was remanded into custody and held at Lewes; there, he was visited by his solicitor, Thomas Duerdin Dutton. Dutton was another member of the Craft involved in this case. He had been initiated into the Elliot Lodge No. 1567 in Middlesex in 1876 and by the time of the trial was also a member of Tuscan No. 14 in London. He would later join two other London lodges—Welcome No. 1673 and Jubilee Masters No. 2712.

By this time, Mapleton's account of the events on the London to Brighton train had changed. He now claimed that there had been a third person in the railway carriage and this unknown man was the murderer of Isaac Gold. As his solicitor, Brother Dutton spent considerable time and effort to find this new suspect, travelling the length and breadth of the country. Unfortunately, it was a complete fiction; there had only been two men present during the murder—the victim and Mapleton.

Despite the murder being committed in Sussex and the arrest being made in London, the trial was held in Maidstone, Kent. Up until 1971, when Crown Courts were created, trials were tried before a judge at the Assizes Court. These judges were known as 'circuit judges' as they moved from place to place. As the crime had been committed in Sussex, it fell into the Home Circuit (which also included Kent, Essex, Hertfordshire, and Surrey), hence the trial was held where the judge was timetabled to sit at that time.

Mapleton pleaded 'not guilty', but little evidence was produced in his favour. When Dr Bond gave evidence of the gruesome injuries suffered by Mr Gold, one spectator at the murder trial fainted at the back of the court, further adding to the drama of the proceedings. The accused man seemed to believe that a smart appearance would be an indicator of innocence and wore full evening dress (it will be recalled that when he returned to the police in Brighton, he had put on a new collar and tie). The jury were not influenced by Mapleton's attire and were so convinced by the case against him that it took them only ten minutes to convict him of murder. Mapleton shouted, 'Gentlemen of the jury, some day, when too late, you will learn that you have murdered me.' Ignoring this claim of innocence, there was only one punishment available to the judge—death by hanging.

Mapleton was held in Lewes Prison and there confessed to a further murder that had occurred four months before the railway killing. Lieutenant Percy Roper had been shot in the Royal Engineers barracks in Chatham, Kent. The condemned man later withdrew this confession and some eminent medical men attempted to convince the Home Secretary to rescind the death sentence and place Mapleton in a lunatic asylum. One such doctor was William Netherclift, the Medical Superintendent of the Chelsea Infirmary and a member of Phoenix No. 257 in Portsmouth (the same lodge as Sir Arthur Conan Doyle). He made a public appeal to the Home Secretary that stated, 'the law may be vindicated and society protected by the execution of a responsible murderer, but justice is outraged and society imperilled by the hanging of a lunatic.' He ended it with a poignant question: 'Which is Lefroy?' Some believed that Mapleton was completely innocent and had been the victim of a miscarriage of justice.

At the Home Office, however, there was little sympathy for the prisoner who had not mentioned the defence of insanity at his trial. The Home Secretary, Sir William Harcourt (one of the few non-Masons in this tale), was also aware that the condemned man had made a full confession, in a document entitled 'My Autobiography' that he had written in his cell. These papers would not see the light of day for a hundred years, as the Home Secretary decided that they should not be published. While admitting his own guilt, Mapleton had accused witnesses of embellishing their evidence and others of simply lying. He also had claimed to be romantically involved with a famous actress of the day (another Mapleton fiction). Sir William noted 'there are many other persons whose names would be brought into unpleasant notoriety… I will lock this up in my secret cupboard' (Gardner, 2004). While all this was happening, Mapleton was busy planning an escape; he wrote to a lady-friend asking her to hide a metal file in a meat pie. Unfortunately for him, the tool never arrived.

The Masonic Lewis, failed actor, and murderer was hanged in the prison on 29 November 1881. Unlike Brother Gold, it was a quick death; his neck snapped as he fell through the trapdoor. His dead body was then cut down and subjected to the formal *post-mortem* examination required by the authorities. Then, an inquest was held, presided over by Brother Wynne Baxter, who had overseen the enquiry into the victim's death. The court recorded that 'Death was caused by hanging, in conformity with the law'. This infamous killer did, however, achieve the fame he so craved while alive. Until 1997, a wax model of Mapleton was displayed in the 'Chamber of Horrors' at Madame Tussauds in London.

The Commissioner of the Metropolitan Police rewarded Chief Inspector Swanson with a £5 bonus for his work in this case. The same reward went to Inspector William Turpin of the Railway Police for his assistance in bringing Mapleton to justice. Turpin was also a Mason, having joined the Domatic Lodge No. 177 in 1867. As we shall see, the soon-to-be Chief Inspector Swanson and Coroner Baxter were two Masons involved in the investigation of possibly the most infamous crimes ever committed in London—the Jack the Ripper murders. Interestingly, it has been suggested Brother Swanson may also have solved that mystery.

34

Good Lawyer, Difficult Clients: Corruption, Cheating, Costly Carnal Desires, and Military Conspiracy

Masonic Connection

Lawyers
Famous actor
Grand Master of England
Founder of Rhodesia

Date

1871: Sir Edward Clarke initiated into Freemasonry
1877: Trial of the Detectives
1890–91: Baccarat Scandal
1895: Trial of Oscar Wilde
1896: Jameson Raid trial

Connection to London

Moorgate: Clarke lived above his father's shop
Leadenhall Street: Clarke initiated in tavern in this street
Southwark: Clarke was the MP for this south London constituency
The Strand: Baccarat Scandal trial held at Royal Courts of Justice
Albert Hall: Site of the installation of the Prince of Wales as Grand Master
Albemarle Street: Location of Oscar Wilde's club
King Street: Theatre where *The Importance of Being Earnest* opened
Old Bailey: Trial of the Detectives and later Oscar Wilde

Lodges

Westminster and Keystone No. 10
Royal Alpha No.16
Caledonian No. 134
Domatic No. 177
Phoenix Lodge of Honor and Prudence No. 331
Apollo University No. 357

Churchill No. 478

Zetland No. 511

Bard of Avon No. 778

Cornish No. 2369

Mendelssohn No. 2661 (erased)

Justicia No. 2563

Bulawayo No. 2566

St Michael No. 2747

United Wards No. 2987 (erased)

Guildhall No. 3116

Athlumney No. 3245

Old Cliftonian No. 3340

Canada No. 3527

Sir Edward Clarke No. 3601

Robert Thorne No. 3663

Trinity College No. 357 (Ireland)

University Lodge No. 55 (Mark)

Oxford University Chapter No. 40 (Rose Croix)

This chapter covers the life of the high-ranking lawyer and Freemason who acted for defendants in some of the most famous cases of his day. Brother Sir Edward Clarke was willing to take on seemingly hopeless cases or those where the defendant had offended the morals of the day. Clarke was born in 1841 and was 'called to the bar' (became a barrister) in 1864. He came from a humble background; his father was a jeweller and the family lived over his London shop in Moorgate Street, where he slept on the stairway as a child. He began working at thirteen years old, but studied during any spare moment and was awarded a sponsorship to study law at Lincoln's Inn.

In addition to his legal career, Clarke was also a Member of Parliament, at various times serving constituents in Southwark, Plymouth and the City of London. He was knighted when he was appointed as Solicitor-General (a senior law officer of the government and deputy to the Attorney-General). He served in this high office for some six years.

His Masonic career began in 1871, when he was initiated into Caledonian Lodge No. 134, which met in the Ship and Turtle tavern (now demolished), which stood in Leadenhall Street in the City of London. He was diligent regarding his lodge duties and was installed as Worshipful Master within four years; he was the Master in 1875, the same year as the Prince of Wales (later Edward VII) was installed as Grand Master. At this ceremony in the Albert Hall, Clarke acted as an assistant to the stewards. These two Masons' paths would cross some five years later, but in a hostile court room rather than in a friendly Masonic lodge.

In his capacity as a barrister, Sir Edward regularly appeared at the Old Bailey as the defence counsel for men and women charged with murder and other heinous crimes, but four cases stand out for their Masonic connections:

The 'Trial of the Detectives': in 1877, four Scotland Yard detectives were charged with corruption and accepting bribes. Sir Edward acted for Chief Inspector George Clarke (a

Sir Edward Clarke, the Mason and barrister who was prepared to defend some of the most difficult cases in Victorian times.

member of the Domatic Lodge No. 177). He successfully defended the police officer; the other three Chief Inspectors were found guilty.

The 'Baccarat Scandal': In 1891, the Grand Master would be called to give evidence against Sir Edward's client and was shown no quarter in the witness box.

Trial of Oscar Wilde: Clarke defended the famous actor, author, and Freemason when he was charged with illegal homosexual acts in 1895.

The Jameson Raid Trial: In 1896, a statesman from South Africa led a botched raid on the (then independent) Boer state of Transvaal. Clarke defended Jameson, who had been handed back to the British authorities to face trial in England. Cecil Rhodes (a Mason), founder of Rhodesia and Prime Minister of the Cape Colony, was strongly suspected of having planned the incursion, with the government in London secretly backing the raid.

The Baccarat Scandal involved a senior army officer being accused of cheating at cards. In Victorian society, such ungentlemanly conduct was (literally) unforgiveable. The affair has its origins in late 1890 when Sir William Gordon-Cumming, a lieutenant colonel in the Scots Guards, was invited to Tranby Croft, a large house near Hull in East Yorkshire (at that time, the home of a shipping magnate). Several eminent men were also at the mansion, including a lord, a general, and, most notably, the Prince of Wales, together with wives and other ladies. The future Edward VII had joined Freemasonry in Sweden in 1868 and was a member and founder of several other lodges. By the time of this incident, he was Grand Master of England. Colonel Gordon-Cummings was not a Mason, but he did share other similarities with 'Dirty Bertie' (the Prince of Wales); they were both arrogant, gamblers, and womanisers.

During the course of two evenings, the group played the card game of baccarat (this is often seen on James Bond films), gambling for high stakes, with the Prince of Wales acting as dealer and banker. Throughout the game, a number of the players suspected that the colonel was surreptitiously adding £5 chips to his stake after he had won the game, thereby increasing his substantial winnings at their expense (£5 at that time had the purchasing power of £500 today). The party had, of course, been drinking throughout dinner and therefore later accounts of his methods varied.

The fact that the Prince of Wales was present influenced the manner in which the alleged cheating was dealt with. Not wishing to embroil their royal guest in a scandal, it was decided that a 'quiet word' should be had with Colonel Gordon-Cumming. This initial attempt to resolve the matter failed as the colonel protested his innocence and demanded that the prince be involved; they were, after all, friends. The Prince of Wales was consulted and appears to have quickly and arbitrarily decided that Gordon-Cumming was a cheat. When they spoke, the prince bluntly told the army officer that it was a simple matter of his account against five accusers. Under pressure, the colonel signed a document promising never to play cards again, but not actually admitting that he had acted dishonestly. All parties were then sworn to secrecy, but given the number of people present, something was going to slip out. Gordon-Cumming made his excuses to his hosts and returned south, leaving a letter for a fellow guest, a retired general, in which he protested his innocence.

Back in London, the accused colonel received a reply from the general, also signed by the Prince of Wales, making it clear that they did not believe him and were convinced of his guilt. Rumours then began to spread in polite society regarding the card game. Gordon-Cumming's good name and army career were at stake. Matters were not helped by the fact that the Colonel-in-Chief of the Scots Guards was the Duke of Connaught, the Prince of Wales's younger brother; the Duke also believed that the cheating had occurred. The Duke of Connaught was also a Mason and would succeed his brother as Grand Master on the latter's ascension to the throne. He would remain as such until 1939.

Faced with ruin, Colonel Gordon-Cumming instructed a solicitor to issue writs against five of his accusers for libel. While the Prince of Wales would be called to court as a witness, he was not named as one of the defendants. The trial began on 1 June 1891 in the Royal Courts of Justice and it had a celebrity feel, with entrance by ticket only. The Prince of Wales was no stranger to having to appear in a court of law; he had been summoned to give evidence in a previous scandal—the Mordaunt divorce. There was, however, a difference at this hearing, as Brother Sir Edward was not going to be as gentle with the Grand Master as the lawyer had been in the previous case.

Acting for the colonel and despite the Masonic connection to the Grand Master, Sir Edward quizzed the scandal-dogged prince for some twenty minutes, with the future king forced to admit that he had not seen any cheating taking place. Sir Edward was also able to show that those who alleged to have seen the dishonest acts could not give consistent accounts. The trial rumbled on for several days and appeared to be going in favour of Gordon-Cummings, but some contemporary newspapers noted the biased summing up of the judge, Lord Coleridge, against the case presented by Sir Edward. The case was lost, with the jury deciding against Gordon-Cummings in less than a quarter of an hour. He was dismissed from the army and would never live down the scandal. *The Times* summed up the totality of his ruin:

> He is ... condemned by the verdict of the jury to social extinction. His brilliant record is wiped out and he must, so to speak, begin life again. Such is the inexorable social rule ... He has committed a mortal offence. Society can know him no more.

The (former) colonel would live until 1930, but he was never accepted into London society again. He would end his life an angry and embittered man, well knowing that his life had been ruined for a gambling win of £225, with the vast majority of his 'friends', including the Prince of Wales, deserting him in his hour of need. Sir Edward, however, continued to believe in his innocence and recorded such in his memoirs, *The Story of My Life* (Clarke, 2013).

The Prince of Wales's popularity also waned as a result of this sad case. A cartoon at the time showed the Grand Master's motto as '*Ich Deal*' (rather than the correct '*Ich Dien*'), alluding to his excessive gambling at the Baccarat table. However, while being found guilty of cheating at cards in Victorian England would mean being shunned, being a homosexual could mean being sent to jail; we now turn to the sad case involving the latter.

Perhaps the most famous man defended by Sir Edward was Wilde, the playwright and author. Wilde's father had been a Freemason in Ireland and Oscar was initiated while at Oxford University into the Apollo University Lodge No. 357 on 23 February 1875. He must have been impressed with the ceremony, as just over three months later, he became a joining member of Churchill Lodge No. 478, which met at the Oxford Masonic Hall.

His motives for joining Freemasonry are unknown, but he may have been interested in the secrecy, rituals, and religious overtones of the Craft. Brother Oscar appears to have had a profound interest in Christianity and, despite having been baptised into the Protestant Church of Ireland, often toyed with the idea of conversion to the Roman Catholic faith (which later occurred on his death bed). It is no surprise, therefore, that he did not follow the path of most Freemasons (from the Craft to the Holy Royal Arch, a degree open to men of all faiths), but opted to be 'perfected' into the Rose Croix, the deeply Christian order, with its often written-about thirty-three degrees. He joined the Oxford University Chapter No. 40 of the Ancient and Accepted Rite (as it is also known) in November 1876, under two years after his initiation into Freemasonry. Extravagant as ever, he purchased all manner of expensive regalia, but failed to pay for it. As a result, Brother Oscar was summoned before the university authorities and ordered to pay his debts.

In March 1878, Wilde was 'advanced' into another Masonic order, joining University Mark Lodge No. 55. The candidate in this degree selects the mark, which he would stamp onto his stones; Brother Oscar chose his initials (O. F. W.), written backwards. However, his interest in Masonry was waning. Later that same year, he was expelled from his Mother Lodge, Apollo, for non-payment of fees. He was later dismissed from the Churchill Lodge for the same reason.

After leaving Oxford with a double first, Wilde was able to convert his artistic ability into a career, writing books, poems, and plays, together with lecturing on the arts, as far away as the USA. In 1881, he married and had two children, perhaps in a vain attempt to conceal his homosexuality. By the mid-1880s, however, he had had his first full blown affair with another man; this may well have influenced his classic novel *The Picture of Dorian Gray*, which some contemporary critics attacked for its veiled references to homosexuality.

In the 1890s, Wilde focused on the theatre and writing plays, most significantly, *The Importance of Being Ernest*. Around this time, he was to meet the man whose father was to bring about his downfall. Lord Alfred Douglas was sixteen years younger than Wilde and openly homosexual. He was also a spoilt and reckless young man who took advantage of Wilde's money and infatuation with him. Ironically, Douglas's father was the Marquis of Queensbury, who is famed for the rules of boxing—that most manly of sports. The marquis and his son were at constant loggerheads and the openly homosexual affair caused the rift to deepen. The marquis is often cast as the villain in this story, but he was justifiably angry. Another of his sons had engaged in a homosexual affair, allegedly with a government minister, and had died in a 'hunting accident' shortly afterwards. However, it is possible that this could have been suicide, or even murder.

Angry and aggrieved, Queensbury decided to take direct action to expose Wilde. In February 1895, *The Importance of Being Ernest* was to open at the (now demolished) St James's Theatre, which stood in King Street, near the junction with Duke Street St James's (this street is known to Masons as the headquarters of Rose Croix). The marquis intended to bring matters to a head by throwing a bouquet of rotten vegetables at Wilde, but the plan was uncovered and the angry father was barred from the theatre. This opening night was the zenith of Wilde's career, with the play being given fabulous reviews, but within less than four months, he was to be in prison, disgraced and cast out from Victorian society.

Thwarted in his first attempt, the Marquis of Queensbury now went to one of the clubs where Wilde was a member, in Albemarle Street, Mayfair. Stopped from entering by the porter, he left a card for the playwright critically addressed as follows: 'To Oscar Wilde, posing somdomite', the word 'sodomite' being misspelt. This was a clear and public allegation from Queensbury that Wilde was engaging in sodomy (or buggery, as it was legally known), an offence in Victorian England, if it was true. Making libellous statements was also a criminal offence, also punishable by imprisonment. Encouraged by his lover, Lord Alfred (Wilde later admitted the intention was to have his lover's father put in prison), he took out a private prosecution against the marquis, charging him with Criminal Libel. This was contrary to the advice of many of the author's friends. Some even advised that he should flee to the continent. The prosecution was a foolish move and this trial was the beginning of the end for Brother Wilde. Just like the legendary Grand Master Hiram Abif, he was to face three trials and like Hiram Abif, the third one would ultimately finish him.

The first trial with the Marquis of Queensbury in the dock, accused of Criminal Libel, was held at that most famous of courts, the Old Bailey and opened on 3 April 1895. The prosecution lawyer (for Wilde) was Brother Sir Edward Clarke. Prior to accepting the case, he had demanded that his client assure him that the allegations of his homosexuality were untrue. Wilde, lying, stated that that they were 'untrue and groundless'. The defence team for the marquis was headed by Edward Carson (later famous as the founding father of Northern Ireland). He had studied with Wilde at Trinity College, Dublin, but they were not friends. While at university in 1890, Carson had joined the lodge named after the college, No. 357 on the roll of the Grand Lodge of Ireland.

Sir Edward Carson. Later known as the 'Father of Northern Ireland', he was the Mason who acted as prosecution counsel at Oscar Wilde's trials.

Prior to the hearing, Carson had tasked private detectives to 'dig the dirt' on Wilde; they had scoured the homosexual haunts of London finding much evidence to support Queensbury's accusation. One of the private detectives was retired CID inspector, John Littlechild, who had been recently initiated into Zetland Lodge No. 511. He later joined Mendelssohn No. 2661 (now defunct) and Justicia No. 2563.

Wilde did not help himself by making flippant remarks during the trial; when asked by Carson if he had ever kissed a servant boy, he stated that he would never have done so as the boy was 'unfortunately ugly'. He also lied about his age, perhaps in a fit of vanity, further damaging his credibility. To show the Marquis of Queensbury had been justified in his accusation of sodomy, many receipts were produced as evidence of the expensive presents which Wilde had showered on several young men. Then, the killer blow; Brother Carson announced that he would call several male prostitutes to give evidence that they had had sex with Wilde. On the advice of Sir Edward, Brother Wilde dropped the prosecution and admitted just the 'posing' part, which had been written on the calling card. Hence, Queensbury had no case to answer, and worse still, the court considered that the libellous accusation that Wilde had engaged in sodomy was 'true in substance and in fact'. Moreover, this made the disgraced actor liable to pay for the marquis's legal fees, leaving him bankrupt.

The accuser now became the accused. Even as the first court case was ending, Scotland Yard officers were applying for a warrant to arrest Wilde. The offence alleged was 'gross indecency'; this was an easier crime to prove, as it meant homosexual acts, not amounting to buggery, but it still carried a maximum offence of two years' imprisonment. To aid his escape, the magistrate is said to have delayed issuing the warrant for nearly two hours and friends again urged Wilde to flee abroad, but he appeared to be gripped by inaction and indecision. Languishing in London, he was arrested and remanded into Holloway Prison. The flamboyant and cossetted author and playwright now found himself in the Spartan conditions of a Victorian prison.

Within weeks, Wilde was back at the Old Bailey and now in the dock as the defendant. He found himself charged with twenty-five offences of gross indecency and conspiracy to commit that crime. Brother Sir Edward again represented him, charging no fee. Wilde was asked to explain the famous phrase (in a poem written by his lover Lord Alfred Douglas), 'the love that dare not speak its name'. He attempted to justify by giving several examples of older men having affections for younger men, such as David and Jonathan in the Bible (they are the subject of the Masonic Order known as the 'Secret Monitor', jokingly referred to by some brethren as the 'homosexual degree' due to its subject matter).

While Wilde seemed determined to convict himself, his brother Mason, Sir Edward, was determined to defend his client. His closing speech was powerful and asked the jury to 'gratify those thousands of hopes that are hanging on your decision' and 'clear from this fearful imputation one of our most renowned and accomplished men of letters of today and, in clearing him, clear society from a stain'. This brought tears to Wilde's eye. The speech nearly worked; the jury could not agree on a verdict, so Wilde was allowed free on bail awaiting the third trial. Bail was set at £5,000—a large sum, but it had bought him three weeks of freedom.

The matter could have been dropped and, despite his dislike of his brother Mason, even Edward Carson wished to stop the pursuit of Wilde. Unfortunately for Brother Oscar, forces in the government wanted to put a stop to his decadent lifestyle, which may have been perceived as a threat to society (this is rather similar to the trials involving the Rolling Stones for drugs in the 1960s). The new prosecution team assessed the quality of the evidence presented at the first trial for gross indecency and selected the best witnesses. The case, therefore, would be more focused and so much stronger. The verdict was inevitable; on 25 May 1895, the jury took just three hours to convict Wilde on the vast majority of the charges. Some in the public gallery supported the verdict, while others booed. Brother Oscar turned grey. From a Masonic point of view, there could not have been less bias— defence and prosecution counsel were members of the Craft, but the judge was not.

The sentence was brutal—two years' imprisonment, with hard labour. The merciless judge commented that he wished that it could be more. Brother Wilde was now 'Prisoner C 3.3' and he was sent to Pentonville, then Wandsworth Prison, but his health declined and he was placed in the infirmary. After a campaign, he was transferred to Reading, hence the title of his later poem, *The Ballad of Reading Gaol.* He was to serve the full two years, spending eighteen months in Reading, where there is a Masonic connection. On release, Wilde noted that a fellow prisoner had made the 'Sign of the Widow's Son'; this would seem to be a description of one of the several signs taught to brethren during the Third Degree. He was torn between acknowledging the sign of a brother in distress and complying with the strict prison regulations that forbad communication between inmates. Wilde persuaded the governor to allow him to wear dark glasses, as though he had an eye complaint, so that he could ignore (or not see) the Masonic communication.

It should be recalled that Wilde had ceased membership of all his Masonic lodges and chapters in 1883, twelve years prior to his imprisonment. Freemasonry, however, was not done with him. Philip Colville Smith (later Sir Philip) was the 'Most Wise Sovereign' (Master) of Oxford University Chapter of Rose Croix and a Past Master of Wilde's Craft lodges—Apollo University and Churchill. He was not a man to upset, as he had much influence and was a member of several London lodges (Westminster and Keystone No. 10, Royal Alpha No. 16, Cornish No. 2369, Athlumney No. 3245, and Old Cliftonian No. 3340), one in Middlesex (Bard of Avon No. 778) and two in Cornwall (Phoenix Lodge of Honor and Prudence No. 331 and St Michael No. 2747). His influence was so great that he would subsequently hold the office of Grand Secretary of the United Grand Lodge of England. Smith ensured that Wilde's name was erased from the Rose Croix membership book, despite the many years since his expulsion for non-payment of fees. The disgraced writer was not to be associated with this Christian order.

Wilde was released from Reading Prison in May 1897 and immediately sailed for Europe, spending the rest of his short life in self-imposed exile in France and Italy. His wife refused to let him see his sons, but sent him money. He even rekindled his romance with Lord Alfred Douglas, the young man who had caused his downfall, but this ended when the families of both men threatened to withdraw financial support. Wilde's last address was the L'Hotel d'Alsace in central Paris. On 25 November 1900, he became severely ill with meningitis; on the 29th, he was baptised into the Roman Catholic Church. He died the following day and was buried in the city. Thus ends the life of a very talented Mason, who, perhaps, caused much of his own downfall. Was he a victim of a repressive society or a predatory homosexual who frittered away his talent and exploited young men and boys? Whatever view is taken, he was a Mason, whose artistic works have left their mark on the world.

Oscar Wilde, the famous playwright, author, poet, and Freemason who was convicted of Gross Indecency in 1895.

Now we travel far across the British Empire to what is now South Africa, which consisted of four states in 1895—two British and two controlled by Dutch speaking Boers. The latter included the Transvaal. In an effort to expand British control, Leander Starr Jameson, a Scottish born statesman, led six hundred raiders into the Transvaal to stir up an uprising amongst British supporting inhabitants of the city of Johannesburg. It was alleged by the British South Africans that their countrymen were being oppressed by the Boers, but the recent discovery of gold was the likely reason; a worthless desert area had now become a very valuable asset. Jameson had not planned this alone; he had support from one of the most influential Britons in Africa—Cecil Rhodes. Rhodes was Prime Minister of the Cape Colony and had been a Freemason since 1876, when he joined the Apollo University Lodge—the same lodge that Oscar Wilde had joined the year before. He would also become a member of Bulawayo Lodge No. 2566 in South Africa and donated the ground where the Masonic Temple would be built.

It was not just Brother Rhodes involved; it would appear that the British government was actively, but covertly, engaged in the plan. Later, Sir Edward Clarke would examine all the telegrams that had passed between Jameson, Rhodes, and the British Colonial Office. He was convinced that the raiders had all believed that, rather than being a private army, they had all been in service of Queen and Country. The government would officially deny this; if the raid failed, all responsibility would lie with the 'private' army.

The raid did fail, with the population of the Transvaal refusing to rise up against their Boer 'oppressors'. Worse still, Jameson and much of his force were captured. The Boers handed Jameson over to the British authorities and he was shipped back to England, arriving in February 1896. The raid had badly damaged relations with the Boers (and ultimately led to the Second Boer War) and, more importantly, had shown the British as the aggressors to the German Empire. Jameson and several serving army officers, including a baronet, were charged under the Foreign Enlistment Act 1870, which made it an offence to plan or engage in military expeditions against a friendly state. They had, in short, been hung out to dry and abandoned by the Colonial Office. Once again, Sir Edward Clarke stepped in to defend the underdog. As further evidence of his honourable behaviour, he would later resign from the government due to its aggressive policies in South Africa.

The defendants were taken to Bow Street Magistrates Court (founded by a Freemason, Sir Thomas de Veil) and formally charged. They were then released on bail and given rooms at the Burlington Hotel in Cork Street, possibly paid for by Brother Rhodes, who had a permanent suite at the premises. Jameson and his fellow accused were indicted before a Grand Jury at the Old Bailey, but actually tried at the Royal Courts of Justice.

As the government was determined to hold a show trial, the defendants were tried before three judges and a selected jury to ensure the 'right verdict' and so appease the Boers. Despite the clear evidence of government involvement unearthed by Sir Edward, the men were (of course) found guilty. Jameson was sentenced to fifteen months in jail. Worse still, Rhodes's brother, a colonel, was sentenced to death for high treason. Honour being satisfied with the Boers (and mindful of the need for experienced soldiers, with knowledge of the Transvaal), the convicted men were soon pardoned and released. Jameson was even to take the position of Prime Minister of the Cape Colony, the position Brother Rhodes had resigned from. That said, Rhodes continued to be a major figure in African politics until his death in 1902. He left a fortune to fund scholarships at Oxford University, which are still available today.

Throughout all this time, from the Trial of the Detectives in 1877 to the Wilde case nearly twenty years later, Sir Edward Clarke had been a Member of Parliament and working barrister. However, he was not so active as a Mason. When he was elected as a Member of Parliament in the south west of England, he attended very few meetings. In his autobiography (Clarke, 2013), he gave his reasons as follows:

I kept up my Masonic work until I became member for Plymouth (1880–1900). Then I practically abandoned it for twenty years. Parliamentary duties made it difficult to attend lodge meetings or banquets in London, and I would not take part in Masonic work at Plymouth, partly because I wished to avoid the slightest possibility of its being connected with politics, and partly because I should have been burdened with the necessity of paying equal attention to each of the three lodges which flourished in my constituency.

He did attend some high-profile meetings in London and when he returned to the capital to serve as an MP for the City, he resumed his Masonic interests and was promoted to a very high rank in 1903—Past Grand Warden. By this time, the Grand Master was the Duke of Connaught. Perhaps Sir Edward's challenging questions to the previous Grand Master, the Duke's older brother, during the Baccarat Scandal trial had been forgotten. He wore his new regalia for the first time in Toronto, during a trip to Canada. Sir Edward was highly respected across the Atlantic; he advised on diverse subjects, including the revision of the Canadian Prayer Book and spoke on behalf of the children's charity established by another Freemason, Dr Barnardo. He also wrote on legal matters, including extradition of suspects from Canada to the United States.

Clarke was present at the consecration of several lodges—United Wards No. 2987 (in 1903), Guildhall No. 3116 (in 1905), and Canada No. 3527 (in 1911). Most importantly, in 1912, lodge No. 3601 was consecrated and named in his honour—the Sir Edward Clarke Lodge. He was to be its first Worshipful Master. The lodge originally met at Holborn Viaduct Hotel in London and then in a variety of venues in the capital until 1994, when it moved to Sevenoaks in Kent. In 1917, he returned to the Albert Hall to serve as a Steward at the celebration of the bicentenary of the foundation of Grand Lodge.

He lived his later years in Staines, to the west of London and was instrumental in the founding of St Peter's church in the town. Sir Edward continued to study Christianity and was a deeply religious man. He wrote to a nearby vicar:

As a lawyer, I have made a prolonged study of the evidences for the resurrection of Jesus Christ. To me the evidence is conclusive, and over and over again in the High Court, I have secured the verdict on evidence not so nearly compelling… The Gospel evidence for the resurrection… I accept unreservedly as the testimony of truthful people to facts they were able to substantiate.

Throughout his career he was a well-known court figure. The availability of daily newspapers in the latter part of the nineteenth century made barristers, such as Sir Edward, household names. When one of his clients was found 'not guilty' following a murder trial at the Old Bailey, he was cheered that evening at the theatre.

In 1914, Brother Sir Edward gave up active work. His retirement was reported in The Law Times (Volume 138) in the same paragraph as the retirement of Sir Thomas Bucknill, a fellow Freemason, who presided over the case of murderer, Brother Frederick Seddon. He had a long retirement, enabling him to write his memoirs, and in 1931, to mark his ninetieth birthday, the *Montreal Gazette* (he was, as we have seen, much respected in Canada) praised his work and noted 'small as he is in physical inches, was a giant at the English Bar and a leader in the House of Commons.' He was, by now, the oldest 'silk', the name given to a barrister holding the rank of Queen's or King Counsel (he had been both).

Sir Edward died two months after his ninetieth birthday. The king, George V, sent a telegram offering condolences to his widow (the king was not a Mason—but his father, Edward VII and his sons, Edward VIII and George VI, were all members of the Craft). Sir Edward was a deeply honourable and religious man who championed defendants against whom the might of the British Empire or the attitudes of Victorian society stood. Freemasons should be pleased to be associated with such a fine lawyer who stood up for the underdog, without being paid to do so in some cases. It is a testament to his service to the Craft that a lodge was named in his honour.

35

Jack the Ripper ... Jack the Mason?

Masonic Connection
Lord Mayor of London
Commissioner of Metropolitan Police
Senior officer in charge of investigation
Detectives
Supplier of disguises to detectives
Police surgeons
Coroners
Pathologist
Offender Profiler
Recipients of letters allegedly sent by the killer
Owner of murder site
Lodges in East London
Jack the Ripper?

Date
1888: Year of murders

Connection to London
Durward Street, Whitechapel: Current name of first murder site
Hanbury Street, Spitalfields: Site of second murder
Henriques Street, Whitechapel: Current name of third murder site
Goulston Street, Whitechapel: Site of graffiti supposedly written by the killer
Mitre Square, City of London: Site of fourth murder
Brushfield Street, Whitechapel: London Fruit and Wool Exchange, built over fifth murder scene
Great Scotland Yard: Headquarters of the Metropolitan Police
Charing Cross Police Station: At the time, Charing Cross Hospital and base of the Police Surgeon and analyst of the murders
Wardour Street: Wig maker's shop used to obtain disguises for detectives

Lodges

Grand Master's No. 1
Royal Somerset House and Inverness No. 4
Royal Alpha No. 16
United Mariners No. 30
St George's Lodge of Harmony No. 32
Old Union No. 46
Vitruvian No. 87
Temple No. 101
Old Concord No. 172
St Paul's No. 194
St Andrew's No. 231
Phoenix No. 257
Royal Lodge of Friendship No. 278
South Saxon No. 311
Royal Standard No. 398
Zetland in the East No. 508
Zetland No. 511
Yarborough No. 554
Ryde No. 698
Combermere No. 752
Dalhousie No. 865
South Middlesex No. 858
Lodge of Temperance in the East No. 898
City of London and Baltic No. 901
Doric No. 933
Southern Star No. 1158
MacDonald No. 1216
Upton No. 1227
Victoria No. 1345
Friars No. 1349
Lodge of Equity and Appleton No. 1445
Octahedron and Charles Warren No. 1417
Prince Leopold No. 1445
Athenaeum No. 1491 (erased)
Hotspur No. 1626
Orpheus No. 1706
Alliance No. 1827
Charles Warren No. 1832 (erased)
Shadwell Clerke No. 1910
Eurydice No. 1920
Quatuor Coronati No. 2076
Drury Lane No. 2127

Albert Victor No. 2328

Ixion No. 2501

Train-bands No. 2524

Lancastrian No. 2528

Justicia No. 2563

Borough No. 2589

Mendelssohn No. 2661 (erased)

Widnes No. 2819

Royal London Hospital No. 2845

Cheselden No. 2870

University of Durham No. 3030

Foxhunters No. 3094

St Chad No. 3115

Widnes and Knowsley No. 3581 (erased)

William Harvey Chapter No. 49 (Holy Royal Arch)

Lancastrian Chapter No. 2528 (Holy Royal Arch)

Tranquillity No. 42 (New South Wales)

St Patrick's No. 195 (Ireland)

St Peter's No. 284 (Scotland)

Ubique No. 411 (Mark)

While other murders have far more tangible Masonic connections (for example, the Seddon case), no other case has been associated with Freemasonry more than the infamous 'Whitechapel Murders' committed in London in 1888 by the serial killer known as 'Jack the Ripper'. Some sixty lodges from Britain to Australia can claim some form of link to the investigation (for good or bad). Importantly, there are several individual Masons who are possible suspects, but it is the idea of a Masonic conspiracy to shield the killer that has captured the public imagination and that aspect will be covered first.

If Stephen Knight's book *Jack the Ripper: The Final Solution* (1976) is to be believed, then Freemasons and the British Royal Family were at the heart of a conspiracy to murder several prostitutes. This idea (with different suspects) has also been put forward by Robinson (2015). The conspiracy theory has been further publicised by Hollywood in the film *From Hell* and various television programmes about the serial killer. In a Canadian film, *Murder by Decree*, even the greatest (but unfortunately, fictional) detective, Sherlock Holmes, finds himself embroiled in this Victorian scandal, where 'Jack' is protected by friends in high places. It is unclear what Sir Arthur Conan Doyle—creator of Holmes, and Freemason—would have made of this. He was a member of Phoenix No. 257 in Southsea, Hampshire. However, these is still doubt whether any suspect or those connected to the murders be linked to the Craft.

A major problem with the Jack the Ripper case is that the police at the time, and investigators since, cannot even agree on the number of victims. The number of women believed to have been slain by mysterious killer varies between five and eleven, with potentially linked homicides occurring between April 1888 and February 1891. There are, however, five crimes committed in 1888 that are generally accepted as the 'canonical' Ripper murders (even on the Metropolitan Police website); these are as follows:

1. Mary Ann Nichols: Friday 31 August in Buck's Row
2. Annie Chapman: Saturday 8 September in Hanbury Street
3. Elizabeth Stride: Sunday 30 September in Berner Street
4. Catherine Eddowes: Sunday 30 September in Mitre Square
5. Mary Jane Kelly: Friday 9 November in Miller's Court

All the victims were impoverished women who had turned to prostitution in the East End of London, a poverty-stricken and crime-ridden area of the capital. The attacks involved the throat being slashed, the abdomen being cut open, and, in some attacks, internal organs being removed. It should be noted that all these occurred on a weekend (Friday, Saturday, or Sunday evenings) and two occurred on the same day. It is believed that the Ripper was disturbed while murdering Elizabeth Stride and went on to murder Catherine Eddowes. This further complicated the murder investigation as the latter crime occurred in the area covered by the City of London Police, meaning that a completely separate force from the Metropolitan Police were responsible for the enquiry.

It must also be remembered that crime is difficult enough to solve in modern day London; in the latter years of the nineteenth century, investigation was a far more basic affair. Police photography was in its infancy (the Metropolitan Police did not even employ its own photographers at the time of the murders). Fingerprints would not be used to convict a criminal in England until 1902, and the idea of DNA did not even exist in contemporary science fiction; it was not until exactly one hundred years later that another sexual killer—Colin Pitchfork—would be sentenced to life imprisonment after DNA evidence had been used for the first time. Albeit, as we shall see, this has not stopped at least one modern-day researcher attempting to use this technology in an attempt to identify Jack the Ripper.

The options for the police in 1888 were limited: find an eyewitness who could identify the killer; offer a reward to obtain the name of a suspect who could be arrested and 'persuaded' to confess his deeds; or flood the area with patrols to catch 'Jack' in the act. To fit into the East End, the detectives needed disguises; they used the expertise of a wig maker and theatrical costume designer, William Berry 'Willy' Clarkson, who ran his business at 45 Wardour Street. His shop is now a Chinese restaurant, but a large clock with '*Costumier Perruquier*' is still fitted to the front of the building. Clarkson was a Mason and a member of Drury Lane No. 2127, which attracted the acting profession and those connected to it. Brother Clarkson appears to have aided villains, as well as officers of the law; he died in suspicion circumstances.

To augment the police patrols (in disguise or uniform), it was also proposed to use bloodhounds to find the killer, but Scotland Yard claimed that it had no budget to pay for the dogs (some things never change). Cheaper innovations had to be found—one constable nailed bicycle tyres to silence his noisy hobnailed boots, to give him the element of surprise. This inventive officer, PC Frederick Porter Wensley, would later join Temple Lodge No. 101 in London and went on to be the founder of the unit that became the famous 'Sweeney' or 'Flying Squad'.

Regarding the infamous conspiracy theory, Knight (1976) claimed that the murders were part of an establishment plot to cover up the secret marriage of the grandson of Queen Victoria, Prince Albert Victor, Duke of Clarence and Avondale (the eldest son of the Prince of Wales, later Edward VII). These were not new accusations; such rumours had been around for many years. The prince was already a Freemason at the time of the murders, having been initiated in March 1885 into the Royal Alpha Lodge No. 16. By 1888, when the killer was stalking Whitechapel, Albert Victor was the Master of Royal Alpha. He was subsequently the founding Master of a lodge named after him—Albert Victor Lodge No. 2328, which met in York. He appears to have been a committed Mason, joining the Rose Croix order. He was later a Grand Warden in the Craft and the Mark Degree, and was the Provincial Grand Master of Berkshire for two years until his death in 1892 at just twenty-eight years old.

The other party to the marriage was Annie Elizabeth Crook—a working class Roman Catholic woman who was employed in a tobacconist's shop. It is important to note that such a marriage, if it ever happened, would have been illegal under the Act of Settlement 1791, a law that forbade anyone in line to the throne from marrying a Roman Catholic.

Prince Albert Victor was said to be under the influence of an artist, Walter Sickert, and his Bohemian and theatrical circle of friends at that time. Sickert allowed the prince and Annie to live a secret life in a flat near Sickert's studio at 15 Cleveland Street, London. This

Prince Albert Victor. According to conspiracy theorists, his illegal marriage resulted in a Masonic plot to kill the prostitutes.

clandestine family existence was even more essential when Annie gave birth to a child called Alice. The nurse maid chosen was, according to this Ripper theory, Mary Ann Kelly—the last victim in the 'canonical five' series.

However, wedded bliss was not to last. In 1887, the Queen and her Prime Minister, Lord Salisbury (claimed by Knight to be a Freemason) received information regarding the prince's love nest and moved quickly. Prince Albert Victor was found and confined to his quarters at the palace. Annie, his 'wife', was taken under the charge of Sir William Gull, the Queen's Surgeon (and it is alleged, a senior Freemason) and eventually certified insane. She was to spend the rest of her life in a lunatic asylum. The baby, however, was not found. Little Alice had been out with her nurse maid. Kelly handed the baby to Sickert. Alice grew up and eventually became Sickert's lover. The product of their liaison was a son—Joseph Sickert— who was eventually to expose the whole wicked 'Masonic plot' to Knight and others.

According to Sickert, Kelly attempted to blackmail the authorities—demanding money or else she would expose the illegal marriage of Prince Albert Victor. Rather than pay, a conspiracy was hatched amongst the senior Freemasons named above, together with Sir Charles Warren, the Commissioner of the Metropolitan Police and Sir Robert Anderson, his Assistant Commissioner, to kill Kelly and her accomplices. The actual murders were committed by Sir William Gull, in accordance with the First Degree obligation penalty of 'having the throat cut across'.

Unfortunately, while a 'ripping yarn' (and suitable for a Hollywood film), the story does not stand up to scrutiny. John Hamill, the then United Grand Lodge of England librarian (and now Director of Communications), researched those purported to be members of the Craft and stated:

> The Stephen Knight thesis is based upon the claim that the main protagonists, the Prime Minister Lord Salisbury, Sir Robert Anderson and Sir William Gull were all high-ranking Freemasons. Knight knew his claim to be false for, in 1973, I received a phone call from him in the Library, in which he asked for confirmation of their membership. After a lengthy search I informed him that only Sir Charles Warren had been a Freemason. Regrettably, he chose to ignore this answer as it ruined his story.

On a practical level, it should be noted that by 1888, William Gull was seventy-two years old and had suffered a stroke; hardly a man able to overpower victims and commit violent crime. Perhaps most damning, Joseph Sickert has since admitted making the whole thing up, but the theory still remains popular. The reader should consider the Yorkshire Ripper case—long solved—but imagine if Peter Sutcliffe had not been caught and many years after the event a book was being written on the case. It is doubtful that the author would sell many copies if he concluded that the serial killer was a rather humdrum (but evil) lorry driver from Bradford. The origin of this conspiracy theory may be the result of a sexual scandal that had involved the Prince of Wales (later Edward VII), who was the Grand Master at the time of the murders.

There are, however, several undisputed Masonic links to the murders. Firstly, there were lodges meeting in that area in 1888. These included:

Sir Charles Warren, the Mason who was the Commissioner of the Metropolitan Police at the time of the murders.

St Paul's No. 19: City Terminus Hotel, Cannon Street, City
Yarbrough No. 554: Green Dragon, Spring Garden Place, Stepney
Temperance in the East No. 898: Assembly Rooms, Newby Place, Poplar
City of London No. 901: Guildhall Tavern, Gresham Street
Doric No. 933: Anderton's Hotel, Fleet Street, City
Upton No. 1227: Three Nuns Hotel, Aldgate High Street
Friars No. 1349: Ship and Turtle Tavern, Leadenhall Street
Prince Leopold No. 1445: Three Nuns Hotel, Aldgate High Street

In addition, these and other lodges had 'Lodges of Instruction' or 'LOI' (practice meetings) meeting in the East End and in the City on the nights of the murders. So, there is no doubt that Masons were in the area at the time, but so were members of every other organisation in London. The yard in which Elizabeth Stride's body was found was actually owned by a Mason—Brother Arthur Duttfield of Doric Lodge No. 933; he was never a suspect in the case and Knight missed this link to the Craft.

While Knight can be shown to be wrong when he claims that Lord Salisbury, Sir William Gull, Sir Robert Anderson, and various others were Freemasons, there is no doubt, as John Hamill notes, that Sir Charles Warren was a member of the Craft. Warren was a long serving officer in the British Army. He was commissioned into the Royal Engineers and while serving as such, he was one of earliest archaeologists in the Holy Land, where he tunnelled under Temple Mount in Jerusalem, the site of King Solomon's Temple. Sir Charles was appointed Commissioner of the Metropolitan Police, based at Great Scotland Yard, in 1886; at the time, it was standard practice to appoint a military officer to command a police force.

In Masonic terms, he is Right Worshipful Brother General Sir Charles Warren, District Grand Master of the Eastern Archipelago in Singapore. He had an extensive Masonic career. He was initiated into the Lodge of Friendship No. 278 (now Royal Lodge of Friendship), which still meets in Gibraltar. His Masonry was worldwide: he was member of Zetland in the East No. 508 in Singapore and had a lodge named after him—the Charles Warren No. 1832 in South Africa (this has since been amalgamated to form Octahedron and Charles Warren No. 1417). He was the first Master of the premier lodge of Masonic research—Quatuor Coronati Lodge No. 2076. Sir Charles also joined a Holy Royal Arch chapter, Rose Croix, the Mark Degree, and Knights Templar.

As Commissioner of the Metropolitan Police, Warren played a personal role in the Ripper enquiry and his intervention has fuelled the Masonic conspiracy theory. On the night of the 'double event' (as it is known), when Eddowes and Stride were murdered, a piece of a blood stained apron, possibly belonging to the first victim of the night, was found in Goulston Street, Whitechapel. It is just over half a mile from Berner Street (Eddowes) to Mitre Square (Stride) and Goulston Street lies halfway between the two. Above the blooded item, there was written in white chalk on the wall, 'The Juwes are the men that will not be blamed for nothing'. The reader will recall that the two murders fell into two different police areas and to emphasise the problems that this can cause, a detective constable of the City Force recorded it slightly differently—'The Juwes are not the men who will be blamed for nothing'.

It is one of the tenets of the conspiracy theorists that Warren ordered this to be removed before it could be photographed, to assist the (alleged) Masonic murderers. Knight claimed that the unusual spelling, 'Juwes', was nothing to do with 'Jews'; it was a reference to Masonic ritual. He then suggested that 'Juwes' was a collective word for Jubela, Jubelo, and Jubelum—names for the three Masons who, in the Third Degree ritual, murder Grand Master Hiram Abif when he refuses to divulge the secrets of a Master Mason to them. This story is Masonic legend; Hiram Abif appears in the Bible at King Solomon's Temple, but his death—peaceful or otherwise—is never mentioned. These names no longer feature in English Masonic ritual, but they do appear in an anti-Masonic pamphlet from 1760, *Three Distinct Knocks*. As official rituals were not published at the time, these exposures are a great help to modern day Masonic researchers. Likewise, the names are noted in a further similar publication two years later called 'Jachin and Boaz'. Unfortunately, for conspiracy theorists, there is no evidence of these fictional murderers ever being referred to as 'Juwes'.

Furthermore, it was not Brother Warren who ordered removal of the message; he simply supported the instructions of the local police commander (not a member of the Craft) who told his officers to wash it away. Superintendent Thomas Arnold of Whitechapel Division feared antisemitic riots, with Jews being blamed for the murders; as we will see, a Polish Jew, Aaron Kosminski, is still very much a Jack the Ripper suspect. The Metropolitan Police's actions displeased the City of London Police, who viewed it as part of the crime scene. Some officers at the time were less sure and thought it an irrelevant piece of graffiti, questioning why a murderer would stop between two crimes and scrawl a 'clue' on a wall.

In addition to Warren, the most senior police officer in London, other key figures in the enquiry were (or would become) members of the Craft. When the murders began, the investigation was initially led by the local head of the CID on 'H' (Whitechapel) Division, Detective Inspector Edmund Reid, who in 1894 would join Ixion Lodge No. 2501 in Harlow, Essex; however, as the enquiry grew, Scotland Yard sent one of its investigators to coordinate it.

The officer despatched to east London was Detective Inspector Fredcrick Abberline, who is one of the most famous detectives linked to the Jack the Ripper case (played by Michael Caine in the 1988 series about the murders and later by Johnny Depp in the film *From Hell*). Abberline had served in the East End for much of his police career (despite being from rural Dorset). He was not a Mason at the time of the murders, but he joined as soon as the investigation had quietened down; in 1889, Abberline was initiated into the Zetland Lodge No. 511. In a similar manner, his deputy, Sergeant George Godley (portrayed in films by actors Lewis Collins and Robbie Coltrane) would also join the Craft. Interestingly, in 1902, when Godley investigated poisoner George Chapman, Abberline (retired by this point) named the arrested man as Jack the Ripper (albeit with little evidence). The following year, Godley (by now an inspector) was initiated into Borough Lodge No. 2589 at London Bridge.

Senior to Abberline was an officer tasked by the Assistant Commissioner to oversee the entire Ripper enquiry from The Yard. His duty was to examine 'every paper, every document, every report… every telegram' relating to the case. The officer trusted with this role was Chief Inspector Donald Swanson. He was already a Scottish Mason, being a member of St Peter's Lodge No. 284. The year after the Whitechapel Murders, he was to join a London Mark lodge—Ubique No. 411. Swanson's views on the identity of Jack the Ripper were to come to light many years after his death and will be discussed later in this chapter.

While Swanson was a very experienced detective, the case should have been handled by the officer with the most investigative experience at Scotland Yard—Chief Constable (this was a rank equivalent to commander today) 'Dolly' Williamson. Williamson was the most senior operational officer in the CID, but he was an ill man and suffered from a heart condition. He died the year after the Ripper murders while still serving. He was a longstanding member of the Lodge of Fortitude and Old Cumberland No. 12.

The failure by the police to catch the killer resulted in much criticism in the press and the formation of the Whitechapel Vigilante Committee. In various films, this has been portrayed as a gang of local thugs, but in reality, it was established by local businessmen, concerned at the potential loss of trade due to the ongoing murders. The man selected as their chairman was a builder and decorator, George Lusk—or Brother Lusk of the Doric Lodge No. 933, the same lodge as the owner of the yard in Berner Street, where Stride's body had been found. Another longstanding member of Doric was Brother Charles Digby, an Inspector in the Metropolitan Police who also served on 'H' Division.

On 16 October, over a fortnight after the murder of the fourth victim, Eddowes, Brother Lusk received a small brown paper parcel. This contained part of a human kidney and the infamous 'From Hell' letter, which read, with (possibly deliberate) spelling mistakes:

From hell
Mr Lusk
Sor
I send you half the
Kidne I took from one women
prasarved it for you tother piece
I fried and ate it was very nise. I
may send you the bloody knif that
took it out if you only wate a whil
longer.
signed
Catch me when
you Can
Mishter Lusk

A kidney had been taken from Eddowes' body. This was noted by the City Police Surgeon, Dr Frederick Brown, who had attended the murder scene in Mitre Square and conducted the *post-mortem* examination. Brown was a very active member of the Craft. He had been initiated into St Paul's Lodge No. 194, which is now based in Southgate, but at the time met in the City. He later went on to join Grand Master's No. 1 in 1878 and was a founding member of two other London lodges—Train-bands No. 2524 and Cheselden No. 2870.

The piece of kidney sent to Brother Lusk was taken to the London Hospital and examined by Dr Thomas Horrocks Openshaw, who held the post of Curator of the Pathology Museum. Openshaw was a Lancastrian and a Freemason. He had been initiated in Newcastle-upon-Tyne in the Hotspur Lodge No. 1626, while studying at Durham University. He went on to join several other lodges, which met in London, with several connected with his birthplace, university, and work—in 1890, the Old Concord No. 172; in 1894, the Lancastrian No. 2528; in 1901, the (now Royal) London Hospital No. 2845; in 1904, he was the founder Junior Warden of University of Durham Lodge No. 3030; and in 1908, Foxhunters No. 3094. He was also a founder of a Bristol lodge, Robert Thorne No. 3663. Dr Openshaw was also active in the Holy Royal Chapter and was the first 'MEZ' of Lancastrian Chapter No. 2528 and a founder of William Harvey No. 2682 (now No. 49). It was initially reported that he had identified the organ as a left kidney belonging to a heavy-drinking woman (fitting the description of Eddowes), but he later refuted giving such an accurate description, stating that it was simply human and may have been preserved in spirits. Dr Openshaw later received a letter signed 'Jack the Ripper' stating 'you was rite it was the left kidny ... ' (badly spelled in the style of the letter sent to Brother Lusk).

Despite this seemingly important clue being in the hand of the authorities, the killer remained at large and the Police Commissioner was heavily criticised by the press and politicians for his failure to catch the serial killer. The message sent to Brother Lusk and the various other letters allegedly sent by the killer also distracted the enquiry (in a similar manner to the Yorkshire Ripper investigation one hundred years later). Furthermore, Warren's time as head of the Metropolitan Police was beset with internal squabbles,

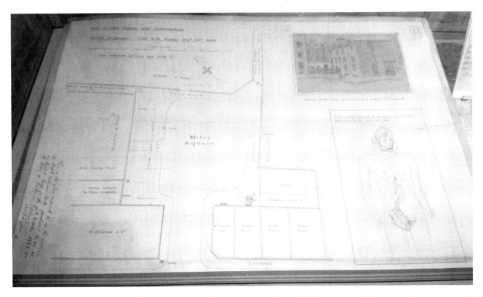

Sketch of Mitre Square and Catherine Eddowes: an original drawing of the murder scene and victim's injuries.

particularly with Assistant Commissioner James Munro, the first head of the CID (detective department). Despite Dr Robert Anderson having taken over this post from Munro, the previous relationship between the CID and the Commissioner cannot have aided the Jack the Ripper enquiry. Adding to the problems facing Scotland Yard, as has been noted above, was the fact that Chief Constable Williamson, the operational head of the detective branch, was at death's door.

Perhaps as a result of a combination of these factors, Warren resigned his post, strangely (or coincidentally), just hours before the murder of Kelly, the final victim. The lack of a commissioner in charge of the Metropolitan Police further hindered the enquiry. Warren had ordered officers not to enter murder scenes if they were believed to be connected to the Jack the Ripper case. As the constables on duty had not been informed of his departure, the scene of Kelly's death—potentially a gold mine of clues—remained sealed for several hours.

One of the officers who visited this scene was Detective Constable Walter Dew. Later in his career, he would become famous as the officer who arrested Dr Crippen. Dew knew Mary Ann Kelly as a local prostitute and later described seeing her mutilated remains as 'the most gruesome memory of my police career.' Her murder in Miller's Court off the long-demolished Dorset Street was, indeed, a terrible sight; she had been butchered. It was Dew who noted that an attempt was made to identify the killer by photographing the open eyes of the dead woman; the contemporary belief was that the eyes would retain the last image seen. Dew would later join Masonry, being initiated into the Dalhousie Lodge No. 865 in Middlesex. This officer would later write his account of the investigation, in which he attributed several earlier deaths to the Jack the Ripper (see Parlour, A., and Parlour, S., 2013). Dew, however, did not name any suspects.

Masonic Jewels belonging to Dr Thomas Openshaw, the doctor who examined the kidney sent with the 'From Hell' letter.

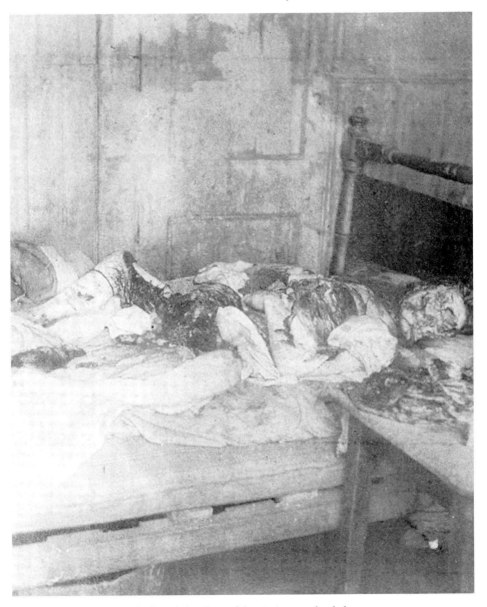

Body of Mary Ann Kelly. The brutal slaughter of the victim can clearly be seen.

Another future Mason involved in the hunt for the killer was Detective Constable Henry Cox of the City of London Police. He was tasked to conduct surveillance on a man believed to be Jack the Ripper, following the death of Kelly. He would later describe the suspect:

> About five feet six inches in height, with short, black, curly hair, and he had a habit of taking late walks abroad. He occupied several shops in the East End, but from time to time he became insane, and was forced to spend a portion of his time in an asylum in Surrey.

He did not, however, name the man and stated that no evidence existed against him; the only hope was catching him in the act of committing a further murder. Cox would later join the Vitruvian Lodge No. 87 in London and, as a detective inspector, arrested Brother Samuel Dougal, another Masonic murderer.

Further to physical descriptions of suspects recorded by officers, a detailed assessment of type of person involved in the killings was provided to Scotland Yard by Dr Thomas Bond, the Westminster Division Police Surgeon. He examined the bodies of all the victims and carried out what today would be called 'offender profiling'. Bond had been initiated into the Old Union Lodge No. 46 in London in 1876, though his membership had lapsed by the time of the Ripper murders. His profile of the killer was as follows and also fits the Yorkshire Ripper:

> He had 'no scientific nor anatomical knowledge'.
> He worked alone and was a 'man of physical strength and of great coolness and daring'.
> He was likely to be a 'quiet, inoffensive looking man probably middle-aged and ... respectably dressed' but, who suffered 'periodical attacks of Homicidal and erotic mania'.

Critically, Dr Bond suggested that those living with him would have some suspicions and may come forward if there was a reward. No financial inducement was ever offered to the public to identify the Ripper, as Sir Charles Warren believed this would result in even more false leads. He did, however, offer immunity from prosecution for any accomplice who came forward and identified the killer. As with all previous tactics, this failed to result in an arrest and like the victims in this case, Brother Bond would come to a sad end; he committed suicide in 1901 by jumping from a window.

The last Ripper killing (if one considers only the 'canonical five') occurred on the second Saturday in November, the day of the Lord Mayor's Parade. This is the day when the old Lord Mayor leaves office and the new one takes the post. The mayor leaving office was Sir Polydore de Keyser—a Belgian Catholic by birth, and a Freemason. He had been the Lord Mayor at the time of the Ripper Murders and given his religion, had a possible connection that Knight failed to play on. De Keyser was a founder member of MacDonald Lodge No. 1216, which was in (what would become) the Territorial Army Centre in Camberwell, south London.

In a further Masonic connection, the coroners at the inquests for the four canonical victims found in the Metropolitan Police District were also members of the Craft. Sussex Freemason Wynne Baxter (a member of South Saxon Lodge No. 311) was the coroner for the County of

Middlesex (Eastern District), which covered the East End. Hence, he was responsible for the inquests into the deaths of Nichols, Chapman, and Stride. In relation to Kelly, the authorities decided that body was found just outside Baxter's part of Middlesex (even the jury at the hearing could not understand why he had not been appointed to deal with the case). Hence, the inquest for the last victim was heard by Thomas Bramah Diplock, who had been initiated into the Royal Somerset House and Inverness Lodge No. 4 in 1854. He later joined United Mariners (then No. 33, now No. 30) and South Middlesex (then No. 1160, now No. 858).

With the city inquest, it has been claimed that the coroner, Samuel Langham, was a member of the Craft, but there is no record of him joining any lodge. Those determined to find a Masonic conspiracy may have confused him with the City Police solicitor, Sir Henry Homewood Crawford. He certainly was a Mason and had been initiated into the Grand Master's Lodge No. 1 in 1879 and later joined Alliance Lodge No. 1827 in 1886.

The case seemingly remained unsolved, but that did not stop the police having several suspects or criminals claiming to the infamous murderer. Once such man was William Wallace Brodie, who stabbed a woman to death in Whitechapel in 1889. The victim had screamed 'Jack the Ripper' during the attack and when arrested, Brodie admitted to committing nine murders, due to having a 'worm in my head'. Police enquiries, however, revealed that he was in South Africa in 1888 and he was only convicted of the one offence for which he had been detained. At least one Mason was involved in the arrest of this Ripper 'suspect'—Sergeant Eugene Charles Bradshaw, a member of Prince Leopold Lodge No. 1445, which met in Aldgate High Street. The lodge location is in walking distance of all the murders.

In 1894, some six years after the murders, the case was reviewed by Assistant Chief Constable, (later Sir) Melville Macnaghten, who went on to be the head of the CID. By this time, Brother Abberline had been replaced as the Scotland Yard inspector in Whitechapel by Henry Moore. Moore had been initiated into Southern Star Lodge No. 1158 and later joined St Chad No. 3115. Macnaghten, who was not a member of the Craft, named three possible (non-Masonic) suspects:

1. Montague Druitt: a barrister, who had committed suicide after the murders.
2. Michael Ostrog: a Russian born criminal who was committed to various lunatic asylums, but who may well have been in France in 1888.
3. Aaron Kosminski: a Polish Jew whose links to the crimes are described in detail later in this chapter.

Over the years that followed, many of the detectives involved would name their own suspects. It has already been noted that Abberline considered George Chapman as the killer. Later, retired inspector and Freemason John Littlechild, would name an American, Doctor Francis Tumblety. As with other suspects, Tumblety matches some of the descriptions of Whitechapel killer, but not others. Littlechild was initiated into Zetland Lodge No. 511 in London in 1894 (he is likely to have been proposed by Brother Abberline, who was already a member). Once retired from the police, he joined Mendelssohn No. 2661 (now defunct) and Justicia No. 2563, then in London, now in Twickenham. He was involved in several famous cases as a police and private detective.

Furthermore, in 1910, Sir Robert Anderson (not a Mason), published his memoirs, *The Lighter Side of My Official Life*. In this, the retired head of the CID wrote a most unusual comment—'"undiscovered murders" are rare in London, and the "Jack-the-Ripper" crimes are not in that category'. Here, he is clearly stating that the identity of the killer was known. He then added that the suspect was identified by a witness as a Polish Jew, but did not name him for fear of being sued.

Anderson presented a signed copy to Chief Inspector Swanson (the Scottish Mason and co-ordinator of the Ripper enquiry at Scotland Yard) and this book remained with his family for many years. In 1987, Swanson's great-grandson was surprised to find that the long dead officer had written notes within it; these named the killer. The book was presented to the Crime Museum at New Scotland Yard for further examination and comparison with original reports written at the time. This confirmed that Swanson was, indeed, the author of the pencil annotations. The chief inspector had also noted the reason as to why the Jewish suspect had not been arrested; the witness was a man of the same religion and had refused to give official evidence in case it resulted in another Jew being hanged.

In his notes at the rear of the book, Swanson explained how the police decided to proceed after the witness refused to give evidence; the suspect was placed under surveillance, no doubt in an attempt to apprehend him when he attacked another prostitute. This tactic was doomed to failure, as the notes record that the man named as the Ripper was placed in the Stepney Workhouse. However, the man was not poor; he was mad. He is likely to have been placed in the adjacent Poplar and Stepney Sick Asylum, located in Devon's Road, Bow. For any determined conspiracy theorists, there is a pub named 'The Widow's Son' on this road; there can be no better Masonic name for an inn.

Swanson confirmed the mental state of the suspect as he recorded that he was soon moved to the lunatic asylum in Colney Hatch, in what is now the London Borough of Barnet. In Victorian times, 'Colney Hatch' was a byword for madness. Critically, he ends his notes by stating 'Kosminski was the suspect'. Kosminski was detained in the establishments shown until his death in a Hertfordshire asylum in 1919. At the time of the murders he was only twenty-three years old, but the notes on his condition appear to show that he may well have been a paranoid schizophrenic—as is his namesake, the Yorkshire Ripper. He also hated women and spent much time masturbating in public; this issue was possibly the reason his family finally had him locked away.

In 2014, it was announced that the case against Kosminski had been 'proved' by DNA. An expert in historic DNA analysis, Dr Jari Louhelainen, claimed that a shawl belonging to Catherine Eddowes could clearly be linked to both this victim and the Polish Jewish suspect. He stated that blood on the shawl had been matched to a descendant of the fourth victim and semen stains had resulted a DNA match to a descendant of Kosminski—conclusive proof, it would seem. Unfortunately, the shawl had been passed through many hands. In legal terms, it is contaminated and would never be accepted in evidence. If nothing else, Kosminski was not a Mason. However, it is still unclear if he was the killer.

Two of the men suspected of being Jack the Ripper have been the subject of books and have been identified as members of the Craft. A third suspect has been linked to the killings, but until now, his involvement in Masonry has not been revealed. The fourth suspect was executed for the brutal killing of a woman, but has not been previously suggested as a suspect for the Whitechapel Murders. There is also a famous philanthropist 'in the frame'.

Two siblings from Liverpool have also been added to the list of possible identities of Jack the Ripper. These are the Maybrick brothers: James (born 1838) and Michael (born 1841). James was initiated into St George's Lodge of Harmony No. 32, which met in Liverpool in 1870, but Michael was a far more committed Mason. In 1876, he was initiated in a London lodge, Athenaeum No. 1491, which then met at a venue of the same name (long since demolished) in Camden Road, Islington. He then joined two London lodges—Orpheus No. 1706 and St Andrew's No. 231. Spreading his wings in 1881, he joined a lodge, which met in Surbiton, Eurydice No. 1920 (this now meets in the Masonic Centre in Ealing) and finally, in 1897, Ryde No. 698 on the Isle of Wight. A committed public servant, he was a magistrate in Ryde and the mayor on five occasions.

The evidence against James, a cotton merchant, emerged in 1992, when a diary came to light in rather dubious circumstances, being handed over in a pub, with little, if any, historical provenance. It does not name the older Maybrick brother, but various entries point to him as the author. Several scientific tests on the ink used on the document and studies of the handwriting have failed to confirm the diary's authenticity. There are, however, several twists in the story of the life (and death) of James Maybrick. Firstly, he appears to have had a common-law wife, who lived in East London (close to the Ripper murders), in addition to his teenage American bride, Florence. Secondly, in 1889, James was allegedly murdered by Florence, who was tried in Liverpool and jailed for the crime. Maybrick may well have killed himself; he had become addicted to arsenic, which he self-administered. In Victorian times, this poison was used to treat malaria. In a final twist, his wife was released in 1904 as the biased trial judge had died insane in a lunatic asylum.

Michael Maybrick left his native city to pursue a musical career, studying music across Europe and later composing several tunes that were popular in Victorian theatres and music halls. He even toured America. Part of the 'evidence' against him is that he wrote a song called '*They All Love Jack*'. In a book, using the title of the song, Robinson (2015) claims that the younger Maybrick was the psychopathic killer who was shielded by Freemasons, instead of Sir William Gull. The diary is also attributed to Michael Maybrick, rather than his older brother. Thus, another suspect has been added to the list for Ripperologists to debate.

The third Mason suspected of being Jack Ripper is a convicted killer. Frederick Bailey Deeming (who was also known by several aliases) was hanged for a murder committed in Melbourne in the Australian state of Victoria, just a few years after the Whitechapel Murders. While awaiting trial, several dead bodies were found buried in a house rented by him in northern England. Deeming was a Freemason and had been initiated into the Tranquillity Lodge in Sydney in 1886 (it was then No. 1552 as an English lodge; it is now No. 42 as part of the New South Wales Grand Lodge). His membership of the Craft has never previously been revealed. It is surprising that he found the time to join a lodge, as, in addition to his murderous ways, he spent much of his time travelling the world, committing numerous swindles (as far apart as South Africa and Hull, as well as being arrested in Uruguay). He was also a womaniser and committed bigamy twice.

Deeming was born in Leicestershire in 1853, but, at the age of sixteen, he ran away to sea. His first marriage was in 1881 and he had four children by his wife, Marie—three daughters and a son. On being released from prison (where he had served a sentence for fraud) in 1891, he rented a house, Dinham Villa in Rainhill, then moved to Lancashire (now Merseyside) and a woman and children were seen there. When locals enquired, Deeming explained them away as his sister and her offspring, who were just visiting and had since left. He then approached the owner of the house and sought to permission renew the kitchen floor. Authority was granted and he purchased four barrels of cement to complete the work.

His 'sister' having vanished, Deeming (now calling himself Albert Williams) now married a local girl, Emily Mather. The new couple sailed for Australia and rented a home in the Melbourne suburb of Windsor. Sometime around Christmas Day 1891, Deeming murdered Emily and buried her under the bedroom floor, covering her with cement. He left the house, initially staying in hotel in Swanston Street (he then began using the name 'Baron Swanston'). Using false references, he obtained employment in a mine in the town of Southern Cross in Western Australia. During this time, he proposed to another woman in Melbourne (fortunately for her, she never joined him at the mine) and during the voyage around the coast, he continued his womanising ways.

In March, a new tenant at the house in Melbourne complained of a dreadful smell and the body of Emily was discovered. Her throat had been cut and her skull smashed with several blows. Detectives of the Victoria Police found letters revealing Deeming's new location and arrested him in Southern Cross. One of the officers may have been a Mason, albeit his occupation on initiation is shown as a 'chemist' (it was not unusual for officers to do this—see DI George Greenham for example). Sergeant William Considine appears to have been a member of Combermere Lodge No. 752 (which is still under the control of the English Grand Lodge, despite being in Victoria).

Even though it was the nineteenth century, news travelled swiftly to Lancashire via Scotland Yard of the arrest of Deeming (or Williams) for the Melbourne murder and the police searched the house in Rainhill. This had remained unoccupied for several months as the killer had taken out a long lease. After smashing through several layers of concrete under the kitchen floor, the police made a gruesome discovery—the decomposed bodies of Marie and the four children, all with their throats cut. The *Yorkshire Evening Post* described the temporary mortuary in the house as an 'afflicting sight' (as Masons will recall from the Third Degree). The house was later demolished to prevent ghoulish sightseers visiting the area.

The officer in charge of the Rainhill investigation was Superintendent Joseph Keighley of the Lancashire Constabulary. He had been initiated in Lodge of Equity and Appleton No. 1445 in Widnes in 1890. He was also a founder member of Widnes Lodge No. 2819 (since amalgamated to form Widnes and Knowsley No. 3581). One of the supervisors at the search was Sergeant Ralph Chipchase, who would later join Victoria Lodge No. 1345 in Eccles in 1898, by which time he had been promoted to inspector.

Both Sergeant Considine in Australia and Superintendent Keighley in England would have known that Deeming was a brother Mason. In luggage belonging to the suspect located in a hotel in Liverpool, police found blood stains and items that were described in the press as 'Masonic signs'. When arrested in Southern Cross, Deeming was in possession of his Masonic apron, which had been embroidered with his initials. It should be noted that this had no influence on Considine and Keighley, who did their duty and ensured that damning evidence was gathered against the murderer.

As news broke of the two murder scenes and the method of killing—the throats of all six victims being slashed—newspapers around the world speculated that Deeming was Jack the Ripper. It was only three years since the Whitechapel Murders and so suspects were still being actively sought. Despite pleading insanity, Deeming was found guilty of murdering Emily Mather at Melbourne Supreme Court in April 1892. He was hanged a month later, with the wits of the time cruelly suggesting that Deeming, 'married in haste and cemented at leisure.'

For many years, it was suggested that Deeming could not have been Jack the Ripper as he was in prison in South Africa in 1888. His movements during the time of the murders are, however, unclear and he may have been in England at that time. It should be taken into account that his crimes were always committed indoors and against family members. He also carefully concealed the bodies, unlike Jack the Ripper, who murdered strangers in the street and left their bodies in open view. Deeming did fit the stereotypical description of Jack the Ripper; he dressed as a gentleman and often claimed to be an army officer. This link to the killer and the similarity of his handwriting to the 'Dear Boss' letter sent to the press during the Whitechapel Murders were all reported in the contemporary press.

However, if Deeming is a suspect for these circumstantial reasons, then perhaps, a fourth name should be added to the list of Masons who may have stalked the streets as Jack the Ripper; that new suspect is Samuel Dougal. Like Deeming, he also pretended to be an army officer (so fits the 'gentleman' description) and was violent towards women (he was hanged for murdering one, but is believed to have also killed two of his wives). Critically, Dougal was born in the East End and was in and around London in 1888, so is as much as a suspect as Deeming. When a soldier, Dougal had joined an Irish lodge, St Patrick's No. 195, and later Royal Standard No. 398 in Canada—another suspect for the 'Ripperologists' to study.

Perhaps the oddest Masonic suspect suggested as Jack the Ripper is the great Victorian philanthropist and Christian orator, Dr Thomas Barnardo, whose charity continues to improve the lives of children and young people to this day. Barnardo began his work in the East End and he knew one of the victims; he identified the body of Elizabeth Stride (the third victim) as a woman who had attended one of his sermons a few days prior to her murder. This was not unusual as he often attempted to persuade prostitutes to hand over their children to his care. Barnardo joined Shadwell Clerke No. 1910, the year after the Ripper murders. Again, there is little evidence to actually link him to the crimes; he was in the East End, had met one of the dead women, and vaguely fitted one of the several descriptions.

The Masonic connections to these infamous murders require further thought. Sir William Gull and Lord Salisbury were not Freemasons, but Prince Albert Victor, the Commissioner of Police, Lord Mayor of London, the coroner, a pathologist, police officers, and even the man who received the kidney 'From Hell' were all members of the Craft, as were the Maybrick brothers and convicted killers Deeming and Dougal. The involvement

Death mask of Frederick Deeming, a convicted murderer long suspected of being Jack the Ripper; identified as a Freemason for the first time.

(or suspected involvement) of so many Masons in key parts of the Whitechapel Murders may indicate some dreadful conspiracy, but it may just reflect Victorian society in England, where the Craft could boast several members of the Royal Family and many men of influence among its brethren. The failure to catch 'Jack' may be due to the lack of the many investigative techniques that were not available in 1888 or simply police blundering and bad leadership, rather than the invisible hand of wicked Freemasonry protecting men in high places. It could also be due to the fact that Kosminski was the killer, but was too mad to be tried before a court.

The rumours of Masonic involvement, however, are unlikely to go away, whether there is DNA or other evidence to prove otherwise. For example, in the novel *The Ripper Secret* (Steele, 2012) the story revolves around Sir Charles Warren, a Freemason (a fact), who finds a secret document (fiction) when carrying out archaeological work under Temple Mount (a fact). This is later linked to the Ripper enquiry (fiction) that Warren was ultimately responsible for as Commissioner of the Police (a fact). Add to the mix that Warren was a member of the Masonic Order of Knights Templar, (allegedly) ordered the removal of the

Goulston Street graffiti referring to the 'Juwes', and resigned just before the last murder, it can be seen how writers (and conspiracy theorists) will always find a new angle to a series of murders that occurred over 125 years ago.

For the Mason (or conspiracy theorist) interested in this case, it is still possible to visit a number of the murder sites, although one—the Kelly murder scene—now lies under a car park. 'Ripperologists', as experts on the Whitechapel murders are known, regularly run tours of the sites of significance. Warren's headquarters at Great Scotland Yard, where he directed the enquiry, has been demolished, although the head office for the Metropolitan Police has moved twice to New Scotland Yard on the Embankment and then the current New Scotland Yard in Victoria. There is still a police building on Great Scotland Yard (albeit on the opposite side of the road from the original headquarters) and it is worth wandering down this road to see the origin of the 'Scotland Yard' name that is famous throughout the world.

As all the evidence in the case has been mishandled and contaminated over many, many years, we are unlikely ever to know the truth of Jack the Ripper's identity—or whether he was Jack the Mason—as the list of suspects grows continually. Perhaps the most sensible comment on the identity of the killer came from crime writer, Colin Wilson:

I have always had the feeling that on the Day of Judgement, when all things shall be known, when I and other generations of 'Ripperologists' ask for Jack the Ripper to step forward and call out his true name, then we shall turn and look with blank astonishment at one another when he announces his name and say, 'Who?'

(Parlour, A., and Parlour, S., 1997).

36

The Murder of William Terriss: Actor, Mason, and Ghost

Masonic Connection
Victim
Doctors
Lawyer
Witnesses
Murderer?

Date
1871: Victim initiated into Freemasonry
1897: Murder occurred

Connection to London
Maiden Lane: Murder occurred in outside Adelphi stage door (a green plaque marks the spot)
Bow Street: Killer taken to police station
Old Brompton Road: Victim buried in Brompton Cemetery
Old Bailey: Court where tried and convicted

Lodges
Domatic No. 177
Jerusalem No. 197
Sutherland Lodge of Unity No. 460
Grecia No. 1105
St Peter and St Pauls' No. 1410
Drury Lane No. 2127
Savage Club No. 2190

Tourists (and Masons) wandering along Maiden Lane towards Covent Garden from Charing Cross may note a plaque recording where William Terriss was murdered in 1897. It is said that the ghost of this renowned Victorian actor still haunts the area. Terriss (born William Charles James Lewin in 1847 in Marylebone, London) was also a Mason, but he may have been killed by another member of the Craft. Terriss was subjected to a brutal knife attack, committed in full view of many witnesses by a madman (or perhaps it was a mad Mason).

Terriss was a well-travelled man who fell into acting after a series of failed careers. Despite a good education at Christ's Hospital in the City of London and attending Oxford University, he failed to obtain a degree. Looking for adventure, he sailed the seas with the merchant navy, worked as a tea planter in India, assisted his surgeon brother, and tried his hand at engineering. Not taking to any of these varied roles, he decided to try acting as he enjoyed amateur theatre.

Having changed his name from Lewin, Terriss appeared in minor roles in Birmingham and London, but he was still restless and uncertain where his future lay. From England, he drifted to South America and even the Falkland Islands, where he attempted to make money from sheep farming. By now married and with a child, he was back in London in 1871 and this is when he first became a Mason, joining the Domatic Lodge No. 177 (using his real name). At the time, the lodge met in the Strand, near many of the theatres where Terriss would become a star.

His career now took off and he impressed audiences playing swashbuckling roles, such as Robin Hood, at the Theatre Royal Drury Lane. It would be assumed that he would have grasped this opportunity to build on this success, but Terriss was still not satisfied with life and sailed for the United States to breed horses in Kentucky. Masonry does, however, seems to have been a stabilising force in his life and he joined a lodge in America. This horse breeding venture was, like many of his other 'get rich quick' schemes, a flop and by 1873, he was back in England.

Terriss returned to acting and became extremely popular, with several leading roles. He also proved his versatility as an actor, being able to move from Shakespeare to comedy, as well as adaptations of Charles Dickens's stories. This work took him to several of the West End theatres, which still stand today, including Drury Lane and the Adelphi on the Strand. In 1880, he joined Henry Irving's company at the Lyceum Theatre, where he achieved even more success, including playing the leading part in Romeo and Juliet. He could excite the audience with both love and fighting scenes. Irving was to become a Mason; in 1882, he joined the Jerusalem Lodge No. 197 and five years later, he was the founder Treasurer of the Savage Club Lodge No. 2190. Irving, as we shall see, would later be scathing regarding the attitude of the authorities towards the acting profession.

Through the 1880s and early 1890s, Terriss moved with ease between major roles at the most popular London theatres and twice toured the United States, in a troop of actors led by Brother Irving. He even found time to join Irving's Mother Lodge, Drury Lane No. 2127 in 1887, but resigned the following year. In 1894, he made his last professional move, returning to take leading parts at the Adelphi. His final role would be in 1897 in a play entitled *Secret Service*, where he played the part of Captain Thorne, a Confederate artillery officer who was really a Union Army spy.

During this successful period, Terriss had met a fellow actor, Richard Archer Prince, who originated from Dundee. It was later stated at the Old Bailey that people in the Scottish city referred to him as 'mad Archer, the actor'. Prince had a foul temper and was

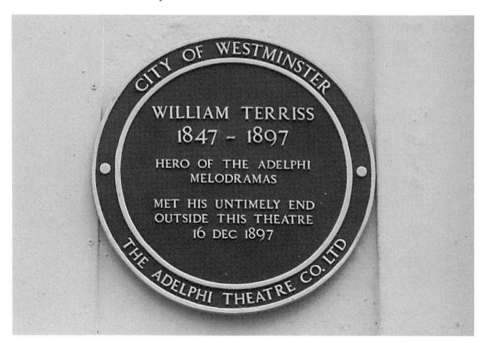

Above: Plaque marking the murder of Terriss, the scene of the crime in Maiden Lane at the stage door to the Apelphi Theatre.

Right: William Terriss. The famous Victorian actor was a Mason, but was he murdered by a Mason?

sacked by Terriss from the Adelphi. Terriss, however, felt pity for the out-of-work actor and sent him small amounts of cash via the Actors' Benevolent Fund. At the later Old Bailey trial, a former employer of Prince, the foreman at the Dundee ironworks hinted that the crazed actor might also be a Scottish Freemason. In evidence to show Prince was insane, the foreman noted that, 'his passions were not those of an ordinary man—on one occasion on a steam-boat trip of one of the Masonic lodges between Edinburgh and Dundee, he had to be locked down in the fore compartment.' This suggests that Terriss's aid for Prince might not have been driven simply by their involvement in the acting profession.

Whatever his motive—looking after a fellow actor or a brother Mason—Terriss appeared to do all he could to assist the deranged Prince, but by mid-December 1897, matters were coming to a head. One medical expert would later diagnose that Richard Archer Prince was suffering from 'delusions of suspicions of persecution.' Prince also believed that he was Jesus Christ and was being blackmailed by Terriss and others. Added to these symptoms of madness, the Scottish actor was drinking heavily and, due to lack of money, not eating. All these factors would contribute to a mind intent on murder. On 13 December, Prince was thrown out of the Vaudeville Theatre on the Strand. Desperate for work, he was becoming even more aggressive. Unfortunately for the Adelphi staff, Prince's wife still worked at the theatre, giving him legitimate access to the building. The evening following the incident at the Vaudeville, Prince and Terriss were heard arguing in the latter's dressing room.

Anger was now boiling within Prince. On 16 December came the straw that broke the camel's back; he was refused any further cash from the Actors' Benevolent Fund. In his crazed mind, the blame for this lay with Terriss. That evening, Prince waited in the shadows of Maiden Lane, just across the road from the stage door at the rear of the Adelphi. Terriss arrived in a carriage and as he walked towards the theatre, Prince moved quickly, stabbing him twice in the back. A friend, Henry Graves, present with Terriss, did not see the knife and assumed that Prince was giving Terriss friendly (but rather too enthusiastic) pats on the back. The dreadful truth was soon all too apparent as a knife was raised and the mad Scottish actor delivered the third and fatal blow. As Terriss turned, Prince plunged the blade into the victim's chest, piercing his heart. The actor cried, 'My God, I am stabbed'. However, the killer did not flee; he allowed himself to be taken into custody by Mr Graves and a local constable, who marched Prince to Bow Street Police Station. The prisoner was continually muttering about 'blackmail' during the short walk to the cells.

Dr William Curling Hayward was called from nearby Charing Cross Hospital (now Charing Cross Police Station) at 7.30 p.m. He found the dying man with a block of ice on his chest. Terriss was barely conscious and never spoke. Within minutes of the doctor's arrival, the famous actor was dead. The body was transported to the hospital and Dr Hayward carried out a *post-mortem* the following day, when he established that death was due to the last stab wound. The knife had penetrated between the fourth and fifth ribs with such force as to break the bones. There were also defence wounds on the right wrist where Terriss had tried to shield himself from the blade. Dr Hayward would later join Masonry far away from London, in Cairo. In 1902, he was initiated into the Grecia lodge No. 1105, an English lodge that met in Egypt. An influential lodge, Lord Kitchener had been Master twenty years before.

At Bow Street Police Station, Prince was questioned by the Duty Inspector, who demanded, 'Where is the knife?' No doubt in dramatic style, the detained man threw back his cape, took out the blood-stained weapon (this is now in the Metropolitan Police Crime Museum), and handed it to the officer without any resistance. Prince was not in the mood for denials; he fully confessed his guilt and his motive. Indicating the knife, he stated: 'that is what I stabbed him with, he had due warning, and if he is dead he knows what he had to expect from me; he prevented me from getting assistance.' The murder weapon was a cheap bread knife and enquiries revealed that it had been purchased by the suspect in October. Prince was charged with wilful murder and simply nodded as the charge was put to him. The investigation was dealt with by Bow Street officers and not Scotland Yard; this was not a complex case to crack.

Within days, the dead body of William Terriss was buried at Brompton Cemetery. According to contemporary news reports, a crowd of up to 50,000 attended the funeral, including Masons Sir Henry Irving and Herbert Beerbohm Tree, also of the Drury Lane Lodge. Tree (an Anglicised version of his Dutch surname) became the manager of the rebuilt His Majesty's Theatre on Haymarket. Tree himself is an interesting character; due to his several affairs, he was the grandfather to the wild British actor, Oliver Reed. Even the Prince of Wales, later King Edward VII and at the time the Grand Master of the United Grand Lodge of England, sent a wreath.

Christmas 1897 delaying the murder trial, so Prince appeared at the Old Bailey on 10 January. The prosecution team featured barrister Horace Avory, who had been initiated into the St Peter and St Pauls' Lodge No. 1410. Avory was a regular performer at the Central

Covent Garden Tube Station is said to be haunted by the ghost of Terriss.

Criminal Court and later a judge. The case was watertight, with several witnesses to the attack, a full confession, and the murder weapon recovered.

While a guilty verdict and execution seemed inevitable, Prince's counsel focused on the defence of insanity. Several members of his family, including his mother, brother, and niece, together with associates from Dundee, gave evidence of his extremely bizarre behaviour and fierce temper. It was also noted that two of his brothers had been declared mad. A theatre manager, Ralph Croydon, stated that Prince was 'peculiar, eccentric and dramatic', with a hatred for William Terriss, whom he had called a 'dirty dog'. Croydon was also a Mason; he had joined the Sutherland Lodge of Unity No. 460 in Staffordshire. Critically, Prince was said to be insane by three medical specialists, including Doctor Theophilus Bulkeley Hyslop. Dr Hyslop was later to join a lodge, the Edinburgh University No. 2974 in 1916.

The tactic worked; Prince was found guilty but insane. He was spared the hangman's noose and committed to Broadmoor Criminal Lunatic Asylum in Berkshire. This did not please Brother Irving who believed that the authorities did not take the death of an actor seriously. Prince was never released and died in Broadmoor in 1936.

However, some believe that William Terriss lives on. His ghost is said to have been seen at the Adelphi, the Lyceum, and in Covent Garden tube station. Wearing Victorian dress, the spectre appeared from a green mist in the theatre. At the tube station, the sad faced Terriss is said to have walked through a closed café door. The tube station was not opened until years after the actor's murder, but it is said to stand on the site of a bakery from which he purchased his favourite cakes. Unfortunately for ghost hunters, Terriss has not been seen since 1972, but Masons using the nearest tube station to Grand Lodge in Great Queen Street may want to keep their eyes open for possibly the only Masonic spectre in London; after a few glasses of wine at the Festive Board, he may well appear.

37

The Mason who Applied to be the Hangman, but Found his Own Head in the Noose

Masonic Connection
Murderer
Attendance at a lodge used as an alibi
Victim of theft
Police officers
Ballistics expert

Date
1885–1903

Connection to London
Alfred Street, Bow: Place of birth
Millbank: Applied to be a hangman at the prison on this site (now marked by a buttress with plaque near Vauxhall Bridge)
Charing Cross Road: Committed fraud at Cox and Co. bank
Civil Service Supply Association, Bedford Street: Evidence from this establishment led to forgery conviction
Bow Street Magistrates Court: Appeared at this court charged with forgery
Old Bailey: Convicted of forgery at this court
Bank of England: Attempted to change stolen money
Cheapside: Attempted to escape once arrested in this street

Lodges
Vitruvian No. 87
Old Concord No. 172
Tyrian No. 253
Lodge of Good Fellowship No. 276
Royal Standard No. 398
Priory No. 1000
St Andrew's No. 1817

Woodgrange No. 2409 (erased)
St Patrick's No. 195 (Ireland)

This is a tale of a Victorian rogue and womaniser who was a Freemason and long-serving soldier. The three times married Samuel Herbert Dougal certainly murdered one woman and may have killed two others; his first two wives died in quick succession, but their deaths were not subject to scrutiny. However, it is possible that he killed other women too.

Never short of lady-friends, several 'common law' wives made allegations of cruelty against him, while he moved around England, Ireland, and Canada fathering numerous children. What makes this sad tale rather ironic is that Dougal had applied to be a hangman, while in the end, he had to face the noose himself. Also, in a previous trial for a more minor matter (stealing from a brother Mason), he tried to use attendance in a Masonic lodge as an alibi.

Dougal was born at 18 Alfred Street, Bow in the East End of London in 1846, but he does not seem to have to have lived in poverty (like many in that deprived area of the capital city). Additionally, he received a good education and qualified as a civil engineer. By the age of nineteen, he had decided on a military career and, in 1866, young Samuel enlisted in the British Army with the Royal Engineers.

Samuel Dougal, Victorian rogue and Freemason.

After initial training at the Royal Engineers depot in Chatham, Kent, he served throughout the United Kingdom, which then included southern Ireland, with postings in Cork, Glamorganshire, and Chester. During the latter tour of duty, he met and married Lavinia Griffiths, who hailed from Northop in Flintshire. She was twenty years old when the marriage took place in 1869.

At that time, many servicemen were illiterate and Dougal was able to use his education to his advantage. In 1877, as a sergeant, he was posted to Halifax, Nova Scotia as the commanding officer's chief clerk. His wife and children accompanied him on this posting to Canada and for many years, all seemed well. Dougal received further promotion to quartermaster sergeant in 1880. His work as an Army draughtsman was much respected by his colleagues, who nicknamed him 'Jim the Penman'.

It was also in 1880 that Dougal joined the Royal Standard Lodge No. 398 in Halifax, Canada, but he was not new to Masonry. He is shown, not as an initiate, but as a joining member from St Patrick's Lodge No. 195, an Irish lodge, which met in (what is now) Northern Ireland.

In 1885, after sixteen years of marriage, his first wife became ill and died suddenly on 29 June. As the death occurred in a married quarter in the military garrison, no inquest was ever held. Lavinia (who was thirty-seven years old at the time of her death) was buried quickly and Quartermaster Sergeant Dougal was allowed to return to England on compassionate grounds. He did not, unfortunately, show any compassion to his children; he put them in a home.

Dougal did not spend much time in mourning. Within two months, he had found a new lady-friend, Maria Boyd. She had an Army background, as her father had been a Medical Officer. This also meant that she was not without money. The couple were soon married and the second Mrs Dougal accompanied her husband back to Canada. The happiness was not to last long. On 6 October, Maria Dougal was also dead, apparently the victim of a tuberculosis epidemic. Some accounts state that Dougal had claimed that poisonous oysters were to blame. Whatever the case, once again, no inquest was held. Given that Dougal had now had two wives die within fewer than four months of each other, it should have caused alarm bells to ring, but it did not. Dougal continued with his Army service and finding new women.

Less than a year later, in May 1886, he had made another girl pregnant. Bessie Stedman was from a farming family in Nova Scotia. Dougal passed her off as his wife by forging a marriage certificate and took her to England, as he had been posted to Aldershot in Hampshire. The couple then moved to the Shaftesbury Park Estate in Battersea, south London. It was not to last. Bessie left him due to ill-treatment and took their daughter back to Canada. There she passed herself off as a widow. As well as his dishonesty, here we have an indication of another flaw in Dougal's character—a violent temper.

Dougal's violence and dishonesty were to emerge continually throughout his life. He claimed that, towards the end of his Army service, he had been made a commissioned officer. In truth, he had left the Royal Engineers with the rank of quartermaster sergeant after twenty-one years of service to Queen Victoria. He received a pension and his Long Service and Good Conduct Medal. Many former soldiers joke that this award is really the 'Long Service and Not Getting Caught' medal; in Dougal's case it may well have been true.

As a civilian, Dougal worked in a variety of jobs in London and on the Isle of Wight. He also found time to father two more children by a widow in Maidstone, Kent. She was to be another woman who left Dougal due to his cruel behaviour. He then moved in with another widow and became the landlord of a small public house, the Royston Arms, in Ware, Hertfordshire to the north of London. His next relationship was to result in his first brush with the law.

For whatever reason (we can suspect violence), the widow and her children left the pub and it would seem that Dougal had a new scheme to obtain money—insurance fraud. A passing constable found the premises on fire and, suspiciously, the landlord had only left a short time before. In December 1889, the former quartermaster sergeant stood trial in the Shire Hall, Hertford for arson and attempting to defraud the insurance company. Luck was with Dougal; he was acquitted, but as we will see, the authorities noted his conduct.

In 1890, a vacancy arose for a hangman and applicants were interviewed at the National Penitentiary, the Millbank Prison. This jail stood in the Pimlico area of London, on the banks of the Thames, between Lambeth and Vauxhall Bridges. Prisoners were committed here for serious crimes and faced hanging or transportation to Australia. There was a Masonic connection to the prison. Its construction was in the charge of Robert Smirke, a Freemason, who also designed the British Museum. It had opened in 1821, but by the time of Dougal's application, all prisoners had been moved to the newer jail at Pentonville and Millbank Prison would be demolished a few years later. All that remains is a wide concrete

The site of Millbank Prison. This is where prisoners were transported to Australia and where Dougal applied to be the hangman.

post with a memorial plaque on the north side of the Thames (opposite the M15 building); this post was one of the bollards where ships were tied up as prisoners were loaded to be taken to Botany Bay.

As a hangman, Dougal would (seemingly) have been an ideal candidate. He had the military discipline to deal with prisoners and his engineering skills would have been useful in calculating the drop required to kill the condemned man. He was not, however, invited to an interview. Concerned at his recent conduct following the fire at his pub (even though he had been acquitted of arson and fraud), the committee responsible for finding a new executioner decided that he was not a suitable man for the post. His current job, as the landlord of a public house, was also held against him (dubious types, these publicans). Instead, the committee appointed a Yorkshire stonemason (not Freemason) named Thomas Scott. He was eventually removed from the post for having sex with a prostitute in a cab—not the best choice, either, it would seem.

Dougal does not appear to have been downcast by not getting the hangman's job and continued with his wicked ways. To demonstrate the womanising nature of the former soldier, it seems that he appears twice in the 1891 census with two different 'wives' and families.

Dougal is recorded as living with a 'wife', Henrietta. She was an Irish woman, Sarah Henrietta White (or 'Hennie' as Dougal referred to her) with children at 254 Southampton Street in Camberwell, south London. This appears to have been the home of his younger brother, Henry, who is also shown with a family at the address.

A Samuel H. Dugall (note variation in spelling of surname, but correct middle initial) with a slightly different birth date is shown with 'wife' Marian and children, as a live-in steward at the Conservative Club, Stapleton Hall Road, Hornsey in north London.

No doubt his pub experience helped the retired soldier (and rogue) to obtain the job in the Conservative club. Importantly, Dougal then took up a similar steward post at the club in Southend, Essex. It has been suggested that Dougal was initiated into the St Andrew's Lodge No. 1817 around this time (see Feather and Lockwood, 2010). The lodge now meets in Southend, but at the time, it held its meetings at the Cambridge Hotel in Shoeburyness just along the Essex coast. There is, however, no record of him being a Joining Member and he was certainly not initiated there (as we have seen, he joined Freemasonry some years before in Ireland). Neither is there any record of him visiting this lodge. As we will see, at least one lodge member would meet Brother Dougal—Alfred Marden, a local police officer. This, however, would not be a harmonious meeting of two brother Masons.

At this point in his life, Dougal returned to Ireland, where he had served as a young soldier. He had obtained a better paid job, as a quantity surveyor at the rebuilding of the Royal Barracks in Dublin. He continued to visit Masonic meetings while living in the Emerald Isle, but it is unclear if he regularly attended or if he continued his membership of his Mother Lodge.

We can be sure, however, that Dougal focused on his most favourite hobby—the pursuit of women. In 1892, he appears to have officially married Hennie in the country of her birth, despite her parents' objections. Dougal was not in Ireland for long and was soon on his travels again. This time, he went to Cudham and Biggin Hill in Kent, where new homes were being built. Next stop was south London, where in Camberwell, he met a well-to-do lady named Emily Booty. The two set up home in Watlington, Oxfordshire. Dougal had initially told Emily that he was a widower, but he then invited his Irish bride, Hennie, and their children to stay with them. This bizarre arrangement, or perhaps *ménage à trois*, lasted for several months until the old Dougal resurfaced and he was violent towards Emily. Emily needed to be rid of the violent, former soldier.

Emily decided to use official channels to remove Dougal and accused him of the theft of her belongings. Hence, in 1895, Dougal found himself in front of a court for a second time. It was not the most serious offence held at Oxford Quarter Sessions that year; that was the theft of dusters, tea cloths, and other such property, valued at just over five shillings (25 pence). While the court criticised his wicked behaviour towards Miss Booty, he was acquitted and walked free. This second acquittal seems to have emboldened him and further crimes were to follow. All had a similar motive—to obtain funds to keep him in the lifestyle that he believed he deserved.

While Miss Booty was glad to be rid of Brother Dougal, wife number three, Hennie, was glad to have him back. Leaving Oxfordshire, the married couple returned to Dublin, where they moved into 2 Liffey Street in the Inchecore district; this address was to feature in later evidence against Dougal. Once settled in, he took a job as a messenger at the Royal Hospital. This involved working in the administrative offices of senior officers and, importantly, gave him access to their desks.

Colonel Childers was one such officer. During the time of Douglas's employment, the colonel's cheque book went missing, but he does not seem to have noticed; Dougal, no doubt, stole it. He was, however, sacked for other reasons in mid-September; this dismissal is noted in the later trial, but never fully explained. Perhaps other dishonesty was discovered or Dougal was violent or over-familiar with a woman employed at the hospital; all are plausible theories given his previous conduct.

Dougal's downfall was now approaching. A few weeks after he had been dismissed, on 16 October, a man matching the retired Quartermaster Sergeant's description entered the Cox and Company bank at 16 Charing Cross Road in London. This bank was used by wealthy Army officers who served throughout the British Empire. A cheque, purportedly signed by the most senior Army officer in Dublin, Major-General, the 3rd Viscount Frankfort de Montmorency, was cashed for £35.

On the same day, a man entered the Civil Service Supply Association on nearby Bedford Street and ordered boots and shoes. This organisation was established to supply goods as cheaply as possible to government employees. The building is still marked by a clock on the wall at the junction of Bedford Street and the Strand. Significantly, the purchaser requested that they be posted to 'Mrs Dougall, 2 Liffey Street, Inchecore, Dublin' (the misspelling of name was likely an administrative error). Despite foolishly giving his home address, Dougal appears, however, to have tried to cover his tracks. In his diary, he attempted to show that he was nowhere near London on the day in question. According to him, on 16 October, he was in Ireland. He noted, 'At home most of day, went into town and made a few small purchases.' To further show that he was in not in England, he claimed that on 17 October, he had 'Attended Masonic Lodge in evening with Brother Shore; no business'. Despite all the teachings of Freemasonry, he appears to have shown no compunction regarding using the Craft as an alibi and lying about attendance at a lodge meeting. To make matters worse, the Major-General and victim of the theft was also a Mason, who had been initiated (when a colonel) into a Derbyshire lodge, Tyrian No. 253. So, in addition to Dougal falsely claiming to have been at a lodge meeting to cover his tracks, he had also stolen from a brother Mason.

Perhaps aware that the police would catch up with him, Dougal left the Inchecore address and moved to the village of Prosperous in County Kildare, about 25 miles from Dublin. The reader should not be fooled by the name of Dougal's new home town; it was run down and not very 'prosperous' at all. In the meantime, the bank had contacted Colonel Childers and confirmed that the cheque was a forgery. Scotland Yard were called in and enquiries at Royal Hospital in Dublin resulted in Dougal being identified as a suspect. A handwriting expert was also employed, casting further suspicion on the dishonest Mason.

Dougal was soon located in Prosperous and Detective Inspector Richards of Scotland Yard obtained a warrant for his arrest on charges of forgery and uttering a fraudulent cheque. Accompanied by two Royal Irish Constabulary sergeants, the detective detained Dougal and searched his Kildare home. Damning evidence was found—the bill for the footwear addressed to his wife in Liffey Street. The diary referred to was also seized. There were some flaws in the case; neither the bank cashier nor the sales woman who took the order for the boots and shoes were able to pick out Dougal at an identification parade. However, Dougal seems to have sealed his fate by keeping the bill from the Civil Service Supply Association. As we will see, this was only the first time that footwear was to provide decisive evidence against him.

The former soldier was taken back to London and appeared before Bow Street Magistrates Court. Dougal was remanded in custody and appeared at the Old Bailey on 9 December 1895. The trial was to last just one day. Prosecution counsel was the unfortunately named Mr Lawless (perhaps not the best name for a lawyer). Dougal pleaded not guilty; this resulted in Brother Viscount Frankfort de Montmorency being dragged away from Army duties in Ireland to give evidence. This will not have impressed the judge in such an open and shut case. Inevitably, Dougal was found guilty; this was his first conviction and must have come as quite a shock to a man who had (seemingly) led a charmed life. The jury, recognising his long service in the Royal Engineers, recommended mercy, but the judge, Sir Charles Hall QC, was having none of it; Dougal was sentenced to twelve months' hard labour. Additionally, his Army pension was forfeited. This was to give Dougal even more reason to swindle and steal cash later in life.

He was confined in Pentonville Prison. On 26 January, Dougal attempted to hang himself; attempting to commit suicide was a crime in itself at that time. The authorities, however, decided not to take further punitive actions. Dougal was declared insane and locked in the London County Lunatic Asylum at Cane Hill, Coulsdon, just to the south of Croydon. The site still exists, but most of the buildings have been demolished.

The idea of shortened sentences and release on parole was not part of the Victorian prison system; Dougal was released on 8 December 1896, having served the full 12 months. He now faced an uncertain future. He was an unemployed fifty-year-old convict with no Army pension to fall back on and no home to go to. His brother, Henry, came to the rescue and allowed him to live in his home at Biggin Hill. Dougal must have retained some of his charm as Hennie, his Irish third wife, came to live with him. This respite was not to last. Hennie returned to Dublin due to his cruel conduct and, appalled at his older brother's behaviour, Henry booted Dougal out of his house in Biggin Hill. Hennie's love for her husband was, as we shall see, still not dead. Dougal's movements are now shrouded in mystery. Ultimately, his next relationship would lead to two deaths, including his own.

On his travels, the out-of-luck former soldier met Camille Cecile Holland. Dougal had little to offer, but the old charm worked (again) and he was soon in a relationship with the rich spinster. At this time, Britain was involved in the Boer War in South Africa, so he was able to play on his military background to impress ladies. How could she resist 'Captain Dougal' as the violent, scheming womaniser was now styling himself?

Camille (or 'Cecily' as Dougal called her) was a good catch; she lived in fashionable Notting Hill and had several thousand pounds to her name. Miss Holland was also attractive, looking far younger than her fifty-six years. She was also proud of her particularly small feet; her shoe wear, as we will see, was to produce critical evidence later. Dougal was able to stay at her home in west London and the couple frequented the Royal Hotel, Southend.

Over time, Dougal confessed to Cecily that he had been unhappily married. He also persuaded her to rent a house with him or 'live in sin' (as it was called at one time for an unmarried couple to reside in the same house). Their first home was in Hassocks, a large village in Mid-Sussex. Eventually, the two decided to purchase Coldhams Farm in Saffron Walden in Essex. Dougal attempted to have the deeds made out in his own name, but Miss Holland was having none of it; she was supplying all the cash (£1,550 was a substantial sum at that time) to purchase the property and the contract was changed to reflect this arrangement. The property required renovation and in the interim period, Camille and Dougal were to stay in rooms owned by Mrs Henrietta Wiskin, who was to become an important witness at the later trial.

In early 1899, the building work was completed and the seemingly happy couple moved into their new home. The name of the premises was changed to Moat Farm and all could have been well, but Dougal's roguish behaviour was to come to the fore. On 13 May, a young servant, Florence Havies, was employed and it was only a matter of hours before Dougal was molesting her and attempting to get into her bed; 'Florrie' had to bolt the door to her quarters to stop him breaking in. Camille became so sick of his behaviour that she slept in the spare room with the young servant girl. Florence also felt safer with someone else in her room. Dougal now realised that the game was up. Camille wanted him out of the house, meaning that he would be homeless and without a penny to his name. It would seem that, at this point, he decided that murder was the only course left to him.

Less than one week after Florence arrived, on 19 May, Dougal and Camille left the farm on a pony and trap. This is the last time that Miss Holland would be seen alive. Later that evening, Dougal would tell the servant girl that Camille had 'gone to London.' By the morning, he was claiming that she had written a letter to him stating that she had gone on a 'little holiday' (even the Victorian Post Office did not deliver letters that quickly). Not wanting to remain at the farm with what can only be described as a 'dirty old man', Florence left; her mother had obtained her two month's wages.

For nearly four years, Dougal kept up the pretence that Camille was on holiday. He kept himself in cash by forging cheques, signing them 'Miss Holland' and informing the suspicious National Provincial Bank that a hand injury had resulted in a variation to the usual signature. He also duped her broker into selling her stocks and shares. By this means, he was able to move nearly £3,000 of Camille's wealth into his own account. He also transferred the farm into his own name by fraudulent means. Neither did he hide his new-found wealth; he was one of the first owners of a motor car in Essex.

Perhaps the greatest example of his bravado (or stupidity) was to invite his estranged wife, Hennie, to live at the farm just one day after Camille had vanished. Having forgiven him for his last bout of cruelty at the house in Biggin Hill, Mrs Dougal returned. The brash, former soldier initially told locals that Hennie was his widowed daughter, but this pretence was not to last for long. Hennie admitted her true identity to the vicar's wife.

Once again, Dougal's violence and womanising got the better of him. Hennie left the farm (and her husband) for good in January 1902. She had fallen for a local man and they went to live in Wales. Dougal obtained a divorce and, despite being nearly sixty years old, managed to seduce two more young servant girls (the Cranwell sisters), making both pregnant. He was also believed to have had sex with a third sister and their mother. There was also local gossip about naked bike riding lessons at the farm.

Being flash with money and womanising was a foolish move for Dougal as it drew attention to him and his wealthy circumstances. His conviction for the Dublin forgery also came to light when he was called to court in January 1903. He had refused to pay child maintenance for one of his latest (illegitimate) children. The rumours and innuendo were building up and eventually, they reached the ears of the local police constable. When added to the facts that Camille Holland had vanished into the night and Dougal was a convicted felon, it can be understood why PC Drew reported the matter to his superiors in the Essex Constabulary. This resulted in Superintendent Charles Pryke and the newly promoted Detective Inspector Marden being appointed to investigate the case. Both investigators have a Masonic connection: Brother Marden was already a member of St Andrew's Lodge and several years after this investigation, Superintendent Pryke would join Priory Lodge No. 1000, which still meets in Southend.

On 4 March, the superintendent visited Moat Farm and informed Dougal that he was under investigation. It was now nearly four years since Camille had last been seen on 19 May 1899. The police suspected that she may have been imprisoned in the farmhouse against her will. A search by the superintendent put to an end to this theory. When questioned, Dougal maintained that Camille had gone to London and he had dropped her at Stansted Railway Station with her luggage. The Victorians were so efficient that, even several years after the night in question, the ticket office could show that no tickets had been purchased for such a journey on that date.

Further police enquiries by DI Marden and Scotland Yard detectives quickly revealed the extent of the disgraced former soldier's dishonesty and fraud. Dougal, however, kept withdrawing the ill-gotten money and travelled to London and Bournemouth, accompanied (unsurprisingly) by a lady—Georgina Cranwell, the third sister of this family to fall for his charms.

Despite his violence and cad-like behaviour, it was dishonesty that was to prove to be Dougal's final downfall. In Victorian times, a £10 note was of great value. Hence, all serial numbers were recorded and anyone handing over a note had to sign it. Thus, the police were able to stop the banknotes that Dougal had obtained. On 18 March, he attempted to change several £10 notes at the Bank of England into smaller denominations. Again, Victorian efficiency came to the fore; the cashier spotted that the serial numbers were of interest to the police. Dougal knew matters were coming to a head and signed the note with a false name, 'Sydney Domville'. At this, the cashier politely asked him to step into a private office where he was confronted and arrested by Detective Inspector Henry Cox, who rightfully suspected that 'Domville' was really Dougal. Cox, who had been involved in the Jack the Ripper enquiry, had been a member of Vitruvian Lodge No. 87, since 1897.

DI (and Brother) Cox began to escort Dougal to the Force Headquarters, which was then located in Old Jewry, less than a five-minute walk away. As they proceeded from Threadneedle Street onto Cheapside, Dougal made a break, running as fast as he could. He may well have escaped, but he foolishly ran up a dead end; this was probably towards Grocers' Hall. He was arrested for a second time and when searched at the police station, he was found in possession of £600 in cash and gold. He also had jewellery known to belong to Camille and a left luggage ticket. This resulted in additional items of Miss Holland's belongings being found at Liverpool Street Station. The case was building up against him. While the murder enquiry was being conducted, Dougal was charged with forgery and fraud and returned to Essex. He was marched, in handcuffs, from the railway station to the court in Saffron Walden; the police were not having him escape again. He was remanded in custody and sent to Cambridge Prison. The former Quartermaster Sergeant would never taste freedom again.

Essex police officers now began to search Moat Farm and did so for several unproductive weeks until a witness came forward with information that Dougal had filled in a drainage ditch. The location of the ditch was established and on 27 April, human remains were recovered; it appeared to be a woman, wearing a dark dress and boots, well-preserved considering the time it had been in the ground. Other items, including hairpins and a comb, were recovered; these would prove to be vital clues as to the identity of the deceased as more modern means of putting a name to the victim were unavailable. Fingerprint identification was in its infancy at this time and, in any case, there would have been no reason to have Miss Holland's finger marks on record as she was a woman of good character.

The items were eventually identified as belonging to Camille by Mrs Wiskin, with whom the couple had stayed prior to moving into the farm. Likewise, Florence, the maid whom Dougal had lusted after, could state that the property recovered had been worn by the lady of the house. Most damningly, it will be recalled that Camille was proud of her small feet. Her footwear was handmade by a shoemaker named George Mold; despite the boots being buried for four years, the maker's mark, an 'M' made out in brass tacks on the heel, could still be made out. Mold was visited by the Metropolitan Police at his shop in Edgware Road, London and verified that the boots had been purchased by Miss Holland. For the second time, footwear evidence was critical in the case against Dougal.

The dead body was examined by Professor Joseph Pepper, the senior pathologist at St Mary's Hospital in London. He was assisted by an Essex Police Surgeon, Doctor Kenneth

Storr, who would join the Lodge of Good Fellowship No. 276 at Chelmsford a few days after the *post-mortem* examination. Pepper was not 'on the square', but his pupils included Freemasons Bernard Spilsbury and William Willcox, whose scientific work would solve many of the most infamous crimes of the early twentieth century. Professor Pepper was able to state that the cause of death was a bullet wound to the right side of the head. The bullet was still inside her skull. He added that the injury was not self-inflicted and it appeared that Camille had been shot at close range by someone stood behind her.

Ballistics was another emerging forensic science at this time and Scotland Yard were requested to find an expert to further link the crime to Dougal. Those involved in this line of enquiry had Masonic connections. The police officer, Detective Inspector Elias Bower, would later join Woodgrange Lodge No. 2409 (now defunct) in London. Bower approached a gun-maker, Edwin Churchill, whose shop was near the Strand. Churchill's experiments (shooting sheep) enabled him to conclude that the bullet found in the skull was very similar to rounds of ammunition found at Moat House Farm. The gun shop owner had been initiated into Old Concord Lodge No. 172 (also in London) in 1897.

Camille's funeral was held on 12 May and some six weeks later, on 22 June, Dougal stood trial in Chelmsford before Mr Justice Robert Samuel Wright. To the charge of murder, he pleaded 'not guilty'. The jury, however, were satisfied with the identification of the body as Camille Cecile Holland and Dougal does not seem to have helped his cause by not giving evidence. As a result, the trial was to last just two days and the jury took less than an hour to convict the former soldier. The judge then sentenced Brother Dougal, the Mason, who had applied to be a hangman, to face the gallows himself. He appealed, claiming (rather belatedly) that the death had been a terrible accident. In a statement to the Home Secretary, Dougal pleaded that he had unintentionally shot his beloved Cecily while unloading his pistol after a day's shooting. It was all to no avail and, on 14 July, at the prison in Chelmsford, this Victorian rogue, murderer, and Mason finally met his maker. Given his presence in London in 1888, his violence towards women and obsession with sex, perhaps he should have been interviewed by police in relation to the Whitechapel Murders.

38

Rival Forensic Science and Rival Masons: the Birth of Fingerprint Evidence

Masonic Connection
Fingerprint expert
Detectives
'Untrustworthy' expert witness

Date
1902: First crime in England (burglary) solved with fingerprint evidence
1905: First English murder trial with fingerprint evidence

Connection to London
New Scotland Yard, Victoria Embankment: Original location of Fingerprint Branch
Denmark Hill, South London: Burglary occurred
Deptford, South East London: Murder location
Old Bailey: Court where tried and convicted
Wandsworth Prison: Site of executions

Lodges
Temple No. 101
Lodge of Temperance No. 169
Canonbury No. 657
Camden No. 704
Dalhousie No. 860 (erased)
Quadratic No. 1691
University of Edinburgh No. 2974

As the nineteenth century turned into the twentieth, the use of forensic evidence to solve crime and identify criminals from items left at crime scenes was rapidly developing. However, there were different ideas as to how best to identify an offender. In France, a system called 'Anthropometry' had been developed by Alphonse Bertillon of the Paris police department. This involved measuring eleven or nine parts of the body, including height, width of head, length of arms, and size of left foot, but this method was useless with identical twins.

In India, then part of the British Empire, a different method was being pioneered by Sir Edward Henry, the Inspector-General of Police in Bengal—fingerprints. Aided by Indian officers, Sir Edward devised a method of classification of fingerprints, so that marks found at crime scenes could be quickly compared and persistent offenders identified (to prevent such criminals giving false names to the court and claiming to have no previous convictions, thereby avoiding a long sentence).

While this section will focus on the first cases in Britain to be solved by fingerprint evidence (and the Masons involved in such), the foremost case solved in this way was in India by Sir Edward (who was not a member of the Craft). Comparing bloodstained marks on a book where a man had had his throat cut, he was able to match the fingerprints to those of a former servant of the deceased.

The Belper Committee was set up in London in 1900 to evaluate the two rival systems of identification. Sir Edward Henry returned to Britain to explain his classification system and the committee recommended that fingerprints should be used instead of anthropometry. During this time, Sir Edward was appointed as Assistant Commissioner in charge of the Metropolitan Police's CID. It is no surprise, therefore, that on 1 July 1901, the Fingerprint Branch opened at New Scotland Yard.

One of the officers who transferred from the Anthropometric Registry, where the measurements of criminals were held, was Detective Sergeant Charles Stockley Collins. He had been a Mason for some time, having been initiated into the Camden Lodge No. 704 in 1894 (he was shown as a 'Detective Officer' on the register). The lodge then met in Anderton's Hotel on the Strand. DS Collins was an innovator and was prepared to use new inventions to aid the detection of crime: for example, he developed the use of photography to record finger-marks left at crime scenes.

The initial focus of the Fingerprint Department, as per Sir Edward's work in India, was confirming the identity of those criminals suspected of giving false names. This was to change with the first conviction for burglary using the new techniques of the department. The villain in this case was Harry Jackson, who broke into a house in Denmark Hill in south London and stole some billiard balls. Examining the scene of the crime, Brother Collins found a dirty thumb print on a freshly painted window sill. This was captured on camera and checked against the classified fingerprints at Scotland Yard. Jackson was identified and brought to trial. On 13 September 1902 at the Old Bailey, DS Collins explained the new fingerprint system to the court. The jury were convinced and Jackson was sentenced to seven years' imprisonment. Not everyone was impressed; a letter appeared in *The Times* newspapers from 'A Disgusted Magistrate' mocked the method: 'Scotland Yard… will be the laughing stock of Europe it if insists on trying to trace criminals by odd ridges on their skins.'

Undeterred, the Fingerprint Department continued to expand its records. The next breakthrough would come three years later, with the first murder case involving fingerprint evidence. By this time, Brother Collins's efforts (in the police and in the lodge) had been rewarded with promotion; he was now a Detective Inspector and Worshipful Master of the Camden Lodge. The murder in question occurred in a shop in Deptford High Street on 27

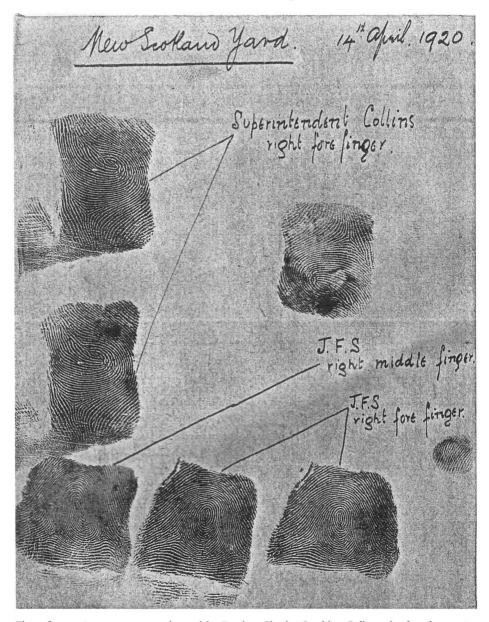

New Scotland Yard.   14ᵗʰ April. 1920.

Superintendent Collins
right fore finger.

J.F.S
right middle finger.

J.F.S
right fore finger.

These fingerprints are an example used by Brother Charles Stockley Collins, the first fingerprint expert, and show his own marks.

March. The elderly shopkeeper and his wife, Thomas and Ann Farrow, had been badly beaten with a blunt instrument, possible a jemmy, causing terrible head wounds; the old man was dead and Mrs Farrow would die four days later in hospital, having never regained consciousness.

Detective Inspector Arthur Hailstone of 'R' Division, the local CID, attended the scene soon after the crime was discovered. He was also a Mason; he had joined the Dalhousie Lodge No. 860 in 1892, which met at Anderton's Hotel, Strand (a popular venue for lodges at that time). Interestingly, the next member to join after him was a Detective named Harry Callaghan; it would seem that 'Dirty Harry' of movie fame may have been a member of the Craft.

A search of the premises by DI Hailstone revealed that a cash box had been opened, and it was estimated that £13 had been stolen. He had a good awareness of forensic evidence and later explained his actions regarding the cash box at the Old Bailey: 'I gave orders that it should not be moved or touched by anybody.' The detective inspector also found two stocking masks with eye holes cut into them; these took on significance with the crime being reported as the 'Mask Murders' in the press. The masks are still in existence and are displayed in the Scotland Yard Crime Museum.

As a murder had been committed, the case was passed from the Divisional CID to Scotland Yard and the detective tasked to solve the crime was Chief Inspector Frederick Fox, also a London Mason. He had a member of Temple Lodge 101 since 1897. On arrival in Deptford, he was met by DI Hailstone and shown the cash box. Fox also understood the potential of obtaining fingerprint evidence:

Stocking Mask: one of the masks used by the Stratton brothers during the murder of Thomas Farrow.

I saw a tin cash box with the tray lying close by it, I took a piece of paper and removed the tray, and took two pieces of paper and removed the box by the corners with the paper between my fingers and the box, to avoid any print of my fingers. I removed them a few feet to the right and took charge of them to prevent anybody touching them.

This cash box was now taken to Scotland Yard for examination by DI Collins. In the meantime, local enquiries revealed several witnesses, who had seen two men leaving the crime scene—Albert Stratton (aged twenty) and his brother Alfred (aged twenty-two). Both men were known to the police as local criminals. Initially, they could not be found, but further damning evidence was obtained from Alfred's girlfriend, when she was interviewed by Chief Inspector Fox. Miss Hannah Cromarty refused to give Stratton an alibi for the night of the murder and stated that he had asked her for a pair of old stockings (the very thing used to make the masks). With this information, a warrant was issued for the arrest of the brothers on suspicion of murder.

On 2 April, a local officer, Detective Sergeant Frank Beavis, spotted Alfred in a Deptford public house, the King of Prussia. An arrest was made and the older Stratton was taken to Blackheath Police Station. There is some irony in the venue of this arrest as Frank Beavis would later join a Masonic lodge, which did not permit the drinking of alcohol, the Lodge of Temperance No. 169. Once at the station, Alfred was questioned, during which he attempted to protect his brother, telling DS Beavis, 'I have not seen him for a long time; I think he has gone to sea'; Albert had been in the navy, so there was a possibility of this being the truth.

Despite Scotland Yard having taken over the enquiry, DI Hailstone was still keeping a sharp lookout for the missing brother in the local area. His diligence was to pay off and the day after Alfred's arrest, Hailstone spotted Albert Stratton near the scene of the crime, walking along Deptford High Street. He was taken into custody and frogmarched to join his brother at Blackheath Police Station.

Just a month after the first arrest, the case was heard at the Old Bailey with both brothers charged with the murder of Mr Farrow (at that time, defendants could only be indicted with one murder at each trial). The Strattons pleaded not guilty; they were aware that there were no witnesses who could place them at the scene of the crime. A milkman, who had initially claimed to have seen the brothers leave the shop, had failed to pick them out at an identification parade. There was, however, some circumstantial evidence. In addition to Alfred's girlfriend giving damning evidence, Albert's lady-friend stated that he had not spent the night in question with her, despite usually doing so.

With the eyewitness testimony done, the barrister for the prosecution called DI Collins to the stand. His evidence was the most important part of the prosecution case. A clear explanation of the fingerprint system was related to the jury and then Brother Collins produced a photograph of the mark found on the cash box. He stated that the mark matched the right thumb print of Alfred Stratton and showed the eleven points of similarity between the print recovered from the scene and the thumb print taken at the police station.

The defence, however, called their own 'expert' who was prepared to state that the thumb print match was an error. This witness was Doctor John Garson, a member of the Royal

College of Surgeons and another Mason, but one who would not be taking 'brotherly love' into the court room. He was to observe that Brother Collins was talking 'a great deal of nonsense'. By this time, Dr Garson was a member of three lodges: Quadratic No. 1691, into which he was initiated in 1882, Canonbury No. 657 (joined in 1885) and University of Edinburgh No. 2974 (joined 1903).

The doctor had the benefit of his medical qualifications to sway the jury, telling them that he was 'a scientific man', no doubt much cleverer than a common policeman. His evidence was clear: the thumb print did not match that of Stratton. On cross-examination, Garson's evidence began to unravel. The prosecution was able to show that he was an expert in anthropometry, rather than fingerprints and he had supported the former at the Belper Committee. More damningly, it had been established that Dr Garson had offered himself as a witness for the defence or the prosecution, depending on which side paid him the most. The trial judge was scathing, describing Garson as 'absolutely untrustworthy'. So, as well as leaving 'brotherly love' at the courtroom door, Dr Garson also seems to have forgotten another of the Masonic Three Grand Principles—'truth'.

After just a two-day trial and two hours of deliberation, the jury found both brothers guilty of murder. The judge, wearing the black cap, sentenced them both to death. The executions took place at Wandsworth Prison at 9 a.m. on 23 May (it should be noted that the murder occurred on 27 March, just eight weeks before the hangings). Albert died easily—his neck was broken—but it appeared that Alfred died the hard way, with some evidence of asphyxia; the rope strangled him to death.

Fingerprints had proved themselves to be a valuable new weapon in Scotland Yard's armoury and their use spread across the world. The involvement of Masons—as fingerprint experts, investigators, arresting officers, and, unfortunately, as an 'untrustworthy' witness— had been significant in these early cases. The evidence of finger-marks found at crime scenes would play a vital role in many later investigations, including the identification of the Great Train Robbers some sixty years later.

39

When Suicide was a Crime:
A Masonic Tragedy

Masonic Connection
Masonic suicide victim (or criminal?)
Request for assistance from lodge

Date
1908: Suicide

Connection to London
Wellington Street: Death occurred near Covent Garden

Lodges
Morton No. 89 (Scotland)

Unusual as it may now seem, to commit suicide was a crime in England until 1961. This was of little consequence if the person succeeded in their aim, but a failed suicide attempt could mean imprisonment or detention in a lunatic asylum. Furthermore, many people regarded taking one's own life as a sin and an inquest verdict of 'suicide' could bring shame on the family left behind.

This sad case involves Warrant Officer George Samphier, a Gunnery Instructor with the Royal Navy, who although born in Portsmouth, joined the Craft at Lerwick on Shetland on 25 October 1899. He had served on numerous ships since joining the senior service in Portsmouth in 1892. At the time of his initiation, he was serving on a battleship, HMS Rodney. Samphier was one of many naval personnel based at Scapa Flow to join a Scottish lodge. He quickly took his Second and Third Degrees, and also the Mark, which is traditionally taken in a Scottish Craft Lodge (unlike in England, where the Mark has its own Grand Lodge). By 1908, Samphier was serving on HMS Swale, a torpedo boat destroyer based at Harwich, Essex.

Now the tragedy unfolds, but some parts of the mystery remain as no reason for the suicide was ever established. On the evening of Monday, 7 September, an unconscious man, later identified as Samphier, was found near death in the public lavatories in Wellington

Street. He had shot himself in the right temple with all chambers loaded, save the one fired round; a revolver was found at the scene. The man was taken to Kings' College Hospital but did not survive his injuries. He was described in one newspaper article as having the appearance of 'a sea-faring man'. Enquiries to identify him were side-tracked as the vest he was wearing was marked 'E. N. Mortimer'; it can only be surmised that this was a colleague on the same ship. The suicide victim also appeared to be 'poor and penniless' (as noted in the First Degree in Masonry) as he had no money in his possession.

In those days, shirt collars and cuffs were detachable and made of cardboard. On one of the cuffs, the dead man had written: 'Will some philanthropic Freemason educate my poor bairns? My lodge is Morton, Shetland Islands. Goodbye dearie. God bless you and our bairns! Forgive me and blame the captain'. This tragic message attracted a lot of press attention at the time and the matter was reported across the country, including the police investigation to identify the dead man in Scotland and England.

In relation to the motive for the suicide, alluded to in the note on the cuff, it has never been established what the commanding officer of HMS *Swale* had done. Samphier's Royal Navy record does show that his career had not been without blemish; in 1906, he had been held 'principally to blame' for the collision of two torpedo boats and it further noted a case of 'neglect of duty' committed during the month before his death. Something had obviously disturbed this man who had been in the service for some sixteen years, as four days prior to his death (3 September), he had been recorded as 'absent without leave'—a very serious breach of military discipline, especially for a warrant officer.

Oddly, the Westminster coroner began the inquest before the body had been identified. The jury appeared sympathetic and endeavoured to return a verdict of suicide during temporary insanity; then, it would not be a crime and his dependants would be more favourably treated. The coroner, however, insisted on a verdict of straightforward suicide.

Enquiries had established that Samphier had left a wife and three small children who lived in his home town of Portsmouth. His body was identified by his brother and the family travelled to London, as Samphier was to be buried in Nunhead cemetery, south of the Thames. Despite the coffin being ready for burial and the grave dug, the superintendent of the cemetery refused to allow the service to take place as the official records still showed the deceased as 'man unknown'. This, no doubt, caused further distress to Mrs Samphier and the rest of the mourners who were sent away for the night.

If nothing else, the warrant officer's appeal on his suicide note did work; the Morton Lodge granted a donation of three guineas. If there can be a happy ending to such a tragedy, it would seem that the wife married another Royal Navy serviceman.

In a further twist, Samphier's daughter later moved to London to work for the Post Office. Her address is listed as Rillington Place, an address that achieved infamy in the 1950s with the trials of Timothy Evans, who was wrongly hanged for the murder of his wife and daughter. In 1953, further dead bodies were found in number 10, and the previous occupant, John Reginald Christie, was tried and hanged for the murder of his wife. In addition to Mrs Christie, Mrs Evans, and baby Geraldine Evans, he was believed to have killed five other women. Fortunately, the only Masonic connection with this tragic case appears to be one of the constables, who searched the house for dead bodies.

40

The Real Sherlock Holmes and Dr Watson: Brothers Spilsbury and Willcox

Masonic Connection
Pathologists
Author of Sherlock Holmes

Date
1905–1947: Numerous cases solved during this period

Connection to London
St Mary's Hospital: Spilsbury's laboratory
St Bartholomew's Hospital: Spilsbury's laboratory

Lodges
Gihon Sancta Maria No. 49
Phoenix Lodge No. 257
St. Mary Magdalen No. 1523
Drury Lane No. 2127
Rahere No. 2546
Sancta Maria No. 2682 (erased)
Misericordia No. 3286.
Rahere Chapter No. 2546 (Holy Royal Arch)
Abernethy No. 569 (Mark)

As the nineteenth century came to an end, forensic science and pathology were in their infancy. The examination of the dead was seen as a 'beastly science', no doubt fuelled by cases such as that of Burke and Hare, the Edinburgh murderers, who killed to provide doctors with fresh bodies to examine. Likewise, it seemed a Dr Frankenstein-style occupation (Shelley's novel was published in 1818), with wicked doctors not allowing the dead to rest and meddling in things that were best left alone. Mason Benjamin Franklin also appears to have been involved in secret experiments on dead bodies.

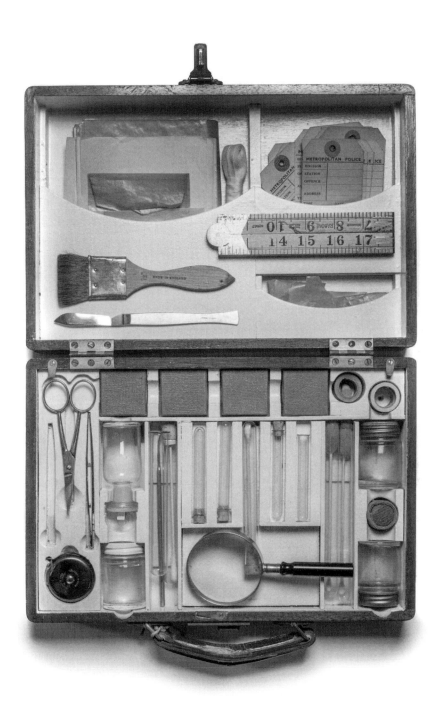

The 'Murder Bag'. Mason Sir Bernard Spilsbury suggested the contents of the bag, which standardised and improved evidence gathering at murder scenes.

This was to change; in the first half of the twentieth century, Bernard Spilsbury (later Sir Bernard) became a famed pathologist and household name. Newspaper sellers would shout 'Spilsbury called in!' after a gruesome murder and in 1934, the American magazine *Time* was calling him 'the living successor to mythical Sherlock Holmes'. Holmes was never a Mason, but his creator, Sir Arthur Conan Doyle was a member of Phoenix Lodge No. 257 in Southsea, Hampshire. Indeed, the equipment and systematic manner that detectives and forensic scientists employ when searching for evidence at crime scenes are still influenced by Spilsbury. Following the 'Crumbles Murder' in Eastbourne, Spilsbury designed the 'Murder Bag', which standardised the kit issued by Scotland Yard to detectives and included evidence labels and containers, tweezers, swabs, a ruler, and even a magnifying glass. The 'Crumbles' case involved Patrick Mahon killing his lover, Emily Kaye, and then cutting up her body. On arrival at the scene of the crime, Spilsbury was 'struck with horror', not at the 'dreadful and afflicting sight' of the dismembered body (he had seen plenty of these), but at the detectives picking up body parts with their bare hands. Hence, rubber gloves were also included in the 'Murder Bag'.

MARCH 14, 1928.]   PUNCH, OR THE LONDON CHARIVARI.   305

by George Belcher

Sir BERNARD SPILSBURY.

When arsenic has closed your eyes,
This certain hope your corpse may rest in :—
Sir B. will kindly analyse
The contents of your large intestine.

MR. PUNCH'S PERSONALITIES.—LXIV.

Sir Bernard Spilsbury, the Mason who pioneered Forensic Pathology.

In many cases, Spilsbury was supported by Dr (later Sir) William Henry Willcox, the senior scientific advisor to the Home Office. It may be fair to call Willcox the 'Dr Watson' to Spilsbury's 'Sherlock Holmes'. These men both worked at St Mary's hospital in London. While Spilsbury would conduct the *post-mortem* examination on murder victims, Willcox was responsible for tests on blood samples, often to prove cases of poisoning or links between the victim and suspect. Numerous landmark and famous cases would feature their involvement.

Both men were also Freemasons and were ultimately members of the same lodge—Sancta Maria No. 2682 (now Gihon Sancta Maria Lodge No. 49), which, at the turn of the century, met at the Imperial Hotel in Regent Street, London. Willcox was initiated into this lodge in 1906 and, the following year, he was a founder member of the Misericordia Lodge No. 3286 (the rather sad sounding name is Latin for 'mercy').

Spilsbury was to become a very committed Mason; in 1920, he was initiated into Rahere Lodge No. 2546, named after the medieval founder of St Bartholomew's hospital (where Spilsbury had his laboratory after leaving St Mary's). He joined the Holy Royal Arch Chapter of the same name less than two years later and, in 1923, he joined the Mark Degree (Abernethy Mark Lodge, then No. 722, now No. 569). He served as Master of Rahere Lodge in 1932, Master in the Mark in 1933, and First Principal of his Chapter in 1937. He also joined several other lodges, including Sancta Maria Lodge and St. Mary Magdalen Lodge No. 1523, serving as Master of both. He later held Grand Rank in the Craft and in the Holy Royal Arch.

So, while Freemasons in the Third Degree would hear about the recovery of Hiram Abif's body and the ancient brethren 'viewing the gaping wound still visible on the forehead' of the dead man, Spilsbury and Willcox spent much of their time doing exactly this (and examining all types of other brutal injuries). Between them, they would send many men to the gallows; it will be described in this book that those hanged as a result of their evidence included several of their Masonic brethren.

Willcox was seven years older than Spilsbury and came to prominence first, in what is believed to the first murder of a woman on a train in England. The crime occurred on 24 September 1905, just a few months before Willcox was initiated into Freemasonry. Late on the evening of that day, a railway worker found the body of a woman in the railway tunnel at Merstham, on the main line between London and Redhill in Surrey. The body was still warm, but the dead woman had a fractured skull and other injuries, which at first appeared to be consistent with falling from, and then being hit by, railway carriages. It was initially believed to be a case of suicide, with the victim walking into the tunnel with the intention of being hit by a train.

An initial police examination of the tunnel soon disproved the theory that the woman had entered the tunnel on foot. Soot on the walls had been disturbed at the height of someone standing in a carriage, indicating that she had fallen from a train. The last one to pass through the tunnel prior to the discovery of the body had been the 9.33 p.m. from Charing Cross to Reading. She could also have been on the earlier London Bridge to Brighton train.

The victim had no money or identification on her person and police circulated a description. It seems odd that Robert Money, who lived some distance away in Kingston Hill, had put a name to the corpse by the following afternoon. Quite how he saw the information so soon is unknown. In any case, he identified the body as his sister, Mary Money (aged twenty-two years old).

At the coroner's inquest, Dr Willcox gave evidence of the injuries and made it clear that, in his expert opinion, the victim had been alive when she had fallen from the carriage. Despite his work and that of the police, the case remains unsolved. Returning to the brother of the victim, Robert Money was to turn murderer in 1912. The police were called to a burning house in Eastbourne and made a very grisly discovery. Money, a bigamist, had shot his two wives (one of them survived) and three children. He had then turned the gun on himself. Given the speed of the identification of his sister after her death, it is worth questioning whether he know more about that than he had stated at the time.

The case that was to bring Spilsbury into the public eye was the infamous murder committed by Dr Hawley Harvey Crippen, covered in detail in Chapter 41. Spilsbury and Willcox assisted in another murder enquiry, which resulted in another first in forensic science. On 29 April 1911, George Baron Pateman approached his fiancé, Alice Linford, and her sister in the street in Finchley, north London. According to Rose Linford, Pateman was in a foul mood and was threatening to commit suicide. Alice refused to go with him, at which he turned violent and slashed her across the throat with a razor; the attack was so vicious that the handle broke off. The victim and her attacker were covered in blood; Pateman made off, but poor Alice staggered fifty yards before collapsing and dying. The police attended and took her blood-stained clothing as evidence. Enquiries revealed that Pateman had lodgings in nearby High Barnet; early in the morning, police raided the premises and arrested him. Bloodstained items, including an overcoat, were seized.

It was a straightforward case and Spilsbury conducted the *post-mortem* examination on the unfortunate woman. He noted that the victim had died from heart failure as a result of massive blood loss from the neck wound. Willcox's involvement was far more innovative. He conducted what he referred to as a 'special test' on the blood saturated overcoat and other clothing and could state 'definitely and positively that they were human blood stains'; this was a world first. Prior to this investigation, scientists could only state with certainty that blood was from a mammal, not necessarily a human. Justice was much swifter at that time and, on 3 July, Pateman was found guilty of murder and sentenced to death. This was later commuted to a life sentence as it was deemed that the killer was mentally ill.

Spilsbury was also to play a critical role in the infamous 'Brides in the Bath' case, where serial killer George Smith murdered three of his wives, whom he had married bigamously. Smith was from the East End of London and lawfully married in 1898, but after being forced to commit theft on his behalf, his wife left him. At the time, the British population was unevenly distributed between male and female; lots of young men had left to seek their fortunes in the colonies. As a result, spinsters were easy prey for the flashy and smooth-talking Londoner.

His killings followed a similar pattern—marry a woman (using a false name), ensure that she took out life insurance or made a will, and then drown her in the bath. He was also prepared to move his victims from one end of the country to another, no doubt, in an attempt to stop the police linking the crimes. Local doctors were content to issue a death certificate based on Smith's account that the victim had fainted or suffered an epileptic fit while bathing. The murders were as follows:

1. 13 July 1912 in Herne Bay, Kent: Bessie Mundy (married in Bristol)
2. 12 December 1913 in Blackpool, Lancashire: Alice Burnham (married in Southsea, Hampshire)
3. 18 December 1914 in Highgate, London: Margaret Lofty (married in London)

Smith's murderous ways may have continued if the father of the second victim had not read of Margaret Lofty's death and noted the similarities to the demise of his daughter. He alerted the police and Smith was arrested on 1 February 1915, in Uxbridge Road, London as he went (unsurprisingly) to discuss the pay out from Margaret's will with his solicitor.

Kent Police now contacted Scotland Yard to link the first death to the case. The three bodies were then exhumed and Spilsbury examined them. He could find no signs of violence or foul play, but he thought it was highly suspicious that Bessie Mundy, in death, had been gripping a bar of soap. Surely if she had suffered a fit or had fainted, she would have let the soap drop. It seemed that she may have been the victim of a very sudden attack, with no opportunity to fight back.

Working with Scotland Yard, Spilsbury conducted experiments with baths, using lady volunteers to play the parts of the deceased women. This resulted in the theory that Smith had suddenly grabbed the legs of his victims and pulled them vertically, resulting in their heads being forced under the water. The sudden rush of water down the throat was found to cause the victim to faint, whereupon they would die from drowning.

This method was demonstrated using a woman police officer (in a bathing suit) at Smith's Old Bailey trial. The display took place in a side room as it was deemed to be unacceptable to have a half-dressed lady in a court of law. The unfortunate (but brave) police officer was rendered unconscious by the demonstration—there was little concern for 'Health and Safety' at that time—but it did provide a powerful example of the technique possibly used by Smith.

Smith was found guilty of the murders and, within six months of his arrest, was hanged in Maidstone Prison. In a bizarre twist, his barrister then suggested that Smith may have hypnotized the women; we shall never know if that was the case. The use of 'similar fact evidence' to show a pattern of behaviour was also utilised for the first time in this case; previously, other similar crimes committed by the defendant could not have been mentioned during the trial.

Jumping ahead to 1934, Brother Spilsbury conducted a *post-mortem* examination on another member of the Craft, Brother Willy Clarkson (Drury Lane Lodge No. 2127). He was the wig-maker, who had assisted detectives with disguises during the Jack the Ripper enquiry. Clarkson also claimed to have sold disguises to Dr Crippen. Just prior to his death, he was found unconsciousness in his bedroom with a large gash on his head. The autopsy revealed no evidence of foul play, but he may well have been murdered. Several years later, it was established that Brother Clarkson had been involved with a gang of arsonists and many of his businesses had been burnt down. These fires had resulted in several large (and fraudulent) insurance pay-outs. Perhaps Clarkson's involvement with criminals resulted in his demise.

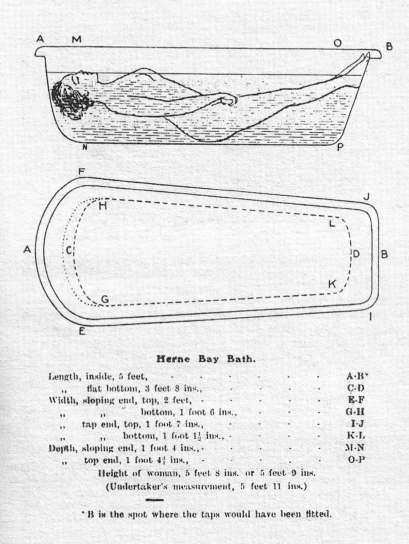

Herne Bay Bath.

Length, inside, 5 feet,	· · · · ·	A-B*
,, flat bottom, 3 feet 8 ins.,	· · ·	C-D
Width, sloping end, top, 2 feet,	· · · ·	E-F
,, ,, bottom, 1 foot 6 ins.,	· · ·	G-H
,, tap end, top, 1 foot 7 ins.,	· · ·	I-J
,, ,, bottom, 1 foot 1½ ins.,	· · ·	K-L
Depth, sloping end, 1 foot 4 ins.,	· · ·	M-N
,, top end, 1 foot 4⅞ ins.,	· · ·	O-P

Height of woman, 5 feet 8 ins. or 5 feet 9 ins.
(Undertaker's measurement, 5 feet 11 ins.)

—

* B is the spot where the taps would have been fitted.

Brides in the Bath: a sketch by Spilsbury used during the trial of George Smith.

41

Dr Crippen:
Captured by a Mason

Masonic Connection
Arresting officer
Pathologist
Toxicologist

Date
1910: Murder and recovery of body occurred

Connection to London
Hilldrop Crescent, Holloway: Scene of the crime
Old Bailey: Court where tried and convicted
Pentonville Prison: Site of execution

Lodges
Gihon Sancta Maria No. 49
Grove No. 410 (erased)
Dalhousie No. 865
St. Mary Magdalen No. 1523
Drury Lane No. 2127
Aeculapius No. 2410
Rahere No. 2546
Sancta Maria No. 2682 (erased)
Misericordia No. 3286.
Rahere Chapter No. 2546 (Holy Royal Arch)
Abernethy No. 569 (Mark)

Dr Hawley Harvey Crippen is still remembered as an infamous murderer. What is less well known is that he was brought to justice by a police officer and forensic scientists who were all Masons. This was also first case where wireless telegraph was used to catch a killer.

Crippen was an American who was born in Michigan in 1862. His first wife died of natural causes (in hindsight, perhaps more investigation was required) and, in 1894, he married Cora Turner, a musical hall singer who used the stage name 'Belle Elmore'. Three years later, the couple moved to England, but Crippen was unable to use his American qualifications to practice 'alternative' medicine. He therefore had to take several (usually lowly paid) jobs. On the other hand, his wife socialised with the stars of the day and had several (open) affairs, even with a lodger at the Crippen family home, 39 Hilldrop Crescent in Holloway, north London. Crippen in turn, took a mistress—a Norfolk born girl, Ethel Neave (which she changed to 'Le Neve'), who worked for him as a typist in the home for the deaf, where he was the manager. Ethel was more than twenty years younger than her lover.

Matters between husband and wife seem to have come to a head after a party at the Crippen home on 31 January 1910. At this point, Cora disappeared, with Crippen informing friends that she had returned to America. Suspicions were raised when young Ethel Le Neve began to wear Mrs Crippen's jewellery. As a result, Scotland Yard detectives attended Hilldrop Crescent to conduct initial enquiries, but a cursory search yielded nothing of importance. Crippen was then interviewed by Chief Inspector Walter Dew, who had much experience of the investigation of crime. Dew had served in the CID throughout London, including being part of the Jack the Ripper enquiry team in 1888. During police questioning, Crippen changed his story; he had been telling his wife's friends that she had died of pneumonia in Los Angeles, but he now claimed that she had eloped with another man. Crippen stated that his initial story was to protect his wife (and himself) from being involved in a scandal. At this time, Chief Inspector Dew had no grounds to detain Crippen and the doctor was released without charge.

As well as being a long-standing detective (he had joined the CID in 1887), Dew was also Mason, having been initiated into a Middlesex lodge, Dalhousic No. 865, which met in Hounslow Town Hall. This lodge should not be confused with the London lodge of the same name and very similarly numbered (No. 860) that features in Chapter 38. The popularity of this name appears to come from the Earl of Dalhousie, a Grand Master of Scotland.

While Brother Dew may have been satisfied with the answers given to him, the search and interview appear to have panicked Crippen. He and Le Neve left London immediately, sailing to Belgium and quickly boarding the SS Montrose, bound for Canada. This sudden disappearance resulted in Dew becoming more suspicious, searching the house far more thoroughly. In the Third Degree, the body of the murder victim (Hiram Abif) is found after a Mason finds that the ground has been recently disturbed. In Dew's case, while prodding the floor of the cellar with a poker, he found that the bricks came up too easily. Digging down about nine inches, he discovered what were later confirmed to be human remains.

Extensive searches failed to find the main parts of the body; the skeleton, head, and limbs had vanished, with lime seemingly used to hasten the decomposition. What did remain was recovered by the detectives for examination by forensic scientists. The two responsible for identification and testing of the remains were Dr William Willcox and Dr Bernard Spilsbury. As we saw in the previous chapter, both were Masons and at the time of the Crippen case, Willcox had been a member of the Craft for some four years and was a member of two lodges—Sancta Maria No. 2682 and Misericordia No. 3286. Spilsbury would join the Craft some ten years later, firstly into the Rahere Lodge No. 2546. A full list of his substantial Masonic career in the Craft, Royal Arch, and Mark is shown in the previous chapter.

Despite the lack of body parts, Spilsbury was able to state that a piece of scar tissue matched that from an abdominal operation that the missing woman had undergone. Willcox conducted toxicology tests and found that Mrs Crippen had been poisoned with a large quantity of hyoscine. Crucially, it could be shown that this drug had been purchased by Crippen from a chemist in Oxford Street. It was also worthy of note that, while he frequently purchased other drugs including (the then legal) cocaine on several occasions, he had only requested hyoscine on one occasion. This sedative is still used today, particularly to treat travel sickness.

Crippen's luck was running out, with the captain of his transatlantic liner, the SS Montrose, becoming highly suspicious about the middle age man, calling himself 'John Robinson' who was accompanied by a highly effeminate 'boy'. Captain Kendall made use of new technology to inform the police in England that he believed that Crippen and Le Neve were aboard. Using the new ship-borne telegraph, Kendall ordered the following message to be transmitted, 'Have strong suspicions that Crippen London cellar murderer and accomplice are among saloon passengers. Moustache taken off growing beard. Accomplice dressed as boy. Manner and build undoubtedly a girl.'

Chief Inspector Dew now followed the example set by another Mason, Inspector Tanner, and boarded a faster ship to pursue a wanted man across the Atlantic. There was, however, a key difference; in 1864, ships could not communicate with each other, unless in very close proximity, but in 1910, the arrest could be coordinated by telegraph across thousands of miles of ocean. Dew's capture of his quarry would also be swifter than Tanner's. Crippen was bound for Canada—part of the British Empire—and so there would be no requirement for extradition proceedings. If he had sailed to the United States, his route to justice would have been much slower.

Dew, in possession of an arrest warrant, arrived in Quebec before Crippen's ship. On 31 July 1910, as the SS Montrose entered the St Lawrence River estuary, the Scotland Yard detective, accompanied by Canadian police officers, boarded the vessel disguised as river pilots. Kendall then invited 'Mr Robinson' to meet the 'pilots', whereupon Dew identified himself as a police officer, saying, 'Good morning, Dr Crippen. Do you know me? I'm Chief Inspector Dew from Scotland Yard.' An initially startled Crippen replied, 'Thank God it's over. The suspense has been too great. I couldn't stand it any longer.' Crippen was arrested on suspicion of murder and mutilation of his wife's body. He was handcuffed as Dew had found a letter on him where he had threatened to commit suicide by jumping overboard. Le Neve, who had been travelling in the name 'John C Robinson', was also taken into custody. Both suspects returned to London in the charge of the chief inspector.

The cuckolded doctor was tried at the Old Bailey in the October. By now, he was described as a dentist. It is suggested by some that, in an attempt to save himself from aggressive cross-examination, Crippen made Masonic signs to the judge during the trial. This included inter-lacing his fingers and putting them above his head. This does sound very similar to one of the 'Sign of Distress' used by Masons; however, in the English

Left: Chief Inspector Walter
Dew, the Mason who pursued
Crippen across the Atlantic.

Below: Dr Crippen in the dock
at the Old Bailey.

ceremony, this version (or one like it) is explained to be the European method of giving the sign. The American version is very different. Furthermore, there is no evidence that Crippen was a member of the Craft in the USA, England, or mainland Europe. He was also wasting his time. The judge, Lord Alverstone, was in a 'lodge' but this was a lodge of the 'Royal Antediluvian Order of Buffaloes'; perhaps, Crippen was also a 'Buff' and was using one of their signs.

The evidence provided by the real Freemasons—Dew, Spilsbury, and Willcox—proved damning. Another Mason was called to verify the tests conducted by Dr Willcox to identify the poison in the body. Dr Arthur Luff was an expert, having written a book, the *Text Book of Forensic Medicine and Toxicology* in 1895. He fully supported Willcox's findings. In 1897, Luff had been a founder of Willcox's lodge, Sancta Maria No. 2682. He had joined the Craft in 1891, being initiated into the (now defunct) Grove Lodge No. 410 in Ewell, Surrey and was also a member of Aeculapius No. 2410 in London.

Despite the defence calling their own medical experts, Crippen was found guilty of murder; the jury took less than thirty minutes to reach a verdict. He was hanged on 23 November 1910 in Pentonville Prison. Le Neve was tried separately and acquitted. She immigrated to the USA on the day of Crippen's execution and her lover was buried in an unmarked grave within the grounds of Pentonville Prison, with, at his request, a photograph of his beloved Ethel. The scene of the crime has long since gone; 39 Hilldrop Crescent was destroyed by bombs dropped by the German Luftwaffe during the Second World War.

As an aside, Brother Willy Clarkson (Drury Lane Lodge No. 2127), the wig-maker, who assisted detectives with disguises, bizarrely claimed that Dr Crippen had been one of his customers. The bald doctor is not recorded as having worn false hair, but a disguise or wig may have been used by Ethel when she dressed as a boy. Given that he could have been prosecuted for assisting a wanted murderer, it is unclear why Clarkson would make such an admission. It may have been that the flamboyant wig-maker was still useful to Scotland Yard, but he later died himself in suspicious circumstances.

42

Masonic Poisoner, Masonic Judge, and Masonic Sign at the Old Bailey

Masonic Connection
Doctor, who signed death certificate
Pathologists
Judge
Sign and phrase used in court
Murderer

Date
1911: Murder committed
1912: Trial at the Old Bailey

Connection to London
Tollington Park, Finsbury Park: House where murder was committed
Buck's Head, Camden: Ownership of this public house was possible motive for the crime
Old Bailey: Court where tried and convicted
Pentonville Prison: Site of execution

Lodges
Lodge of Friendship No. 6
Neptune No. 22
Lodge of Good Report No. 136
Royal Sussex Lodge of Hospitality No. 187
St Kew No. 1222
Stanley No. 1325
Empire No. 2108
Old Westminsters' No. 2233
Ebbisham No. 2422
Stephens No. 3089

There have been many claims that Masonic signs have been made in court to ensure a 'not guilty' verdict or a lighter sentence. These signs have been attributed to various villains of the past, notably Dr Crippen, who was not really a doctor and certainly not a Freemason. So, let us turn to a real story of the Masonic sign made in court.

Frederick Seddon, the villain and Mason in this case, was born in Liverpool in 1872 and was initiated into a local lodge, Stanley No. 1325 in 1901. He moved south and, in 1905, he was a founder member of Stephens Lodge No. 3089 in Buckingham. He resigned from both lodges in 1906 and this is the end of his time in the Craft, but it was not the last time he would make use of Masonic phrases and signs.

By 1909, he was the supervisor of a number of insurance collectors in London and he purchased a large house at 63 Tollington Park. Seddon, his wife Margaret, their five children, and other family members all moved into this home. Seddon appears to be obsessed with making money and despite the fourteen bedrooms, he managed to squeeze his father and several servants into one room. He also charged the insurance company a fee for the use of one of the rooms as his office.

The following year, a rich but eccentric spinster named Eliza Barrow moved into the house. She had several business interests, including the lease on the Buck's Head public house near Camden Market (the pub is still there), a barber's shop next door, and had money invested in stock. She also distrusted banks and particularly liked gold coins (and bank notes), something Seddon also enjoyed collecting. We cannot be sure how many of these coins were in her possession, but at the trial, it was suggested that there was at least £400 in gold in a cash box (today this would be worth over £20,000).

Seddon persuaded Barrow to allow him to take charge of her assets and she signed over £1,600 in stock (today's value around £90,000). In return, Seddon would pay her an allowance and allow her to live rent free in his home. As the prosecution counsel at the trial would later allege, this was the motive to kill Barrow. Once dead, no allowance would have to be paid and the stock (and other items) would belong to Seddon. Critically, Seddon's teenage daughter, Maggie, attended on Barrow, bringing meals to her. This enabled the Seddons to control the food and drink consumed by their wealthy lodger.

This cosy arrangement continued for over a year and, in the summer of 1911, Seddon, his wife, and Barrow went on holiday to the seaside resort of Southend in Essex. On their return home, Maggie Seddon was sent by her father to purchase a small pack of fly paper; this was to prove a critical issue at the later trial. The fly paper contained arsenic, but the identification evidence was hotly disputed by the defence as the chemist claimed that he clearly remembered Maggie Seddon purchasing fly paper some six months after the event. It was suggested that arsenic extracted from the paper was mixed into a dose of 'Valentine's Meat Juice', an American potion that became popular in Edwardian Britain for treating stomach problems. As arsenic is virtually colourless and tasteless, it could easily have been concealed in this manner. A piece of the 'Mather's Chemical Fly Paper' was later produced in court and is now in the Crime Museum at Scotland Yard.

Whatever the method used to administer the poison, Elisa Barrow was soon in agony, suffering from violent stomach pains. The local doctor, Dr Henry Sworn, was called and attended several times over a fortnight period. He was also a Mason, having been initiated

63 Tollington Park; the victim, Eliza Barrow, occupied rooms on the top floor.

Frederick Seddon, the Mason who famously made Masonic signs at the judge during his murder trial.

into Neptune Lodge No. 22 in 1885. On her deathbed, on 13 September, Barrow made a will. This did not make Seddon the beneficiary, but he was named as the executor of the will and was the only person to know the full extent of her worldly goods. At 11.30 p.m. that night, Barrow cried out 'I am dying'; by the following morning, she was found dead. The doctor foolishly signed a death certificate without seeing the body. He would later tell the court that he had been too busy dealing with a local epidemic to follow the correct procedures. The cause of death was recorded as 'epidemic diarrhoea and exhaustion'.

The Barrow family had a vault in a church in Islington where she should have been interred. Seddon, however, quickly organised an inexpensive funeral and Barrow was buried in a cheap plot in Islington Cemetery within two days of her demise. Her family were not informed. Greedy as ever, Seddon obtained commission from a local undertaker for giving him some business. Once convicted, he was later to claim that 'it was quite a respectable funeral.'

In the meantime, the Barrow family had become aware of Elisa's death. Her cousin, Frank Vonderahe, visited Seddon on 20 September and demanded to see her will and insurance policy. Seddon claimed that all her funds had been spent on the funeral. Given the low cost of the 'arrangements' and the suddenness of the death (and burial), Vonderahe was rightly suspicious. Seddon also announced that the pub and barber's shop now belonged to him and soon departed on holiday for two weeks with his wife, returning to Southend. This apparent lack of grief for their departed lodger aroused further suspicion. Vonderahe soon communicated his fears to the local police and Scotland Yard detectives were placed on the case.

In November, the police were satisfied that there were reasonable grounds to the relatives' suspicions and Eliza Barrow's body was exhumed and taken to Finchley mortuary. It was examined by Dr (later Sir and Worshipful Brother) Bernard Spilsbury, who had come to public prominence at the trial of Dr Crippen. Crucially, he demonstrated that the death was due to poisoning. Hence, he was the ideal choice of pathologist to assist in the Seddon investigation.

At Finchley Mortuary, Spilsbury's examination of the body of Eliza Barrow (who had been buried for nearly two months) revealed no evidence of any disease that could have caused her death. He did note that, 'The body was remarkably well preserved, both externally and internally. This would suggest that death was due to some poison having a preservative affect'. Arsenic can have such an effect and blood tests were to reveal at least two grains (and possibly even five) of the drug in her body—a large amount that was more than capable of killing an adult in days rather than weeks. This indicated that Barrow had not been poisoned over a long period. She had been given a substantial amount, possibly in one dose. In a further Masonic connection, these blood tests were conducted by Dr William Henry Willcox, senior scientific advisor to the Home Office, who (as we have seen) was a member of the Sancta Maria Lodge in 1906, a lodge which Spilsbury would also join.

On 4 December, police visited Tollington Park and arrested Seddon on suspicion of murder. The senior detective recorded that Seddon claimed that the allegation was 'Absurd … Are you going to arrest my wife as well? Have they found arsenic in her body? She has not done this herself'. It sounds extremely suspicious that he should mention arsenic and he appears to have attempted to lay the blame on Mrs Seddon. He later vigorously denied that he had tried to shift suspicion in this manner.

Seddon was remanded in custody and appeared at the inquest into the death of Barrow held on 14 December. He did not give evidence. The jury returned the following verdict: 'That the said Eliza Mary Barrow died … of arsenical poisoning at 63 Tollington Park, the arsenic having been administered to her by some person or persons unknown'. The police subsequently arrested Mrs Margaret Seddon and she too was charged with murder. She was found to have changed thirty-three £5 notes for gold coins (a considerable amount of cash at that time, so much so that when changing a 'fiver' you had to give a name and address) and she had given a false name and address to the bank clerk when doing so. The police strongly suspected that this money came from Eliza Barrow's cash box.

The scene was now set for the Masonic murder trial. On the 4 March 1912, the Seddons appeared at the Old Bailey. The judge was His Honour Mr Justice Bucknill, or in Masonic terms, Right Worshipful Brother (later Sir) Thomas Bucknill, Provincial Grand Master for Surrey, a very senior Mason; he had also been the Member of Parliament for Epsom in the same county. By the time of the trial, Bucknill had been a member of the Craft for nearly forty years as he had been initiated into a London lodge in 1873 at the Lodge of Good Report No. 136. He was a very dedicated Mason, joining the Old Westminsters' Lodge No. 2233 in 1891, being the first master of Ebbisham Lodge No. 2422 in Surrey the following year, and joining Lodge of Friendship No. 6 in 1903 with his son. He was appointed as the Provincial Grand Master of Surrey in the same year as joining the latter lodge, and would hold the position until his death in 1915.

Rather unusually (and scandalously) for a judge at that time, Bucknill had been divorced and then remarried a divorced woman. His first wife had committed adultery with a Royal Engineers officer. Bucknill then married Annie Hare, who had divorced her husband, John Strachey Hare, on grounds of cruelty. The couple had lived in Clifton, Bristol and rather ironically, the cruel Mr Hare was also a Mason, being initiated into the Royal Sussex Lodge of Hospitality No. 187 in Bristol in 1866 and later joining the St Kew Lodge No. 1222 in Weston-Super-Mare.

Returning to the Old Bailey, the trial was to last for ten days—lengthy at that time. The case against the Seddons was circumstantial as no one had witnessed any poison being given to Eliza Barrow. Both Frederick and Margaret Seddon gave evidence in their own defence, which they had no need to do. Mrs Seddon was able to explain away the £5 note changing and use of a false name, stating that she had frequently done this to assist Eliza Barrow. Giving evidence back-fired for Frederick Seddon; a contemporary account describes the manner of his performance in the witness box as 'cold and hard as a paving stone'. It was a fatal error on his part.

Right Worshipful Brother, His Honour, Sir Thomas Bucknill, the Mason who sentenced Brother Seddon to death.

Mr Justice Bucknill's summing up appears to have been kinder to Mrs Seddon than to her husband. He may also have had knowledge that Seddon was (nominally) a Freemason (he had resigned in 1906), as towards the end of his speech to the jury he advised them:

> It matters not what religion a man belongs to, what nationality he is, what sect or brotherhood or anything else he may belong to, he who lives under the protection of the laws of the country in which he abides must keep them, and if he breaks them he must pay the penalty, even although the penalty be his life.

This statement sounds like part of The Charge After Initiation, where the tenets and rules of the Craft are related to a new brother—'you are to be exemplary in the discharge of your civil duties ... by paying due obedience to the laws of any State which may for a time become the place of your residence or afford you its protection.'

Given what was to happen after sentence, this advice takes on significance, possibly suggesting that the judge had been warned that Seddon would attempt to use Freemasonry to his advantage. This part of the speech has echoes of part of the Third Degree (Master Mason) obligation, which every candidate recites:

> That my breast shall be the safe repository of his secrets when entrusted to my care— murder, treason, felony, and all other offences contrary to the laws of God and the ordinances of the realm being at all times most especially excepted.

The jury took just one hour to reach a verdict. Margaret Seddon was acquitted, but her husband was found guilty of murder. Seddon then made a lengthy statement, claiming that the police had tried to force his wife to give evidence against him, that he had been convicted on circumstantial evidence, and (oddly) that Miss Barrow may have committed suicide by poisoning herself. Then came the famous statement, '...I declare before the Great Architect of the Universe that I am not guilty, my lord'; it is unclear how he knew that the judge was a Mason. The 'Great Architect of the Universe' is the name used by Freemasons in the initiation ceremony. He is also said to have made a Masonic sign, either the First Degree sign or the sign of 'Grief and Distress' (from the Third Degree).

At that time, there was only punishment for murder—death by hanging—and, in line with English court tradition, Mr Justice Bucknill donned a black cap to deliver the sentence. He appeared to be shocked by Seddon's appeal to the Great Architect, but told him:

> From what you have said, you and I know we both belong to one brotherhood, and it is all the more painful to me to have to say what I am saying. But our brotherhood does not encourage crime; on the contrary, it condemns it. I pray you again to make your peace with the Great Architect of the Universe....

Then the sentence was delivered:

> that you be taken from hence to a lawful prison, and from thence to a place of execution, and that you be there hanged by the neck until you are dead; and that your body be

buried within the precincts of the prison in which you shall have been confined after your conviction; and may the Lord have mercy on your soul!

At this time, photography was permitted in court and a photograph was taken of Seddon in the dock, with Brother, Mr Justice Bucknill wearing the black cap. This image, captured at the moment of the death sentence, was thought to be unacceptable. It was mentioned during a Parliamentary debate some thirteen years later and led to the current prohibition on photography during court hearings.

Seddon appealed against his conviction, but the sentence was upheld. He continued to protest his innocence up to the very end and made what he called his 'Final Statement'. This contained a seemingly Masonic reference to the 'creator, to whom all secrets are revealed'. His statement was as follows:

I am Not Guilty of the Murder of Eliza Mary Barrow. I swear that I have never purchased arsenic in my life in any shape or form, neither have I at any time instructed, directed, or influenced the purchase of arsenic. I did not administer arsenic to her in any shape or form, or any other poison, neither did I advise, direct, instruct, or influence the administration of arsenic, or any other form of poison to the deceased. And I further swear that I had no knowledge that she died from arsenical poisoning; I believed she died from epidemic diarrhoea as per Dr Sworn's certificate. I solemnly swear before my Creator, to whom all secrets are revealed, that this is a true statement, and the Law, in its seeming blindness and misguided justice, has condemned an Innocent Man.

He was hanged on 18 April 1912 in Pentonville Prison, London, less than two miles from the scene of the crime. His body was buried there, in unconsecrated ground with just a marker showing his initials. That then is the end of the trial where the Masonic sign was used, but to no avail. Seddon may have been a member of the Craft, but all the other Freemasons involved in this case—the judge (Bucknill) and the pathologists (Spilsbury and Willcox)—performed their duties with utmost integrity, following the rules of the Craft taught to them in the First and Third Degrees. Sadly, not all Freemasons thought well of the judge, who had clearly done his duty, legally and Masonically. A letter written by Bucknill to a friend named as 'A. Mosses', a few days after the sentence, is on display in the Crime Museum at New Scotland Yard:

12 Embankment Gardens SW
16.3.1912
My dear Mosses
Thank you so much for yours of 14th. I have been too upset since last Thursday to write letters, although I have had to do my Court work. I am gratified that you came to the Court, for it was to see part of a case that has had no like Ever.
It was a <u>very</u> trying time for me for 10 whole days and it ended in such a dramatic way, for never has a poor creature addressed a Judge like he addressed me at such a time. I don't blame him for (illegible words).

Since then I have been receiving many kind letters, but some cruel ones, condemning me for sentencing a Brother Mason to Death-generally anonymous ones.

What a cruelty! for how could I escape doing my duty, and I feel quite sure that Seddon had a fair trial, and that I put every point in his favour to the Jury.

I think you won't care to see another murderer sentenced, will you?

And we Judges have to do this horrible work even although one should object to capital punishment, as I do.

Very truly yours

T.T. Bucknill

It would appear that the recipient of this letter was Alexander Mosses, who had been initiated into Empire Lodge No. 2108. He resigned in 1913; we shall never know if the treatment of Brother Bucknill by his fellow Masons influenced his decision.

There is a postscript to this tale. When the Scotland Yard Crime Museum visitor's book was checked, it was found that Brother Seddon had visited in 1905, perhaps suggesting that he was looking for ideas for the perfect murder.

43

Masonic Murder Mystery:
Who killed the Chairman of Harrods?

Masonic Connection
Victim
Man, who accused him of dishonesty

Date
1872: Victim initiated into Freemasonry
1899: Lord Mayor of London
1921: Died of poisoning

Connection to London
Victoria Embankment, near the Temple: Monument names Sir Alfred Newton as the Lord
    Mayor when Queen Victoria last visited the City of London
Knightsbridge: Died outside Harrods

Lodges
Royal Clarence No. 271
Khyber No. 582
Abbey No. 624
Anerley No. 1397
United Studholme Alliance No. 1591
Alliance No. 1827 (erased)
Grafton No. 2347
London County Council No. 2603 (erased)
Alfred Newton No. 2686
White Rose of York and Addeys' No. 2840

The life (but not death) of Worshipful Brother Sir Alfred Newton is similar to the tale of
Dick Whittington—a young man from the provinces who journeyed to London to make
his fortune and became Lord Mayor. The difference for Sir Alfred, however, is that he

died in very suspicious circumstances, after drinking poisoned medicine dispensed from Harrods, the famous department store of which he was chairman.

Alfred Newton was born in Hull in the East Riding of Yorkshire in 1846. By the age of nineteen, he was working for himself as a yeast merchant. Being based in a port, this young entrepreneur soon extended his interests into steamships and soon owned his own boats. In 1872, he took his first step in Freemasonry, joining the lodge, which bore the name of the river on which his ships sailed—the Humber Lodge No. 57. He also had business interests in Burton-on Trent, Staffordshire and joined the Abbey Lodge No. 624 there in 1880.

With London being the centre of the greatest empire ever known, Newton was drawn to the 'streets paved with gold' that offered many opportunities for an ambitious and clever man to make money; Newton fitted both categories. Having moved south, he settled with his family in the affluent area of Chislehurst, on the Kent and London border; there, he soon established himself into both business and Masonic life in the capital. In 1888, he is recorded as a joining member of Alliance Lodge No. 1827 (now amalgamated to form part of United Studholme Alliance No. 1591), which at the time met in Gresham Street in the City of London. The lodge records describe him as a 'steamship owner', with a business address in nearby Leadenhall Street. Within two years, he had joined another London lodge, Grafton No. 2347.

Newton's business interests were extremely varied—railways, insurance, real estate, breweries, gold mining across the world, and even a theatre. One area, which would ultimately bring his name into disrepute (and possibly a motive for his murder) was his involvement with the Mendel Group, a syndicate of rich business owners, who saw the new idea of department stores as a way to make even more money.

While extremely busy in business and Masonic terms, Newton was also progressing in public life and in 1888, he was appointed as a Sheriff of London. The holder of this ancient office had, at that time, important judicial duties and sat at the Old Bailey as a Justice of the Peace. The appointment is a prerequisite of being made the Lord Mayor, in similar vein to a Masonic lodge, where a member must be a warden, before he is the master. During Newton's year of office, the Prince of Wales, then the Grand Master of the United Grand Lodge of England and later King Edward VII, was granted the Freedom of the City.

The following year—1889—his interest in department stores was to reach its zenith; he was appointed as the first chairman of Harrods. The history of the store describes him as 'shrewd', but he also had to override the decisions of his board members and could be ruthless with them. This may also have been a motive for his later murder. If his directors did not like him, Masons certainly did and in 1897, a lodge was opened bearing his name (Alfred Newton No. 2686); he became the first Worshipful Master.

His influence in the City was also forever increasing, with him being the master of three livery companies (Framework Knitters, Girdlers and Fan makers) and an Alderman. Most importantly, in November 1899, he was made Lord Mayor of London—not bad for a yeast merchant from Hull—but as we shall see, at the time of his appointment, he was under the cloud of a business scandal.

As Lord Mayor, he launched an appeal for a fighting force to assist in the Boer War. Newton raised a small fortune to equip the City of London Imperial Volunteers, who sailed to South Africa to take part in several successful actions during the Boer War. Their

Honorary Colonel, Field Marshal Lord Roberts, was (unsurprisingly) also a Freemason (Khyber Lodge then No. 852 in India, now No. 582 in London). This work in supplying the empire with much needed troops was to result in the boy from Hull being knighted by Queen Victoria and becoming Baron Newton of the Wood, Sydenham. A plaque celebrating the last visit of Victoria to the City was placed on the Embankment, near the Temple and displays Sir Alfred's name as the Lord Mayor at that time; this plaque is just near the griffin that marks the border between the cities of London and Westminster. Despite all these accolades in London, he refused to forget his northern roots and, in 1901, he was the first Worshipful Master of a lodge of which he was a founding member—White Rose of York Lodge No. 2840 (now known as White Rose of York and Addeys').

Newton's life then seems to take on a slower pace. He remained an active Mason and Chairman of Harrods throughout the Great War, until his death in June 1921. At the age of seventy-five years old, the chemist at his store dispensed him some indigestion medicine— all very routine, or so it would seem. This was delivered to his home, where he appears to have taken just one dose. Having complained of its bitter taste, Sir Alfred died suddenly in his motor car, outside Harrods. Medical evidence would show that he was already a very sick man, but the massive dose of strychnine added to the medicine hastened his end. The medicine was laced with enough poison to kill sixty men. This leaves little doubt that someone was determined to see him dead.

No murderer, however, was ever identified, so the question of who killed the Harrods chairman and former Lord Mayor of London remains. The critical piece of evidence is the medicine bottle, but an extensive enquiry at the Chelsea Coroner's Court failed to establish where or when the poison could have been added to the medicine. The coroner even noted that the movement of the bottle, which had passed through many hands, reminded him of the 'wandering of Ulysses.' There appear to be four groups of possible suspects: former business associates; a Harrods employee; a servant at his Chiselhurst house; and a family member.

Newton's involvement in the Mendel Group, around the time he was Lord Mayor, no doubt made him several enemies among his former business associates. The Mendel Group formed the 'Industrial Contract Corporation' with the intention of buying up department stores across London. It managed to buy only one—a shop in Clapham—for £17,000. In a rather dubious move, the shareholders then sold it to themselves for nearly three times the amount, sharing the 'profit' between themselves. Not all at the company saw this as an honest business practice and one, Sir John Blundell Maple, demanded an enquiry by the Board of Trade. Maple was also a self-made, successful businessman who had made his money in the furniture trade, but, like Newton, had branched out into other areas. In another parallel, Sir John was also a politician, being the Member of Parliament for Dulwich and an active Freemason. Maple was a member of three lodges—Anerley No. 1397, which met in south London, the (now defunct) London County Council No. 2603 and the Royal Clarence No. 271, which stills meets in Brighton. Contrary to the oft suggested Masonic cover-ups and 'back scratching', here we have a Freemason demanding that another member of the Craft be held to account for what were alleged to be dishonest business practices. The enquiry was held in 1899 and although the judge, who chaired the proceedings, called the buying and selling of the Clapham store 'nothing short of a scandal', Newton was not found to have breached any rules. His accuser, Sir

Plaque naming Sir Alfred Newton as Lord Mayor. This can be seen on the Embankment at the start of the City of London.

John, would die within four years and some fifteen years before the poison was administered. Newton's wheeler dealer business methods continued and it is not unreasonable to suggest that perhaps some other aggrieved business associate added the fatal dose.

Newton was the chairman of the department store for over thirty years and it is known that he could ride rough-shod over his directors. This, no doubt, would cause bad feeling and importantly, the evidence is clear—the poisoned medicine was dispensed from the store. At the inquest, the Harrods chemist and her assistant were closely questioned, but no fault was found with their work and they demonstrated that the medicine was correctly prepared, placed in a sealed envelope, and despatched to Sir Alfred's home. Hence, it would appear that the poison was added after it left the store. It should also be noted that the poisoner appears to have had little expert knowledge; the large amount of strychnine used appears to show the poisoner was an amateur, rather than a trained chemist who would have been aware of the strength of poisons and the dose needed to kill.

The culprit could have been one of the several servants. The arrival of the bottle at the house appears to have been an important aspect of this case, which was not pursued by the coroner. The driver of the delivery van recalled the bottle being in the sealed envelope, but the kitchen maid who took possession of it was uncertain if the bottle was in any such envelope. This was critical to the case, but was never resolved. The medicine was placed in the pantry and later taken to the landing near Sir Alfred's bedroom when the old bottle ran out. None of the servants had seen any rat poison in the house (the most common household use of strychnine), and no other source of the poison was identified. Another suspicious factor was the washing of the medicine glass. The parlour maid stated that she always took this away and washed it, but on the day of the fatal dose, someone else had removed the glass and cleaned it; perhaps a disgruntled servant added the strychnine.

A family member could have been responsible; Lady Newton acted strangely at the time. She was unable to attend the inquest due to 'precarious health', but managed to outlive her husband by some fourteen years, dying in 1935. It is unknown whether his son was in the family home at the material time. From 1910 until just after his father's death, he was the Member of Parliament for Harwich and so was likely to have been away. Later, he too would be the Master of the Alfred Newton lodge. With his father gone, he would inherit a title and be known as Sir Harry Kottingham Newton, 2nd Baronet and he may also have inherited his father's fortune. The evidence, however, provides no indication that the son was the poisoner. Importantly, Sir Harry highlighted to the authorities his father's complaint that the medicine had a bitter taste and therefore created the suspicion that the death was murder; the real poisoner, would not wish to draw such attention to the crime. If he had not done so, it is unlikely that a *post-mortem* examination would have been held and the death recorded, due to the elderly victim's ill health, as natural causes.

And so, the Masonic murder mystery remains unsolved. The most likely suspects appear to be those working or living in the Chislehurst family home of the Newtons. The police and coroner do not seem to have focused on the possibility of the sealed envelope containing the medicine having been interfered with or why someone other than the parlour maid washed the glass used by Sir Alfred. As we will see with the 10th Duke of Devonshire, this would not be the only time that a Freemason would be murdered and the killer escape justice.

44

Mason, Media, Members of Parliament, and a Massive Swindle

Masonic Connection
Swindler
Accomplice

Date
1885: Bottomley initiated into Freemasonry
1905: Elected as a Member of Parliament
1921: Imprisoned for fraud

Connection to London
Bethnal Green: Birthplace
Paternoster Square: London Stock Exchange
Southwark Bridge Road: London offices of the Financial Times
Houses of Parliament: Served as an MP
High Courts of Justice: First trial at this court
Guildhall, City of London: Second trial
Old Bailey: Third trial
Wormwood Scrubs, Hammersmith: Served sentence in this prison
Windmill Theatre, Great Windmill St, Soho: Collapsed on stage

Lodges
St Alban's No. 29
Cadogan No. 162
Tranquillity No. 185
Lodge of Israel No. 205
Polish National No. 534
Drury Lane No. 2127
Fairfield No. 2224

The life of swindler Brother Horatio Bottomley is not a tale of 'rags to riches', it is a tale of 'rags to riches to rags' or 'three strikes (or three fraud trials) and you are out'. According to one biographer, he could 'tempt the banknotes out of men's pockets'. Bottomley was born in 1860 in Bethnal Green to a working class 'East Ender' family. Tragically, both his parents died in his youth and he spent five years in the dreadful surroundings of a Victorian orphanage in Birmingham, far away from home. Determined to improve his lot, Bottomley worked as a solicitor's clerk, but then decided that he could make his fortune in trading in shares at the London Stock Exchange. His knowledge of the law would prove useful in his financial dealings. He would also establish one of the most famous newspapers in Britain and become a Member of Parliament. He became a Freemason by joining the Polish National Lodge No. 534 in 1885.

Having gained experience of publishing local newspapers, Bottomley founded the *Financial Times* some six years after joining the Craft. The paper was established to give independent advice on the Stock Exchange. That said, Bottomley was able to slip in false reports to manipulate the value of shares, hence he could devalue companies that he wished to buy and boost the price of his own stock. He also engineered a deal to publish Hansard reports, the official record of Parliamentary debate. This company initially appeared successful and attracted much investment, but Bottomley was falsely inflating the profits, enabling him to claim excessive dividend payments. In May 1891, he drew too much of the spotlight on his activities by taking £100,000 out of the company and then applying for bankruptcy. The government's Board of Trade investigated and Bottomley was charged with fraud, together with the company's directors. This included the Lord Mayor-Elect of London and fellow Freemason, Sir Henry Isaacs, who had been initiated into the Lodge of Israel No. 205 in 1853. He had then joined several other London lodges, including Tranquillity No. 185 in 1857 and Drury Lane No. 2127 in 1886.

Bottomley and his directors appeared at the High Courts of Justice in January 1893 for a mammoth three-month trial before Judge Henry Hawkins. By using the legal knowledge gleaned during his early career, great oratory, and charm, Bottomley painted a picture of a conspiracy involving several government departments, which were, he alleged, intent on bringing him down. Judge Hawkins (not a Mason) aided the defendants' case with a summing up that was heavily in their favour. Despite a very strong prosecution case, Bottomley, Isaacs, and the other directors were acquitted. Despite the 'not guilty' verdict, such a trial could have destroyed the reputation of some, but Bottomley turned the affair to his advantage, with many believing that he was a financial wizard.

Climbing the social ladder, Bottomley became the Liberal Party Member of Parliament for Hackney in 1905, but his financial dealings would result in a second accusation of dishonesty that would put the brakes on his political aspirations. Around this time, Bottomley began to work with Ernest Hooley, who made several fortunes by buying companies and selling them at inflated prices. These fraudulent schemes involved several famous brands of today—Schweppes, Bovril, Dunlop, and Raleigh cycles. Hooley was also 'on the square'; he had been initiated into the Fairfield Lodge No. 2224 in his home town of Long Eaton, Derbyshire in 1899.

In 1908, Brother Bottomley was summoned to appear at the Guildhall in the City of London, where he was accused of a further fraud. Bottomley had exploited the excitement (and greed) created by the discovery of gold in Australia and had been selling worthless shares in a mining business. His failure to keep proper records of the transactions aided his cause and he again walked free from court. This time, however, Bottomley was not unscathed; the Liberal Party temporarily suspended him. Worst still, his reputation in the city was damaged.

During the 1910 general election, Bottomley fought his seat as a Liberal, despite having an increasingly antagonistic relationship with the party. His Conservative opponent was also a Freemason: Sydney King-Farlow, a barrister who was a member of Cadogan Lodge No. 162. Determined to keep his seat, Bottomley used all manner of tactics to disrupt King-Farlow's electioneering. This included hiring groups of men to march around the Conservative meetings in steel toe-capped boots, so that no one could hear the speeches. King-Farlow also alleged that Bottomley had encouraged children to throw stones at his supporters. Once Bottomley had regained his Hackney seat, the two rivals engaged in a most un-Masonic exchange of letters in *The Times*, where further allegations of dubious tactics were made and denied. Oddly, this was not the first election campaign that had resulted in King-Farlow falling out with a brother Mason. In 1909, at the Sheffield Attercliffe by-election, he had clashed with opponent Arnold Muir Wilson (a member of St Alban's Lodge No. 29), calling him a 'cad and a liar'. The disagreement became so bitter that Wilson took King-Farlow to court, alleging that he had assaulted him and damaged his bowler hat—a very British offence. The charge, however, was dismissed as Brother Wilson engaged in bizarre behaviour while giving evidence, including throwing his damaged hat at King-Farlow's counsel.

In 1914, the world was about to tear itself apart, but rather than seeing a global conflict as a disaster, the First World War presented Bottomley with another opportunity to make money. While Samuel Johnson famously remarked that 'patriotism is the last refuge of a scoundrel', Bottomley would turn it into a money-making scheme. Returning to the publishing industry, he transformed his magazine *John Bull* into the journal for the British 'Tommy', as rank and file soldiers were known. While the British Army was relatively small at the outbreak of war, it soon grew to contain millions of men—all potential purchasers of the publication. As a great speaker, Bottomley was soon a recruiting voice for the Army—good for the country, but also good for his pocket. He was accused of profiteering and ensuring that prize draw wins benefitted close friends (and his own pocket), but using the legal knowledge from his early work, he was able to successfully sue for libel. His oratory in court was so excellent that one judge even offered him his wig. He was also welcomed by Field Marshals and Admirals during his tours around France and the Royal Navy fleet to boost the morale of the British servicemen.

Despite his obvious shortcomings (greed and vanity among them), Bottomley's efforts in the First World War had made him very popular with the public; in 1918, he was re-elected into his old seat, but this time as an independent candidate. While his political career was back on course, his income was about to reduce and Bottomley had a life style to maintain—a big country house in Sussex, a love of champagne, horse racing, and several mistresses. Unfortunately, for the media magnate, the readership of his magazine was set to drastically reduce as the number of British servicemen was cut, with the war having ended. To bolster his business, Bottomley played on the patriotic fervour created by the victory over Germany and established the John Bull Victory Bond Club. This was a form of lottery where investors had the chance of winning a large cash sum each month. Regrettably for the participants, not all the money was correctly invested, with Brother Bottomley diverting large sums into his own accounts.

In 1921, a pamphlet was printed, attacking Bottomley and accusing him of swindling the investors in his scheme. Now he became the architect of his own doom; having won several libel cases, he was, no doubt, confident of another victory, when he sued the author of the document for criminal libel. Unfortunately, like Brother Oscar Wilde, he lost the libel case, and the accuser became the accused. For the third time, Bottomley was on trial, charged with fraud—this time at the most famous of London courts, the Old Bailey. He denied the charge and used all his bluff and bluster to try to convince the jury of his innocence. Bizarrely, he convinced the court to allow an adjournment of fifteen minutes each day so that he could drink a pint of champagne (for medicinal purposes of course). This time, Bottomley's charm and oratory would fail him. The weight of the evidence was such that the jury took less than half an hour to convict him. The prosecuting barrister later noted that Bottomley was 'a drink-sodden creature whose brain would only be got to work by repeated doses of champagne'.

The Member of Parliament, media magnate, and champagne addict was sentenced to seven years' imprisonment—a spectacular crash. To add to his demise, as a bankrupt, he was expelled from Parliament. While in Wormwood Scrubs prison, he had to sew mailbags. When the prison chaplain saw him in the workshop, he remarked, 'Ah, Bottomley, sewing?' Bottomley replied 'No, *padre*, reaping.' At least, he could see dark humour in his downfall

Horatio Bottomley. The Mason and swindler can be seen wearing a top hat arriving at court.

Crime and the Craft

and he was not completely alone: Brother Hooley was also imprisoned in 'the Scrubs' at the same time; fraud had also brought him down.

On his release in 1927, Bottomley began to rebuild his fortune by going on stage as a one-man show, telling the story of his life and showing how he had committed his fraud, as a warning to the audience. Unfortunately, many provincial theatres refused to book him. Bottomley therefore took his show to the Windmill Theatre in London's Soho, where he gave his lecture in between the performances of naked girls. He continued to be a serial womaniser, so he would have enjoyed watching lots of pretty women who stood like statues (at the time the rule was 'move and it is rude').

In 1933, Bottomley collapsed on stage at the Windmill, having suffered a heart attack. He was taken to hospital and survived the operation, but died within days of a stroke. He was cremated in Golders Green, but he was so unloved that it took four years for a relative to collect Bottomley's ashes and scatter them at his former home in Sussex. He was a very talented man, but all his obituaries spoke of a wasted life. His love of money certainly was the root of evil, which ultimately destroyed him. In the Ancient Charge, a new Mason is told to use 'the talents wherewith God has blessed you, to His Glory and the welfare of your fellow creatures.' Brother Bottomley chose to use his talents—oratory, business skills, and legal knowledge—to line his own pockets. He ignored the teachings of Freemasonry and suffered the consequences.

45

Murder Most Foul … Murder Most Mason! With an Opera Connection

Masonic Connection
Poisoner and murderer
Chemist, who sold arsenic
Intended victim
Pathologist
Magistrate
Jury foreman
Crown Court architect
Composers: Gilbert and Sullivan

Date
1906: Murderer initiated into Freemasonry
1921: Wife died
1922: Found guilty of murder

Connection to London
Scotland Yard: Crime investigated by Metropolitan Police
Madame Tussauds: Killer appeared as waxwork model

Lodges
Lodge of Antiquity No. 2
Lodge of Harmony No. 255
United Studholme Alliance No. 1591
Bayard No. 1615
Loyal Hay No. 2382
Rahere No. 2546
Lodge St Machar No. 54 (Scotland)

Now we turn to the case of Major Herbert Armstrong, the only solicitor in Britain to be hanged for murder. The victim was his wife. Armstrong had been the Worshipful Master of his lodge in Hay-on-Wye, Wales, but despite his Third Degree obligation regarding his brother Masons—that he would 'not injure or cause or suffer it to be done by others' them—he also tried to poison a fellow lodge member. This later poisoning was to prove his downfall (literally). This is the case possibly involving, as we shall see, more Freemasons than any other. Armstrong was also a fan of two Masons who wrote operas; these will be considered at the end of this chapter.

Armstrong was born in Devon in 1870 and studied law at Cambridge University. He returned home to Newton Abbott to practice as a solicitor, but then transferred his work to Liverpool. In 1906, he joined a practice in Hay-on-Wye in the Welsh border country, but lived just on the English side in the village of Cusop Dingle in Herefordshire. By this time, he had married a family friend from Devon, Katherine Friend—known as 'Kitty' to her husband—by whom he was to have three children. The Armstrong family soon moved into a larger house in Cusop Dingle named 'Maysfield'.

His lodge, Loyal Hay No. 2382, met above a bank in the town and, to demonstrate the cross-border nature of the area, it changed from being part of the Masonic Province of South Wales to the Province of Herefordshire (without physically moving) at the time of Armstrong's nefarious deeds. Armstrong had joined the lodge in the same year as his arrival in the town.

Herbert Rowse Armstrong:
Mason, solicitor, and poisoner.

The newly arrived solicitor went on to become a well-respected member of the community; he was appointed Clerk to the Justices (the legal advisor to the local magistrates) and served as a captain in the Territorial Army, being promoted to the rank of major when he served in the First World War. He was also a church warden and progressed quickly in his Masonic career, being made Worshipful Master in just six years and later served as Chaplain of the lodge. In the year of his arrest, he had been appointed Provincial Senior Deacon.

Life at home, however, does not appear to have been as successful. Major Armstrong (as he was referred to by now) was a slight man with a wife who was very domineering. She set petty rules regarding when and where he could drink alcohol or smoke in the house. Mrs Armstrong was also known to embarrass her husband in public and in front of the servants.

Armstrong enjoyed gardening (perhaps to keep himself out of the house and out of the way of his wife). The First World War also proved to provide more opportunities for freedom and the major had several affairs while away from home. However, despite all the killing and death that he may have seen on the Western Front, it would seem to be his time in his perfectly kept garden that gave him the means to commit murder. His obsessive desire to get rid of dandelions ensured that he had a plentiful supply of arsenic-based weedkiller. The squirting device that he used to spray and eradicate the unwanted plants would later be used as evidence against him. To add to the Masonic links, the arsenic was purchased from the local chemist, Mr John Davies, a fellow member of the lodge (and the brother-in-law of Brother Oswald Martin, the man Armstrong later attempted to poison).

In mid-1919, not long after the end of the First World War, Mrs Armstrong began to suffer with a condition where the nerves in her upper body became inflamed. She was examined by the local general practitioner (and Freemason), Dr Thomas Hincks, and that seemed to be the end of the matter. Her health, however, both mentally and physically, took an unexpected turn for the worse in the autumn of the following year so much so that she was admitted to the Barnwood Asylum for the mentally ill, in nearby Gloucester. Physically, she was suffering from vomiting, heart problems, and fever, together with paralysis in her feet and hands. Mentally, she was suffering from delusions. Dr Hincks believed that her condition related to the illness she had suffered in 1919. Armstrong took advantage of this freedom. While on a trip to London, he had dinner with a lady-friend, whom he had first met while in the Army in 1915. Significantly, he amended his wife's will so that he became the sole beneficiary, with no provision for their children.

Away from home, Mrs Armstrong's health improved and she was able to return home to Herefordshire in January 1921. This return home proved fatal; she was dead on 22 February, exactly a month after her discharge from the asylum. Dr Hincks appears to have been mystified by her death, but he duly signed the death certificate, concluding that she had died from a combination of illnesses relating to the stomach lining, heart, and kidneys.

No one appears to have suspected Major Armstrong of any wrongdoing. He was seen as the perfect husband; he had spent much time caring for his wife, reading to her, and reducing the time he spent at work during the time of her illness. His true feelings towards his wife can perhaps be seen in his actions after the death; the servants had closed the curtains in the house (as was the tradition at that time) as a mark of respect. On Major

Armstrong's return home, the first thing which he did was to open them all. The funeral was held soon afterwards and the matter (and Mrs Armstrong) was laid to rest. If Worshipful Brother Armstrong had committed murder, he had got away with it this time.

On the business front, Armstrong had only one rival solicitor to compete with in Hay-on-Wye—Mr Oswald Martin, or in Masonic terms, Brother Martin, who was also a member of the Loyal Hay lodge. Armstrong had tried to persuade the rival company to become a joint practice, but this was not to be and having failed to neutralise the opposition by peaceful means, he appears to have decided on more radical tactics.

Some eight months after the death of Mrs Armstrong, the two solicitors were in dispute over a property sale; it appeared likely that Armstrong would lose the case and would cost him a large sum of money. A meeting was arranged on 26 October 1921 at the major's home and Martin attended. Armstrong, in a typically English well-mannered way, picked up a buttered scone and gave it to his Masonic brother, saying 'excuse fingers'. The scone, however, was not all it seemed as on arriving home, Brother Martin became violently ill. For an Englishman, Major Armstrong did not seem to be 'playing with a straight bat'; he was being very ungentlemanly.

This was not the first time that a member of the Martin family had become ill after eating something. A box of chocolates had arrived at their home a few weeks before—an anonymous gift, but a very unpleasant one. At least one member of the family had suffered vomiting after eating the sweets. Fortunately, the remaining chocolates were not thrown away and would later be used as evidence.

These occurrences were not lost on the local chemist, who had supplied arsenic to Major Armstrong. You will recall that this chemist (Davies) was Martin's brother-in-law and had been a member of the same lodge (he had resigned at the turn of the century). Dr Hincks also noted that Oswald Martin's illness was very similar to that suffered by Mrs Armstrong. The three Masonic brethren—Martin, Davies, and Hincks—agreed that the Martin family should be very wary of any gifts received from Major Armstrong. Dr Hincks sent a sample of urine to the Clinical Research Association and traces of arsenic were found. He decided to report the matter to the authorities.

Just one year before, another solicitor had been acquitted in a very similar case in North Wales. A major factor was information leaking out of the local police force prior to arrests being made. The Home Secretary was keen, therefore, not to see similar failings and by-passed the Herefordshire Constabulary, tasking Scotland Yard to take charge of the case.

Major Armstrong seems not to have suspected any police involvement, as during their investigation, he continued to invite Mr Martin for tea. His Masonic brother had to find more and more excuses to avoid these invitations (the plot begins to look like an Ealing Comedy at this point). Such was Armstrong's seeming naivety to the police activity that, when arrested on New Year's Eve 1921, he was found to have a packet of arsenic in his pocket. More of the drug was discovered at his home.

Armstrong appeared at the Bredwardine Magistrates' Court on 2 January 1922, the very court where he was the clerk (confusingly, three sets of magistrates sat in the Hay courtroom—two Welsh and this English one). The initial charge related to the attempted murder of his rival solicitor and lodge brother, Oswald Martin. The fact that the clerk was now in the dock resulted in a farce, as Armstrong had to give advice to his replacement, who was 'hard of the hearing and slow of the pen'. When remanded in custody for seven days, to appear at 10 a.m. the following week, Armstrong had to remind the bench that they had a licensing session at that time and 11 a.m. would be far more convenient. The bench agreed with the prisoner and changed the time of the hearing.

In the meantime, Mrs Armstrong's body was exhumed and a *post-mortem* was conducted by Bernard Spilsbury, who had been Raised to the Third Degree just several months before in Rahere Lodge No. 2546. His experience in the Crippen and Seddon cases would have proved invaluable. Spilsbury was to find damning evidence as the dead woman's body was riddled with arsenic. The Scotland Yard detectives also seized the chocolates sent to the Martin household. Traces of arsenic were found and a small hole was discovered in each of the sweets, which matched the tip of the nozzle of a weed eradicator owned by Armstrong. For all this evidence, the police focused on the death of Mrs Armstrong and the attempted murder charge was dropped.

Worshipful Brother Major Armstrong was now charged with murder on his return to the magistrates' court, where the chairmen of the three magistrates was Worshipful Brother C. E. Tunnard Moore, also a member of Loyal Hay lodge. Armstrong denied any responsibility for the death. His response to the accusation was unequivocal: 'I am absolutely innocent'. Armstrong was now remanded in custody to await trial at the local Assizes.

The trial took place in Hereford in April 1922 in the Shire Hall, an impressive building designed by Sir Robert Smirke (the architect of the British Museum in London and a member of Lodge of Antiquity No. 2 in 1808). The judge at the trial was Mr Justice Darling. Given all the Masonic connections, it is surprising to find that this judge was not a Mason. The defence attempted to argue that Mrs Armstrong had committed suicide, but this meant that in her weak condition, she would have had to walk downstairs and take ever increasing amounts of arsenic without anyone noticing. Brother Spilsbury's evidence was critical; he stated with certainty that the fatal dose was given within twenty-four hours of her death. Brother Hincks made it clear that it was 'absolutely impossible' for Mrs Armstrong to have taken the drug herself. Armstrong gave evidence in his own defence, but his inability to explain to the judge why he was in possession of a packet of arsenic at the time of the arrest further wounded his credibility. Critically, the judge allowed the details of Oswald Martin's poisoning to be included in the trial evidence; Armstrong had not been charged with this offence and his defence counsel attempted to stop this matter being put before the jury.

The jury found Armstrong guilty of murder and he was sentenced to death. Even the foreman of the 'twelve good men and true' was a member of the Loyal Hay Lodge—Brother William Rees. The sentenced was appealed, but to no avail and on 31 May 1922 in Gloucester Prison, Worshipful Brother Major Herbert Armstrong was hanged by the neck until he was dead. He continued to protest his innocence to the very end. The Armstrong children were taken into the care of an aunt, but they were not told the circumstances of their parent's deaths. Tragically, one his daughters found out the truth when she visited Madame Tussauds 'Chamber of Horrors' in London and saw a lifelike wax model of her father with details of his crimes.

There ends the tale of another Masonic poisoner, a case with possibly more connections to the Craft than any other: murder most foul, murder most Mason. Importantly, it should be noted that as with the Seddon case, no favouritism was shown to the poisoner. All members of the Craft involved did their duty. It may have been the professionalism displayed in this case that resulted in Spilsbury being knighted by the king. He became Sir Bernard in 1923.

As a postscript, it is worthy of note that Armstrong was a fan of fellow Masons Gilbert and Sullivan (the famous composers) and, rather aptly, his favourite opera was *Trial by Jury*. Arthur Sullivan was initiated in 1865 into the Lodge of Harmony No. 255 in Middlesex and joined the United Studholme Alliance Lodge No. 1591. William Gilbert began his Freemasonry in Scotland in 1871, when he was admitted to the Lodge St Machar No. 54. He then joined a London lodge, Bayard No. 1615. While Sullivan died in his bed, Gilbert died in a rather odd manner. He drowned while attempting to save a nineteen-year-old girl to whom he was giving swimming lessons to in his private lake.

46

Did an English Freemason Cause the Wall Street Crash?

Masonic Connection
Swindler
Solicitor
Judge

Date
1910: Swindler initiated into Freemasonry
1929: The Wall Street Crash

Connection to London
St Paul's, City of London: Attended school
Piccadilly: Location of two businesses
Upper Brook Street, Mayfair: Luxury home, with swimming pool
Charing Cross: During lunch at the station hotel, swindler confessed his crimes
Old Bailey: Court where tried and convicted
Horseferry Road: Died in Westminster Hospital

Lodges
St Peter and St Pauls' No. 1410
United Northern Counties No. 2128 (erased)

The Wall Street Crash of 1929 ruined many lives and businesses, resulted in the Great Depression and contributed to the rise of extreme governments in Europe, with the Second World War the inevitable consequence. There is some speculation that a crooked English Freemason contributed to the start of the worldwide crash in the financial markets. The Mason in question is Clarence Charles Hatry, who was born in Hampstead, north London in 1888 to wealthy parents, who were German immigrants. His father, Julius, established 'Hatry and Co', silk-merchants in the City of London and was wealthy enough to send his sons to the nearby fee paying school, St Paul's (adjacent to the cathedral). The Hatry family had five servants to run a large house in Belsize Park and a second home in France.

Clarence began his professional career as an electrical engineer in nearby Hendon and then took employment as an insurance clerk in central London. When his father died, his mother inherited the silk company and Clarence joined the firm as a director. This is the description of his employment on the records of United Northern Counties Lodge 2128, which he joined in 1910. The lodge then met in the Inns of Court hotel, which stood in High Holborn (the lodge was closed in 2007, due to lack of members). Hatry turned the silk merchants into a limited company in the same year as joining the lodge, but within months, the company had gone bankrupt.

The solicitor who represented him at the bankruptcy hearing, Harry Dade, was 'on the square'; he was a member of the Centurion Lodge No. 1718, which met in the Inns of Court, the heart of the legal profession in London. Hatry got away lightly as he was discharged from personal bankruptcy as early as 1911 without having to meet his debts.

Having seemingly wrecked the family silk company, Hatry returned to the insurance business, buying a company based at 180 Piccadilly. He acquired a small firm for £60,000 and, in less than six months, sold it for four times the value (today, this would be in region of £22 million). As with the other Masonic swindler, Horatio Bottomley, the First World War (1914–18) also presented a chance to make lots of money. During this period, Hatry became involved in several major businesses, becoming the Managing Director of the Commercial Bank of London, a director of Leyland Motors, Chairman of the British Glass Industries, and several other senior roles in the food producing and agricultural business.

Throughout the 'Roaring Twenties', Hatry diversified even more and was a 'wheeler dealer' making fortunes (and often losing them) in all manner of businesses—loan companies, transporting Eastern European immigrants to the USA, and investing in new technologies, such as vending machines and automated photographic machines in railway stations. Despite being declared bankrupt on several occasions, he managed to emerge richer each time, often claiming vast insurance payments for failed deals. At one point, he pawned his wife's considerable collection of jewels to pay off debts, but turned the affair in his favour, adopting the slogan 'The man who always pays.'

He made no secret of his wealth, owning his own yacht and living in a mansion in Mayfair, one of the first to have its own swimming pool. His desirable home at 56 Upper Brook Street was just a stone's throw to the former location of Mark Masons' Hall at number 40. Hatry also owned several racehorses, including one named 'Bobby Dazzler', to further show off his affluence.

Hatry was also politically active and was on the executive committee of the British Empire Union. This was anti-communist and, originally, during the First World War, vociferously anti-German. Given that he was the son of German parents, this does seem odd, but perhaps he was trying to prove his loyalty to Britain. The Earl of Harewood, who was later Grand Master of the United Grand Lodge of England (1942–47), was described as a 'prominent member' of the Union on its posters. Harrods is also shown as a business supporting the organisation (the chairman of this famous store was also a member of the Craft).

In 1929, Hatry's greed resulted in the gamble that would prove his nemesis—the creation of a vast British iron and steel corporation by merging several companies. The finance involved is no small amount now ($40 million), but at the time, it was an unimaginable amount of money. The Stock Exchange investigated and established that Brother Hatry was involved in fraud; he had printed forged and duplicated share certificates to the value of $1 million to hide the fact that his businesses were failing. In late September, the Stock Exchange suspended trading in Hatry's companies. These had once been valued at £24 million; now, they were massively in debt.

In rather gentlemanly fashion, the (non-Masonic) Director of Public Prosecutions had lunch with the failed businessman at the Charing Cross Hotel, during which Brother Hatry admitted fraud and forgery. He was then taken into custody awaiting trial. In the meantime, due to the shock created in the London Stock Exchange, the Bank of England introduced financial measures that resulted in British investors transferring assets from the United States back to England. The American *Time* Magazine (21 October 1929) pointed the finger of blame at Hatry, noting that he had committed 'gigantic frauds' that 'unsettled confidence in The City and hastened Depression'. It would seem, indeed, that a Freemason from England played a key role in causing the Wall Street Crash.

It was, however, another Freemason, who ensured that Hatry was punished for his crimes. In January 1930, Hatry appeared at the Old Bailey before the 'Hanging Judge', as Brother Mr Justice Avory was known. Avory had been initiated into the St Peter and St Pauls' Lodge No. 1410. The death penalty no longer being available for the crime of fraud, Hatry received a lengthy sentence—fourteen years' imprisonment with two of hard labour,

The Wall Street Crash, the source of misery across the world, but was it caused by Mason Clarence Hatry?

crushing rocks. He later had to sew mailbags like Brother Bottomley. A big fall for a man who used to swim each day in his private Mayfair pool. He would serve nine years before being released on parole.

Despite declaring 'My name has become a byword, and I am irretrievably ruined.' Hatry continued to make money once released and soon was living in a large house, this time in Dover. He managed to attract the ire of the local population in 1946, by employing thirty workmen to make alterations to his home; the number of men gives some idea of the size of his home. This was at a time when the town was still badly war-damaged and many residents needed rehousing. Such was the strength of feeling that a question was asked in the House of Commons. He appears to have made his new fortune in the publishing business, with a new business at 187 Piccadilly.

Hatry died in 1965, aged seventy-six in the Westminster Hospital, which then stood in Horseferry Road. At the time of his death, he was living in Onslow Square, a large house in a garden square in Kensington. Given the location of this home and his previous residence in Dover, it appears odd that his estate was worth less than £1,000. It is unclear if the Mason who brought about the biggest financial crash in history died with little money or had hidden it away. In any case, while a Mason may have caused financial chaos across the globe, it was another Mason, Mr Justice Avory, who put him in prison for doing so.

47

Hangmen, the Hanging Judges, and Hanged Masons

Masonic Connection
Ruthless judges
Unsuccessful applicant for hangman role
Hangman, who executed Masons
Murderers and traitors

Date
1850: William Hardman initiated into Freemasonry
1874: Horace Avory initiated
1916: Casement treason trial

Connection to London
Judge sat at the Old Bailey
Judge sat at Newington Sessions (now Inner London Crown Court)

Lodges
Robert Burns No. 25
Cadogan No. 162
Phoenix No. 257
Lodge of St John and St Paul No. 349
St Peter and St Pauls' No. 1410
United Northern Counties No. 2128 (erased)

The records of the United Grand Lodge of England show that none of the hangmen who were employed by the British government were members of the Craft. Samuel Dougal was a Mason who applied to be a hangman, but was turned down due to his rather dubious conduct. Some years after his attempt to take charge of the gallows, he suffered a rather ironic fate.

One hangman, John Ellis, was responsible for hanging two Masonic murderers—Frederick Seddon and Major Herbert Armstrong. Ellis also was in charge of the hanging of Crippen; Irish Nationalist Roger Casement, who may have been linked to the Craft; and George Smith, the Brides in the Bath killer. Ellis himself came to a tragic end after being deeply affected by the execution of a female prisoner. The condemned woman had to be tied to a chair with the noose placed around her neck. Ellis later committed suicide and in a report on his death, the *Nottingham Evening Post* (26 August 1924) noted that 'a lodge of Freemasons once declined to admit an executioner to its membership, even though he was otherwise well qualified.' The source of this information is not quoted in the article, but it does appear that hangmen were not welcome in the Craft.

While no hangmen were Masons, several judges who sent men to the gallows certainly were members of the Craft. Most famously, these included Right Worshipful Brother Sir Thomas Bucknill. It was Bucknill who sentenced Seddon to be hanged, despite the prisoner giving Masonic signs from the dock. Despite Seddon and Sir Thomas Bucknill passing into Masonic folklore, the Mason actually known to the criminal fraternity of the day as the 'Hanging Judge' was Brother Sir Horace Edmund Avory. Sir Horace was also nicknamed 'Acid Drop' due to the caustic comments included in his summing-up speeches to juries that were rarely in favour of the defendant. Avory was wont to give bizarre statements in court, once defining a lunatic as someone who 'sometimes thinks he is the Lord Chancellor; sometimes he thinks he is a fried egg and cannot sit down except on a piece of toast.'

The 'Hanging Judge' became a Mason in 1874, when he was initiated into St Peter and St Pauls' Lodge No. 1410, which stills meets in Newport Pagnall in Buckinghamshire. His Masonic career was quite short and he appears to have done little after being 'raised' to the Third Degree. At that time, he was a barrister and, as such, represented Harry Benson and subsequently, Worshipful Brother Edward Froggatt (a member of Robert Burns No. 25) during the corruption scandal that engulfed the Scotland Yard Detective Department in 1877. Unfortunately for Avory, both his clients were convicted. Avory was, however, part of the prosecution team that (eventually) successfully convicted Brother Oscar Wilde. Wilde's defence counsel, Worshipful Brother Edward Clarke, was another Masonic barrister who often appeared in court with Avory, albeit sometimes on opposing sides. During the Trial of the Detectives, the two both appeared for the defence. In the Wilde case, one appeared for the defence, the other for the prosecution.

Avory was subsequently appointed as a judge at the Old Bailey where he would preside over many criminal trials, involving murder, treason, and felony. During his time on the bench, he showed little mercy to convicted villains, sending a goodly number to the gallows. This famously included Sir Roger Casement, a supporter of Irish nationalism who was convicted of treason for attempting to obtain German support for the Easter Rising in Dublin in 1916. Hilaire Belloc (1870–1953), an Anglo-French writer and Member of Parliament, claimed that Casement was hanged to show that the British Government would show no favour to an Ulster Protestant and a Mason. There is, however, no record of Casement being a Mason in England or Ireland. A Roger Casement from Ulster was initiated into St John and St Paul No. 349 (a Malta lodge that still exists), but this was a relative of the man convicted for treason who shared the same name. That is not to say that he was not initiated elsewhere. There is, however, a more certain Masonic connection to Sir Roger. When he had been sentenced to death, Sir Arthur Conan Doyle, a member of Phoenix Lodge No. 257, attempted to save Casement from the hangman's noose. The creator of Sherlock Holmes argued that the Ulsterman was insane, but the campaign failed and Casement was executed.

Despite being a member of the Craft throughout his time as an Old Bailey judge, Avory showed no favour to Masons appearing before him. As described in the previous chapter, Brother Sir Charles Hatry, the Mason and swindler, received no special treatment and was given a substantial prison sentence. Hatry was a member of United Northern Counties Lodge No. 2128.

Brother Avory continued to hold sway over the fate of many a convicted murderer and felon throughout his long life. Such was his dedication to duty that he collapsed while at the bench during a trial. In 1935, at eighty-three years old, the Grim Reaper would finally catch up with Avory. The judge was found dead from a heart attack, entangled in his bed sheets; Brother Acid Drop had passed to the Grand Lodge Above. His death was mourned by the Lord Chief Justice, who observed, 'He will have no successor. To the English Bench it is a sad and irreparable loss, but to me it is a devastating shock! I am almost too overcome with tears to speak... No sweeter spirit ever adorned the earth.' Criminals of the age may have disagreed.

Sir Roger Casement:
hanged for treason, but
was he a Mason?

In a Masonic twist, long after his burial, Sir Roger Casement's remains were moved from London to Ireland. Just as Hiram Abif's dead body was removed from the original grave and re-interred in a more fitting burial place in Jerusalem, so Casement's remains were taken from an unmarked grave in Pentonville Prison to a tomb in Dublin. The mystery of whether a Mason was sentenced to be hanged by another Mason remains.

While he does not seem to have condemned anyone to death, it is worth noting the sentences handed out to criminals by Sir William Hardman QC, a member of the Cadogan Lodge No. 162 and judge at Newington in south London and Kingston, Surrey. They show a very different attitude to crime and punishment. This ruthless Lancastrian was known as the 'hard man' by criminals who appeared before him in the latter part of the nineteenth century. Hardman was criticised by at least one radical newspaper for his harsh sentences; a man who stole a pair of boots received five years' imprisonment, and a female thief received seven (with hard labour). When a child molester appeared before him, he stated in court that a 'sound flogging… was the only sensible punishment.' Hardman was a man of many parts; he was also involved in politics and journalism, as the chairman of the Conservative 'Primrose League' and editor of the *Morning Post* newspaper.

48

Bodies in Trunks:
More Cases for
the Masonic Forensic Scientist

Masonic Connection
Pathologist

Date
1927: Charing Cross trunk murder
1934: Brighton trunk murder
1976: Acquitted murderer admitted guilt

Connection to London
Pathologist based at London hospital
Charing Cross murder occurred in London
Murder victim's legs discovered at King's Cross

Lodges
Gihon Sancta Maria No. 49
St. Mary Magdalen No. 1523
Rahere No. 2546
Sancta Maria No. 2682 (erased)
Rahere Chapter No. 2546 (Holy Royal Arch)
Abernethy No. 569 (Mark)

Anyone standing in Charing Cross station in central London will see lots of men in black jackets and striped trousers carrying their briefcases; for here is the nearest mainline railway station to Great Queen St, with just a ten-minute-walk to Grand Lodge. However, not many of the brethren passing through this terminus realise that it was the site of a grisly find, which was to lead to another murder being solved by one of their number, Worshipful Brother Sir Bernard Spilsbury.

On Friday, 6 May 1927, a large trunk was placed in the station left luggage office. The man depositing made a simple request—it was to be handled carefully. He then left in a taxi. As the weekend passed, the staff in the left luggage department began to notice a dreadful small emanating from the trunk and the police were called on 10 May. The constable forced open the locks on the left luggage and a search revealed five packages, wrapped in brown paper and tied with string. No doubt with trepidation, the officer cut the string and there found (as the Masonic Third Degree ritual describes it) a body 'very indecently interred'; in each package was a body part wrapped in towels, clothing, and importantly, as we shall see, a duster. The trunk also contained clothing, which provided clues as to the identity of the victim. Underwear bore the named 'P. Holt'; there were also laundry marks.

The different body parts were removed to Westminster Mortuary, where they were examined by Brother Spilsbury. He was able to state that the victim was a large lady, in her mid-thirties, who had been dead in the region of seven days. The limbs had been cut off—legs at the hips and arms at shoulder level. She had bruising all over her body, but it could be demonstrated that the injuries had been sustained while she was unconscious. Importantly, the cause of death could be established; the victim had been asphyxiated.

The clothing in the trunk quickly led the Metropolitan Police to a Mrs Holt, a well-to-do lady, who lived in fashionable Chelsea, but she was (forgive the Third Degree pun) 'yet alive' and had not 'suffered death'. It established that the underwear had been stolen by one of her servants and when Mrs Holt attended the mortuary, she was able to identify the victim (from her facial features) as 'Mrs Rolls', who had been in her employ. However, 'Rolls' was a pseudonym; the dead woman's real name was Mrs Minnie Alice Bonati. She was English, but had married an Italian waiter. This marriage was not to last; she had left Bonati and entered into a 'common law' marriage with a Mr Rolls, hence her use of that surname.

Spilsbury's estimation of her age was very accurate; she was thirty-six years old at the time of the murder. He was also correct regarding the time of death; a witness had seen her

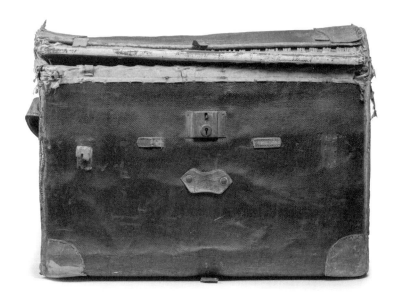

The trunk used by John Robinson to conceal the body of Minnie Bonati.

alive and well in Chelsea during the afternoon of Wednesday 4 May (two days before the trunk was deposited). She had been working as a prostitute.

The police investigation was proving very slick and made use of the media to find the origins of the trunk. Photographs were published of the piece of luggage in London newspapers and a shopkeeper was able to describe the man who had bought it—dark complexion, average height, and with a military bearing (it must be considered that this was not unusual as much of the male population had served in the First World War). Next, a cab driver came forward with further vital evidence; he had picked up a man with a large trunk in Rochester Row (a few minutes away from Charing Cross) and had dropped him at the station. The driver was able to point out the place he had collected his fare, 86 Rochester Row.

All the occupants were interviewed but one could not be found. The second-floor rooms were used as the office of Edwards and Co estate agents by a man named John Robinson (also aged thirty-six). Suspiciously, he had vacated the premises on or about 9 May, telling the landlord that he was bankrupt. Robinson was also a former Army sergeant fitting the description given by the cab driver. Hence, the estate agent became the prime suspect in the murder enquiry.

The police now endeavoured to trace Robinson who had links in several parts of London. He had lodgings south of the River Thames in Kennington, but these were empty. There was, however, a telegram addressed to 'Robinson, Greyhound Hotel, Hammersmith'. Police officers went to this west London public house and found Mrs Robinson, or rather a woman who thought she was Mrs Robinson. The suspect had married her bigamously without her knowledge. The police were to utilise her anger when she was informed of this fact. In the meantime, Robinson had contacted her, not knowing that she was now assisting the detectives. A meeting was arranged on 19 May at the Elephant and Castle (the district adjacent to Kennington). The police allowed the couple to meet, then pounced; Robinson was conveyed back to New Scotland Yard.

He was interviewed by a senior detective and denied any involvement in the murder or disposal of the body. He was then placed on an identification parade and shown to the shopkeeper (who sold the trunk), the taxi driver (who had collected the fare in Rochester Row), and a porter from Charing Cross; none could positively identify him as the man with the trunk. At this point, there was no other evidence against him so he was allowed to leave Scotland Yard.

The investigating officer was not satisfied; he believed that Robinson was the killer. He ordered that the duster in which a body part had been wrapped should be washed to reveal any identifying features. His diligence paid off; the clean duster now revealed the word 'Greyhound', the name of the pub where Robinson had lived with his 'wife'. A further search was then conducted at 86 Rochester Row and a tiny object proved to be the final piece in the jigsaw; a blood-stained match was recovered from a wastepaper bin. Robinson was re-arrested on 23 May and returned to Scotland Yard. There, he made a full confession, admitting that, 'I met her at Victoria and took her to my office… I done it and cut her up.'

In less than two months, Robinson appeared at the Old Bailey, charged with the murder of Mrs Bonati. He claimed that he had taken her back to his office, but she had demanded money and this led to an argument. She had become violent (her ex-husband appeared

Crime and the Craft

for the defence to state that this was likely). Robinson claimed that he defended himself, resulting in the woman falling over and hitting her head on the coal-scuttle, a small shovel kept by the fireplace. This 'accident' had knocked her unconscious. He left the office, hoping that on his return, she would have recovered and left; however, she was still there and dead. He claimed that he panicked; he then bought the trunk and a sharp knife to cut up the body.

Brother Spilsbury offered a different version of events to the court. He stated that his examination of the body suggested that the killing had been a deliberate act. It appeared from the bruising that Robinson had knelt on the victim to hold her down, while at the same time suffocating her. The jury believed the eminent pathologist and took only an hour to find Robinson guilty of murder. On 13 July, he was sentenced to death by hanging and he was executed within a month at Pentonville Prison.

Robinson's case was not the only trunk murder where Sir Bernard would act as an expert witness. In June 1934, at the railway station in Brighton, a seaside resort on the south coast of England, another foul-smelling trunk was opened to reveal the torso of a pregnant woman. The local Chief Constable called in Scotland Yard and the victim's legs were found in a suitcase in London at King's Cross station. The deceased was never identified. A month after this discovery, the police in Brighton conducted searches of the houses near the station, which resulted in another suspicious trunk being found in the bedroom of 52 Kemp Street (less than five minutes-walk from the Brighton terminus). Another decomposing female body had been discovered, but this time there was an identification. The victim was Violet Kaye (also called Saunders), a forty-two-year-old woman, who lived with a man named Tony Mancini. Mancini (who was known by several aliases, including 'John Notrye', the name used at his trial) was a convicted thief and local waiter. Like Minnie Bonati, Violet was a prostitute, but she was also a heavy drinker and user of illicit morphine. She had last been seen two months before her body was found and enquiries revealed that Mancini had told friends that, after an argument, Violet had gone to live in Paris.

The dead body had been examined by Brother Spilsbury and, in his opinion, death had been caused by a violent blow to the head. As a result, an arrest warrant was issued for Mancini, who by this time, had fled Brighton. On 17 July 1934, the suspected murderer was spotted by two constables in Eltham, South East London. He was arrested and taken to Lee Road Police Station. Despite the bizarre coincidence of one body in a trunk leading to the discovery of another, he was only charged with the murder of Violet.

At his trial at Lewes Assizes in Sussex, Mancini claimed that he had returned home and found his lover dead, but had hidden the body out of panic (an all too familiar defence, as we have seen). Perhaps influenced by the defence focusing on the victim's lifestyle, the jury found Mancini not guilty. Sir Bernard's view that the defendant was responsible for fatally wounding Violet was vindicated many years later; in 1976, Mancini confessed to the killing to a *News of the World* journalist prior to his death. Mancini said that Violet had drunkenly attacked him with a hammer, but he had wrestled from her grasp and struck her on the left temple. At the time, English law did not allow a murderer to be retried if he had already been found not guilty. War was now approaching and Spilsbury's skills would also prove vital to the war effort.

49

Crimes against Humanity, Crimes against Masonry: The Impact of the Second World War on Freemasonry

Masonic Connection

Fascist persecution
Death of Dutch Grand Master
Possible origin of Forget-Me-Not flower emblem
Destruction of Temples
Prisoner of War camps
Pathologist, who aided war effort

Date

1930s to 1945: Period of Nazi control of Germany

Connection to London

Carlton House Terrace: Location of embassy of Nazi Germany in London
De Hems Public House, Macclesfield Street: Unofficial headquarters of the Dutch
    Resistance
Retired Metropolitan Police officer sent to Nazi concentration camp
London-based Masonic pathologist aided the war effort

Lodges

Gihon Sancta Maria No. 49
Frederick Lodge of Unity No. 452
Lodge La Cesaree No. 590
Royal Alfred No. 877
St. Mary Magdalen No. 1523
Rahere No. 2546
Sancta Maria No. 2682 (erased)
Loge Liberté chérie (Belgium)
Rahere Chapter No. 2546 (Holy Royal Arch)
Abernethy No. 569 (Mark)

The Nazi war machine was to be responsible for millions of deaths as it swept through Europe; many groups of people were to suffer from this wicked regime—Jews, gypsies, and, most relevant to this book, Freemasons. Hatred of Freemasonry extended to other Fascist rulers who brought much misery to mankind. This policy was to have a terrible impact on Masons high and low throughout Europe and across the world. The reaction to it, especially in England, was sensible at the time, but was to later result in a poor public image of the Craft that continues to this very day.

The warnings were there for all to see. In the mid-1920s, Hitler had written in his book *Mein Kampf* that Freemasonry had 'succumbed' to the Jews and Hermann Goering, the President of the *Reichstag* (German Parliament) and later head of the Luftwaffe, also observed that 'in National Socialist Germany, there is no place for Freemasonry.' The Italian Fascist dictator, Benito Mussolini, dissolved Masonry in his country aided by his 'Blackshirts'. When one brave brother, General Luigi Cappello, chose the Craft over the Fascist Party, he found himself under arrest on trumped-up charges. He was later sentenced to thirty years' imprisonment for trying to assassinate Mussolini or as he preferred to be called, '*El Duce*'. In Spain, General Franco made membership of a lodge a specific crime with an automatic sentence of twelve years in jail. For Spanish Rose Croix Masons of the 18th degree, the punishment was much worse—death. Franco's views were quite clear: 'The whole secret of the campaigns unleashed against Spain can be explained in two words: Masonry and communism ... we have to extirpate these two evils from our land.'

In 1934, the Nazi Ministry of the Interior ordered the abolishment of the Craft in Germany, with all lodge property passing into state ownership. The Nazi secret police, the Gestapo, were present at the final meetings to ensure that the three Grand Lodges that existed at that time were permanently closed. At least one Freemason, a young lawyer named Walter Plessing, committed suicide.

Freemasons were also banned from holding positions in the government. The hatred of Masonry was so great that 'B3', a special section of the Gestapo, was tasked to deal with the issue. Any German detained for Masonic activity could be sent to a concentration camp, where they were treated as political prisoners. These unfortunate brethren were forced to wear an inverted red triangle on their prison uniform to designate their status. Heinrich Himmler, leader of the dreaded SS, who provided the guards at the camps, listed the Craft as one of the key enemies of the Nazi state; SS personnel were taught that 'Jewry, Freemasonry and Bolshevism' were the equivalent of a poisonous snake ready to destroy the German race.

The strict and swift enforcement of these measures was so great that in August 1935, Hitler felt able to announce in the Nazi Party newspaper that Masonry had been eradicated in Germany. Much of the lodge property, which had been seized as part of these measures, was to find itself part of the 1937 'Anti-Masonic Exposition'. These exhibitions, which took place all over Nazi controlled Europe, included entire lodge rooms and were the brain-child of Josef Goebbels, the propaganda minister.

Masonic legend has it (because there is no direct proof) that it is in this period that German Freemasons began to use the Forget-Me-Not flower as a secret means of recognition, instead of the square and compasses. Rather fortunately, another German organisation, the *Winterhilfswerk* (in English, 'Winter help volunteer scheme') also used the same emblem.

The German Embassy in England prior to the outbreak of war was in Carlton House Terrace; this is the only place in London where the swastika flag flew. In the present day, the building houses the Royal Society—how odd that the same premises should at one-time house those who attempted to destroy Freemasonry (the Nazis) and also an organisation, which many Masonic historians believe was extremely influential in the formation of the Craft as we know it today; the first known speculative Masons in England (Sir Robert Moray in 1641 and Elias Ashmole in 1646) were founder members of the Royal Society. At least five of the first ten Grand Masters were fellows and several Masons have been presidents of the Royal Society, including Sir Christopher Wren, the Duke of Sussex, and Sir Joseph Banks.

Returning to the Second World War, despite war being declared on Germany by Britain and France on 3 September 1939, in the rest of Europe, all seemed calm. This was the 'Phoney War'; however, lodges in 'vulnerable areas' such as London, which may have been subjected to air raids, were cancelled until early 1940. The fear at that time was not a German invasion, but air raids and the dropping of poison gas on urban areas.

Freemasons in Belgium and the Netherlands must have felt especially secure; the war was none of their business as the governments of these nations had declared themselves neutral. Holland had not been involved in war since the time of Napoleon and maintained just a small army; indeed the Grand Master of the Dutch Freemasons was Hermanus van Tongeren, an elderly retired major-general. On the Channel Islands, the British Crown Dependencies just off the northern French coast, life (and Freemasonry) rumbled on. One Mason there was retired Metropolitan Police Station Sergeant Herbert Groome. A member of the Frederick Lodge of Unity No. 452 who had worked at Bromley Police Station in south London, he must have thought that he had made a sound decision to move to such a beautiful place. The Provincial Grand Master of the Channel Islands was Right Worshipful Brother Charles Edward Malet de Carteret, a retired British Army officer who presided over the Masonic Temple on Jersey. This impressive building was full of Masonic furniture and artefacts and, most importantly, Grand Lodge yearbooks containing the names and details of all senior English Freemasons. De Carteret was from a distinguished Channel Islands family and was a member of at least two lodges on Jersey; he had been initiated in Royal Alfred No. 877 in 1891 and later joined Lodge La Cesaree No. 590.

The persecutions in Germany had caused the Grand Master of the United Grand Lodge of England to advise Masons not to discuss the Craft with 'outsiders'. This was sound advice in the circumstances, but was to impact greatly on the public perception of Masons in the years after the war. As a precaution, valuable documents from Grand Lodge were sent to Canada, South Africa and the United States, in case of a German invasion.

The calm ended suddenly on 10 May 1940, when German forces swept into Holland and Belgium, ignoring their neutrality, to out flank the British and French armies. The ruthless bombing of the city of Rotterdam four days later was conducted by the Luftwaffe to show the consequences of resistance. Almost all the city centre was destroyed, and thousands of civilians were made homeless. The ornate Masonic hall, built in 1882 for the Lodge of Three Columns, was reduced to rubble. Only pieces of a marble plaque and some keys could be found. Their queen having fled to Britain, the stunned and leaderless Dutch surrendered in less than one week.

Worse was to come. The British and French forces stationed in France and Belgium were overwhelmed in just over two weeks. The Germans quickly reached the Channel coast and the remnants of the Allied army was evacuated at Dunkirk. France surrendered on 22 June. The British Government, well knowing the vulnerability of the Channel Islands to bombing given their proximity to the French coast, demilitarised them. German troops began to land on Jersey and Guernsey at the end of June and beginning of July 1940. The occupying forces decreed that no Masonic activity must take place, but gave an assurance that no property would be interfered with. Perhaps unwisely, the Provincial Grand Master ordered that the Temple in Jersey should simply be locked and all items left in situ. This would be a decision he would regret.

In the Netherlands, there was no such initial restraint on the part of the Germans. Masonic temples were wrecked, and property and funds were seized; this even included a solid gold gavel used by the Grand Master. Prior to the surrender, the Dutch brethren well knew that Major-General van Tongeren was in grave danger as the Grand Master and offered him safe passage to England. His reply to this offer was unequivocal: 'I have enjoyed the pleasures of being Grand Master, now I must also carry the burden.' This bravery and sense of duty was to prove fatal. He was arrested in October 1940 and placed in Sachsenhausen concentration camp in Germany. He died in March 1941. He was a man of honour who was murdered for being a Freemason.

The death of the Dutch Grand Master who was steadfast in the face of wickedness will resonate with many Freemasons; it is not unlike the death of Hiram Abif, the builder of King Solomon's Temple, who is beaten to death, but maintains his honour until the end. The next part of the story has similarities to the account related in the Holy Royal Arch chapter, where an invading army (the Babylonians) loot and destroy the temple.

The Nazi promises in Jersey did not last long. On 27 January 1941, members of the German Secret Field Police sent from Berlin entered the Masonic Temple and committed acts of looting and wanton vandalism over a period of two days. Nearly all furniture, regalia, books and lodge warrants were stolen. A *Wehrmacht Oberst* (colonel) seized the 'squared pavement' (the black and white chequered carpet) for use in his office and eventually took it back to his homeland. All funds and property were then transferred out of the hands of the Masonic authorities. If nothing else, the Nazis proved to be slightly better than the soldiers of Babylon; at least the Germans did not burn the temple down after looting it.

Nor was it just Masonic property that was to suffer. Retired police officer, Brother Groome, found himself in a dire situation. He was not Channel Islands born, and the Germans decreed that all such men would be deported. He was to spend the rest of the war in a camp in Nazi Germany. He was fortunate to return to England, alive and well after the war.

Many of the items seized from lodges in the Channel Islands, the Netherlands and across the rest of Europe ended up in as additional exhibits in Goebbels Nazi Anti-Masonic displays in Munich and later in Berlin. In 1942, Alfred Rosenberg, an influential Nazi, was commissioned by Hitler to wage an 'intellectual war' against the Jews and Freemasons. Building on Goebbels' work, Rosenberg's special unit was tasked to seize and research Masonic books and documents. German troops were required to assist in this work, no doubt diverting them from fighting the ever-stronger Allied forces, especially the Red Army in Russia.

German tactics at sea could also be against the accepted laws of combat. During the Battle of the Atlantic, Freemason George Smith of Frederick Lodge of Unity No. 452 was the captain of a merchant vessel, the *King John* sailing from Vancouver to England. During this voyage, he was attacked by a German raider, the *Widder*, and sunk. He was eventually hauled off the ship by the German captain, who then refused to take on board the British seamen, leaving them to their fate. Captain Smith spent the rest of the war in a Prisoner of War camp—Marine POW Camp X13.

He returned to the lodge in 1945 and the following year, King George VI awarded him the OBE for his bravery. *The London Gazette* records that, 'Capt. Smith displayed coolness and courage and he did not leave his ship until she was a mass of wreckage and on fire.' The German captain suffered a very different fate. He was tried after the war for failing to obey the laws of the sea, and sent to prison for failing to pick up survivors.

The tide of war eventually turned against the Germans. It should be noted that the leaders of the Western allies were Masons—King George VI, Winston Churchill, the British Prime Minister, and the two American wartime presidents, Roosevelt and Truman. Perhaps one of the major turning points of the war was the Soviet victory at Stalingrad, which destroyed two German armies. The commander of the German forces in the Russian city, Field Marshal Friedrich von Paulus, surrendered on 31 January 1943, enraging Hitler, who thought that such a high-ranking officer would commit suicide rather than hand himself over to the Soviet army. The Nazi regime denounced Von Paulus as a 'high grade Freemason'.

In the same year as the defeat on the Eastern Front, the Axis armies would face a British and American thrust into Europe, starting with an invasion of Sicily. To convince the Germans that the intended targets were, in fact, Greece or southern France, British intelligence agents hatched a strange scheme named 'Operation Mincemeat'. This involved placing a dead body, dressed as the fictitious 'Major William Martin, Royal Marines' in the Mediterranean Sea, with plans showing the false invasion sites. A body had to be found that would be believed to have died from drowning. The authorities turned to Sir Bernard Spilsbury, the eminent pathologist and Mason.

Sir Bernard found a body of a man who had died from eating rat poison. He noted that this would be very difficult to detect at a subsequent *post-mortem* examination. He was correct and the plan worked. The Spanish authorities were convinced that 'Major Martin' had drowned in the sea and handed over the fabricated plans to Nazi agents. As a result, German troops were moved from Sicily to cover Allied landings elsewhere. Brother Spilsbury's knowledge of dead bodies—gleaned from many murder investigations—had helped to save the lives of many British and American soldiers during the invasion of Sicily. The Mark Degree warns its members to 'avoid the danger of indulging in deception or attempting fraud'. Given the circumstances, Brother Spilsbury can be forgiven for engaging in this wartime deceit.

Victory, of course, came in May 1945, when Hitler, Goebbels, Mussolini, and many other Fascist Anti-Masons were dead. Goering and Himmler would soon take their own lives. Tragically, much of the Masonic furniture, regalia and books looted from temples across Europe were lost forever; they were either destroyed by the devastating Allied bombing campaign, which grew in strength throughout the war, or seized and taken back to the Soviet Union by Red Army units to be hidden away in Soviet archives.

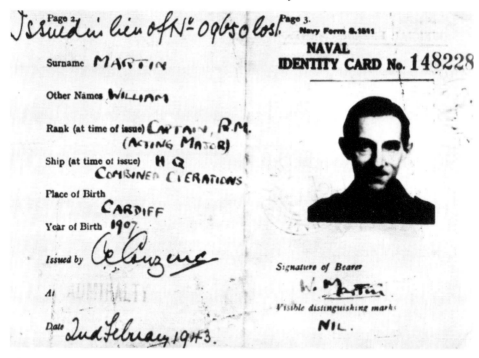

The fictitious identification card of Major William Martin. The body used for Operation Mincemeat was selected by Mason, Sir Bernard Spilsbury.

During the war, Allied prisoners of war had organised lodges of instruction; British and Australian PoWs did not hold full lodge meetings as they had no 'warrant' from a Grand Lodge. In German camps run by the *Wehrmacht* and Luftwaffe, the main enemy for PoWs was often boredom and learning ritual offered an escape. For those captured in the Far East, the Craft offered the opportunity to practice one of the Grand Principles of the Order— 'relief' or charity for their fellow man. In Japanese camps, where the guards systematically starved the inmates and committed all manner of war crimes, the British and Australian Freemasons donated cigarettes to the patients in the camp 'hospital' (a euphemistic name for a building from which medical supplies were deliberately withheld by the Japanese). Not constrained by the same rigid following of rules by Anglo-Saxon Masons, at least one lodge was formed by European members of the Craft. In 1943, seven Belgian Masons, who had been imprisoned in Esterwegen concentration camp as 'terrorists' (resistance fighters) formed the *Loge Liberté chérie* (Lodge of Beloved Liberty). The lodge conducted all three degrees in the camp, out of sight of the Nazi guards. Tragically, several of the founders died in this or other camps before the Allied armies liberated the inmates. Only one founder and the candidate who had joined in the camp survived. A memorial stands to record their efforts to keep the light of Masonry shining in that dreadful place.

The consequences of the Second World War on Freemasonry were far reaching. Many Masons died on active service, including the Grand Master of the United Grand Lodge of England, the Duke of Kent. The crash of his flying boat in the mountains of Scotland has generated all manner of conspiracy theories. Thousands of Masons died in concentration camps, including the Grand Master of Holland; we will never know the exact number as many members of the Craft may have been classified by the Nazis and their collaborators as 'political prisoners' or 'Jews'.

In Britain, lodge membership increased and many new lodges were opened. The men leaving the Armed Forces were looking for the comradeship they had enjoyed during the war and Masonic lodges offered such. However, as these men died, Freemasonry is left with as many Masons as there were in Edwardian times, but five times more lodges, leaving many unsustainable. Perhaps the most damaging effect of the Second World War was the continuance of the policy of secrecy after the conflict had ended. This resulted in criticism going unanswered and all manner of accusations being thrown at the Craft. While this policy has been rescinded and Masons encouraged to be open about their membership, it will take many years to recover the reputation enjoyed by Freemasonry prior to 1939.

50

Grand Master Murdered!
The Case of the Evil Dr Adams

Masonic Connection
Death of Grand Master
Witness at murder trial

Date
1919: Duke of Devonshire initiated into Freemasonry
1947: Duke installed as Grand Master
1950: Death of the Duke
1956: Suspect tried for murder

Connection to London
House of Lords: The Duke sat on Churchill's cabinet
Old Bailey: Court, where trial took place

Lodges
Royal Alpha No. 16
Tyrian No. 253
Hartington No. 916
United No. 1629 (erased)
Dorothy Vernon No. 2129
Royal London Hospital No. 2845
Royal Colonial Institute No. 3556
Westminster and Keystone Chapter No. 10 (Holy Royal Arch)
Phoenix Chapter of St Ann No. 1235 (Holy Royal Arch)

Of all the Grand Masters since 1717, only one has died under suspicious circumstances—Most Worshipful Brother Edward William Spencer Cavendish, 10th Duke of Devonshire and Grand Master of the United Grand Lodge of England from 1947 to 1950. This case is also an establishment cover-up even worse than those involving Jimmy Savile and Cyril Smith; in this case, a mass murderer was seemingly allowed to escape justice.

The Duke was born in London, but his family's seat was at the magnificent Chatsworth House set in the beautiful Derbyshire Dales. The family had long been connected to Freemasonry in the county with the sixth, eighth, and ninth Dukes being Provincial Grand Masters of Derbyshire. The family were also major land owners on the Sussex coast and played a major part in the establishment of the town of Eastbourne. The Victorian belief in the medicinal benefits of sea air and the arrival of the railway in 1849 made this a very valuable asset. The seventh Duke engaged a renowned architect to design a fashionable town built 'for gentlemen by gentlemen'. Unfortunately, the connection to this town was to feature significantly in the demise of the tenth Duke and Grand Master.

The Duke, known as the Marquess of Hartington before his father (the ninth Duke) died, joined the local Territorial Army regiment, the Derbyshire Yeomanry in 1913. He then served throughout the First World War in France and the Middle East, being twice mentioned in dispatches. He continued to serve in the regiment and eventually became the commanding officer, as Lieutenant Colonel in 1935. He also served his county as a magistrate (Justice of the Peace) and later as the Lord Lieutenant, an office where the holder represents the monarch in the county.

He was also active in local politics, winning the West Derbyshire seat in 1923; he remained as the Member of Parliament for the area until his father's death in 1938. At that point, he inherited the title Duke of Devonshire and moved to the House of Lords. The Second World War then broke out and the Duke held two ministerial positions in (fellow Mason) Churchill's government. In a political twist that may have influenced later events, his sister, Lady Dorothy Cavendish, married Harold McMillan, a Conservative MP who went on to be the Prime Minister from 1957 to 1963.

The Duke's Masonic career began in 1919, when he was initiated in Hartington Lodge No. 916 in Eastbourne. The following year he joined the Dorothy Vernon Lodge No. 2129 in Bakewell, Derbyshire and was installed as Worshipful Master in 1927. He went on to join several other Craft lodges—Royal Alpha No. 16, Royal Colonial Institute No. 3556, United No. 1629 (all in London), and Tyrian No. 253 (Derbyshire). He followed in his forefathers' footsteps in 1938 by becoming Provincial Grand Master of Derbyshire. Further Masonic advancement was to follow. In 1947, the Earl of Harewood, the Grand Master, died and the Duke of Devonshire was selected to replace him. The Duke was installed as Grand Master by Most Worshipful Brother, His Majesty King George VI, who held the rank of Past Grand Master. The Duke's Royal Arch career is equally impressive. He was exalted into Phoenix Chapter of St Ann No. 1235 in Buxton, Derbyshire in 1922 and joined Westminster and Keystone Chapter No. 10 in 1944, serving as First Principal in the same year. He was to be promoted to the highest rank possible, First Grand Principal of the Supreme Grand Chapter, in the same year as he became Grand Master.

We now turn to the man suspected of murdering the Duke—Doctor Bodkin Adams, a man who was not a Freemason, but is possibly one of the worst serial killers in history. He is an early version of Dr Harold Shipman, the murdering Manchester General Practitioner. Adams was born in Antrim, Northern Ireland in 1899 into a deeply religious family; his father was a 'fire and brimstone' lay preacher in the austere and evangelical Plymouth Brethren, who would think nothing of beating his son as punishment for 'sin'. Adams studied medicine in Belfast before training in a Bristol hospital. He arrived in Eastbourne in 1922, having successfully applied for a position as a General Practitioner in a Christian medical practice. The town was still a seaside home for the Duke of Devonshire. It was also a retreat for the rich and powerful of the day. To this day, Eastbourne is seen as a retirement town with many a rich widow; it was even more so in the middle of the twentieth century.

Dr Adams then set about obtaining a great deal of money, taking a substantial loan from one patient to buy an eighteen-bedroom house. More suspiciously, he began to be left money in the wills of his elderly (usually female) patients. One lady, Matilda Whitton, left him nearly £8,000—equivalent to nearly £500,000 today. This was contested by the relatives, but the court upheld Adams's rights to the money. His austere Christian upbringing appears to have failed to teach him that 'the love of money is the root of all evil.' Adams also appears to have been very careful to cover his tracks. He was often the sole executor of the will and many of his patients expressed a wish to be cremated rather than buried. Hence, any evidence of large quantities of drugs being pumped into their bodies would (literally) go up in smoke.

Dr Bodkin Adams, a serial killer who escaped justice.

Rumours circulated about Adams and his dubious methods from the 1930s; he even received anonymous postcards alleging that he was 'bumping off' those in his care. It appears that rather than administering drugs to ease the pain of his elderly patients, he was, in fact 'putting them to sleep'. It would seem, however, that the polite and respectful manner of Britain at that time, with its 'keep calm and carry on' attitude—especially the genteel nature of Eastbourne—protected him from open enquiry.

Adams took full advantage of the situation and became a very rich man, perhaps the wealthiest doctor in the country. There can have been few medical practitioners at that time, who owned two Roll Royce luxury cars. By some means, he was able to attract the great and the good to his practice. This included an admiral, the Chief Constable of the local police, a member of parliament, many Sussex businessmen and, sadly for Freemasonry, the Duke of Devonshire.

On 26 November 1950, the Duke suffered a heart attack while resting in Eastbourne; he was only fifty-five years old. Suspiciously, he died in the presence of Dr Adams, who signed a death certificate stating that the Grand Master had died of natural causes. Even more suspiciously, Adams failed to notify the local coroner in breach of regulations as the Grand Master had not seen a doctor in the fortnight prior to his death. The motive is not clear. His property would pass automatically to his son. In the Harold Shipman case, the prosecution suggested that one of his motivating factors to commit murder was the enjoyment of having power over life and death; this could have been Adams's motive.

While the Duke was an establishment figure and the most senior Freemason in the land, Adams, the lowly doctor had the power now. There may be another explanation. It has been suggested by Cullen (2004) that the murderous medic may have had an even more sinister reason to kill the Duke. As a member of the deeply religious Plymouth Brethren, he would have hated Freemasons and the Grand Master would have been viewed as the 'devil incarnate'. A search of the Plymouth Brethren website as recently as 2013 showed that it contained a reference to the 'evil nature of Freemasonry' with much mention of 'Lucifer'. However, the death seemingly aroused no suspicion and there was no police investigation. It was another death that resulted in Dr Adams facing a charge of murder.

Whatever his motivation to kill the Duke, religious zeal was certainly not the motive for the death of another patient of Adams—octogenarian widow Edith Morrell, who had suffered a stroke while staying with her son in the north of England. Such was Adams's caring nature (or greed, depending on your viewpoint) that he travelled all the way to the hospital in Cheshire to bring her back to Eastbourne. To reduce her pain, Adams administered an ever-increasing dosage of morphine. At the same time as being given this powerful drug, Mrs Morrell made several wills. In these, Adams was due to receive a variety of valuable assets—large sums of cash, antique furniture, and possibly most attractive to the greedy doctor, a Rolls Royce motor car.

It took fifteen months of this treatment before Mrs Morrell died. Adams issued a death certificate stating that the widow had died of a stroke. To make sure, he slit her wrist. Her body was cremated with Adams declaring that he had no reason to believe that he would benefit from her death. This was, no doubt, a lie; he later received the Rolls Royce and some valuable furniture by the terms of her will. By making such a statement, he ensured that a *post-mortem* examination would be deemed unnecessary. He also billed the family for over one thousand visits to the old lady, charging in modern day terms the best part of £100,000 for his services.

Adams continued in his nefarious manner for six years. The fact that he received property and valuables from the wills of over one hundred and thirty more patients added to the gossip in the quiet seaside town. Action was finally taken in July 1953. An actor, Leslie Hanson, was very suspicious that his elderly friends, Mr and Mrs Hullett, had been patients of Adams and both had died within four months of each other. Hanson contacted Eastbourne Police anonymously and made a complaint. Possibly to cover his tracks, Adams was to claim that the widow, Gertrude Hullett, had told him that she wished to commit suicide as she was so depressed after the death of her husband. When a *post-mortem* examination was conducted, Mrs Hullett was found to have twice the fatal dose of sodium barbitone in her body, prompting questions of whether it was suicide or murder. In any event, Adams was to benefit from the death of the couple—another large quantity of cash and another Rolls Royce luxury car (worth over £60,000 today).

At that time, the many small police forces did not have the resources to deal with murder investigations, hence Scotland Yard was called in. The enquiry into Dr Adams fell to Detective Superintendent Herbert Hannam, a successful detective of his day; the Teddington Towpath Murders were possibly his most celebrated case. Hannam found evidence to prosecute on four counts of murder; the death of the Grand Master was not one of these cases. The law, however, suited Adams; he could only be tried for one murder at a time (the law would change the following year), so the jury was unlikely to hear of the numerous other deaths.

The police faced unprecedented interference and hindrance by the medical and legal establishment. Detective Superintendent Hannam expressed his concern about this at the time. Brother 'Nipper' Read, then a junior detective, recalled that many officers were aware that the investigation was doomed to failure. Several parties conspired to achieve this aim. Firstly, the British Medical Association (the BMA is a form of trade union for doctors) sent a letter to all doctors in the area advising them that they would breach patient confidentiality if they discussed matters with the police (despite the patients being dead). Official reports on the case were then leaked by the Attorney-General—Sir Reginald Bullingham-Manner, a government official—to the BMA and General Medical Council (GMC), when there was no lawful reason to do so. In addition to doctors 'closing ranks', another possible motive for a cover up was protection of the new National Health Service (only nine years old at this time). The last thing it needed was an NHS doctor swinging from the end of a rope. The service was in a financial mess, and a general practitioner being sentenced to death could have led to many doctors leaving the NHS.

The Attorney-General, responsible for prosecuting the case at court, was a member of the Cabinet, and therefore responsible to the new Prime Minister, Harold Macmillan. It will be recalled that Macmillan was married to the Duke of Devonshire's sister. She had been in a long-term affair with another politician, Lord Boothby, and if Adams was tried several times for different murders, this unfortunate matter may have become public information. Bullingham-Manner was a distant relative of the deceased Grand Master. Perhaps he had a personal reason for stopping the whiff of scandal reaching Chatsworth House.

Sir Reginald Manningham-Buller, the Attorney-General who was responsible for the failed prosecution of Dr Adams.

Bullingham-Manner decided that the first trial would relate to the death of Edith Morrell, which appeared to the police to be an odd choice. Mrs Morrell had been cremated, so there was no forensic evidence to present to the court. Hence, Superintendent Hannam's suspicion of underhand behaviour seems entirely justified. In March 1957, Adams appeared at the Old Bailey before Lord Justice Patrick Devlin. The defence already had the upper hand, as the police report leaked by Manningham-Buller to the BMA and GMC had found its way to them. Further, the Attorney-General had failed to pursue a serious loss of evidence; a number of nurses' notebooks had 'gone missing' from a file. The case was further weakened by expert medical evidence provided (ironically) by a Freemason, Worshipful Brother Michael Ashby, a consultant neurologist (who later worked at the Royal Masonic Hospital). Unlike other medical professionals, Ashby was not convinced of his fellow doctor's culpability and the judge noted that his 'borderline evidence' could make it unsafe to convict Adams. Ashby was a member of Royal London Hospital Lodge No. 2845. Tragically, the expertise of pathologist and Mason, Sir Bernard Spilsbury, was not available. He had committed suicide in 1947, distraught at the death of his sons (one of them, a doctor, was killed in the Blitz).

All these factors contributed to the inevitable; Adams was found not guilty of murder. However, the Establishment cover-up did not end there. The Attorney-General then entered a plea of *nolle prosequi*—relating to the murder of Mrs Hullet, meaning that the prosecution were unwilling to proceed with further charges. Lord Justice Devlin described this as 'an abuse of power', but once the plea had been made, it was too late. Adams, however, was to be found guilty of something. He had failed to keep records of the dangerous drugs in his possession and he was 'struck off' as a doctor, but only for four years

There are other possible factors in the cover-up these evil crimes, including the death of the Grand Master. There were rumours of a homosexual affair between a doctor, a magistrate, and the Deputy Chief Constable of Eastbourne. There was a clear implication that Adams was the doctor in this *ménage à trois* at a time when homosexual acts were a criminal offence.

It is a great injustice that Adams went on to live until 1983; he died when eighty-four years old, having enjoyed the many luxuries that his ill-gotten gains had brought him. The Home Office pathologist, Francis Camps, believed that he was responsible for at least 163 suspicious deaths. The Grand Master, the tenth Duke of Devonshire, is buried in the churchyard of St Peter's Church in Edensor, Derbyshire, not far from Chatsworth House. He is the only Grand Master to have died at the hands of a killer. His successor as Grand Master was the Earl of Scarborough.

51

The Great Train Robbery:
How a Mason found Ronnie Biggs

Masonic Connection
Police officers
Source of information used to locate wanted man

Date
1963: Robbery committed
1973: Biggs located in Brazil

Connection to London
Robbery gang composed of London villains
Scotland Yard detectives investigated the crime

Lodges
Temple No. 101
St Mary's No. 1763
Paddington No. 3267
Glevum No. 7385
Alexander Woods No. 8661
Manor of St James's No. 9179

Fortunately for the Craft, there were no Freemasons in the gang of London villains who carried out this audacious robbery on a British train in the English countryside and stole (in today's value) around £45 million. Members of the Craft did, however, play major roles in cracking the case and bringing the robbers to justice. Most interestingly, information obtained at a lodge meeting in a far-off country led to one of the robbers being found after he had fled to the other side of the world.

The planner of the raid has never been identified; he was known as 'the Ulsterman' (due to the style of his coat, rather than being from Northern Ireland). The robbery required inside information regarding train timings, security arrangements, and the best time to strike. As an example of the type of detail that an unknown post office employee was supplying, it should be noted that the raid took place just after a Bank Holiday in Scotland, so far more money was being carried than usual.

The gang was led by Bruce Reynolds who was born in Charing Cross Hospital (bizarrely now Charing Cross Police Station) and a building with a foundation stone laid by the Duke of Sussex, the first Grand Master of the United Grand Lodge of England. Reynolds gathered together a group of villains whose names have become infamous—'Buster' Edwards, Charlie Wilson, and petty south London criminal Ronnie Biggs. The raid involved meticulous planning; the gang required specialist railway skills, vehicles, and a hide-out. In June 1963, on behalf of the gang, a dishonest solicitor purchased Leatherslade Farm in the Buckinghamshire countryside, between Aylesbury and Oxford. This secluded three-bedroom farmhouse was nearly twenty miles from the intended scene of the robbery—an ideal place for the gang to 'lie low' once the crime had been committed.

The robbers moved from London to the farm on Tuesday 6 August. All that was required now was the tip-off that the train was carrying a large quantity of cash. They had expected to 'do the job' that evening, but the robbery was postponed for twenty-four hours. The go-ahead information came the following day and so, on the evening of Wednesday 7 August, the gang disguised themselves as an army unit and drove to the Bridego Railway Bridge (now called 'Train Robbers' Bridge') in a military style lorry and two Land Rovers. This location was well chosen as it was near the quiet hamlet of Ledburn, an ideal place to commit crime as it is an out of the way country location, policed by a very small county constabulary. Once *in situ*, the robbers changed from army uniforms into railway-style overalls.

At 6.40 p.m., the 'Travelling Post Office' train left Glasgow Central Station en-route to Euston Station in London. The train was made up of twelve carriages, filled with Post Office workers, who sorted and dropped off mail as the train travelled south. The second carriage behind the engine was the robbers' target; this was the 'HVP' (High Value Packages) coach. During a standard journey, this would have contained £300,000, but due to the banks having been closed in Scotland for the Summer Bank Holiday, it contained nearly ten times as much: £2.6 million—a fortune in 1963.

By 3 a.m. on the morning of Thursday 8 August, the train was passing through rural Buckinghamshire, just over forty miles from the final destination. Suddenly, there was an unexpected red signal; it was a fake. The green light had been covered with a glove by the robbers and a red lamp put in its place. The train driver's assistant (still known as the 'fireman' despite steam engines being replaced by diesel) climbed down onto the track, intending to use a track side telephone to ring the local signalman. He found that the telephone wires had been cut and was then thrown down the railway embankment. The Great Train Robbery had begun.

The robbers stormed the engine and seized the driver, Jack Mills. The meticulous planning now began to unravel. The plan was for one of the gang (who has never been identified) to drive the train the short distance to Bridego Bridge, where the loot could be easily unloaded. The appointed driver, however, had been learning to drive the wrong type of train—small shunting engines, not a large modern diesel. Now the robbery turned violent. Mills was ordered to drive his own engine to the bridge. He initially bravely refused, but was badly beaten; this was to affect him for the rest of his life. Ronnie Biggs's role had been to supervise the robbers' train driver. This individual having proved a failure, Biggs was sent to so something more useful: to help carry the bags of cash down to the lorries.

The robbers detached the rear carriages, leaving only two coupled to the engine—the first carriage and the HVP. This also eliminated the threat of the many postal workers who would be left stranded in the other trucks. The engine was now driven down the track to the bridge. The gang attacked the HVP carriage and quickly subdued the five workers inside, with the robbers using coshes. Given the enormous amount of cash on board, it is surprising that there were no security staff or police officers present to protect it. Mills, the engine driver, and his assistant (dragged back up the railway embankment) were also moved to this part of the train and handcuffed.

The gang worked quickly and by using a 'human chain', they removed nearly all the 128 sacks from the carriage in under half an hour, coming in at over two tons of valuables. With their ill-gotten gains loaded onto the truck, they drove off into the night. To confuse any potential witnesses, the two Land Rovers were both displaying the same registration number and drove off in different directions. A railway man on the train eventually raised the alarm by obtaining a lift on a goods train to Cheddington Station.

The robbers made it to Leatherslade Farm, intending to stay for some time. Charlie Wilson was the gang's 'treasurer'; unlike the version in a Masonic lodge (who spends his time trying to get money out of the members), Wilson actually gave the cash out. The loot was divided up evenly between the sixteen members of the gang, together with several smaller payments set aside for those who had played minor roles. The robbers then spent some of their time playing the board game 'Monopoly' with real cash; even they could not believe their luck. This activity was to form part of their ultimate downfall.

By listening to the police radio transmissions, the robbers realised that the police were convinced that they had 'gone to ground' in Buckinghamshire and searches were being made to flush them out. In consequence, the plan to leave the farm was brought forward. Unfortunately, a petty (unnamed) villain was tasked to clean up (or burn down) the hideout to destroy any traces of forensic evidence, especially fingerprints. This was not done and later presented the police with a major lead.

By 5 a.m. on the morning of the robbery, the head of Buckinghamshire CID had attended the scene and called in Scotland Yard's Flying Squad, whose role was to target armed robbers. This famous unit, also known as 'The Sweeney' (in Cockney rhyming slang, 'Sweeney Todd' stands for 'Flying Squad'), had been founded by two Masons. In 1919, Detective Chief Inspector Frederick Porter Wensley ran a 'Mobile Patrol Experiment' using a horse drawn carriage to target robbers and pickpockets. Porter had been initiated into the Temple Lodge No. 101 in London in 1908. When Walter Edward Hambrook took charge of the unit, it became officially known as the Flying Squad and had authority to work in all areas of London. As a Detective Inspector, Hambrook had joined another London lodge, Paddington No. 3267.

Returning to the events in Buckinghamshire, a team from the Flying Squad left London to aid the small constabulary; this included Detective Sergeant Jim Nevill, later head of the Anti-Terrorist Squad and a Freemason. Later in his career, he would become a founder member of the Manor of St James's Lodge No. 9179. Another Detective Sergeant was 'Nipper' Read (of Kray Twins fame), who is a member of Alexander Woods Lodge No. 8661.

The local police also began to scour the countryside to find any hideout. Some five days later, on 13 August, they received a tip off from a farm worker about suspicious behaviour at Leatherslade Farm. A sergeant and the village constable for the Brill area attended; the constable was John Woolley, a former Royal Military Policeman who would go on to join St Mary's Lodge No. 1763 (an Oxfordshire lodge). A large truck and two Land Rovers were parked there; the fact that the latter two vehicles had the same registration plates confirmed that the farm-worker may well have been justified in calling the police.

An upstairs window was seen to be open. The now retired PC Woolley recalls that, as the junior officer, it was his duty to climb up and search the premises. The robbers had long gone, but the story now begins to sound like the Holy Royal Arch ritual. In that ceremony, the candidate plays a Mason who finds a vault under the ruins of King Solomon's Temple. On climbing down, a search reveals a vital clue to the lost secrets of Freemasonry, but being unable to read it, due to the darkness, he is (symbolically) lifted out of the vault to the 'light of day'. In the Buckingham farmhouse, PC Woolley found his own version of the secret vault—a trap door near the kitchen that led to a dark cellar. On entering, he found some sacks, but due to the 'want of light', he was unsure if they were significant. Like the Mason in the ceremony, the truth was revealed once he could see. He had in his hand a mail sack full of the wrappings from bundles of bank notes and the cellar was full of similar bags.

Leatherslade Farm, the hideout of the Great Train Robbers was found by a young police officer who is now a Mason.

The police had been looking for a breakthrough in the Great Train Robbery investigation and now the gang's hideout location had been discovered. PC Woolley, like the Royal Arch Mason, could announce, 'it is found'.

Scotland Yard detectives and fingerprint officers were soon swarming all over the farm. The interior was extensively searched and large quantities of food (over two hundred eggs), other essentials (over thirty toilet rolls), and bedding were noted, together with post office bags, wrappings from bank notes and the Monopoly board. In the farm grounds, more mail bags were found buried.

In London, the head of the Flying Squad, Detective Chief Superintendent Tommy Butler coordinated the small 'Train Robbery Squad', which consisted of six officers, including Detective Sergeant Jack Slipper (neither Butler nor Slipper appear to have been Masons). Slipper later went on to be head of the Flying Squad and, as we shall see, continued to be involved in the case for many years.

With fingerprints and other evidence from the farm being quickly utilised, the Flying Squad were able to arrest many of the robbers over the next month, but Reynolds and Edwards were still on the run. Much of the money was never recovered. The trial of those apprehended was held in Aylesbury in January 1964; the local court was too small, so the council offices had to be converted. The hearing, with hundreds of witnesses and court exhibits, was to last nearly three months. Thirteen of the gang were found guilty and seven of them, including Biggs, were sentenced to thirty years' imprisonment. The judge told the gang that they had participated in 'a crime of sordid violence inspired by vast greed'.

The robbery has an international dimension. Reynolds and Edwards both spent time in Mexico, where they were joined by Wilson, who managed to escape just four months into his sentence. All were eventually captured and sentenced to long prison terms. It is Ronnie Biggs who is of interest to the Masonic crime reader. On 8 July 1965, less than two years into his thirty years' sentence, Biggs escaped from Wandsworth Prison by climbing a rope ladder and dropping onto the roof of a waiting furniture van.

Having broken out of jail, Biggs met with his wife and children and travelled by boat to Belgium, and then to Paris, where he underwent plastic surgery to change his appearance. The following year, the Biggs family were on the move again, this time to Australia. They were to live there in Adelaide and Melbourne for two years, until it was announced on the local television news that the police were aware of Biggs being in the country and would soon be making an arrest. The wanted fugitive left his family and boarded a boat to Panama, arriving in Brazil in late 1969. He settled in Rio de Janeiro. He soon had a new wife and a son but maintained a low profile, hidden from the British authorities. Unhappily, in 1970, the train driver, Jack Mills, died of leukaemia, but his family remained convinced that his ill-health was directly related to the actions of the robbers.

In 1973, Detective Sergeant Brian Marshall of Gloucestershire Police was seconded to the Central Drugs and Illegal Immigration Intelligence Unit, a national squad, based at New Scotland Yard; this unit was a forerunner of the National Crime Intelligence Service and Serious and Organised Crime Agency. At this time, rumours began to surface of Biggs's hideaway in Rio. Marshall was tasked to track him down, but as he was travelling alone, Brother Brian, a member of Glevum Lodge No. 7385 in the Province of Gloucestershire,

Ronnie Biggs, the Great Train
Robber who was located in Brazil
as a result of information gained at
a Masonic Festive Board.

decided to spend an evening with Masonic brethren in Brazil. He contacted the United
Grand Lodge of England and established the details of a lodge in Rio that was 'recognised'
and could be visited by an English Mason. While seeking out top criminals, the last thing he
needed to do was to commit a 'Masonic' offence of his own by visiting an 'irregular' lodge.

At the Festive Board that followed the meeting, DS Marshall asked the brethren (most
of them ex-pat Englishmen) if they had come across any new British men in Rio. One man
stated that he had—a recently arrived man calling himself 'Michael' was offering to do
odd-jobs or gardening work. As a result, the detective sergeant arranged to meet the odd
job man in the café near the iconic Christ the Redeemer statue, which overlooks the city,
on the pretext of offering him some work. While the fugitive robber had undergone plastic
surgery, the officer still suspected that 'Michael' was Biggs. In order to prove his hunch,
once the meeting had ended, he carefully placed the cup and saucer used by the mysterious
man in a bag. DS Marshall took these items to the British Embassy and they were quickly
transported to the Fingerprint Branch at New Scotland Yard. The fingerprint officers were
soon able to confirm that the man in Rio who had held the cup was indeed Ronald Arthur
Biggs, the missing Great Train Robber. Herein lies an important lesson for criminals: you
can change your face, but you cannot change your fingerprints.

Anyone giving 'serious contemplation to the Volume of the Sacred Law' (as Freemasons are told to do at their first meeting) will note that in 1 Timothy, St Paul warns 'the love of money is the root of all evil'. In the case of the Great Train Robbers, it also seems to be the root of all unhappiness. In 1994, 'Buster' Edwards was found dead in a lock-up garage in south London; he had hanged himself. In 1990, Charlie Wilson, who had continued to be involved in major crime, was assassinated by an unnamed hitman (Wilson had been laundering cash from the Brinks Mat Raid). Having enjoyed the protection of the Brazilian authorities for many years, Ronnie Biggs voluntarily flew back to England in 2001 and was returned to prison. After a series of strokes, he was released on compassionate grounds. Biggs observed to a journalist, 'Even in Brazil I was a prisoner of my own making. There is no honour to being known as a Great Train Robber.' Reynolds, the leader, died in 2013 after living part of his later life in a council flat in Croydon. He noted, 'I became an old crook living on handouts from other old crooks.'

In contrast to the (non-Masonic) villains, the (Masonic) police officers in this case retired after long careers; both live happy lives and both still attend their lodges. Brian Marshall holds the British Empire Medal; the year after finding Leatherslade Farm, he bravely tackled a man armed with a shotgun and other weapons. Brother 'Nipper' Read went onto very high rank in the Police Force and was decorated for his service. Once again, members of the Craft had played critical roles in bringing violent and greedy criminals to justice.

52

The Kray Twins:
Brought to Justice by a Freemason

Masonic Connection
Senior officer in charge of enquiry
Detectives

Date
1962: 'Nipper' Read initiated into Freemasonry
1966: Ronnie Kray murdered George Cornell
1967: Reggie Kray murdered Jack 'the Hat' McVitie
1969: Twins convicted of murder

Connection to London
Vallance Rd, Bethnal Green: Home of the Kray family
Tower of London: Kray Twins held in custody at this fortress
Whitechapel Road: Murder committed in Blind Beggar public house
Evering Road, Stoke Newington: Murder committed in a flat
Old Bailey: Kray Twins tried and convicted in this court

Lodges
Alexander Woods No. 8661
Lodge of Quality No. 9356

The Kray Twins, Ronnie and Reggie, were notorious gangsters from the East End of London during the 1950s and '60s who ran a criminal empire known as 'The Firm'. Despite their standard attire of dark suits and black ties, the twins were not Masons, but they were ultimately brought to justice by members of the Craft.

Born in 1933, Ronnie and Reggie lived for most of their childhood in 178 Vallance Road in Bethnal Green with their fearsome mother, Violet, and older brother, Charlie. Influenced by their grandfather and aided by a predisposition to violence, the twins became successful boxers at an early age. Ronnie, in particular, was prone to aggressive behaviour, aggravated by paranoid schizophrenia.

The Kray Twins. Their reign of terror was ended by a Freemason.

As young men, they were involved in all manner of offending, but avoided borstal—the young offender's prison of the day. They were soon to get their first taste of life behind bars. In 1952, the nineteen-year-old twins were called up for National Service. They were to serve in the Royal Fusiliers, a regiment based at the Tower of London. Due to their ill-disciplined and violent conduct, they were soon, like villains of old, to find themselves not serving at the Tower, but instead locked in it; they were two of the last prisoners ever held there. Their short army service ended with a dishonourable discharge, having served periods of custody in military prisons in Shepton Mallet, Somerset and Canterbury, Kent.

Returning to the East End of London, the Krays then took over a snooker hall named The Regal, and raised further money by running protection rackets targeting local businesses. The Twins were later given a nightclub by the notorious slum landlord, Peter Rachman. The club, Esmeralda's Barn, in fashionable Knightsbridge was to attract many celebrities, including Frank Sinatra and other stars of the era. The Krays soon became celebrities themselves, being photographed (as were many 1960s icons) by David Bailey.

Despite their overt violence and involvement in crime, the twins had no need of Masonic conspiracies to aid them. They had something far more powerful—the Establishment. Ronnie had enjoyed homosexual liaisons with Lord Boothby, a Conservative peer (who had also had an affair with the Prime Minister's wife) and Tom Driberg, a Labour Member of Parliament. Thus, neither of the two main political parties put much pressure on Scotland Yard to tackle The Firm, as it risked their 'dirty linen' being washed in public.

In 1964, the press set about exposing the high-level protection enjoyed by the twins and the *Sunday Mirror* newspaper ran a story about a relationship between an unnamed 'peer and a gangster'. To ensure this story remained 'buried', the Krays and Boothby dealt with it in their own ways. The twins threatened the journalists with violence; Boothby threatened legal action and the newspaper agreed to pay him £40,000 in an out of court settlement. This affair, no doubt, confirmed to the brothers that they were untouchable.

An example of their brazen attitude to authority (and the Twins ruthlessness when confronted with a problem) can be seen in the case of the escape of Frank Mitchell—the 'Mad Axeman'. Mitchell had been sentenced to life imprisonment in 1958 for robbery with violence. He had later escaped and held an elderly couple hostage; he was armed with an axe taken from their shed, hence his nickname. Ronnie had befriended Mitchell in Wandsworth Prison and their friendship continued once Ronnie had been released. Later, Mitchell was sent to Dartmoor Prison, in the remote West Country of England, and was allowed to wander the countryside as part of work parties. He was aggrieved as he had been given no possible release date. Ronnie and Reggie decided to 'spring' him, claiming that the intention was to highlight his case to the media.

The escape (if it could be described as such) was easy. A pick-up was arranged outside the prison. Mitchell wandered out and was then driven to a flat in East Ham. Unfortunately, he was a big, violent man with the mind of a child. He found that he had swapped a lax prison (Dartmoor) for one with far more ruthless guards—The Firm. He began to threaten the lives of Ronnie and Reggie (who had not bothered to visit him) and became an inconvenience. As a result, he vanished. His body has never been found, but the Krays were cleared of any involvement in his death; however, in more recent times, their contemporaries have admitted that Mitchell was killed on their orders with the body thrown into the sea.

The Krays' downfall began when they committed two further murders, the first in front of numerous witnesses. On 9 March 1966, Ronnie shot George Cornell in the Blind Beggar pub in Whitechapel. Cornell had been a member of the rival Richardson gang and had infuriated Ronnie by calling him a 'fat poof' some weeks before. The fact that Ronnie felt able to gun a man down in front of several witnesses demonstrates the power they held in the East End. The following year, Reggie killed Jack 'the Hat' McVitie. McVitie had worked for the Twins, but owed them money. Reggie had initially felt sorry for him, but egged on by his brother, he went on to murder him. McVitie was lured to a flat in Stoke Newington, believing that he was going to attend a party. Once there, Reggie tried to shoot him, but the gun failed to fire. McVitie was then killed by being brutally stabbed several times with a carving knife. His body has never been found; again, it has been suggested that it was thrown out to sea.

The man tasked by the Assistant Commissioner in charge of the CID at Scotland Yard to bring down the Krays was Detective Superintendent Leonard 'Nipper' Read. A small man, he was a police lightweight boxing champion, hence his nickname. Read was already a Freemason; he joined in 1962. Originally in a London lodge, he was appalled when another police officer member attempted to have a local villain initiated in the Craft. Nipper's objections worked; the man was not admitted, but he still feels disappointed that anyone could think of making such an unacceptable man a Mason. He then joined Alexander Woods Lodge No. 8661 in Hertfordshire.

How apt that one boxer was going to take on two other boxers—Ronnie and Reggie. To ensure tight security and prevent leaks, Read moved the enquiry from Scotland Yard to Tintagel House, a non-descript police building on the south side of the River Thames. The first task was to coordinate intelligence against the twins; this was no easy task as time and time again, Detective Superintendent Read was to come up against the East End wall of silence, where no one would 'grass' (give information) to the 'Old Bill' (the Metropolitan Police). The hand-picked unit had several Masons within, including (the then) Detective Sergeant David Eager, a member of the Lodge of Quality No. 9356 in Surrey.

Using criminal informants, a case was built up against the Krays, but many witnesses were still unwilling to give evidence while the twins roamed free. A decision was made to arrest them and as many members of The Firm as possible, in an attempt to break the cycle of fear. On 8 May 1968, teams of officers left West End Police Station; by the end of the day, Ronnie, Reggie, and fourteen members of their gang were under arrest. Critically, they were remanded in prison awaiting trial, thus removing much of the threat of witness intimidation. The barmaid from the Blind Beggar pub now felt able to pick out Ronnie on an identification parade as the killer of George Cornell.

In 1969, the twins stood trial at the Old Bailey charged with the two murders. Their attempts to evade justice were dealt a serious blow when members of The Firm (and even a cousin, Ronnie Hart) gave evidence against them, including giving a detailed account of the death of Jack 'the Hat'. The Krays' fate was sealed; both were sentenced to thirty years imprisonment without parole. Their brother, Charlie, received a ten-year sentence. Ronnie was never to be free again; declared insane, he was sent to Broadmoor secure hospital and died there in 1995. While suffering from cancer, Reggie was released on compassionate grounds in 2000 after serving more than thirty years. He died within a fortnight and was buried next to his twin in Chingford cemetery in East London.

Nipper Read went on to be the Assistant Chief constable in his native county of Nottinghamshire and then to command the National Crime Squad. He was awarded the Queen's Police Medal to mark his exceptional detective career. He is still a Mason and proudly wears a badge to show that he has been a brother for over fifty years. He has never been 'through the Chair' as being the Master of a lodge is, in his opinion, 'too much work'—an amusing comment from a man who dedicated his life to catching the most violent and devious criminals. He is held in respect by police officers of all ages and the villains he helped to put in prison for long periods; he is rightfully seen as a decent and honest man, who played by the rules. David Eager is also still a very active Mason who has been recognised for his charity fundraising.

53

Not So Great Architect:
Brother John Poulson and
Corruption at the Heart of Government

Masonic Connection
Corrupt businessman
Arresting officer
Judge

Date
1953: Poulson Master of a lodge
1960: Poulson Master of a lodge
1974: Convicted at Leeds Crown Court

Connection to London
Cannon Street Stations: Designed by Poulson
East Croydon Station: Designed by Poulson
Waterloo Station: Several buildings around the site designed by Poulson

Lodges
Pentalpha No. 974
De Lacy No. 4643
Tateshall No. 7645
St Michael's No. 8186

Many Masons will have travelled to work in London and passed through the railway stations at Cannon Street, Waterloo, and East Croydon, but few are probably aware that these were designed by a corrupt architect who was also a Freemason. Brother John Garlick Llewellyn Poulson was a devious and greedy man (even his lawyer was to later describe him as 'hypocritical, self-righteous and perhaps something of a megalomaniac') and his downfall led to the resignation of one of the most senior politicians in the land. He is also very damaging to Freemasonry; a search of the many anti-Masonry websites on the internet could easily convince the reader that the dishonesty of Brother Poulson is further proof of Masonic skulduggery at the highest levels of British society. Unfortunately for the conspiracy theorists, the truth is never that simple and while Poulson was a dishonest Mason, he was brought to justice by other members of the Craft.

Poulson was born in Pontefract in West Yorkshire in 1910. He managed to dodge military service during the Second World War and married into a family of influence; his sister-in-law was married to a member of the House of Lords. He then managed to build one of the most successful architectural businesses in the United Kingdom, despite his first employer claiming that he could not 'design a brick shit house'; it was so big that even Poulson could not believe the size of his empire.

In addition to his zeal in building a business empire, Poulson was also a keen Mason, being a member of several lodges, which met in his native county—Pentalpha No. 974 (in Bradford), De Lacy No. 4643, and Tateshall No. 7645 (both in Pontefract). He also appears to have had a holiday home in Devon as he was a member of St Michael's No. 8186, which then met in Teignmouth. His interest in the Craft was so great that he was a founder member of two of these lodges. In 1953, he was installed as the Worshipful Master of De Lacey and seven years later, he was Master of Tateshall. Of course, his fellow members would have had no reason to suspect his villainy, to them he would have been seen as a successful businessman.

Brother Poulson's business method was simple and effective, offering a complete building service. Prior to his company, all roles in architecture and the building industry were clearly defined—designer, planner, builder. Poulson combined them all and cut out the 'middle men'. He also had luck on his side. Given the post-war rebuild of Britain and the housing boom of the 1960s, this was an ideal time for an innovator to make money, and lots of it. Poulson was able to make over £1 million per year—a vast sum in that decade. Furthermore, the nationalised industries also offered many opportunities to make a 'fast buck', with some dishonest officials ready to award contracts to those who would pay. Amusingly (or tragically for the author, who is a Northerner), Poulson found that it was often cheaper to bribe Labour councillors in the north of England than their Conservative counterparts in the south. His tactic was to lavish his targets with gifts and dinners in top hotels.

The leader of Newcastle council fitted the bill and corrupt Labour politician T. Dan Smith (who was not a Mason) was eventually jailed for six years. Further bribery resulted in him being paid another fortune to develop the Aviemore winter sports complex in Scotland. It was not just the north that offered opportunities to make money. In London, it was the nationalised railways that offered Poulson a chance to make money with the help, of course, of a greedy British Railways employee. Graham Tunbridge held a senior position in the south region and was able to ensure that Poulson received the contracts to rebuild Waterloo, Cannon Street, and East Croydon Stations. These large deals came at a very reasonable price—£25 per week and the loan of a car. Demonstrating his ability to corrupt Conservative, as well as Labour politicians and the influence he had with the highest government officials in the land, Poulson also enticed the Home Secretary, Reg Maudling (not a Mason), into becoming a business partner.

It was not just in the United Kingdom that his web extended. With the British Empire ever decreasing, the newly independent nations offered ever more opportunities to make money. Poulson's business extended to West Africa and he was aided by paying British

MPs to ask questions in Parliament on his behalf. In Malta, he obtained a hospital building contract after Maudling put pressure on the government.

Poulson's star was, however, starting to wane. His empire was overreaching itself and a failure to pay the taxman was the start of his downfall. Matters were to come to a head on New Year's Eve 1969 when he was formally prevented from controlling his own company. Within two years, he had filed for bankruptcy, but it was clear to anyone who was prepared to review his case that there had been much corruption involved in his business dealings. Thus, in 1972, the Metropolitan Police Fraud Squad began an investigation. The team was led by George Churchill-Coleman, a Freemason who would eventually hold very senior offices in the police (Commander, Anti-Terrorist Squad) and in the Craft (Assistant Provincial Grand Master, Surrey).

If the conspiracy theorists are to be believed and Freemasonry is a wicked organisation, Worshipful Brother Churchill-Coleman would have attempted to cover the tracks of his Masonic brother, John Poulson. This, however, did not happen as Churchill-Coleman pursued his quarry with vigour and in June 1973, Brother Poulson was arrested and charged with fraud and corruption. This development was to end the career of Maudling, the Home Secretary. As head of the Home Office, he oversaw the Metropolitan Police. His position was untenable and he resigned.

In February 1974, Poulson was tried at Leeds Crown Court before Mr Justice Waller, a senior Freemason and Grand Officer of the United Grand Lodge of England. As with

Commander George Churchill-Coleman, senior officer and senior Freemason, who ruthlessly prosecuted other members of the Craft, including John Poulson and Tony Williams, the Laird of Tomintoul. He also stopped the corruption enquiry that targeted DCI Lundy.

his police brother, George Churchill-Coleman, the judge was to show no favouritism to his Masonic brother, sentencing Poulson to five years' imprisonment. Mr Justice Waller described the prisoner as an 'incalculably evil man'. Poulson, however, saw fit to blame everyone else, stating, 'I have been a fool, surrounded by a pack of leeches.' Even when released in 1977, he continued to maintain his innocence, but he was a broken man and a bankrupt.

The scandal resulted in the 'Register of Members' Interests' being introduced for Members of Parliament. It also was the basis of the television series *Our Friends in the North*, which tells a tale of corruption in local government. It must be noted that, while Poulson was a member of the Craft, he was a happy to bribe anyone—Masonry does not seem to have played any part in these decisions. Importantly, Worshipful Brothers Churchill-Coleman (the police officer) and Waller (the judge) displayed the highest standards of integrity in ensuring that fellow Mason Poulson faced justice.

54

Something Moody in the West End: Dirty Books and Dishonest Masons?

Masonic Connection
Corrupt police officers
Honest police officers

Date
1956: Bill Moody initiated into Freemasonry
1964: DS Moody joined the Obscene Publication Squad
1977: Moody tried for corruption

Connection to London
Soho: Corruption occurred in 'Dirty Book' shops
Old Bailey: Court where tried and convicted

Lodges
Lodge of Amity No. 137
All Souls No. 170
Tredegar No. 1625
Edmonton with Chandos No. 4339
Irenic No. 4797
Deptford No. 4847 (Erased)
Broadstone No. 8641
Manor of St James's No. 9179
Irenic Chapter No. 4797 (Holy Royal Arch)

The word 'moody' in London slang means 'dodgy' and this could certainly be said of Detective Chief Superintendent Alfred William 'Bill' Moody. Moody was also a Mason and possibly the most corrupt officer to serve in the Metropolitan Police, challenging John Meiklejohn, who some one hundred years previously was also taking massive bribes from London villains. Indeed, the scandals caused by both officers resulted in the command structure of Scotland Yard's detectives being changed in an attempt to prevent corruption, with better supervision of plain clothes officers. Importantly, while the Moody case is often presented by detractors of the Craft as an example of Masonic conspiracy and criminal activity, the truth is not so simple. Other members of the Craft would play major parts in rooting out his wickedness and ensuring that justice was served.

Moody was born in 1925 in south London to Anglo-German parents. His surname was originally Schwarz, but his father had used the name 'Smith' to serve in the British Army during the First World War. Just before the Second World War, the family officially changed their name to Moody. Bill Moody joined the Metropolitan Police in the post-war years and soon transferred from the uniformed branch into the CID. In 1956, he was initiated into Deptford Lodge No. 4847 and later the same year, he was exalted into Irenic Chapter No. 4797. He appears to have been a keen Mason as in 1960, he joined the Irenic Lodge, which bore the same number as the Chapter. All these Masonic units met in central London.

By 1964, he had achieved the rank of detective sergeant and was posted to the Obscene Publications Unit, whose role it was to prevent the sale of pornography that was rife in Soho and arrest those responsible for this illicit trade. The unit was known as the 'Porn Squad' or 'Dirty Squad' and it was the making of Moody, who rose from the rank of sergeant to Detective Chief Superintendent in just eight years—a meteoric rise. While his senior officer, Commander Wally Virgo (a non-Mason), would later appear in the dock at the Old Bailey with Moody, there was no doubt as to who was really in charge of the corrupt practices in the Dirty Squad; it was Moody. The prosecution counsel at his later trial had no doubt that the 'deplorable web of corruption' revolved around the Detective Chief Superintendent. In his opening speech, the barrister stated, 'In the nine years from 1964 to the spring of 1972, when the process of discovery began, Mr Moody was the principal architect of this criminal behaviour … The evidence will show he was organising corruption on a very large scale'. It was little wonder that Brother Moody was known by the nickname 'Wicked Bill'.

Moody's corruption was a well-organised racket, where traders in illegal pornography had to purchase a 'licence' from his team 'authorising' them to sell their wares. Typically, the licence would cost an initial fee of £4,000, followed by payments of £100 per week in brown envelopes. Once the licence had been bought, the corrupt officers under Moody's command would actively protect the pornographer from police investigations. They would also offer assistance, selling them dirty books that had been seized from shops whose owners had not paid the required bribes and taken advantage of the (corrupt) Moody protection plan. At the later trial, one pornographer stated that he had been given a CID tie so that he fitted in when taken to Holborn Police Station to buy obscene material.

Occasionally, other police units, such as the Regional Crime Squad, would interfere with the licensing system and raid pornographers 'authorised' by Moody. In such an eventuality, the proprietor of the dirty book shop could pay an additional bribe to the Porn Squad to have the case dropped. On one occasion, Brother Bill took £14,000 to corruptly interfere in an investigation and assist a pornographer who had been found in possession of a large quantity of 'blue' movies. This term apparently came into use as the censors used blue ink to mark unacceptable language or scenes.

During his wicked reign over Soho, Moody did not just take cash bribes from those who he should have been bringing to justice. The pornographers also bought him a set of gold

Chief Superintendent Bill
Moody, the Mason and
dishonest officer who was
known as 'Wicked Bill'.

sovereign cufflinks, paid for foreign holidays, and entertained him in top London hotels. It was not, however, a one-way street. Moody took pornographers, including Ron 'the Dustman' Davey (so called due to his previous work with the council), to Masonic events. At the time, Moody's Mother Lodge (Deptford) met in the Horseshoe Hotel in Tottenham Court Road, a stone's throw away from the dirty book shops in Soho. The Irenic lodge was nearby too, meeting in the Café Royal in Regents Street.

Moody's quest to obtain ever more money meant that even police officers had to pay him cash; one officer was so disgusted with the culture of bribery and corruption in the Porn Squad that he demanded a transfer. This was allowed by DCS Moody, but only after payment of £100. The head of the squad was, however, getting greedy and 'flash'; this would draw attention to his conduct. He thought nothing of flouncing around New Scotland Yard, wearing expensive tailored suits and made no secret of having two top of the range cars, bought for him by one of his 'clients'.

In 1972, CID corruption in London was publicly exposed. The *Sunday People* newspaper reported that the Commander of the Flying Squad, Kenneth Drury, had gone on a holiday paid for by a pornographer. Drury is often claimed to be a member of the Craft, but there is no record of his membership at the United Grand Lodge of England.

The new commissioner at Scotland Yard, Sir Robert Mark (a non-Mason), tackled the problem of corrupt detectives head on and set about reforming the CID. It was Mark who famously remarked 'a good police force is one that catches more crooks than it employs,' and Moody was certainly one of the crooks employed by the Met. One of the commissioner's first acts was to create the Anti-Corruption Unit, known as 'A10'. The CID as 'C Department' had always been responsible for the investigation of any form of crime, so giving the responsibility of rooting out dishonest officers to 'A (Uniformed) Department' was a major change. Despite all the talk of Masonic corruption, Mark does not appear to have had any mistrust of members of the Craft. He appointed experienced detective (and Mason) John Morrison as one of the Detective Chief Superintendents in A10. Morrison had been initiated into the Tredegar Lodge No. 1625 in the Great Eastern Hotel at Liverpool Street Station in 1966.

Following the Drury case, another newspaper, *The Sunday Times*, reported on the dishonest activities of the Obscene Publications Unit. Brother Moody's downfall began when the diaries of a pornographer came to light. These documents outlined in great detail the bribes paid to Moody and his officers. Given that the corruption involved a very senior officer of Detective Chief Superintendent rank, Deputy Assistant Commissioner (later Assistant Commissioner) Gilbert Kelland was tasked to investigate the 'Dirty Squad'. Kelland was no stranger to 'A' Department; he had been a uniformed officer for all of his career. Like Morrison, he was also a Mason. He was later to defy police advice on Masonry and was a founding member of the Manor of St James's Lodge No. 9179.

As a founding member of the 'Manor', Worshipful Brother Kelland refused to bow to pressure placed on police officers to withdraw from Masonry. The Commissioner of the Metropolitan Police, Sir Kenneth Newman, had issued all his officers the 'Blue Book' or 'The Principles of Policing'. In this publication, he advised:

> The discerning officer will probably consider it wise to forgo the prospect of pleasure and social advantage in Freemasonry so as to enjoy the unreserved regard of all those around him. It follows from this that one who is already a Freemason would also be wise to ponder from time to time whether he should continue as a Freemason.

Short (1993) made claims regarding Kelland's willingness to deal with corrupt Masons in the CID:

> [They] can be explained partly by the existence of two distinct Masonic traditions in the Metropolitan Police at this time. Gilbert Kelland ... had spent the first twenty-five years of his service in uniform. He was not a 'career detective' and he never allowed his Freemasonry to intrude into, or overlap with, his police work. In contrast Freemasonry in much of the CID had become a cover for crookery and corruption.

This ignores the fact that his right-hand man, Deputy Assistant Commissioner Ron Steventon, was a CID officer (through and through) and would later head A10. Steventon was a member of Edmonton Lodge No. 4339 (now called Edmonton with Chandos) and several other lodges. He achieved high Masonic rank in London and Essex (see Chapter 56 for further details of his Masonic ranks).

As a result of Brother Kelland's investigation, in May 1977, six police officers, including Commander Virgo and recently retired DCS Moody appeared at the Old Bailey. They were charged with twenty-seven charges of bribery and corruption. There was an irony in this, as five years before his appearance in the dock at the same court, Moody had been congratulated by a judge for bringing other corrupt officers to justice.

Brother Moody was convicted and sentenced to twelve years' imprisonment. Including 'Wicked Bill', the work of Brother Kelland resulted in some thirteen corrupt detectives, of ranks high and low, some Masons, some not, going to jail for a total of nearly one hundred years. Moody was not finished with Freemasonry. He remained a member of his lodges and chapter throughout his incarceration, but resigned from them all between 1987 and 1990. He was officially expelled from Masonry in 1991. It should also be noted that at the time of the trial, Deputy Assistant Commissioner Peter Neivens OBE QPM was appointed as the Director of the Complaints Department. Neivens was also a very distinguished Freemason who had been initiated in 1957 and was appointed Deputy Provincial Grand Master of Essex in 1995.

All the Masons described in this sorry affair have now died. After prison, Moody ended his days in Devon. He passed to the 'Grand Lodge Above' in 2012; perhaps his bribery and corruption resulted in him being sent 'downstairs'. It must be noted that several Freemasons—Kelland, Steventon, and others—played key roles in ensuring that another Mason was sent to prison for his involvement in bribery and corruption.

Following on from the Porn Squad investigation, Operation Countryman was initiated in 1978 by the Home Secretary, as a wide-ranging enquiry into corruption in the City of London Police and Met's CID. The operation was named after the corrupt detective, Meiklejohn. An officer from outside London was selected to head the enquiry—Assistant Chief Constable Leonard Burt of Dorset Police, who reported to his own Chief Constable, Arthur Hambleton. Hambleton was a brave man; he had been awarded the Military Cross, while serving as a Royal Marines officer in the Second World War.

Burt led the corruption enquiry with vigour, but the investigation was fraught with inter-force mistrust and rivalries. Hambleton subsequently made allegations that his team had been obstructed by the Metropolitan Police at the highest level. When Hambleton retired, he gave an interview to the 'World in Action' investigative television programme in 1982, during which he and other retired senior officers alleged that the enquiry had not just been frustrated by the Metropolitan Police, but also by the government. It is interesting to note that both Burt and Hambleton were Masons. Burt joined Broadstone Lodge No. 8641 in 1977 and later, Lodge of Amity No. 137, which both met in Poole, Dorset. Hambleton joined the All Souls Lodge No. 170, in Weymouth, in 1980. On *World in Action*, when asked about the potential damage to police morale by Operation Countryman, Hambleton stated 'My first loyalty is to the people of England.' This is important; his loyalty was to the people he served, not to other police officers or Freemasons.

Countryman also gives a very stark example of a Mason who refused to give any quarter to corrupt members of the Craft or the police. City of London Police Detective

Chief Inspector Philip Cuthbert was secretly captured on tape by fellow Mason Detective Chief Superintendent John Simmonds, while gloating about setting up armed robberies and taking bribes from criminals. As a result, Cuthbert was jailed for three years. A convicted villain who gave evidence against Cuthbert described him as 'a criminal, who chose to be a policeman.' John Simmonds would later leave Masonry as he found some members of the Craft sided with Cuthbert. Perhaps, he should have reminded them of the Third Degree obligation.

It can be seen that being a Mason, as Detective Chief Superintendent Moody and Detective Chief Inspector Cuthbert were, is no protection against being investigated and jailed for corruption. Furthermore, the involvement of honest officers who were also members of the Craft in the highest echelons of Operation Countryman demonstrates that Masonic police officers can be trusted to act 'without fear or favour' as their constable's oath demands.

55

Worshipful Master, Worshipful Villain: The Silver Bullion Robbery

Masonic Connection
Robbers
Detectives
Informant
Conspiracy theories

Date
1979: Lennie Gibson installed as Master of his lodge
1980: Robbery occurred
1981: Three Masons convicted of armed robbery
1986: Convicted robber returns to his lodge

Connection to London
A13, Barking: Location of offence
Belgrave Close, Oakwood, N14: Hiding place of stolen bullion

Lodges
Edmonton with Chandos No. 4339
Ilford No. 4442
Olympus No. 5488 (erased)
Bishop Ridley No. 6196
Waterways No. 7913 (erased)
James Terry No. 556 (Mark)

If various anti-Masonic sites on the internet are to be believed, then London lodges are awash with villains who use Masonic temples to plan crimes with corrupt Scotland Yard detectives. Such occurrences are, in reality, very rare, but the Silver Bullion Robbery of 1980 is possibly the closest example of possible Masonic collusion between police and criminals. However, the truth is not so clear cut. As we will see, many of those involved in the crime and subsequent investigations were Masons—some good, some bad. This case also reveals the danger of giving too much credence to Masonic conspiracy theories.

Surprisingly, this case has received little attention in recent years despite the robbery yielding more 'loot' than the Great Train Robbery. The case also highlights a case of rather foolish 'Brotherly love', where lodges or relatives paid the membership fees of convicted robbers, welcoming them back after long prison sentences. This brought shame on Freemasonry and supplied ammunition to those who attack it. However, as we will see, the case is not as simple as bad Masons and good non-Masons; as always in life, the facts are far more complex. The robbery occurred during Operation Countryman, the massive enquiry into corruption within the Metropolitan Police's CID. Hence, the crime caused embarrassment for Scotland Yard as well as the United Grand Lodge of England.

Even without the Masonic connections, the Silver Bullion Robbery is worthy of note as a well-planned and audacious crime. On 24 March 1980, the Samuel Montagu merchant bank arranged the transfer of 321 silver ingots, valued at £3.4 million, from London to communist East Germany. The ingots were packed in a large lorry that was to cross to the continent via Tilbury docks. As the lorry drove along the A13 trunk road through Barking in east London, it was flagged down by a uniformed police officer and two Ministry of Transport inspectors, but this was a trick; the uniforms were bogus and it was the start of an armed robbery.

The 'police officer' was, in fact, Micky 'Skinny' Gervaise, a career criminal, but not a member of the Craft. There were, however, Freemasons in the gang that night—most significantly, Worshipful Brother Leonard 'Lennie' Gibson, who was the Master of Waterways Lodge No. 7913 at that time. Gibson had been installed into the Chair of King Solomon in the October of the previous year at the Southgate Masonic Centre. Gibson and Gervaise were aided by two men of Italian descent—Rudolpho 'Dolf' Aguda and his nephew, Renalto 'Ron' Aguda, who were members of the Ilford Lodge No. 4442, which then met at the (now defunct) Clerkenwell Masonic Centre in central London. Dolf and Ron Aguda seemed to have been keen Masons as they were later joining members of Olympus No. 5488—a now erased lodge that met in the temples of Grand Lodge in Great Queen Street.

These brethren certainly met in their various lodges. A check of the lodge records clearly shows inter-visiting between them, with Gibson visiting the Ilford Lodge at nearly every meeting in 1978 and 1979 as a guest of one or other of the Agudas. There were no police officers in this lodge; a check of the records clearly shows this. There were, however, police officers in Waterways lodge, one of whom had been a detective but returned to uniform. Most importantly, there is no evidence that any of these Masonic officers were involved in the crime. Indeed, as we will see, a Masonic villain and later 'super-grass' accused a non-Mason detective of being the corrupt officer who had aided and abetted the criminals.

The lorry driver, believing it to be a routine check—probably on the roadworthiness of the lorry or his driver hours—pulled into the side of the road. Once the vehicle had come to a halt, the bogus police officer (Gervaise) directed the security guards to come to the front of the lorry. The unsuspecting guards were then confronted by the rest of the gang and quickly overpowered. The sight of a pistol and a shotgun were enough to convince them that the robbers meant business. The driver and guards were tied up and dumped in a garage. By the time they had struggled free and escaped, the silver ingots, and the villains, had vanished into the night. This took some effort—the silver weighed about ten tons.

However, the gang did not go to ground. Dolf and Ron Aguda certainly had cheek (or perhaps commitment to Masonry) as a few days after the raid, they turned up to the Lodge of Instruction to practice for a forthcoming meeting. One member of Ilford Lodge recalls that the raid featured heavily in the *London Evening Standard* newspaper and was actually discussed when they were there. No one at that time suspected the brothers of involvement in the robbery.

Meanwhile, at New Scotland Yard, the Flying Squad had been tasked to investigate the crime, find the silver and catch the robbers. The first officer to obtain an important lead on this case was Detective Chief Inspector Tony Lundy. According to Short (1992), the DCI received a tip off from Roy Garner; that is to say Brother Roy Garner of Bishop Ridley No. 6196, a London lodge, naming some of the gang. Garner had been a Mason since 1973, but had never been the Master of the lodge and does not seem to have achieved even the lowly rank of Steward.

Garner was (seemingly) a petty crook, but he was later sentenced to twenty-two years in prison for his part in a cocaine smuggling racket. That said; no police officer receives information on serious crime if he speaks to people at a vicar's tea-party. Garner's career as a 'grass' is well-documented in several books and in 1986, he was also publicly named as an informant in the House of Commons.

Much has also been written about DCI Lundy, who was an expert at using informants and turning hardened villains into 'super-grasses'—criminals who agreed to give evidence against their partners in crime in return for a reduced sentence. His work resulted in hundreds of armed robbers being convicted, but we will never know if he was corrupt or a very successful detective brought down by jealous colleagues at Scotland Yard. He has been the subject of an investigation by 'World in Action' television journalists and several books have been written putting forward both views. We do know, however, that Tony Lundy was not a Freemason. He is described as 'part mean Northerner among flash Cockneys … part Catholic outsider in a largely Masonic culture …' by Short (1993). As a Roman Catholic, he felt unable to join a Lodge. Indeed, he is one of several officers who have subsequently claimed that Masons had conspired to damage his promotion prospects.

Two very senior officers at New Scotland Yard, both Deputy Assistant Commissioners (and both believed to be Masons) had diametrically opposed views of this (non-Mason) officer. Ronald Steventon observed in an official document that, 'It is my belief that Mr Lundy is a corrupt officer, who has long exploited his association with Garner.' On the other hand, David Powis wrote, 'I have the highest regard for … Ronald Steventon. Nevertheless, I did not agree with all he said or wrote. No evidence was forthcoming of any corrupt behaviour by Mr Lundy … I have no doubts about his fundamental integrity' (Short, 1993). DAC Powis also observed the fantastic work rate of DCI Lundy in catching armed robbers, noting 'His industry in operational work…was on the highest plane.'

There is no doubt as to DAC Steventon's lodge membership—he was Worshipful Master of Edmonton Lodge No. 4339 in 1992—but this was far from being the first time that he had

Detective Chief Inspector Tony Lundy, the detective in charge of the Silver Bullion Robbery investigation who believed that a Masonic conspiracy was hindering his promotion.

been installed in the 'Chair of King Solomon'. He was a Grand Officer (Past Assistant Grand Director of Ceremonies) and member of several lodges. Most significantly, in the Royal Arch, he was the Deputy Grand Superintendent in Hertfordshire, second in command of all Chapter Masons. He was also a member of the Mark and Royal Ark Mariner degrees (James Terry Lodge No. 556). It is not so clear regarding DAC Powis. A former senior officer informed the author that he believed Powis was a Freemason. Retired Commander George Churchill-Coleman stated, 'I am a Mason, but I am not sure about David Powis. He always spoke in vague Masonic terms.' Worshipful Brother Churchill-Coleman's extensive Masonic career is described in Chapter 58.

Returning to the investigation into the robbery, Garner had informed DCI Lundy that Gervaise was involved in the silver bullion heist. Here was one villain who was easy to find; he was already being held in custody at Enfield Police Station for other matters. He had been arrested on 18 May for his part in several crimes, including two unrelated robberies where over £1.2 million worth of jewellery had been stolen.

To try to save his own skin, Gervaise had turned 'supergrass', but a key part of the deal of being allowed this status was that a criminal had to clean his own slate. This meant admitting all of his own previous offending and naming those who had also been involved. In return, he would receive a substantially reduced sentence at court. A dirty, but highly effective, tactic to employ against major criminals. Gervaise, however, had not mentioned his involvement in the silver bullion robbery despite confessing to many other burglaries and violent thefts. Perhaps he was hoping that, if he kept his mouth shut, he could still claim his share of the loot (£500,000) once he got out of jail. More importantly, however, is his belief in a Masonic conspiracy. He eventually admitted his involvement, but, when interviewed in Lundy's office, he stated that he was reticent to do so as he believed that the DCI and Lennie Gibson were in the same lodge. Here lies the danger of seeing a Masonic conspiracy when there is none.

However, it must be noted that Lundy was connected to Lennie Gibson, but not through membership of the Craft. Photographs would later surface in the press showing Lundy and Worshipful Brother Gibson, together with Brother Garner, at a social function related to a boxing club, organised by the 'Lady Ratlings' (the female version of the Water Rats charity). The DCI had helped to run the Finchley Amateur Boxing Club in his spare time. As a fitness fanatic, he had seen this as an opportunity to use his skills to divert youngsters from crime. The children of (seemingly petty villains) Gibson and Garner were taught how to box at the club.

Assured of the lack of Masonic links between the investigating officer and the robbers, the 'supergrass' began to inform on his fellow gang members. Worshipful Brother Gibson and his brother Freemasons—the Agudas—were located and held in police cells across north London. Indeed, Gibson and Dolf Aguda had been arrested together after being spotted in a car in east London.

Lundy used his boxing club link with Gibson to get the robber to talk about his involvement in the robbery. He even allowed Gibson and Aguda to speak together—the tactic worked and they agreed to hand back the bullion. On 4 June 1980, nearly three months after the robbery, Gibson led the detectives to a lock-up garage in Belgrave Close, Oakwood, N14 (not far from the penultimate northern stop on the Piccadilly line). The flimsy door was soon broken open with a crowbar and 309 silver ingots were found. They had been concealed behind wooden pallets. In their haste to find the loot, the police had missed an important clue—the key to the garage was on Dolf Aguda's key ring—at the police station. Unfortunately, the fate of the missing twenty-two ingots has never been determined, leading to further accusations of corruption. Another 'supergrass' alleged that Gervaise had arranged for the missing bullion to be smuggled out of the country.

On 5 January 1981, Gibson and the Agudas pleaded guilty to the silver bullion robbery and were sentenced to ten years' imprisonment each, but DCI Lundy's joy was to be short-lived. His grief was to come from another Freemason and, like the Agudas, a member of the Ilford Lodge. Brother William Young had been arrested for a variety of crimes by the Regional Crime Squad and was known as 'Burglar Bill' (perhaps his true profession), although he had described himself as a 'waterman/lighterman' on his lodge application. He also knew members of the Finchley boxing club; he alleged that Lundy was corruptly involved with Lennie Gibson and had arranged for Garner to receive an informant reward, which he was not entitled to. This would lead to ten years of suspicion and investigation into (by now) Detective Superintendent Lundy's conduct. None of the accusations were proved, but mud sticks and Lundy's career would eventually end in ignominy with a medical retirement.

Smith also made allegations against Dave Spicer, a fellow Freemason and friend of Lundy (and Lennie Gibson). Smith claimed that Spicer was a go-between who paid corrupt detectives bribes on behalf of other villains. Smith now vanishes from the scene (and the lodge); as a 'supergrass', that would have been a wise move. He had joined the Craft in June 1979, completed all three degrees within less than a year, but did not hang around long enough to receive his Grand Lodge certificate (usually presented soon after the Third Degree). The Ilford Lodge secretary recorded that he 'went away … and left no forwarding address.' Smith was duly booted out; no one paid Burglar Bill's subscriptions and he was excluded. As we will see, the other Masons involved seemed to have had more friends in their lodges.

Gibson and the Agudas were eventually released, after serving two-thirds of their sentence. Despite their convictions for violent crime, members of their respective lodges had continued to pay their fees and retained them as 'country members'—lodge members can claim this status if they cannot attend many meetings (for example, if they are working abroad) and it reduces their fees.

On 14 October 1986, Worshipful Brother Gibson was welcomed back into the Waterways Lodge. He attended regularly throughout 1987 and 1988, often inviting Ron Aguda as a visitor. Their presence was, however, an embarrassment to Freemasonry. United Grand Lodge took action and excluded them from the Craft. Gibson's last lodge meeting was on 9 May 1989. He did make an impassioned plea for clemency to the Grand Lodge appeal panel, but the exclusion was upheld. Despite being dismissed, his Masonic record did live on, as, until the lodge was closed in 2016, he was shown on the summons as the Worshipful Master for 1979. Gibson also lasted longer in Masonry than Roy Garner, who had started his downfall. Garner was expelled from Masonry in 1982. The Agudas were also thrown out of the Craft.

As was said at the start of this chapter, the idea of a Masonic conspiracy of villains and corrupt detectives is never clear cut. In this case, we have seen very bad Masons—Gibson, the Agudas and 'Burglar Bill' Smith. It has also been shown that the information leading to the arrest of these members of the Craft came from another Mason, Roy Garner, himself a major criminal. Perhaps he recalled the Third Degree obligation that he was not permitted to keep secrets about 'murder, treason, felony and all other offences against the laws of God and established ordinances of the realm'; such 'ordinances' include the Theft Act 1968, which defines robbery as a criminal offence with a maximum sentence of life imprisonment. Perhaps, he was simply thinking about the reward money; this seems more likely.

Of the non-Masons, Tony Lundy has been much maligned without ever being convicted, despite being accused of corruption by criminal Mason (Brother Smith) and a police Mason (Brother Steventon). Then again, he was supported by possible Mason, DAC Powis. Despite Lundy's suspicion of the Craft, it was Commander (and Worshipful Brother) Churchill-Coleman who finally put an end to the investigation into the detective's alleged corruption. By this time, the enquiry had descended into farce, with the only remaining issue being whether Lundy had received a discount on a garden fence.

It has also been shown that even villains fear Masonic conspiracies, when in reality, the link between Gibson and the investigating officer was a boxing club and not a Masonic lodge. There have been no calls for police involvement in amateur boxing to be registered, unlike lodge membership. As has been observed (Short, 1993), Lundy must have been targeting the right villains as nine out of ten armed robbers arrested by his squad admitted their part in the raids. It must also be noted that more than nine out of ten armed robbers are not Freemasons.

56

Masonic Hanging in London?
The Strange Case of Roberto Calvi

Masonic Connection
Dead man
'Physical penalties' from ritual
Members of Italian Masonry

Date
1982: Year of death

Connection to London
Body hanged under Blackfriars Bridge

Lodges
Propaganda Due or 'P2'

The case of Roberto Calvi, an Italian banker and Freemason found dead under Blackfriars Bridge on the edge of the City of London in the 'Square Mile' (a rather Masonic sounding title in itself), has fascinated conspiracy theorists. At his initiation ceremony, every Freemason is informed of the ancient penalty of the First Degree: 'having the throat cut across, your tongue torn about by the root and buried at low water mark at least a cable tow's length from the shore, where the tide regularly ebbs and flows twice in twenty-four hours'. While Calvi's throat had not been slit, he certainly was dangling by the neck by a rope (or perhaps a Masonic 'cable tow') and he was directly above the ebbing and flowing of the River Thames.

Calvi was born in Milan in affluent northern Italy in 1920. He pursued a career in banking and was appointed chairman of the Banco Ambrosiano in 1975. In 1981, while still holding that key role, he was found guilty of transferring large sums of money (nearly $30 billion) out of the country in contravention of financial legislation. He served a short spell in prison where he attempted to commit suicide; this obviously added another theory to the circumstances of his later death. On his release, Calvi (shockingly) resumed his role as bank chairman. This involvement in financial scandals was a far cry from the original

Roberto Calvi, dishonest banker and Freemason who was found hanged in London.

aims of the bank, which had been set up in 1896 and named after Saint Ambrose for the purpose of 'serving moral organisations, pious works, and religious bodies set up for charitable aims.' Having a convicted fraudster in charge can hardly have aided the bank to achieve such aims.

The link with the church was longstanding and Banco Ambrosiano's main shareholder was the 'Institute for Works of Religion', the euphemistic name of the bank owned by the Vatican, the headquarters of the Catholic Church in Rome. In consequence, Calvi became known as 'God's Banker'. There is, however, no evidence of divine inspiration in the bank's fortunes and in June 1982, Banco Ambrosiano collapsed. The collapse was not an accident; over $1 billion had been stolen or siphoned off, leaving the bank with crippling illegal debts. Calvi had tried to warn the Pope (then John Paul II) of the impending financial crisis, but to no avail. The affair was to cost the church over $220 million, which it paid out in 1984 as the Vatican admitted that it had 'moral involvement' in the matter. Calvi may have been trying to save his own skin by warning the Pope. He well knew that a decade before, when the Roman Catholic Church had lost a vast sum due to the collapse of the Franklin Bank, the owner, Michele Sindona, had been found dead in his prison cell; his coffee had been laced with cyanide. The dead bank owner was from Sicily and, of course, he was linked to the Mafia. Calvi and Sindona were also members of the infamous Italian Masonic Lodge 'Propaganda Due' or 'P2'.

This lodge was founded in 1877 in Turin, with the name 'Propaganda Massonica' or 'Masonic Propaganda'; from the start, it was frequented by the rich and powerful in Italy. Its name, however, is not as sinister as it sounds; the word 'propaganda' is now associated with the evil lies of the likes of Dr Goebbels, but the original use of the word comes from the Roman Catholic Church and a section of the Vatican known as 'Congregatio de Propaganda Fide' (which translates as 'Congregation for Propagating the Faith'). This department was also known simply as 'Propaganda'. Its aim was to spread or 'propagate' the Roman Catholic faith in countries requiring 'conversion'. Hence the name of the lodge could be translated as 'Promotion of Freemasonry', which is less sinister.

During the 1930s, the Craft was outlawed in Italy by the fascist dictator, Mussolini, but once the Second World War ended, lodges re-opened, often due to American encouragement. The Grand Orient (the Grand Lodge) of Italy renumbered the lodges as many had fallen by the wayside during the ban, and 'Propaganda' became No. 2 ('due' in Italian) on its roll, and so was known as 'Propaganda Due', or simply 'P2'.

Membership, however, was in decline by the 1960s and there were less than twenty brethren in the lodge. P2 was soon to be reinvigorated by Licio Gelli, a businessman in the textile industry. His key skill seems to have been gaining access to powerful and influential men in politics and business. He joined the lodge in 1964. Coincidentally (or suspiciously, depending on view point) members of P2 called themselves *frati neri* or, in English, 'black friars'; this could have been the reason for the selection of the bridge where Calvi was ultimately found.

By 1971, Gelli had become such a key player in P2, that the Grand Master of the Grand Orient of Italy, Lino Salvini, approached him to take charge and draw new and influential members into the lodge. Gelli then set about converting the lodge into a right-wing group that could counter what was perceived to be a communist threat to the country and beyond (several members were from Latin America). His extreme political beliefs were longstanding: he had fought with Franco's forces during the Spanish Civil War in the 1930s and during the Second World War, he had been a member of the fascist Italian government, working closely with the German Third Reich, particularly Reichmarshall Hermann Goering, head of the Luftwaffe.

The political aim of P2, promoted by Gelli, was completely contrary to the rules of English Freemasonry, where the brethren are not permitted to discuss religion or politics in the lodge. Indeed, the lodge strayed so far away from its original purpose that 'sleeping members' were not even required to take part in Masonic ceremonies or ritual. Gelli paid the subscriptions of these unofficial members in bulk cash payments. Unfortunately in 1972, the United Grand Lodge of England officially recognised the Grand Orient, thereby legitimising its activities in the eyes of the Masonic world and allowing P2 members to attend lodges all over the world.

Masonic concerns about conduct within the lodge came to a head at the Grand Orient in 1974. After enquiries had been made, Gelli was expelled from the Craft and the P2 lodge was (apparently) also 'struck off the roll' so that it was no longer considered part of 'Regular' Italian Freemasonry. Surprisingly (for those unaware of the nature of politics and intrigue in Italy), the lodge was reissued with a warrant by the Grand Master the following year and Gelli was active again, assisting to raise money to aid the election of a new (and more friendly) Grand Master. To add to the confusion, in 1981, the Grand Orient ruled that the 1974 vote to expel Gelli and P2 was in order. Unfortunately, the other brethren of

Propaganda Due were simply allowed to transfer their membership to other lodges, leaving the issue of politically motivated Masons in the Grand Orient unresolved.

The Italian authorities were alerted to the activities of the Propaganda Due lodge in 1981, when they were investigating the activities of Sindona, the Mafia-linked bank boss. A police raid on Gelli's house found a list of nearly one thousand P2 members. This contained details of government officials, politicians (including a member of the cabinet), generals, and admirals from the Italian and Argentinian armed forces, senior officers in the Italian Secret Service, and even a member of the deposed Italian royal family. Perhaps most notably, both Calvi and the infamous former Italian Prime Minister, Silvio Berlusconi, were shown on the roll of P2 brethren; this caused such a scandal that the Italian government fell in May of that year.

On 11 June 1982, Calvi vanished from his apartment in Rome, with his bank on the verge of collapse. He had been due to stand trial for further banking offences. Six days later, the bank relieved him of his position and within hours of this decision, his personal secretary was found dead—she had apparently fallen from a window of the bank offices. Whether she was assisted in falling to her death remains unclear; the official verdict was suicide. What is certain, however, is that one week after leaving Rome, Calvi arrived in London. His journey from Italy to England has all the hallmarks of a complex spy novel, like much of this tale. He had used several false identities on his travels, which had taken him around Europe, travelling by planes, cars, and even a speed boat. Later enquiries revealed that he had stayed in hotels in Zurich, Amsterdam, and Edinburgh, or had been concealed in private residences. He eventually flew from Innsbruck in Austria to England and arrived, posing as an executive of the Fiat motor car company. Just before his death, he was staying in a room in the Chelsea Cloisters hotel in west London. There he maintained a very low profile; during his time in the English capital, he remained almost completely out of sight.

This invisibility was to end. On the morning of 18 June, a postman found his body hanging from temporary scaffolding underneath Blackfriars Bridge. The river had certainly 'ebbed and flowed' during this time, as when his body was found, his feet were under water. When he was cut down by police officers from New Scotland Yard's Thames Division (River Police), they found several bricks (possibly representing 'fallen masonry') and a large quantity of cash in British, Swiss, and Italian currency stuffed in his pockets (and more bizarrely, in his fly). If there was a murderer involved, he certainly was not interested in robbery. A false passport on the body gave the name 'Gian Roberto Calvi', close enough to his true identity for the police to identify him.

The *post-mortem* examination revealed that he had died as a result of asphyxiation by hanging. His neck had not been broken and it appeared his fall had been broken by hitting the water. No evidence of foul play was established. No physical injuries could be found and it therefore appeared that he had not been restrained or forced into hanging himself, nor were there any traces of suspicious drugs or chemicals in the body.

Calvi's expensive (but not waterproof) watch had stopped at 1.52 a.m.; calculations conducted regarding the length of the rope and tide times for the river appear to confirm this as the approximate time of death.

The first coroner's inquest in the City of London, held in the month after his death, recorded a verdict of 'suicide', but this decision was met with much shock, especially in

Blackfriars Bridge: the arch with the footway was the site of Roberto Calvi's death. This is also where Percy Lefroy Mapleton disposed of Isaac Gold's watch.

his native Italy. It appeared highly unlikely that Calvi could have killed himself in such a bizarre manner. At the time of his death, he was sixty-two years old. To hang himself would have taken the skills of a youthful acrobat, able to climb ladders, swing across several pieces of scaffolding, and put his head in a noose while operating in darkness, with bricks filling his pockets and trousers. There was also no evidence of abrasions to his hands, rust under his fingernails or damage to his clothing, which would have indicated such a trapeze-act style ascent of a London bridge.

At the High Court in London, the Calvi family's demand for a new inquest was granted. In consequence, in July 1983, a second hearing was convened to decide on the mode of death and this time the jury decided on an 'open verdict', meaning that they were unsure of the cause of death; it could have been murder or suicide. Police enquiries in England drew a blank. It could not even be established how he travelled from his Chelsea hotel to the scene of his death. It would appear, however, that he had intended to move again; a search of his hotel room revealed two suitcases packed and ready to go.

If Calvi had been murdered, there were a number of suspects. The Mafia, the Vatican, and the powerful brethren of the P2 lodge may all have had reason to kill him. Members of all three groups had lost vast sums of money due to the collapse of Calvi's bank. The investigation into the death took a positive turn in the summer of 1991, some nine years after the body had been found. The Italian Police received information from a Mafia informer that the order to murder Calvi had been made by a Godfather, Giuseppe Calo, and the Venerable Master of the P2 lodge, Licio Gelli. The informant added that the actual killing was carried out by two members of the Camorra, the Mafia-style organisation based around Naples. They in turn had been murdered, no doubt to ensure that their silence was assured.

Enquiries rumbled on and six years after this information had been obtained, the Italian authorities further implicated several other dubious businessmen and Mafia-style criminals in the death. Calvi's body was exhumed in December 1998, as his family continued to insist that he had been murdered, but this revealed no new evidence. By 2003, now twenty-one years into the enquiry, prosecutors in Rome announced that in their view, Calvi had been murdered to prevent him blackmailing members of the Mafia, the 'Institute of Religious Works', and of course, the P2 lodge.

In a further twist, in 2005, Gelli was formally informed that the Italian police were treating him as a suspect in relation to the murder of Calvi. Here we have the Master of the P2 lodge accused of killing one of the brethren. In the end, Gelli was not charged, but in October 2005, five men, including at least one Mafia member, appeared in a secure court in Rome on charges of murdering 'God's Banker'. Unsurprisingly, given the web of intrigue surrounding the case, all were acquitted, much to the anger of the Calvi family. So, the strange death of this Italian Freemason remains unsolved.

The law did, however, catch up with Venerable Master Gelli, the linchpin of the P2 lodge. He was jailed for his part in the Banco Ambrosiano collapse. He was also found guilty of 'obstructing justice' in relation to the investigation into the deaths of eighty-five people in the bombing of the Bologna railway station in 1980. Devious as ever, he escaped from a Swiss prison and spent time in South America and France, but he was extradited back to Italy in 1998. He has since told journalists 'I will die a fascist'.

The crimes committed by Gelli, the suspicious manner of Calvi's death, and the existence of the P2 lodge are, no doubt, stains on the Craft. We are unlikely to ever know how Calvi died, but the assassins are likely to be part of an unholy alliance of the Grand Orient of Italy, the Vatican, and the Mafia. This is an unlikely combination, as since 1738, when Pope Clement XII issued his 'bull' against the 'depraved and perverted societies of Freemasons', the Roman Catholic Church and the Craft have been at loggerheads and the church Inquisition have punished and tortured those who are Freemasons.

If nothing else, the Calvi affair proves that (in Italy and elsewhere) the allure of money and power can overcome all theological differences. Calvi was one of the money lenders in the (Masonic) temple and The Vatican. He paid a terrible price for involving himself in this Italian financial skulduggery and it all came to an end with his odd death under Blackfriars Bridge in the City of London.

57

Evil Man, Evil Criminal, Evil Freemason: Brother Kenneth Noye

Masonic Connection
Career criminal and murderer
Police officers

Date
1980: Noye initiated into Freemasonry
1986: Noye acquitted of murdering a police officer
2000: Noye convicted of 'road rage' murder

Connection to London
Old Bailey: Trials occurred at this court

Lodges
Sydney No. 829
Hammersmith No. 2090 (erased)
Manor of Bensham No. 7114
Manor of St James's No. 9179

Kenneth Noye was a career criminal, vicious killer, and Freemason, but many have questioned how this evil man came to join a fraternity whose 'Grand Principles' are 'brotherly love, relief and truth'. This will be explored in this chapter and the truth revealed for the first time. It should also be noted that not all Masons linked to this case are evil or corrupt. As we shall see, the most senior police officer involved in the Brinks Mat robbery investigation was a Mason, but his input was to aid solving the crime, not covering it up. It will also be shown that while Noye attempted to use a Masonic handshake to influence a police officer, his efforts had no impact on the detective (also a Mason) who continued to do his duty.

Noye was born in 1947 into a hard-working family in Bexleyheath in South East London. His parents both worked—his father had served in the Royal Navy in the Second World War—and his criminal career would have seemed very unlikely as he grew up in this quiet part of the capital on the outskirts of Kent. However, at an early age, he set on the path that

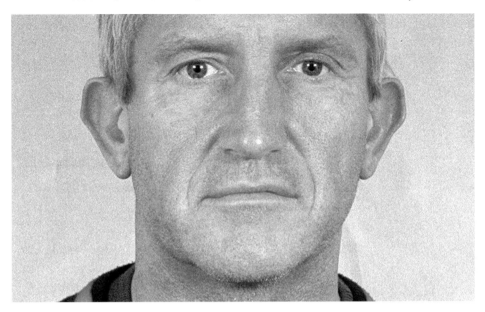

Kenneth Noye, Mason and vicious criminal.

would lead him to a life of crime and lengthy prison sentences. Possibly the first indication of his dishonesty was when he was found with money stuffed into his Wellington boots. He had stolen it from the till in the shop where his mother was employed. Noye was just five years old. By the time he was a teenager, he was running a 'protection racket' at school, demanding money with menaces from fellow pupils and was making further cash by selling stolen bicycle parts. He was also selling programmes at the local greyhound track— legitimate employment for a teenager—but the track attracted local villains and Noye was to find kindred spirits. He also had a violent streak and he soon established that violence could help him to achieve his aim to become very rich.

When still a teenager, he had his first taste of prison. He had moved up to dealing in stolen motor vehicle parts, but he was arrested and convicted of handling stolen goods. The Magistrate sentenced Noye to twelve months' imprisonment in a borstal (young offender prison) in Wiltshire. Noye would learn more from his fellow inmates and would hone his skills as a 'fence', the nickname for a criminal who receives and trades in stolen items.

As an adult, Noye moved to West Kingsdown, a quiet north Kent village, and established a haulage firm that would provide cover for his dishonest activities. Despite living in the countryside, he still felt drawn to south London, especially around the Old Kent Road, where his family had originated. This was a hot bed of villains, especially armed robbers; it should be recalled that many of the Great Train Robbers came from south of the Thames. It is alleged that he made money by informing on other criminals, bringing him into contact with Metropolitan Police detectives—some hard-working officers intent on catching villains and some as dishonest as Noye.

With businesses, criminal and legitimate, booming, Noye was able to buy a bigger plot of land in the village. The dilapidated bungalow (suspiciously) burnt down shortly after

Noye moved in and the insurance money helped to pay for a Mock-Tudor ten-bedroomed mansion, complete with swimming pool. He endeared himself to locals by making donations to local good causes and allowing the Scouts to use the pool. The youngsters, however, had to return to the Scout hut and be collected by their parents from there. Noye did not want anyone nosing around 'Hollywood Cottage' as he had named his home.

The haulage business was sold for a vast profit and Noye started to trade in gold. He started to import Krugerrand coins from South Africa, well aware that by melting them down and selling them on, he could avoid paying Valued Added Tax (VAT) and make more money. This is the start of his love of this precious metal. His criminality spread to other areas; he illegally imported a gun from the United States and received a further conviction for handling in 1977.

Despite his previous convictions and his ever-expanding criminal activities, Noye found time to join the Hammersmith Lodge No. 2090 on 10 January 1980, which at the time met at the Star and Garter Hotel, Kew Bridge Road in Brentford, West London, a long way from West Kingsdown. The minutes of the lodge record, 'Mr Kenneth James Noye being within hail and properly prepared was admitted to the mysteries and privileges of ancient Freemasonry.' The Charge was delivered by a Brother Price. The newly made Mason obviously did not pay attention to the section relating to 'paying due obedience to the laws of any state, which may become the place of your residence.'

On the subject of Noye's involvement in Masonry, Clarkson (2006) stated, 'According to one police source inside the Freemasons, Noye's membership was actually proposed and seconded by policemen'. An internet site embellishes this further, noting that Noye, 'later rose up the ranks to become Master of the Lodge. A sizable proportion of this lodge was made up of Police Officers. Even though his notorious past as an underworld gangster was well known to them. There were also a sizeable number of gold bullion dealer members of this lodge.' Unfortunately for conspiracy theorists, this is not the case and the facts are somewhat at variance to their bold statements, in particular:

Proposal into the lodge: Noye was proposed and seconded by Peter Green and Francis Kenny, two scrap metal dealers from Wembley, not police officers.

Lodge made up of gold bullion dealers: in addition to the scrap metal dealers Green and Kenny, the lodge in 1980 had the feel of a working men's club, with the membership consisting of several builders and taxi drivers, together with a dairy manager, a bank official, and an electrical tool repairer. There were certainly no traders in valuable metals.

Lodge made up of police officers: there was only one member who was a police officer and he was a sergeant in the British Transport Police. Unless Noye was considering becoming a train robber, this officer (even if corrupt) was of little use to him. On the night of his initiation, a Metropolitan Police officer was present as a guest of another member and there is no evidence of any link to Noye.

Lodge aware of Noye's 'notorious past as an underworld gangster': the lodge would have had no reason to suspect that Noye's occupation, as shown on his application form, was incorrect—he described himself as a 'haulage contractor'. As described above, when he joined the Craft, Noye had a juvenile conviction for stealing car parts and adult convictions for handling stolen goods and illegally importing a gun. While the lodge could have challenged these matters (if he declared them), they hardly make him a 'gangster' and such convictions do not amount to a 'notorious past'.

Master of the Lodge: Noye never achieved any rank in the lodge, not even the lowest rank of Steward, who serves wine at the Festive Board.

So, the truth of his Masonic career is revealed. Efforts to confirm these details took some time as the secretary of Hammersmith Lodge died in 2012, quickly followed by his wife, leaving one hundred years of minutes and records in the loft of their home in Hither Green, south London. As the author found when he visited the new owners, all these documents had been thrown into a skip when the house was renovated and lost forever. Fortunately, another member of the lodge had retained copies of the documentation from the relevant period.

Moving back to Noye's criminal enterprises, in 1981, he spread his wings, setting up a business in the Netherlands to trade in gold, which was imported from Kuwait and then melted down to disguise its origins. As ever, it was then sold on for vast profit; next came gold from Brazil. Within a year, Noye was running an international smuggling operation, working with the American Mafia, which was making him £3 million per year. As his villainy became international, his interest in Masonry quickly waned; Noye was Passed to the Second Degree and Raised to the Third in the first year of joining, but once presented with his Grand Lodge Certificate in March 1981, he became an irregular attender. These certificates are not unusual; they are presented to all Master Masons when they have completed all three degrees.

Now to the robbery that would result in much Scotland Yard interest in Noye's activities. During the early morning of 26 November 1983, a gang of armed robbers raided the Brinks Mat security depot near Heathrow Airport. They had been aided by an employee who gave them access to the premises. The Metropolitan Police soon established that the corrupt employee was the brother-in-law of career villain, Brian Robinson. The gang of robbers on that day included Robinson and 'Mad' Micky McAvoy, both of whom would later be found guilty and given long prison sentences. Noye had no involvement in the raid at this stage.

To obtain the codes to the vaults, the ruthless robbers poured petrol on the genitals of one of the guards and threatened to shoot him. The gang had expected to find £3 million in cash. They had struck lucky: there were also large quantities of diamonds and travellers' cheques and, most importantly, £26 million in bullion—nearly seven thousand bars of gold. The handling of this vast stolen horde of precious metal needed an expert, and Kenneth Noye was the ideal man.

The key witness in the case was the corrupt employee who soon broke under interrogation and told the police all he knew about the robbers. Scotland Yard detectives were mindful that if he was sent to prison to await trial, he could be 'persuaded' to change his evidence by associates of the gang who were already serving sentences for other matters. Hence, a successful application was made to detain the corrupt security guard in police cells until the trial. The most senior officer involved in this decision was Assistant Commissioner Gilbert Kelland, a Freemason and founder member of the Manor of St James's Lodge

No. 9179. Kelland was a thoroughly honest officer who ruthless purged dishonest officers, Masons or not. Hence, a key individual in ensuring that the robbers were brought to justice was a member of the Craft. Brother Kenneth had also attended his last Masonic meeting; he was not seen at Hammersmith Lodge after January 1984.

With the vast amount of gold missing, police attention was soon drawn to Noye. This was to lead to tragic results. On 26 January 1985, as part of an undercover operation against Noye, two police officers, including DC John Fordham (who was not a Mason), crept into the grounds of Hollywood Cottage to carry out surveillance. Unfortunately, Noye's guard dogs alerted their master, leading to Noye, his wife, and his criminal associate, Brian Reader, confronting DC Fordham. The officer was found with ten stab wounds. Noye was arrested and charged with murder. Disappointingly, given the officer's injuries, at the Old Bailey trial, he was to be found not guilty after claiming self-defence. The force used to justify such a defence is supposed to be 'reasonable'—how this can mean stabbing a man so many times is unclear. When the verdict was announced, Noye thought not of the dead man's widow and children, but rather mouthed vulgar comments at the investigation team.

Despite the acquittal, Noye was kept in custody. During the search of his home after the killing of DC Fordham, gold bars had been found near a garage, connecting him with the Brinks Mat raid. Noye's incarceration was to cost the Hammersmith Lodge. His attendance at formal meetings had ceased, but he did, however, like to attend Ladies' Festivals— large dinner dance parties where he could show off to friends and, as they would say in London, be 'flash'. Unfortunately, the lodge Ladies' Night fell after Noye was put in prison on remand. The twenty places booked by him had to be paid for; the other members had to cover the debt.

Proof of his lowly status in the lodge was found by dog handler Police Constable Jim Gillett of Kent Police, who was a Master Mason at the time (and is still a member of a Kent lodge). During a search of Noye's home, PC Gillett found a Masonic apron identical to his own—light blue with three rosettes. This clearly shows that Noye had not been the Worshipful Master of his lodge. Jim Gillett was not the only Mason involved in the search of Noye's residence. DS (later Chief Inspector) Neil Johnstone also took part. He later became a high-ranking officer in the Holy Royal Arch in Kent. Again, his concern was the administration of justice; whether Noye was a Freemason was an irrelevance.

The subsequent trial in May 1986, again at the Old Bailey, resulted in Brother Noye being found guilty of handling the stolen bullion and VAT fraud; just like Al Capone, while he was not convicted of murder, he was found guilty of tax offences. The sentence was severe— thirteen years' imprisonment. This vile man and Freemason had not helped himself. When found guilty, he had told the jury 'I hope you all die of cancer.' The judge, no doubt, took that comment into account. A few months later, he received an additional four years in jail as he had been found guilty of handling stolen china ornaments, which had been stolen from the home of the tenth Earl of Darnley. There is a Masonic twist to this tale: the second Earl had been Grand Master in 1737.

The co-defendant in the china case was Micky Lawson, a fellow Freemason who had visited the Hammersmith Lodge as a guest of Noye. Lawson was a member of Sydney Lodge No. 829 in Sidcup, Kent, not far from West Kingsdown. While he was acquitted of the charge of assisting Noye to handle the stolen ornaments, justice would eventually catch up with Lawson. He was later jailed for twelve years for his part in a massive cannabis smuggling conspiracy.

While serving his sentence, Noye decided to focus on a different type of criminal enterprise. Drugs were a far easier and more lucrative commodity than gold and even while in open prison, he was establishing himself as a major dealer in the new substance called ecstasy. He was aided in his work by the corrupt detective, DS John Donald, who warned Noye of any interest from investigators, home or abroad, including the US Drugs Enforcement Agency. While Noye's drug dealing career may have been moving forward, his Masonic career was not. In 1989, while in Swaleside Prison on the Isle of Sheppey in Kent, he was informed by the United Grand Lodge of England that he had been expelled from Freemasonry. Noye's membership of the Craft had come to an end, but he would still attempt to use the 'secrets' of Masonry for his own ends, as we shall see.

Noye was released in the summer of 1994, having served just eight years of the thirteen-year sentence. It was not, however, going all his way. Loss adjusters forced him to hand over £3 million, which their investigations had linked to the Brinks Mat bullion. Never one to be short of money for long, he made up much of this lost cash by importing large amounts of cheap ecstasy from the Netherlands, where he still had criminal contacts from his gold trading days.

His freedom to move around England would soon end and once again, a knife (and his violent temper) would play a role, as it did with the death of DC Fordham. Noye became involved in a 'road rage' incident at the M25 and M20 interchange near Swanley in Kent on 19 May 1996. The other car was driven by Danielle Cable, a nineteen-year-old girl who was with her fiancé, Stephen Cameron. On the roundabout, a fight took place between Noye and Cameron, a much younger man. Possibly because he was about to lose face and be beaten, Noye pulled a knife and killed his opponent; this was all witnessed by Miss Cable who was to be the critical witness at the subsequent trial.

Noye fled the scene and within hours, he had flown to France by helicopter; he then made his way to Spain. The vehicle he had been driving at the time of the murder, a Land Rover Discovery, had been crushed in a scrapyard by a criminal associate. Noye also spent time in Northern Cyprus, but eventually used various out-of-the-way villas in southern Spain to evade arrest. When he was located, Danielle Cable was flown to Spain to identify him as the man who had murdered her fiancé. This undercover procedure (she and the detectives pretended to be tourists) took place in a pizzeria in an inland Spanish village where Noye had been spotted. The identification would have been difficult; Noye had dyed his hair and paid a plastic surgeon to change his nose. He was not arrested at that moment and further enquiries had to be made, but the British police, aided by Spanish anti-terrorism officers (all were mindful of the death of DC Fordham) finally arrested him outside a restaurant in the town of Barbate.

After much legal wrangling, Noye was finally extradited back to England on 20 May 1999 and arrived in back in familiar territory—Dartford. It was almost three years to the day since the murder of Stephen Cameron. When questioned at the local police station, his initial ploy was to deny everything, while at the same time trying to control and manipulate the investigating officers. As retired DCI Tony Brightwell of the Flying Squad (and a Freemason at the time, now lapsed) recalled about his dealings with Noye, 'As soon as I walked in the interview room and saw Noye he came towards me to shake my hand, which I immediately recognised as the handshake of a Freemason. And I formed the opinion that here was a man that was showing out to me in hope that I was a fellow Mason that would help him.' Here, the Masonic handshake went against Noye; DCI Brightwell was a man of integrity. He knew that Mason or not, Noye was a vicious criminal.

In March 2000, Noye returned to the Old Bailey. Again charged with murder, he used his all too familiar tactic—pleading self-defence. He would tell the court that Stephen Cameron was a younger and bigger opponent and so he had to use the knife. This time not all the jury were so easily convinced and on 13 April, Noye was found guilty by a majority verdict of 11–1. The sentence was mandatory—life imprisonment—and the former Freemason cannot apply for parole until 2018. The verdict was welcomed by many, including the family of DC Fordham as well as the family of Stephen Cameron. Just as the United Grand Lodge of England wanted rid of Noye, many South London criminals were also glad that he was off the streets. A violent criminal, who kills a police officer, brings lots of unwanted attention from the 'Old Bill'.

As with the Great Train Robbery, the Brinks Mat raid is further proof (if any was ever needed) that 'the love of money is the root of all evil'. It is estimated that in the thirty years since the crime occurred at Heathrow Airport, more than twenty people connected to it are dead. This includes Train Robber Charlie Wilson, who was assassinated by criminals in Spain, where he was using the proceeds of the Brinks Mat robbery to finance a drug dealing empire. The list of the dead also contains the name of Worshipful Brother Alan 'Taffy' Holmes, who in 1987 was Master of the Manor of Bensham Lodge No. 7114, which meets at Croydon. Worshipful Brother Holmes was a Detective Constable who had served on the Brinks Mat investigation team and was being interviewed by the Metropolitan Police complaints branch regarding links between Noye and the police. DC Holmes shot himself in his garden.

Despite Noye being 'on the square', Masonic police officers from the highest ranks to the lowest played their parts in bringing Noye to justice; amongst them Assistant Commissioner Kelland, DCI Brightwell, DS Johnstone and PC Gillett. Unfortunately for the conspiracy theorists, all these Masons did their police duty and ensured that Brother Noye was sent to prison. The Hammersmith Lodge closed in February 2016, due to lack of membership. The last link between Noye and Masonry has finally gone, but the truth of his involvement in the Craft has at last been told.

58

The Scotland Yard Swindler: Surrey Mason and Scottish Laird

Masonic Connection
Fraudster
Senior police officer
Judge

Date
1995: Trial held

Connection to London
New Scotland Yard: Fraud committed within the headquarters of the Metropolitan Police
Old Bailey: Court where tried and convicted

Lodges
Methuen No. 631
Herschel No. 1894
Guildhall No. 3116
Buckinghamshire Masters No. 3305
Old Harrovian No. 4653
Guildford No. 5443
South West Surrey Masters No. 5965
Oxshott No. 7622
Castlemartyr No. 8420
Claydon No. 9178
Manor of St James's No. 9179
Andredesleah No. 9423 (erased)
Methuen Chapter No. 631 (Holy Royal Arch)
Addington Chapter No. 1787 (Holy Royal Arch)
Wineslai Chapter No. 2435 (Holy Royal Arch)
Richard Eve Chapter No. 2772 (Holy Royal Arch)

The decommissioned New Scotland Yard in Victoria, with its revolving triangular sign, was one of the most famous police buildings in the world, but lurking within the administrative offices in the early 1990s was a fraudster who was defrauding the Metropolitan Police out of millions of pounds. The man involved was a Mason. If the conspiracy theorists are correct, this crime should have been covered up by Masonic senior officers and judges; the truth is somewhat different.

Throughout the ages, detectives have paid criminal informants for information—a dirty but essential business that helps to bring many serious offenders before the courts. It is also a very secretive area of police work as a leak could result in an informant being seriously beaten or even killed by other criminals. In consequence, the fewer people knowing any details of informants, the better. Tony Williams, a senior administrator in the Metropolitan Police, was to take advantage of this situation. As Deputy Director of Finance at Scotland Yard, he was authorised to sign cheques for large sums of money to pay informants and only his signature was required. Fertile ground for embezzlement, if the man holding the cheque book is dishonest. Williams was a Freemason, being a member of Oxshott Lodge No. 7622, which met at Surbiton in Surrey.

Unknown to his colleagues in the police (or lodge), Brother Williams was living a double life. In England, he lived a seemingly uneventful existence in the London suburbs. In Scotland, however, he (literally, as Londoners might say) 'lorded it about' as Lord Williams of Tomintoul. A title that he had purchased, unbeknown to the local people, with his ill-gotten gains.

Tomintoul is a small village in the Highlands and the local people were thrilled when an 'aristocrat' arrived and spent a fortune on local properties, including the Gordon Hotel with its twenty-nine bedrooms. He also established a company, 'Tomintoul Enterprises', through which he purchased a restaurant, other businesses, and several residential properties. To emphasise his status, Williams also invested in the local country club, which was even used by the Royal Family. Lord Williams or 'the Laird' was even more popular when his investment resulted in employment for some forty residents of the local area. Unfortunately, it was all based on fraud. The swindling finance director had stolen over £4 million from the Scotland Yard accounts to finance his exotic Scottish lifestyle.

An investigation was launched and the Fraud Squad (not having far to travel) established that money was being syphoned away from the Yard by one of its own employees; Williams was soon identified as the culprit. This information was passed to a senior Mason and senior officer at Scotland Yard—Commander George Churchill-Coleman OBE QPM, who had recently been appointed as head of the Anti-Terrorist Squad. Worshipful Brother George was also an Assistant Provincial Grand Master in Surrey and a member of four Surrey lodges—Guildford No. 5443, South West Surrey Masters No. 5965, Castlemartyr No. 8420, and Andredesleah No. 9423. He was also a founder member of the much-maligned Metropolitan Police lodge, the Manor of St James's No. 9179. According to Short (1993), this lodge is the epitome of Masonic police corruption. We have already seen a challenge to this view as two of the most senior officers who tackled corruption in the Metropolitan Police were members of this lodge—Assistant Commissioner Gilbert Kelland and Deputy Assistant Commissioner Ron Steventon. Worshipful Brother Churchill-Coleman was also going to demonstrate that Freemasons could deal ruthlessly with other members of the Craft who have committed crime.

In August 1994, the Commander ordered the arrest of 'Lord' Williams, taking umbrage at the detective sergeant (who knew his Masonic rank) who asked 'Guv'nor, do you know he is a Mason?' He informed the author that his answer was 'I don't care who he is, get him arrested.' Williams was brought into custody, charged with fraud, and bailed to appear at court.

His trial was to be held at that most famous of courts—the Old Bailey. As we have seen throughout this book, several Masons have been tried and convicted at this courthouse, including murderers Frederick Seddon. As with Seddon, Williams would appear before a very senior Mason. The trial judge on this occasion was Right Worshipful Brother Sir Lawrence Verney, at the time the Deputy Provincial Grand Master of Buckinghamshire.

His Honour Mr Justice Verney, a senior Mason who was less than impressed when Brother Tony Williams made Masonic signs at his trial.

He was also the Recorder of London, the most senior judge at the Old Bailey. Sir Lawrence was a very active Mason, being a member of several London and Buckinghamshire lodges, including Methuen No. 631, Herschel No. 1894, Guildhall No. 3116, Buckinghamshire Masters No. 3305, Old Harrovian No. 4653, and Claydon No. 9178. He was also a dedicated Royal Arch Mason and a companion in several Chapters: Methuen No. 631, Addington No. 1787, Wineslai No. 2435, and Richard Eve No. 2772.

In May 1995, Commander Churchill-Coleman was present at the trial and witnessed Williams give several Masonic signs directed at the judge. Sir Lawrence was less than impressed. He informed the senior police officer that he had also recognised the defendant's efforts to use Masonry in an attempt to secure an acquittal. This had failed and Williams was sentenced to over seven years' imprisonment. In consequence, he was also dismissed from the Craft.

As with Worshipful Brother Churchill-Coleman, Judge Verney was a great servant to Freemasonry. In addition to his provincial duties, Sir Lawrence also simplified and tightened up Masonic disciplinary procedures. He ensured that brethren convicted of crime could not slip back into their lodges by temporarily resigning before being formally dismissed.

Despite all the suggestions of the detractors of the Craft, this is yet another case where the Masons involved in the investigation of crime and dispensing of justice acted in accordance with the law. 'Lord Williams', the fraudster and dishonest Mason, was swiftly arrested and properly sentenced for his crimes despite his efforts to influence the judge with 'secret signs'.

59

Conclusions

Lodges

Temple No. 101
York No. 236
Lodge of Friendship No. 750
Royal Edward No. 1088
Beauchamp No. 1422
Albert Lucking No. 2717
Lodge of Newton No. 3024
Duchy of Cornwall No. 3038
Paddington No. 3267
Acacia No. 3436
Woolwich Polytechnic No. 3578
Connaught Army and Navy No. 4323
Archbishop Tenison No. 5163
Liberty No. 5573
East Surrey Masters No. 5888
Tilehurst No. 6526
Radlett No. 6652
New Jubilee No. 7056
Torkington No. 7359
County Gate No. 7849
Richard of Bordeaux No. 8333
Stockport Lodge of Installed Masters No. 9562 (erased)
Chapter of Newton No. 3024 (Holy Royal Arch)
Connal Wilson Chapter No. 9171 (Holy Royal Arch)

This book asks the question: 'Is there a link between Freemasonry and crime?' Throughout the previous chapters, Masonic connections to nearly every famous (and infamous) criminal deed and scandal that has occurred in Britain have been highlighted. It has been shown that there are, no doubt, villains who have been Freemasons, but time and time again, dishonest and wicked members of the Craft have been punished for their crimes, even when appearing before judges who are also 'on the square'.

Perhaps the starkest example is Brother Frederick Seddon, who was sentenced to death by Right Worshipful Brother His Honour Sir Thomas Bucknill, despite the convicted poisoner giving Masonic signs to the judge at the Old Bailey. This is not as isolated case. Wall Street Crash creator, Brother Clarence Hatry, was handed a long jail sentence with hard labour by Brother Sir Horace Avory, who may also have ordered the execution of Irish Nationalist (and possible Mason) Sir Roger Casement. Fraudsters Brother John Poulson and Brother Tony Williams were not just sentenced to imprisonment by a Masonic judge, they were also investigated by a police officer who was a Mason. Being a Mason also did not help Brother Oscar Wilde nor Brother Kenneth Noye. In earlier times, being the Grand Master of Scotland was of no benefit to the Earl of Kilmarnock when he was found guilty of treason and had his head chopped off, nor the Grand Chaplain, the Reverend William Dodd, who was convicted of fraud in less enlightened times than Poulson or Hatry. Dodd had to dangle from a noose on the 'Tyburn Tree' until he was dead, rather than spend several years locked in a cell.

It has been claimed on the internet that the infamous serial killer, Dr Harold Shipman, was a Mason. Some sites go so far as to name a lodge (Liberty No. 5573), but the members of that Lancashire lodge (and indeed, Freemasonry in general) are being besmirched as there is no record whatsoever of the murderous doctor ever joining the Craft. What is clear, however, is that the detective inspector responsible for arresting and charging Shipman certainly was a member of the Craft. The officer in question was Stan Egerton, who became a very active Mason after his initiation into Torkington Lodge No. 7359. He later joined several other Cheshire lodges—Royal Edward No. 1088, Stockport Lodge of Installed Masters No. 9562 (now defunct), and Lodge of Newton No. 3024—as well as two Holy Royal Arch Chapters—Chapter of Newton No. 3024 and Connal Wilson No. 9171. Brother Egerton endured much abuse in the early stages of the murder enquiry as many people in the town of Hyde believed that Dr Shipman was innocent. The detective inspector demonstrated great strength of character in persisting with the enquiry and ensuring that the awful truth was revealed; he was a credit to Freemasonry.

Arguably, most positively for the Craft, the investigation of crime and use of forensic evidence throughout the world has been influenced by the work of two scientists, who were also Masons—Sir Bernard Spilsbury and Dr William Willcox. These two members of the Craft brought forensic science out of the shadows and developed techniques and systems still used today, especially in the investigation of murder and other serious crimes. Some of the most famous and innovative police officers of their day have also been Masons; this has included:

Inspector Dick Tanner: the first officer to bear the accolade 'of the Yard' and may have been the inspiration for Sherlock Holmes.
Sergeant Charles Collins: the first detective to use fingerprint evidence to solve a murder.
Chief Inspector Walter Dew: the officer who pursued Dr Crippen across the Atlantic.

Detective Chief Inspectors Fred Wensley and Walter Hambrook: the founders of the Flying Squad.

Detective Superintendent 'Nipper' Read: the tenacious detective who brought the Kray Twins to justice.

Deputy Assistant Commissioner Ernie Bond OBE QPM: a founder member of the Army's SAS and the first 'Commander X' or head of Scotland Yard's Bomb Squad, which was later renamed the Anti-Terrorist Squad. A very active Mason, he was a member of Woolwich Polytechnic Lodge No. 3578, Connaught Army and Navy No. 4323, and Richard of Bordeaux No. 8333.

Assistant Commissioner Gilbert Kelland: the head of the anti-corruption unit at New Scotland Yard, who ensured that fellow Mason, Detective Chief Superintendent Bill Moody, was sent to prison for receiving bribes.

Commander George Churchill-Coleman: head of the Anti-Terrorist Squad who also showed no 'fear of favour' when dealing with swindling Masons, John Poulson and Tony Williams.

Detective Sergeant Norwell Roberts: the first black officer, who served in the Metropolitan Police. He endured a vicious campaign of bullying on joining, but served his full thirty years and was awarded the Queen's Police Medal. Norwell informed the author that he received a much warmer welcome in Masonry than he did in the police! Norwell is a member of Beauchamp Lodge No. 1422 and Radlett No. 6652, as well as being active in many other Masonic Orders.

Detective Chief Inspector Brian Bowden-Brown: a pioneer of 'cold case' reviews using Low Copy DNA to identify offenders for previously unsolved serious cases. This detective brought to justice Michael Roberts, known as the 'Beast of Bermondsey', who burgled and raped elderly victims in their south London homes. Brian is a member of Albert Lucking Lodge No. 2717 in Essex and County Gate No. 7849 in Kent.

Senior Scenes of Crime Officer Nick Mitchell of Surrey Police was instrumental in obtaining the first conviction in the world using 'Familial DNA' in 2004 as a result of him recovering a brick thrown through a lorry windscreen. The driver had died and the brick was submitted to the Forensic Science Laboratory for DNA analysis. Despite the offender not being found on the DNA database, he was identified by similarities to a relative's genetic profile. Nick is a member of York Lodge No. 236.

Even the author, as Detective Chief Inspector Neville, can claim to have introduced the use of 'Super Recognisers' into the police and made the use of images, such as CCTV, the third forensic discipline to add to fingerprints and DNA. As well as the lodge noted in Chapter 1, he is also a member of Duchy of Cornwall No. 3038, Archbishop Tenison No. 5163, and East Surrey Masters No. 5888.

Other police Masons have died honourable deaths in their service of the public. PC Roger Brereton, who was murdered during the Hungerford Massacre in 1987, was a member of Tilehurst Lodge No. 6526. Despite being shot four times with a high-powered rifle, Brother Roger still managed to use his radio to warn colleagues of the murderous rampage of Michael Ryan. Detective Constable Jim Morrison, a member of New Jubilee Lodge No.

Left: Norwell Roberts, police officer and Freemason, on his first day at Training School.

Below: Mason DCI Brian Bowden-Brown pioneered the use of Low Copy DNA and cold case review to solve serious crime

7056, was stabbed to death after bravely chasing a bag thief from Covent Garden in 1991, while off-duty. In recognition of his bravery, he was posthumously awarded the Queen's Gallantry Medal.

Perhaps most memorably, the man, who played the part of *Dixon of Dock Green*—the epitome of a British police officer—was a Mason. Actor Jack Warner was a member of Acacia Lodge No. 3436. In a further link to the Craft, Warner died in the Royal Masonic Hospital. He also achieved better than Hiram Abif, who was murdered and stayed dead. PC Dixon was shot and killed in the film *The Blue Lamp*, only to come back to life and serve in the Metropolitan Police for twenty-five more years.

There have, of course, been Masonic police officers concerned in poor investigations. Sir Charles Warren resigned, having failed to catch Jack the Ripper. The Yorkshire Ripper enquiry, where numerous opportunities were missed to identify Peter Sutcliffe as the killer, was the responsibility of another Mason—Assistant Chief Constable George Oldfield. Brother Oldfield was a member of Lodge of Friendship No. 750. The stress and strain of the massive investigation to arrest the Yorkshire Ripper contributed greatly to the fatal heart attack suffered by this officer.

If conspiracy theorists are to be believed, Masons meet in lodges and plan all manner of crime and skulduggery. In reality, Masonic afternoons are far more mundane, with degree ceremonies, accounts, charity donation, and administration on the agenda. A problem for the Craft is that no evidence is required to support the outlandish theories of which it is accused. With the Jack the Ripper case (whether the suspect is Sir William Gull, the Maybrick brothers, Deeming, Kosminski, or someone else) unsubstantiated 'facts', rumour, and innuendo (together with a Hollywood movie) are presented as irrefutable evidence of Masonic involvement in the murders. In a more recent example, the 2007 murder of British student Meredith Kercher in Italy was blamed by one blogger on the 'Masonic Order of the Red Rose' (this is unknown in England). It was alleged that the victim and the American convicted of the killing, Amanda 'Foxy Knoxy' Knox, were both members of this Masonic organisation. It should be noted that no evidence of this was ever presented to the investigation and Knox was eventually freed by the Italian court of appeal when the true attacker was identified by blooded fingerprints at the scene.

Other conspiracy theories have also been proved to be without foundation. The Trial of the Detectives in 1877 is often presented as bad Masons corrupting the police, with Chief Inspector John Meiklejohn being portrayed as the dishonest police Mason who conspired with Masonic fraudster William Kurr. However, once the facts are examined, there is no evidence that Meiklejohn was a Freemason and the only reason we know that Kurr was a member of the Craft is due to another Mason (Flintoff) refusing to help 'a brother in distress'. Due to Brother Flintoff's evidence, Kurr went to jail and the corruption was exposed. The detectives arrested (two Masons, two not) were arrested by Superintendent Williamson (a Mason) and while a dishonest lawyer and Mason (Froggatt) was also on trial, Masonic lawyers appeared for the defence (Clarke) and prosecution (Avory). This further highlights the problem of assuming that all Masons are sworn to protect each other, no matter what crime has been committed. It also fails to take into account the obligation in the Third Degree (as explained in Chapter 1), which clearly states that, while a Mason should keep another brother's secrets, this rule does not apply if it relates to 'murder, treason, felony and all other offences contrary to the laws of God and the established ordnances of the realm'. This leaves little that a Mason can keep secret. All serious crimes are covered by 'felony' and theft is contrary to the laws of the land and the 'laws of God'. Keeping secrets about adulterous behaviour, while not a criminal offence, also offends against the Ten Commandments.

Being a Mason does not mean receiving a lighter sentence. During the trial at the Old Bailey, being a member of a lodge certainly did not help Chief Inspector Palmer; he was found guilty of corruption on very little evidence (having allegedly committed just one act—sending a telegram to warn the fraudsters of impending arrest). Despite his limited efforts (if they ever existed) to help the villains, Palmer received the same sentence as non-Masons, Meiklejohn and Druscovich. These officers had been engaged in dishonest conduct over a long period, committing numerous acts of corruption for which they received enormous bribes in the form of cash and jewellery.

The A13 Silver Bullion Raid further highlights the dangers of giving too much credence to Masonic conspiracy theories. There is no doubt that three members of the Craft were involved in the armed robbery, principal among them being Worshipful Brother Lennie Gibson. That said, two conspiracy theories (both false) emerged during the investigation of the crime, hindering the enquiry team. Firstly, the investigating officer, DCI Tony Lundy, believed that Masonic senior officers were blocking his promotion. Secondly, when arrested, one of the non-Masonic robbers was afraid of speaking to DCI Lundy, as he was convinced that the detective was in the same lodge as Gibson. The trouble with conspiracy theories is that it is too easy to make two plus two equal five, or even more.

Perhaps the most ridiculous suggestion is that, while a low-ranking officer is master of his lodge, he has power over senior officers, even at work. This, however, is exactly the theory put forward by Short (1993), where he alleged that a detective inspector in the City of London Police, who was Worshipful Master was 'superior in rank to the Commissioner' (the most senior officer in the force). While this is contrary to common sense, it is also against The Charge to the Initiate, which is recited to every new member. This states that in Lodge, a brother must give 'perfect submission to the master and his wardens, while acting in the discharge their respective offices'; if they are engaged in police work, they are not in their Masonic 'office'.

It should also be noted that if Masons are as powerful as some would believe, it is difficult to imagine that someone could murder the Grand Master and walk away from a court a free man. This is, however, exactly what happened with Dr Bodkin Adams, who (without doubt) murdered the tenth Duke of Devonshire, who was Grand Master of the United Grand Lodge of England at the time of his death in 1950. This case probably shows what is really powerful—the Establishment. If Adams had been convicted it would have undermined several Establishment issues—the survival and reputation of the newly formed National Health Service, the exposure of the Prime Minister's wife's involvement in an affair, and the outing of a homosexual love triangle involving a senior police officer and a magistrate (at a time when such acts were illegal).

An earlier example is the acquittal of Byron for the murder of William Chaworth; the fact that Byron had been the Grand Master of Freemasons seems to have had little influence on the outcome. What proved his lifeline was his membership of the House of Lords and ability to claim the archaic 'Benefit of the Clergy'—designed to protect those in power—which enabled him to escape the death penalty. It is plausible that the Establishment would cover for one of its own when considering how (non-Masons) Cyril Smith and Jimmy Savile were allowed to sexually abuse victims over many years without being brought to justice. It is certain that Freemasons were not the ones protecting them as neither of them belonged to the Craft. The Establishment also protected the Kray Twins and allowed them to run a criminal empire for far too long.

In relation to the cover up of historic sex offences allegedly committed by politicians and other public figures, former minister Norman Tebbitt stated, 'At that time I think most people would have thought that the Establishment, the system, was to be protected and, if a few things had gone wrong…that it was more important to protect the system.' It should also be noted that Freemasonry is becoming less and less part of the Establishment. Whereas it could once boast a whole host of earls, viscounts, and barons as its leaders, there are now fewer and fewer titled men involved in the Craft; below the Grand Master, the next three ranks (Pro Grand Master, Deputy Grand Master and Assistant Grand Master) no longer include, for the first time in centuries, members of the House of Lords.

For all this, it cannot be denied that the Craft is guilty of several things. It has certainly been guilty of unnecessary secrecy in the past and, while this may have been justified at the time of a potential Nazi invasion, to persist with this policy until just a few years ago has brought nothing but woe to Freemasonry. As the world went through the anti-Establishment period of the sixties and seventies, senior Masons would simply stand by as conspiracy theories were published or the likes of Monty Python ridiculed the Craft on television. The method of dealing with the media, which can be summed up by the motto of the United Grand Lodge of England—'Hear, see, be silent'—has been particularly ineffective in a time of twenty-four-hour wall-to-wall news coverage. Too often, what reporters are not told, they simply make up.

For example, in 2015, Lord Janner was accused of sexually assaulting many young boys. A report appeared in the *Daily Mail* claiming that he had been protected by the local Leicestershire police chief, as both were Masons. No attempt to challenge this damaging statement was made by the Grand Lodge, despite it being easily proved that Janner was not (and never had been) a member of the Craft. The publicly available Hansard record of Parliamentary debates includes the following statement from Janner in 1999, when the registration of Freemasons in public offices was being considered by the government. It can clearly be seen that he is not a Mason:

> My Lords, does my noble friend the Minister recall that among the first organisations to be banned and demonised by the Nazis were the Freemasons? Speaking as someone who is not a Freemason, perhaps I may nevertheless urge my noble friend and the Government to take care in the way they deal with an organisation which has among its membership a huge number of very distinguished servants of this country.

When the Hillsborough Enquiry was established to investigate the poor police investigation into the tragic death of ninety-six Liverpool football fans in 1989, the United Grand Lodge meekly accepted the prohibition of Freemasons serving on the investigation team. There is no doubt that the senior officer in charge on the day of the match was a Mason, but the basis of the ban was an unsubstantiated rumour that on the day after the match, a Masonic meeting was held to agree a conspiracy to cover up police failings. The Grand Lodge could have pointed out that the match was on a Saturday and its rules have always forbidden meetings on a Sunday. Furthermore, such a ban was potentially illegal due to a 2007 ruling by the European Court of Human Rights that overturned an Italian local government order that Freemasons had to declare their membership. Hence, the Grand Lodge could have been more robust in defending the honour of the decent and honourable Masons, whose police experience could have aided the enquiry.

In addition to silly secrecy and a failure to defend itself, Freemasonry, especially in England, could also be found guilty of hypocrisy and snobbery. New candidates are told that Masons judge each other by 'honour and virtue and not rank and fortune'. Too often, however, the latter two criteria are applied—the top Masons invariably went to the 'right school' (a fee paying one) or had a high rank in society. Petty rules are also ruthlessly enforced in lodges, especially relating to the ties that Masons are permitted to wear in one province or another. For all this, even in the most repressive societies, failure to challenge false accusations, excessive secrecy, enforcement of petty dress regulations, hypocrisy, and snobbery, while foolish or unpleasant human traits have never been criminal offences.

Freemasonry has also made more effort to vet those men who wish to join. Declarations regarding previous convictions are now required and the master of a lodge has to sign a certificate declaring that a candidate is a 'fit and proper man' to join the Craft. Erring Masons are also far more likely to be expelled than in the past. The United Grand of England notices (*Quarterly Communications*) feature about forty brethren each year who have been dismissed. As the membership (in England and Wales) consists, generally, of middle aged, white men, the crimes committed by them reflect this—expulsions usually relate to convictions for fraud, theft or child pornography. That said, there are some unusual cases—organising cock fighting, football hooliganism and drug dealing. The key issue is that, unlike the time of Lennie Gibson (the 1980s armed robber), positive and decisive action is now taken to dismiss such scoundrels.

So, in conclusion, Freemasonry includes many good men and a few 'bad apples', as do most organisations. Once the facts are analysed, there is no evidence of any Masonic conspiracy to 'control the world' or to commit crime. The Craft, however, could do more to defend itself and challenge attacks. The policy of openness is the way forward; excessive secrecy simply plays into the hands of conspiracy theorists and unscrupulous journalists. There is also the issue of a human failing; throughout history, people have needed a group to blame for their misfortunes. So, while many would baulk at the idea of racism or sexism, they are quite happy to discriminate against Masons and justify their actions by making all manner of questionable accusations. It should be remembered that many members of the Craft have made the world a better and safer place with their contributions to the world of forensic science and detection of crime. A few have been wicked and greedy—such is human nature.

Bibliography

Ascoli, D., *The Queen's Peace: Origins and Development of the Metropolitan Police 1829-1979*, (Hamish Hamilton, 1979)

Berman, R., *Schism: The Battle that Forged Freemasonry*, (Sussex Academic Press, 2013)

Begg, P., and Skinner, K., *The Scotland Yard Files: 150 Years of the CID (1842-1992)*, (Headline, 1992)

Belloc, H., *The Life of Joseph Hilaire Pierre Rene Belloc 1870-1953*, (Farrar, 1957)

Brightly E., *Miscellaneous Library of W Mann, including Record of the Trial of William, Lord Bryon in the House of Peers*, (Inquirer Books, 1874)

Clarke, E., *The Story of My Life*, (Forgotten Books, 2013)

Clarkson, W., *Kenny Noye: Public Enemy Number 1*, (John Blake Ltd, 2006)

Cullen, P., *A Stranger in the Blood: The Story of Dr Bodkin Adams*, (Elliott and Thompson, 2004)

Davis, R., *Annals of the Lodge of Unions 256*, (Blades, East and Blades, 1885)

De Veil, *Life and Times of Thomas De Veil Knt*, (1748)

Elliott, P., and Thompson, A., *Stranger in Blood: The Story of Dr Bodkin Adams*, (1st edition, 2004)

Feather, F., and Lockwood, M., *A Life of Dougal*, (Essex Society for Family History, 2010)

Foot, I., *Notable English Trials: The Seddons*, (William Hodge and Company, 1914)

Gardner, J., *The Trail of the Serpent: The true story of a notorious Victorian murder*, (Pomegranate Press, 2004)

Graef, R., *Talking Blues*, (Collins Harvell, 1989)

Gurney, J., and Gurney, W., *The trial of Edward Marcus Despard, esquire: For high treason, at the Session house*, (1803)

Highfill, P., Burnim, K., and Langhans, E., *Eagan to Garrett: Actresses, Musicians, Dancers, Managers'*, (Southern Illinois University Press, 1978)

Honeycombe, G., *Dark Secrets of the Black Museum'*, (John Blake Publishing, 2014)

Knight, S., *Jack the Ripper: The Final Solution*, (Harrap, 1976)

Lane, B., *Murder Guide*, (BCA, 1991)

Lincoln, H., Baigent, M., and Leigh, R., *Holy Blood, Holy Grail*, (Random House, 2013)

Lomas, R., *The Invisible College*, (Corgi, 2002)

Lord, E., *The Stuarts' Secret Army: English Jacobites, 1689-1752,* (Google books, 2004)

Lushington, *Depositions of the witnesses in the case of the divorce of Lord and Lady Grosvenor,* (J. Russel, 1771)

Neville, M., *Sacred Secrets: Freemasonry, the Bible and Christian Faith,* (History Press, 2012)

Parlour, A., and Parlour, S., *Researches of The Jack the Ripper Whitechapel Murders,* (Ten Bells Publishing Ltd, 1997)

Parlour, A., and Parlour, S., *Inspector Walter Dew CID and the Jack the Ripper Whitechapel Murders of 1888,* (Ten Bells Publishing Ltd, 2013)

Peabody, D., *Exploding the Ripper Masonic link,* (MQ Magazine, 2002)

Robinson, B.,*They All Love Jack: Busting the Ripper,* (Fourth Estate, 2015)

Short, M., *Lundy: The Destruction of Scotland Yard's Finest Detective,* (Harper Collins, 1992)

Short, M., *Inside the Brotherhood,* (Harper Collins, 1993)

Steel, J., *The Ripper Secret,* (Simon and Schuster UK, 2012)

Internet sites

Ancestry: Records of membership of United Grand Lodge of England (1751–1921)

Lane's Masonic Records (1717–1894)

Freemason Fellows of the Royal Society

Old Bailey On-line: Proceedings of the Central Criminal Court (1674–1913)

List of Lodges

Fairfield	2224	44
Foxhunters	3094	35
Frederick Lodge of Unity	452	1, 49
Friars'	1349	35
Gallery	1928	32
Gihon Sancta Maria	49	40, 41, 48, 49
Glevum	7385	51
Grafton	2347	43
Grand Master's	1	25, 31, 32
Grand Stewards	0	7, 12, 15, 27, 35
Grecia	1105	36
Grove (erased)	410	41
Guildford	5443	58
Guildhall	3116	34, 58
Hammersmith	2090	57
Hartington	916	50
Herschel	1894	58
Hotspur	1626	35
Household Royal Brigade	2614	31
Ilford	4442	55
Irenic (erased)	4797	54
Irenic Chapter (Holy Royal Arch) (erased)	4797	54
Ixion	2501	35
James Terry (Mark)	556	55
Jerusalem	197	7, 12, 27, 36
Jubilee Masters	2712	33
Justicia	2563	32, 34, 35
Khyber	582	43
L'Esperance (erased)	369	19
Lancastrian	2528	35
Lancastrian Chapter (Holy Royal Arch)	2528	35
Liberty	5573	59
L'Immortalité de L'Ordre (erased)	303	15
Lodge La Cesaree	590	49
Lodge of Amity	137	54
Lodge of Antiquity	2	19, 27, 45
Lodge of Emulation	21	12
Lodge of Equity and Appleton	1384	35
Lodge of Fortitude and Old Cumberland	12	30, 32
Lodge of Friendship	6	12, 27, 32, 42
Lodge of Friendship	750	59
Lodge of Good Fellowship	276	37

Lodge of Good Report	136	42
Lodge of Harmony	255	45
Lodge of Israel	205	44
Lodge of Newton	3024	59
Lodge of Quality	9356	52
Lodge of St John and St Paul	349	47
Lodge of Temperance (erased)	169	38
Lodge of Temperance in the East	898	35
Lodge of the Nine Muses	235	13
Lodge of Unions	256	22
London County Council (erased)	2603	43
Loyal Hay	2382	45
MacDonald	1216	35
Manor of Bensham	7114	57
Manor of St James's	9179	51, 54, 57, 58
Mendelssohn (erased)	2661	32, 34, 35
Merchants'	241	21, 22, 24
Methuen	631	58
Methuen Chapter (Holy Royal Arch)	631	58
Misericordia	3286	40, 41
Moriah (erased)	176	18
Navy	2612	31
Neptune	22	42
New Jubilee	7056	59
Ockenden	1465	33
Octahedron and Charles Warren	1417	35
Old Cliftonian	3340	34
Old Concord	172	35, 37
Old Harrovian	4653	58
Old Union	46	33, 35
Old Westminsters'	2233	42
Olympus (erased)	5488	55
Orpheus	1706	35
Oxford University Chapter (Rose Croix)	40	34
Oxshott	7622	58
Paddington	3267	51, 59
Pentalpha	974	53
Phoenix	257	33, 35, 40, 47
Phoenix Chapter of St Ann (Holy Royal Arch)	1235	50
Phoenix Lodge of Honor and Prudence	331	34
Polish National	534	44
Prince Leopold	1445	35

Prince of Wales's	259	23, 24, 26, 27, 29, 31
Priory	1000	37
Quadratic	1691	38
Quatuor Coronati	2076	35
Radlett	6652	59
Rahere	2546	40, 41, 45, 48, 49
Rahere Chapter (Holy Royal Arch)	2546	40, 41, 48, 49
Richard Eve Chapter (Holy Royal Arch)	2772	58
Richard of Bordeaux	8333	59
Robert Burns	25	21, 32, 47
Robert Thorne	3663	35
Royal Alfred	780	32
Royal Alfred	877	49
Royal Alpha	16	16, 27, 29, 31, 34, 35, 50
Royal Clarence	271	33, 43
Royal Colonial Institute	3556	50
Royal Edward	1088	59
Royal Lodge of Friendship	278	35
Royal London Hospital	2845	35, 50
Royal Somerset House and Inverness Lodge	4	6, 12, 15, 17, 26, 35
Royal Standard	398	35, 37
Royal Sussex Lodge of Hospitality	187	42
Royal York	315	33
Royal York Lodge of Perseverance	7	25
Ryde	698	35
Sancta Maria (erased)	2682	31, 40, 41, 48, 49
Savage Club	2190	36
Scientific	88	29
Shadwell Clerke	1910	35
Sir Edward Clarke	3601	32, 34
Socrates	373	30
South Middlesex	858	35
South Saxon	311	33, 35
South West Surrey Masters	5965	58
Southern Star	1158	32, 35
St Alban's	29	13, 44
St Andrew's	231	35
St Andrew's	1817	37
St Chad	3115	35
St George and Corner Stone	5	7
St George's Lodge of Harmony	32	35
St Helena	488	33

St Kew	1222	42
St Mary Magdalen	1523	40, 41, 48, 49
St Mary's	1763	51
St Michael	2747	34
St Michael's	8186	53
St Paul's	194	35
St Peter and St Pauls'	1410	32, 36, 46, 47
Staffordshire Knot (erased)	626	29
Stanley	1325	42
Star (erased)	1275	30
Stephens	3089	42
Stockport Lodge of Installed Masters (erased)	9562	59
Sutherland Lodge of Unity	460	36
Sydney	829	57
Tateshall	7645	53
Temple	101	35, 38, 51, 59
Tilehurst	6526	59
Torkington	7359	59
Train-bands	2524	35
Tranquillity	185	44
Tredegar	1625	54
Tuscan	14	33
Tyrian	253	37, 50
Ubique (Mark)	411	33, 35
Union Waterloo	13	30
United—erased	1629	50
United Industrious	31	21
United Mariners	30	35
United Northern Counties (erased)	2128	46, 47
United Studholme Alliance	1591	43, 45
United Wards (erased)	2987	34
University (Mark)	55	34
University Lodge (erased)	74	10
University of Durham	3030	35
University of Edinburgh	2974	38
Upton	1227	35
Victoria	1345	35
Vine Tavern (erased)	60	11
Vitruvian	87	35, 37
Waterways (erased)	7913	55
Welcome	1673	33
Westminster and Keystone	10	34

Lodge of St John and St Paul	349	47
Apollo University	357	29, 34
L'Esperance (erased)	369	19
Socrates	373	30
Royal Standard	398	35, 37
Amphibious (erased)	407	22
Grove (erased)	410	41
Ubique (Mark)	411	33, 35
Frederick Lodge of Unity	452	1, 49
Sutherland Lodge of Unity	460	36
Churchill	478	34
St Helena	488	33
Zetland in the East	508	35
Zetland	511	32, 34, 35
Polish National	534	44
Yarborough	554	33, 35
James Terry (Mark)	556	55
Abernethy (Mark)	569	40, 41, 48, 49
Khyber	582	43
Lodge La Cesaree	590	49
Beadon	619	29
Abbey	624	43
Staffordshire Knot (erased)	626	29
Methuen	631	58
Methuen Chapter (Holy Royal Arch)	631	58
Canonbury	657	38
Ryde	698	35
Camden	704	38
Lodge of Friendship	750	59
Combermere	752	35
Bard of Avon	778	34
Royal Alfred	780	32
Dunheved	789	32
Sydney	829	57
South Middlesex	858	35
Dalhousie (erased)	860	38
Dalhousie	865	35, 41
Royal Alfred	877	49
Lodge of Temperance in the East	898	35
City of London and Baltic	901	35
Hartington	916	50
Doric	933	35

Pentalpha	974	53
Rose of Denmark Chapter (Royal Arch)	975	30
Priory	1000	37
Royal Edward	1088	59
Grecia	1105	36
Southern Star	1158	32, 35
MacDonald	1216	35
St Kew	1222	42
Upton	1227	35
Phoenix Chapter of St Ann (Holy Royal Arch)	1235	50
Star (erased)	1275	30
Stanley	1325	42
Victoria	1345	35
Friars	1349	35
Lodge of Equity and Appleton	1384	35
Anerley	1397	43
St Peter and St Pauls'	1410	32, 36, 46, 47
Octahedron and Charles Warren	1417	35
Beauchamp	1422	59
Prince Leopold	1445	35
Ockenden	1465	33
Athenaeum (erased)	1491	35
St Mary Magdalen	1523	40, 41, 48, 49
Elliot	1567	33
United Studholme Alliance	1591	43, 45
Bayard	1615	45
Tredegar	1625	54
Hotspur	1626	35
United (erased)	1629	50
Welcome	1673	33
Quadratic	1691	38
Orpheus	1706	35
St Mary's	1763	51
Addington Chapter (Holy Royal Arch)	1787	58
St Andrew's	1817	37
Alliance (erased)	1827	35, 43
Charles Warren	1832	35
Chine	1884	32
Herschel	1894	58
Shadwell Clerke	1910	35
Eurydice	1920	35
Gallery	1928	32

Abbey	2030	30, 32
Quatuor Coronati	2076	35
Hammersmith	2090	57
Empire	2108	42
Drury Lane	2127	35, 36, 40, 41, 44
United Northern Counties (erased)	2128	46, 47
Dorothy Vernon	2129	50
Savage Club	2190	36
Fairfield	2224	44
Old Westminsters'	2233	42
Albert Victor	2328	35
Grafton	2347	43
Cornish	2369	34
Loyal Hay	2382	45
Avondale	2395	32
Woodgrange (erased)	2409	37
Aeculapius	2410	41
Ebbisham	2422	42
Wineslai Chapter (Holy Royal Arch)	2435	58
Ixion	2501	35
Train-bands	2524	35
Lancastrian	2528	35
Lancastrian Chapter (Holy Royal Arch)	2528	35
Rahere	2546	40, 41, 45, 48, 49
Rahere Chapter (Holy Royal Arch)	2546	40, 41, 48, 49
Justicia	2563	32, 34 ,35
Bulawayo	2566	34
Borough	2589	35
London County Council (erased)	2603	43
Navy	2612	31
Household Royal Brigade	2614	31
Mendelssohn (erased)	2661	32, 34, 35
Sancta Maria (erased)	2682	31, 40, 41, 48, 49
Alfred Newton	2686	43
Jubilee Masters	2712	33
Albert Lucking	2717	59
St Michael	2747	34
Richard Eve Chapter (Holy Royal Arch)	2772	58
Widnes	2819	35
White Rose of York and Addeys'	2840	43
Royal London Hospital	2845	35, 50
Cheselden	2870	35

Glevum	7385	51
Oxshott	7622	58
Tateshall	7645	53
County Gate	7849	59
Waterways (erased)	7913	55
St Michael's	8186	53
Richard of Bordeaux	8333	59
Castlemartyr	8420	58
Broadstone	8641	54
Alexander Woods	8661	51, 52
Connal Wilson Chapter (Holy Royal Arch)	9171	59
Claydon	9178	58
Manor of St James's	9179	51, 54, 57, 58
Lodge of Quality	9356	52
Andredesleah (erased)	9423	58
Stockport Lodge of Installed Masters (erased)	9562	59

Lodge outside England or Wales	Country	Chapters
Loge Liberté chérie	Belgium	49
Loge Les Neuf Soeurs	France	14
Loge de Bon Amis	France	14
Loge de St Jean de Jerusalem	France	14
Les Amis Réunis	France	15
Lodge of Nine Sisters	France	15
La Parfaite Union	France	19
Minerva of the Three Palm Trees	Germany	13
Lodge of Victorious Truth	Germany	27
Lodge of Independence with Philanthropy	India	32
Ancient Union	Ireland	28
St Patrick's	Ireland	35, 37
Kells	Ireland	31
Trinity College	Ireland	34
Enniskillen	Ireland	31
Lurgan	Ireland	21
Carlow	Ireland	21
Propaganda Due	Italy	56
Tranquillity	New South Wales	35
St John's	Philadelphia	14
Lodge Mother Kilwinning	Scotland	9
Lodge of Edinburgh (Mary's Chapel)	Scotland	3, 9

Lodge Canongate of Kilwinning	Scotland	9
Lodge Scone and Perth	Scotland	3
Kilwinning Scots Arms	Scotland	4
Lodge Dalkeith Kilwinning	Scotland	9
Lodge St John	Scotland	9
Lodge of Dundee	Scotland	9
Lodge St Machar	Scotland	45
Morton	Scotland	39
St Peter's	Scotland	33, 35

Index